I'M NOT ANTI-BUSINESS,
I'M ANTI-IDIOT

A DILBERT™ BOOK
BY SCOTT ADAMS

BOXTREE

First published 1998 by Andrews & McMeel Publishing, Kansas City

This edition published 1998 by Boxtree
an imprint of Macmillan Publishers Ltd
25 Eccleston Place London SW1W 9NF
and Basingstoke

Associated companies throughout the world

ISBN 0 7522 2379 8

www.dilbert.com

1 3 5 7 9 8 6 4 2

A CIP catalogue record for this book is available from
the British Library.

Printed by Bath Press

Blah, blah, blah, Pam. Blah, blah, blah.

Introduction

I'm a misunderstood cartoonist.

The people who misunderstand me the most are the ones who write to tell me they enthusiastically agree with my opinions. Those people scare me. Sometimes they develop irrational attractions to me, based on the fact that our opinions are so similar. They often inquire about the possibilities of mating with me, or—if they are male—drugging me and keeping me in a basement in a big glass container. It's all very flattering.

Other people write to tell me they plan to hunt me down and beat me senseless with ceramic statues because my opinions are at odds with their own well-constructed views of the universe. The people who worship unicorns come to mind. They're a vindictive group.

Still other people call me a hypocrite because their incomplete information about my actions is inconsistent with their misinterpretation of my opinions. I deal with this the only way I know how to—by signing their names to anti-unicorn literature.

The problem with other people's opinions about my opinions is that no one actually knows my opinions. All anyone knows about me is the dialogue I put in the mouths of rotund engineers, talking rats, megalomaniac dogs, and pointy-haired bosses. I might be dumb, but I'm not dumb enough to express my true opinion about anything important. The one thing I've learned about freedom of expression is that you really ought to keep that sort of thing to yourself.

That said, I do feel an irrational need to make one futile attempt to clear up the biggest misconception about my opinions: I'm not anti-*management*. I'm anti-*idiot*. The two groups intersect so often that I use the terms interchangeably, even though I know I shouldn't. Let me set the record straight: If you think you're a smart manager, you have my word that I'm only making fun of other people.*

Sincerely,

S.Adams

Scott Adams

*Unless you worship unicorns.

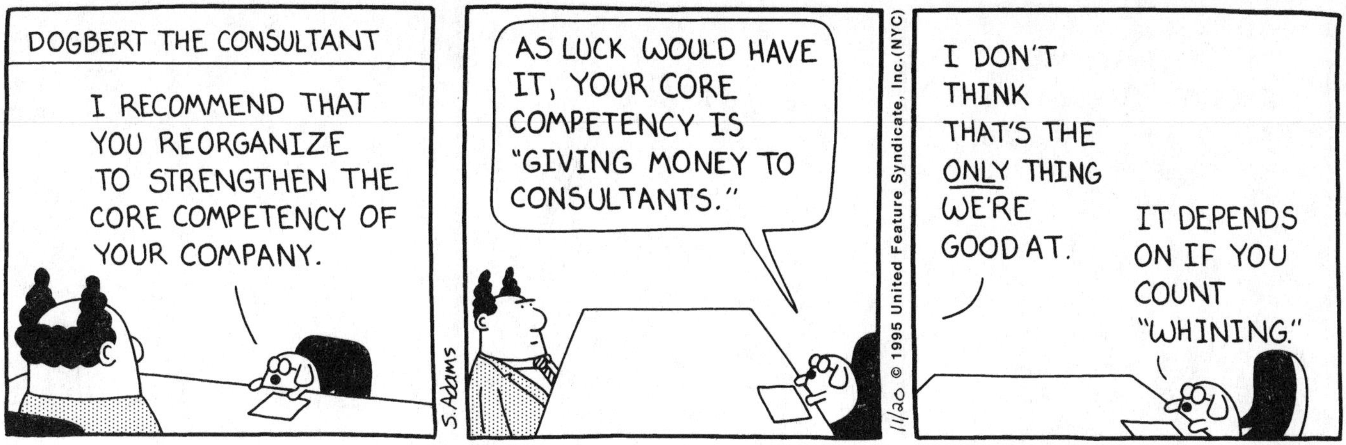
DOGBERT THE CONSULTANT
I RECOMMEND THAT YOU REORGANIZE TO STRENGTHEN THE CORE COMPETENCY OF YOUR COMPANY.
S. Adams
AS LUCK WOULD HAVE IT, YOUR CORE COMPETENCY IS "GIVING MONEY TO CONSULTANTS."
11/20 © 1995 United Feature Syndicate, Inc.(NYC)
I DON'T THINK THAT'S THE ONLY THING WE'RE GOOD AT.
IT DEPENDS ON IF YOU COUNT "WHINING."

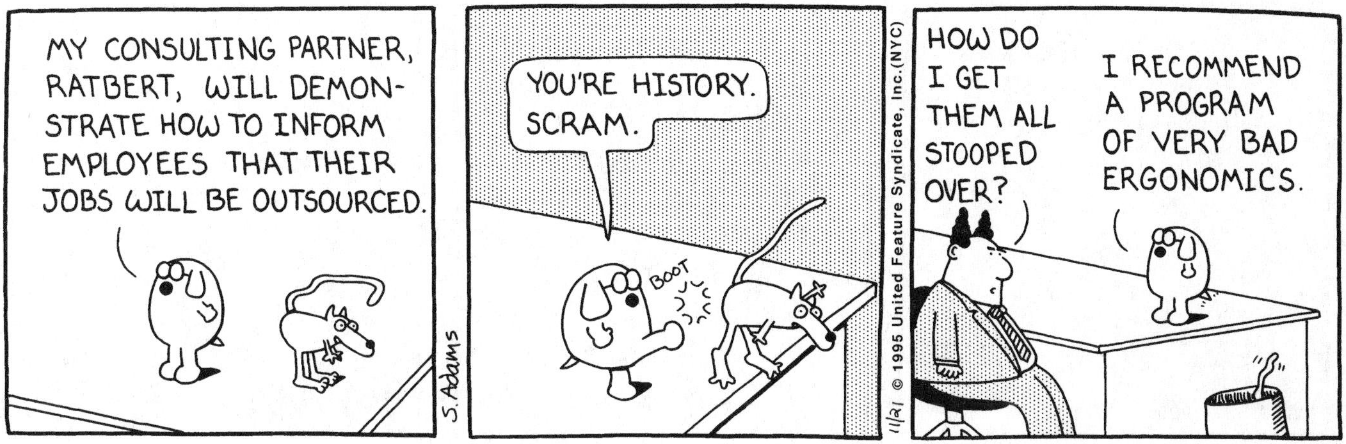
MY CONSULTING PARTNER, RATBERT, WILL DEMON-STRATE HOW TO INFORM EMPLOYEES THAT THEIR JOBS WILL BE OUTSOURCED.
S. Adams
YOU'RE HISTORY. SCRAM.
BOOT
11/21 © 1995 United Feature Syndicate, Inc.(NYC)
HOW DO I GET THEM ALL STOOPED OVER?
I RECOMMEND A PROGRAM OF VERY BAD ERGONOMICS.

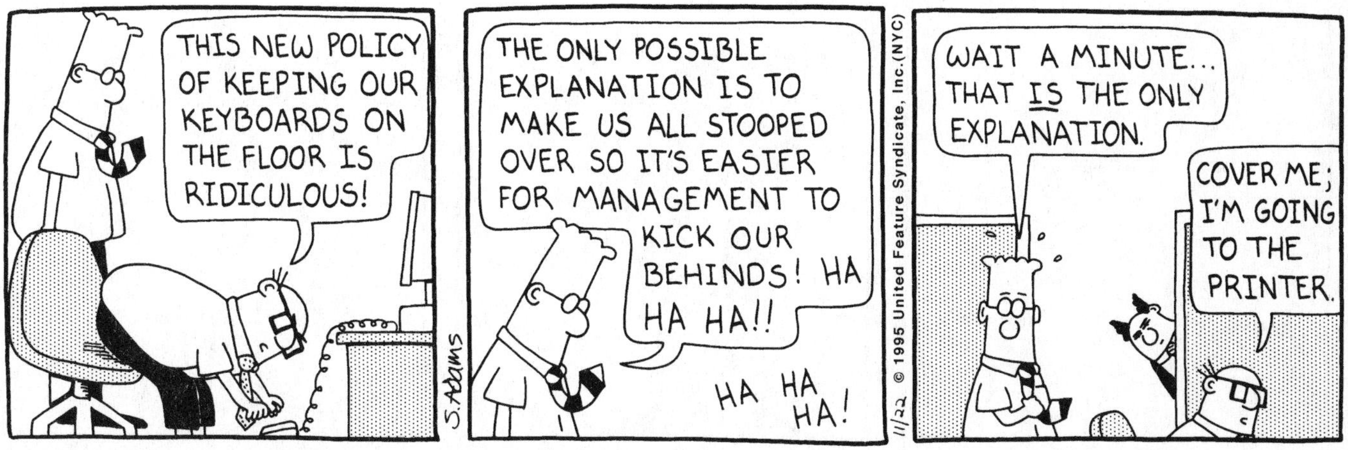
THIS NEW POLICY OF KEEPING OUR KEYBOARDS ON THE FLOOR IS RIDICULOUS!
S. Adams
THE ONLY POSSIBLE EXPLANATION IS TO MAKE US ALL STOOPED OVER SO IT'S EASIER FOR MANAGEMENT TO KICK OUR BEHINDS! HA HA HA!!
HA HA HA!
11/22 © 1995 United Feature Syndicate, Inc.(NYC)
WAIT A MINUTE... THAT IS THE ONLY EXPLANATION.
COVER ME; I'M GOING TO THE PRINTER.

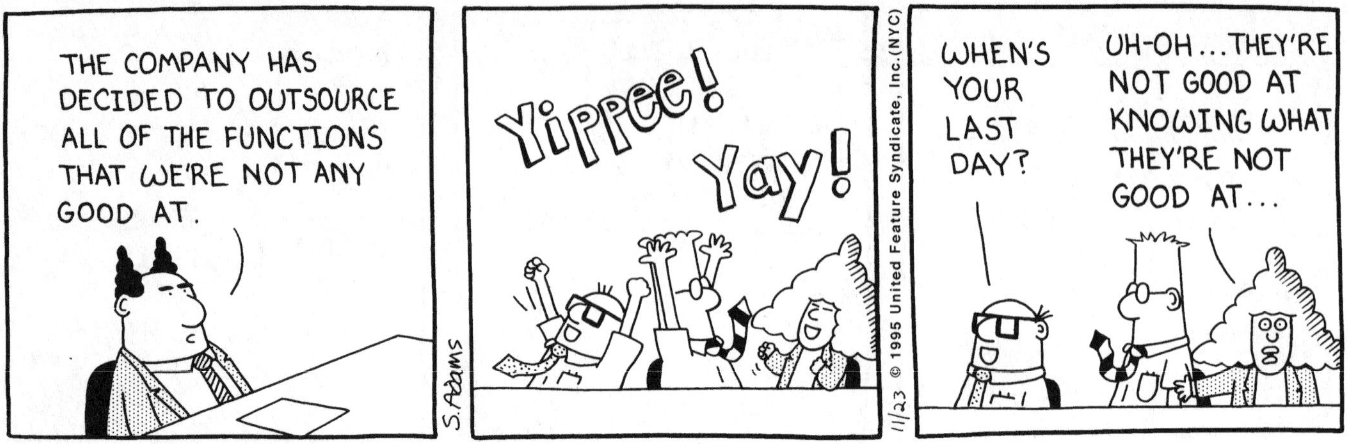
THE COMPANY HAS DECIDED TO OUTSOURCE ALL OF THE FUNCTIONS THAT WE'RE NOT ANY GOOD AT.
S. Adams
Yippee!
Yay!
11/23 © 1995 United Feature Syndicate, Inc.(NYC)
WHEN'S YOUR LAST DAY?
UH-OH... THEY'RE NOT GOOD AT KNOWING WHAT THEY'RE NOT GOOD AT...

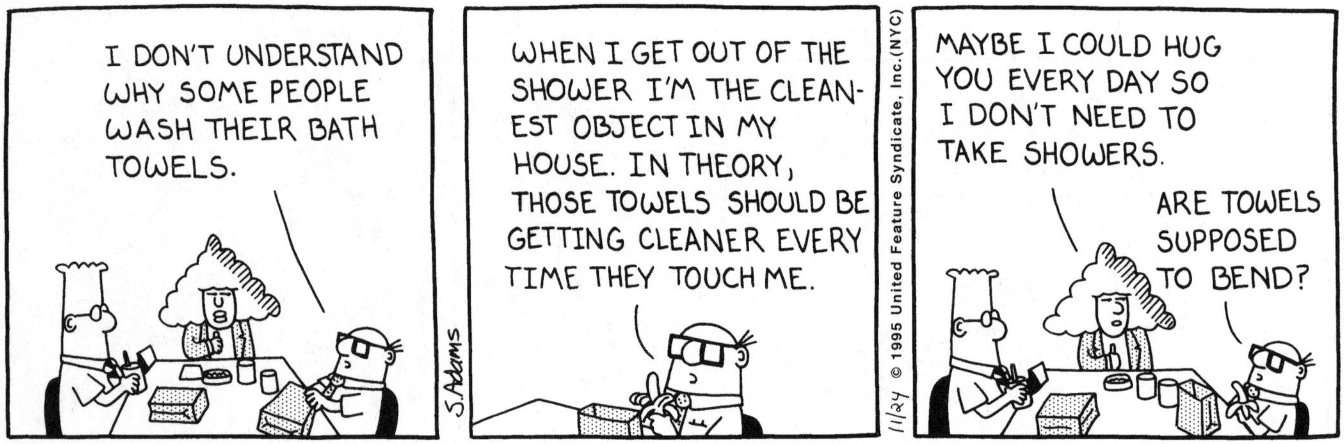
I DON'T UNDERSTAND WHY SOME PEOPLE WASH THEIR BATH TOWELS.
S. Adams
WHEN I GET OUT OF THE SHOWER I'M THE CLEAN-EST OBJECT IN MY HOUSE. IN THEORY, THOSE TOWELS SHOULD BE GETTING CLEANER EVERY TIME THEY TOUCH ME.
11/24 © 1995 United Feature Syndicate, Inc.(NYC)
MAYBE I COULD HUG YOU EVERY DAY SO I DON'T NEED TO TAKE SHOWERS.
ARE TOWELS SUPPOSED TO BEND?

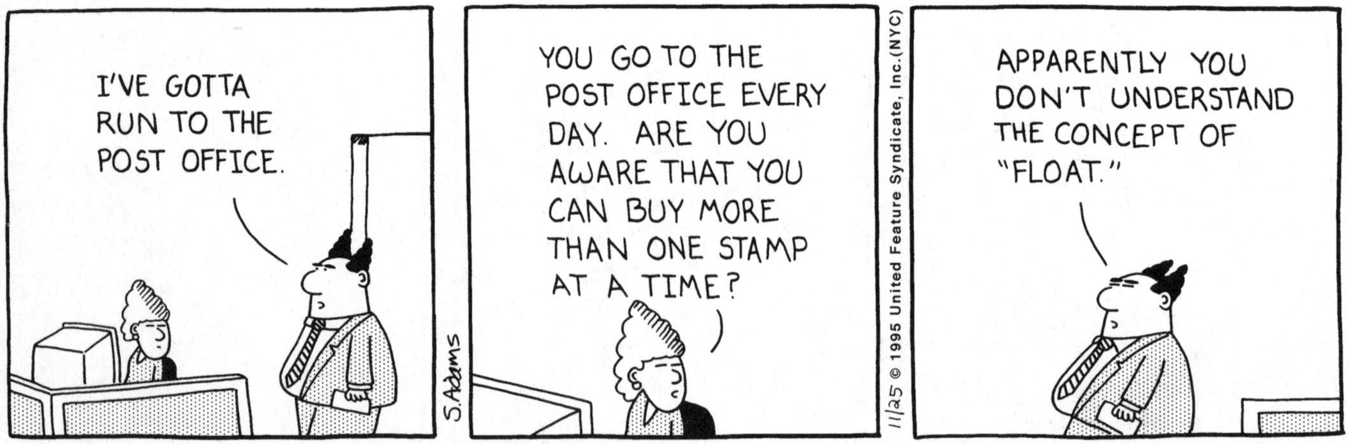
I'VE GOTTA RUN TO THE POST OFFICE.
S. Adams
YOU GO TO THE POST OFFICE EVERY DAY. ARE YOU AWARE THAT YOU CAN BUY MORE THAN ONE STAMP AT A TIME?
11/25 © 1995 United Feature Syndicate, Inc.(NYC)
APPARENTLY YOU DON'T UNDERSTAND THE CONCEPT OF "FLOAT."

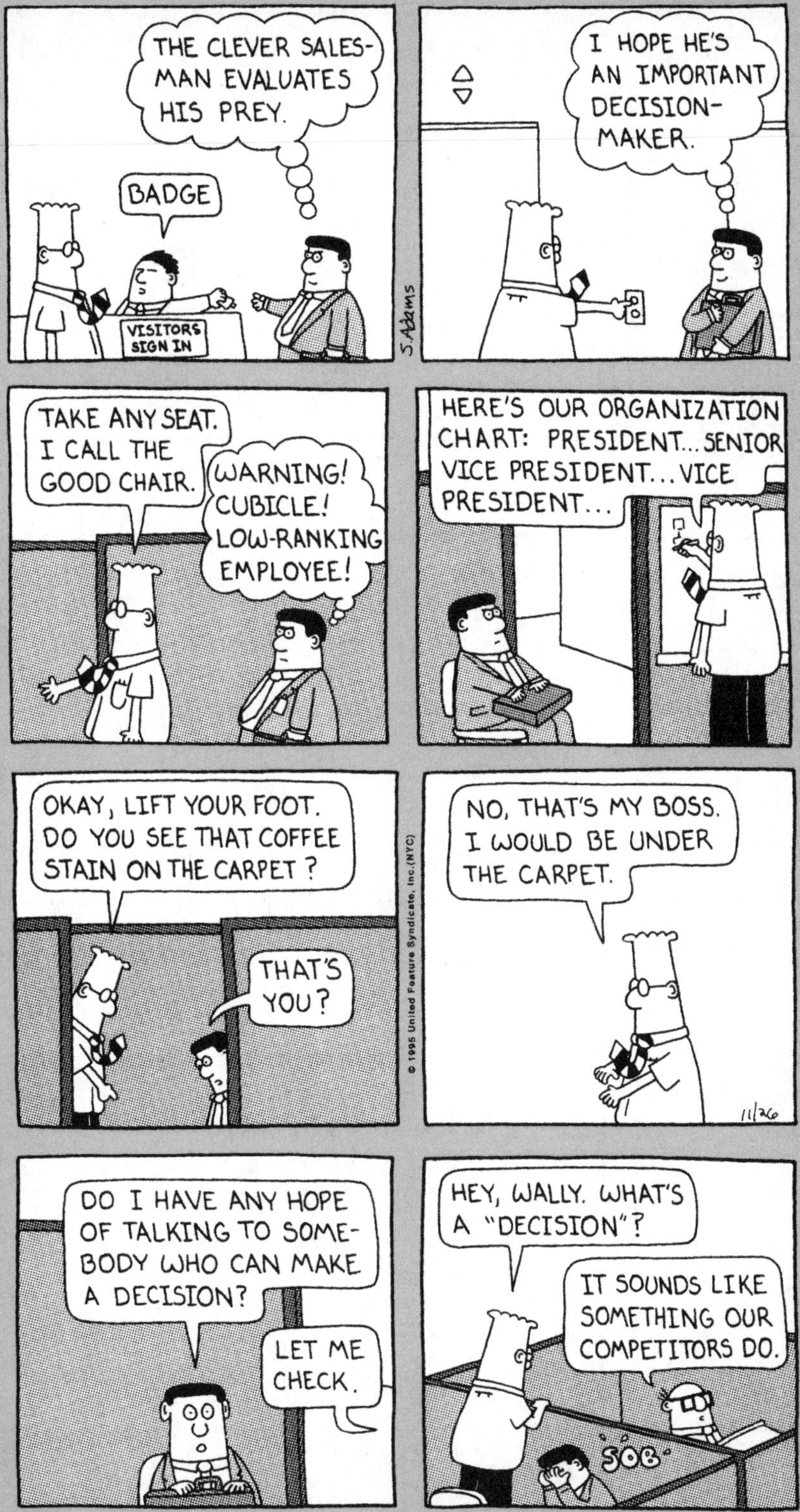
THE CLEVER SALES-MAN EVALUATES HIS PREY.
BADGE
VISITORS SIGN IN
S. Adams
I HOPE HE'S AN IMPORTANT DECISION-MAKER.
TAKE ANY SEAT. I CALL THE GOOD CHAIR.
WARNING! CUBICLE! LOW-RANKING EMPLOYEE!
HERE'S OUR ORGANIZATION CHART: PRESIDENT... SENIOR VICE PRESIDENT... VICE PRESIDENT...
OKAY, LIFT YOUR FOOT. DO YOU SEE THAT COFFEE STAIN ON THE CARPET?
THAT'S YOU?
© 1995 United Feature Syndicate, Inc.(NYC)
NO, THAT'S MY BOSS. I WOULD BE UNDER THE CARPET.
11/26
DO I HAVE ANY HOPE OF TALKING TO SOME-BODY WHO CAN MAKE A DECISION?
LET ME CHECK.
HEY, WALLY. WHAT'S A "DECISION"?
IT SOUNDS LIKE SOMETHING OUR COMPETITORS DO.
SOB

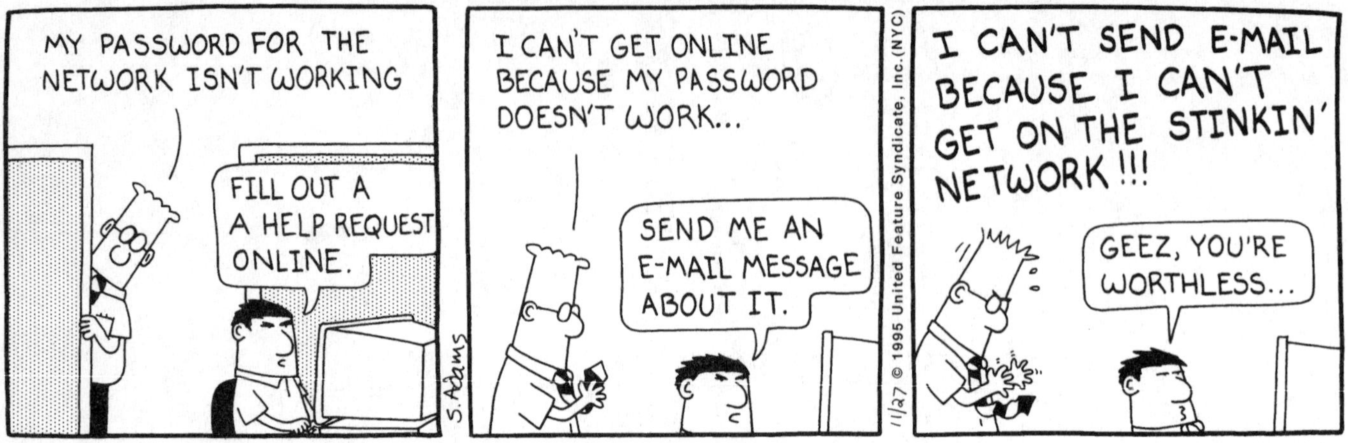
MY PASSWORD FOR THE NETWORK ISN'T WORKING
FILL OUT A HELP REQUEST ONLINE.
S. Adams
I CAN'T GET ONLINE BECAUSE MY PASSWORD DOESN'T WORK...
SEND ME AN E-MAIL MESSAGE ABOUT IT.
11/27 © 1995 United Feature Syndicate, Inc.(NYC)
I CAN'T SEND E-MAIL BECAUSE I CAN'T GET ON THE STINKIN' NETWORK!!!
GEEZ, YOU'RE WORTHLESS...

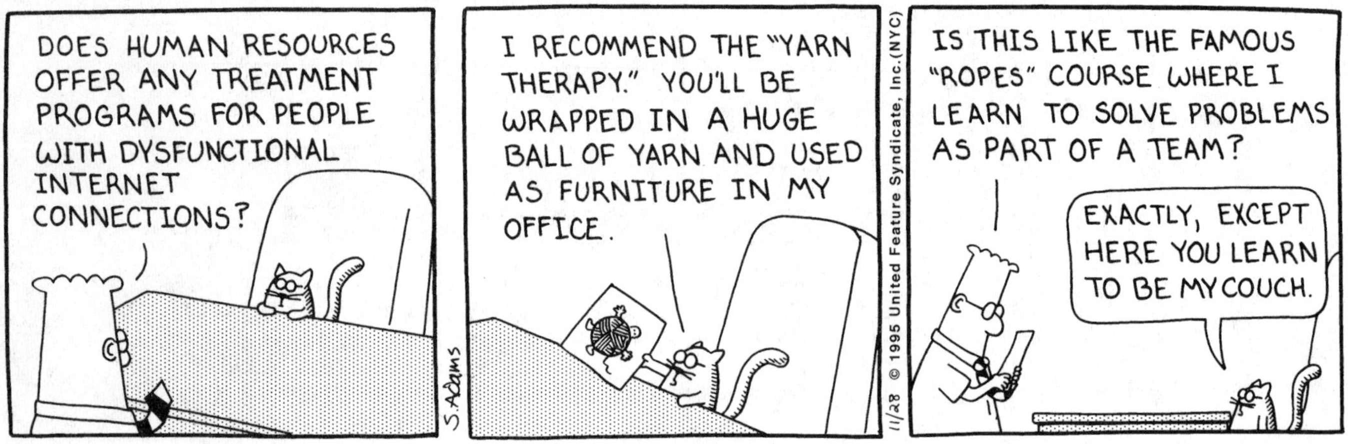
DOES HUMAN RESOURCES OFFER ANY TREATMENT PROGRAMS FOR PEOPLE WITH DYSFUNCTIONAL INTERNET CONNECTIONS?
S. Adams
I RECOMMEND THE "YARN THERAPY." YOU'LL BE WRAPPED IN A HUGE BALL OF YARN AND USED AS FURNITURE IN MY OFFICE.
11/28 © 1995 United Feature Syndicate, Inc.(NYC)
IS THIS LIKE THE FAMOUS "ROPES" COURSE WHERE I LEARN TO SOLVE PROBLEMS AS PART OF A TEAM?
EXACTLY, EXCEPT HERE YOU LEARN TO BE MY COUCH.

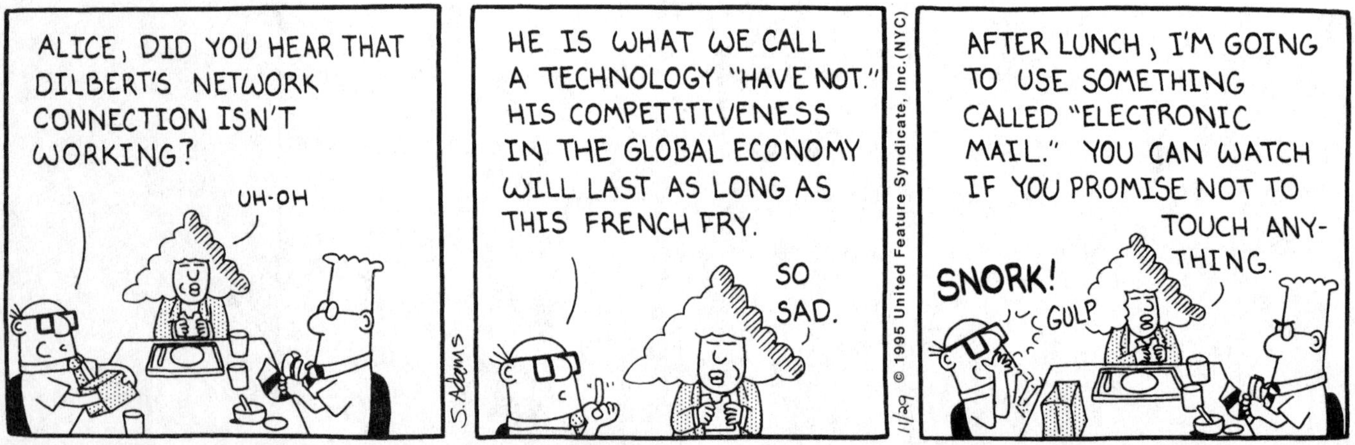
ALICE, DID YOU HEAR THAT DILBERT'S NETWORK CONNECTION ISN'T WORKING?
UH-OH
S. Adams
HE IS WHAT WE CALL A TECHNOLOGY "HAVE NOT." HIS COMPETITIVENESS IN THE GLOBAL ECONOMY WILL LAST AS LONG AS THIS FRENCH FRY.
SO SAD.
11/29 © 1995 United Feature Syndicate, Inc.(NYC)
AFTER LUNCH, I'M GOING TO USE SOMETHING CALLED "ELECTRONIC MAIL." YOU CAN WATCH IF YOU PROMISE NOT TO TOUCH ANYTHING.
SNORK!
GULP

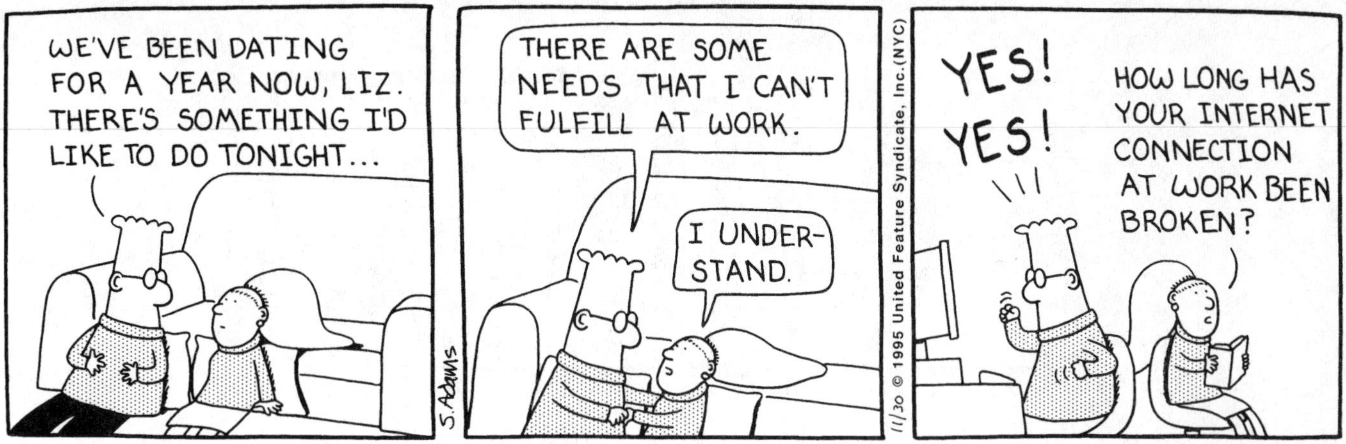
WE'VE BEEN DATING FOR A YEAR NOW, LIZ. THERE'S SOMETHING I'D LIKE TO DO TONIGHT...
THERE ARE SOME NEEDS THAT I CAN'T FULFILL AT WORK.
I UNDER-STAND.
YES! YES!
HOW LONG HAS YOUR INTERNET CONNECTION AT WORK BEEN BROKEN?
S. Adams
11/30 © 1995 United Feature Syndicate, Inc.(NYC)

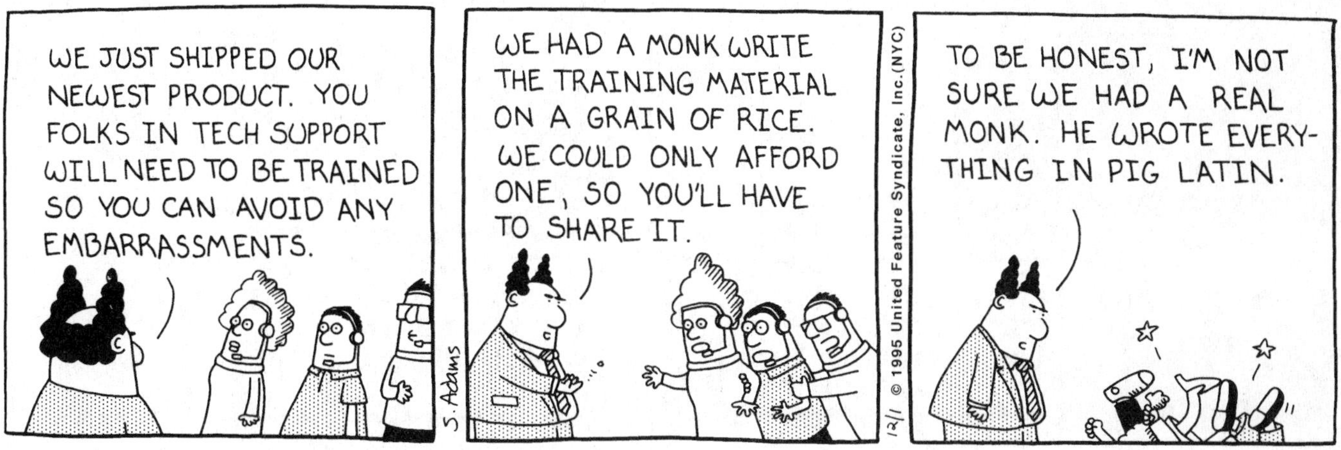
WE JUST SHIPPED OUR NEWEST PRODUCT. YOU FOLKS IN TECH SUPPORT WILL NEED TO BE TRAINED SO YOU CAN AVOID ANY EMBARRASSMENTS.
WE HAD A MONK WRITE THE TRAINING MATERIAL ON A GRAIN OF RICE. WE COULD ONLY AFFORD ONE, SO YOU'LL HAVE TO SHARE IT.
TO BE HONEST, I'M NOT SURE WE HAD A REAL MONK. HE WROTE EVERY-THING IN PIG LATIN.
S. Adams
12/1 © 1995 United Feature Syndicate, Inc.(NYC)

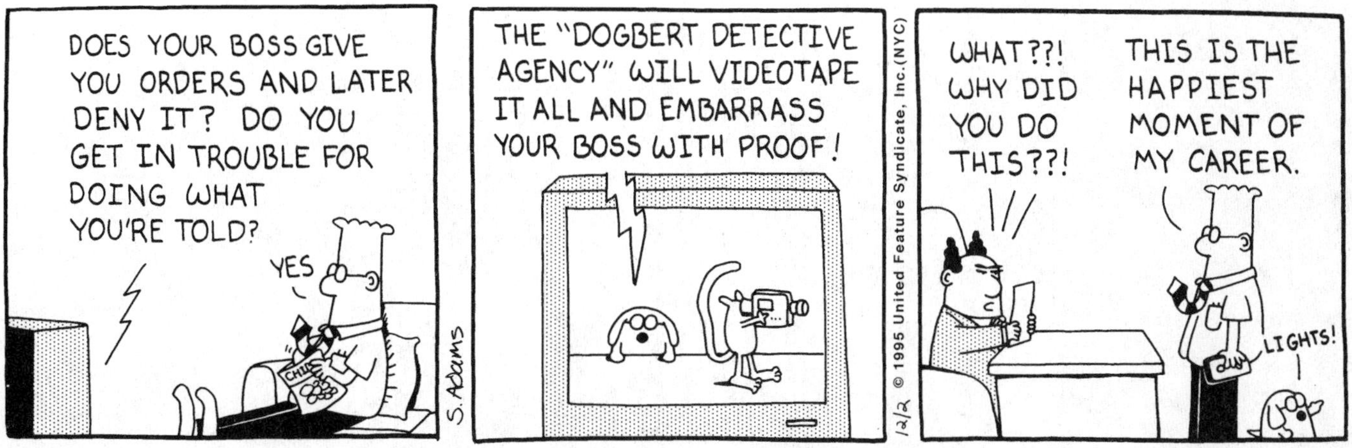
DOES YOUR BOSS GIVE YOU ORDERS AND LATER DENY IT? DO YOU GET IN TROUBLE FOR DOING WHAT YOU'RE TOLD?
YES
THE "DOGBERT DETECTIVE AGENCY" WILL VIDEOTAPE IT ALL AND EMBARRASS YOUR BOSS WITH PROOF!
WHAT??! WHY DID YOU DO THIS??!
THIS IS THE HAPPIEST MOMENT OF MY CAREER.
LIGHTS!
S. Adams
12/2 © 1995 United Feature Syndicate, Inc.(NYC)

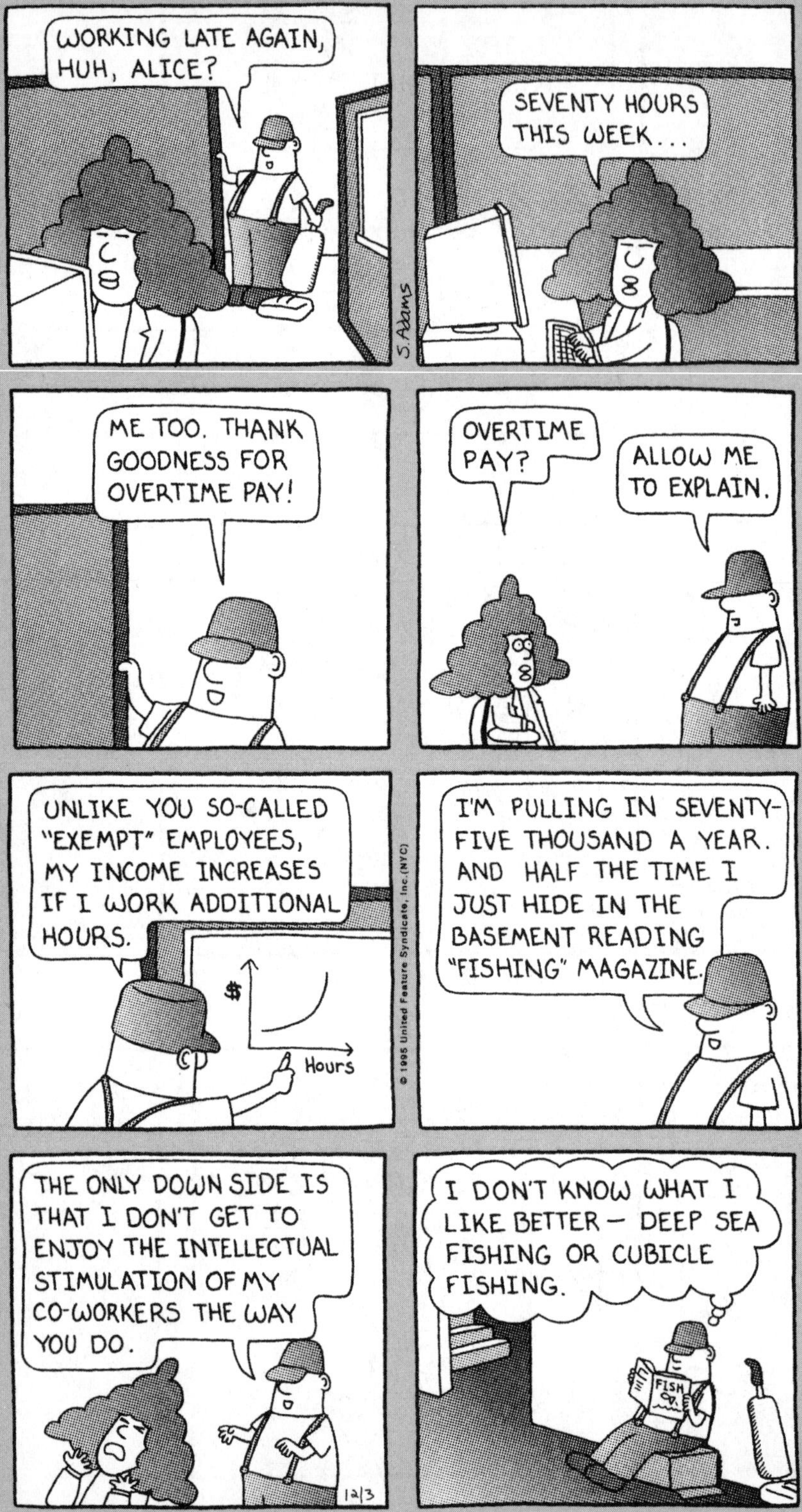
WORKING LATE AGAIN, HUH, ALICE?
SEVENTY HOURS THIS WEEK...
S. Adams
ME TOO. THANK GOODNESS FOR OVERTIME PAY!
OVERTIME PAY?
ALLOW ME TO EXPLAIN.
UNLIKE YOU SO-CALLED "EXEMPT" EMPLOYEES, MY INCOME INCREASES IF I WORK ADDITIONAL HOURS.
$
Hours
© 1995 United Feature Syndicate, Inc.(NYC)
I'M PULLING IN SEVENTY-FIVE THOUSAND A YEAR. AND HALF THE TIME I JUST HIDE IN THE BASEMENT READING "FISHING" MAGAZINE.
THE ONLY DOWN SIDE IS THAT I DON'T GET TO ENJOY THE INTELLECTUAL STIMULATION OF MY CO-WORKERS THE WAY YOU DO.
12/3
I DON'T KNOW WHAT I LIKE BETTER — DEEP SEA FISHING OR CUBICLE FISHING.
FISH

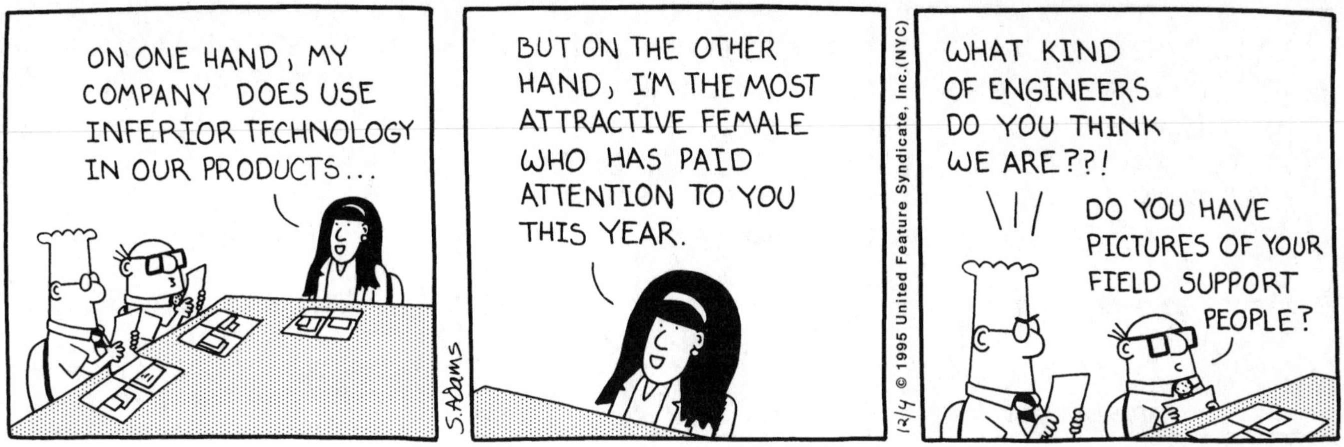
ON ONE HAND, MY COMPANY DOES USE INFERIOR TECHNOLOGY IN OUR PRODUCTS...
BUT ON THE OTHER HAND, I'M THE MOST ATTRACTIVE FEMALE WHO HAS PAID ATTENTION TO YOU THIS YEAR.
WHAT KIND OF ENGINEERS DO YOU THINK WE ARE??!
DO YOU HAVE PICTURES OF YOUR FIELD SUPPORT PEOPLE?
S. Adams
12/4 © 1995 United Feature Syndicate, Inc.(NYC)

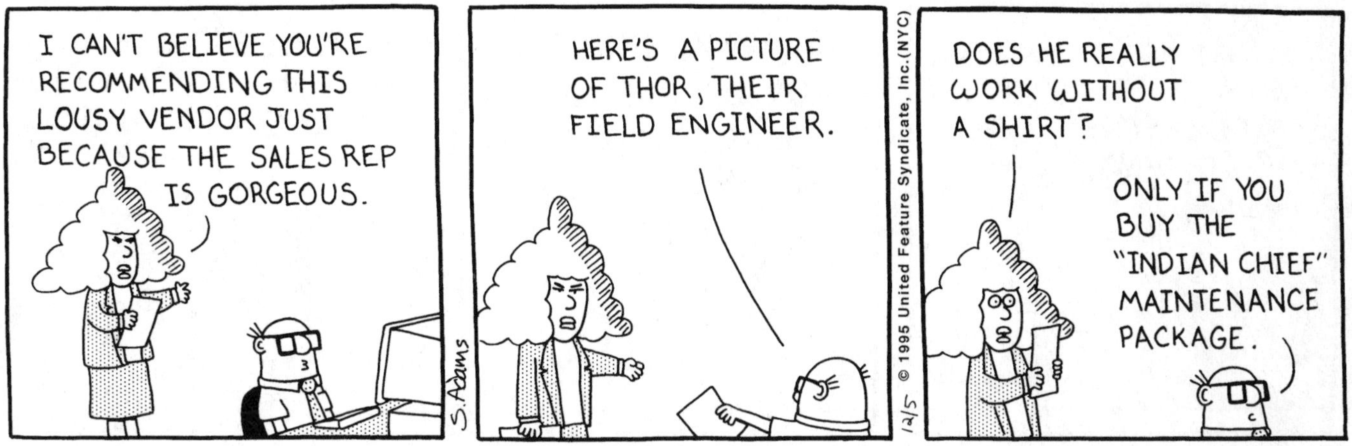
I CAN'T BELIEVE YOU'RE RECOMMENDING THIS LOUSY VENDOR JUST BECAUSE THE SALES REP IS GORGEOUS.
HERE'S A PICTURE OF THOR, THEIR FIELD ENGINEER.
DOES HE REALLY WORK WITHOUT A SHIRT?
ONLY IF YOU BUY THE "INDIAN CHIEF" MAINTENANCE PACKAGE.
S. Adams
12/5 © 1995 United Feature Syndicate, Inc.(NYC)

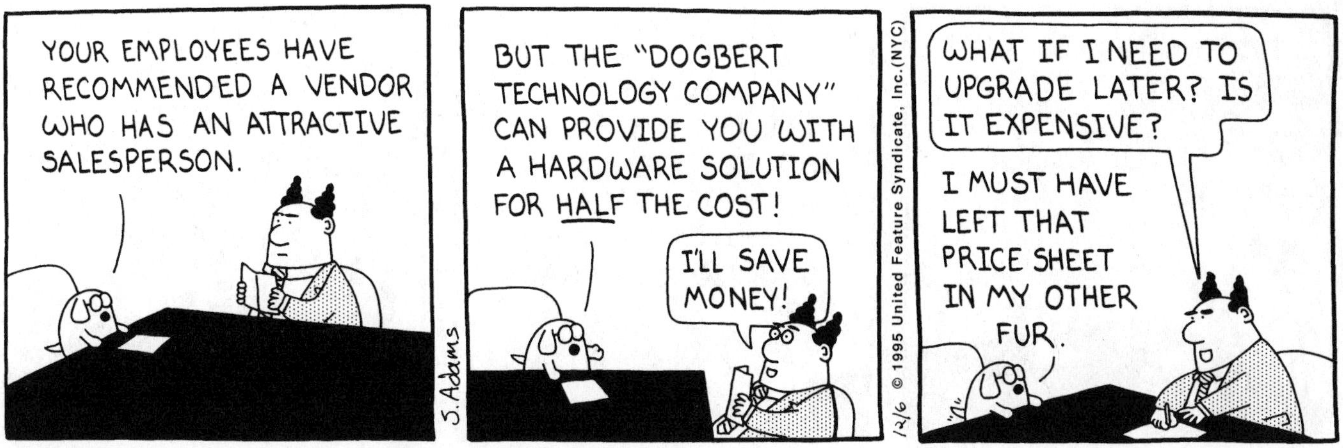
YOUR EMPLOYEES HAVE RECOMMENDED A VENDOR WHO HAS AN ATTRACTIVE SALESPERSON.
BUT THE "DOGBERT TECHNOLOGY COMPANY" CAN PROVIDE YOU WITH A HARDWARE SOLUTION FOR HALF THE COST!
I'LL SAVE MONEY!
WHAT IF I NEED TO UPGRADE LATER? IS IT EXPENSIVE?
I MUST HAVE LEFT THAT PRICE SHEET IN MY OTHER FUR.
S. Adams
12/6 © 1995 United Feature Syndicate, Inc.(NYC)

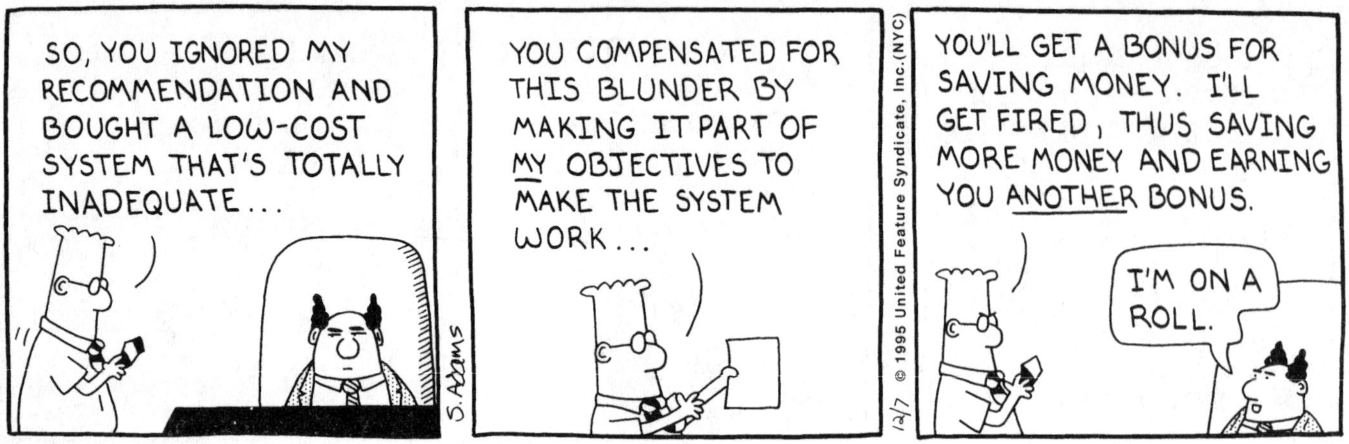
SO, YOU IGNORED MY RECOMMENDATION AND BOUGHT A LOW-COST SYSTEM THAT'S TOTALLY INADEQUATE...
S. Adams
YOU COMPENSATED FOR THIS BLUNDER BY MAKING IT PART OF MY OBJECTIVES TO MAKE THE SYSTEM WORK...
12/7 © 1995 United Feature Syndicate, Inc.(NYC)
YOU'LL GET A BONUS FOR SAVING MONEY. I'LL GET FIRED, THUS SAVING MORE MONEY AND EARNING YOU ANOTHER BONUS.
I'M ON A ROLL.

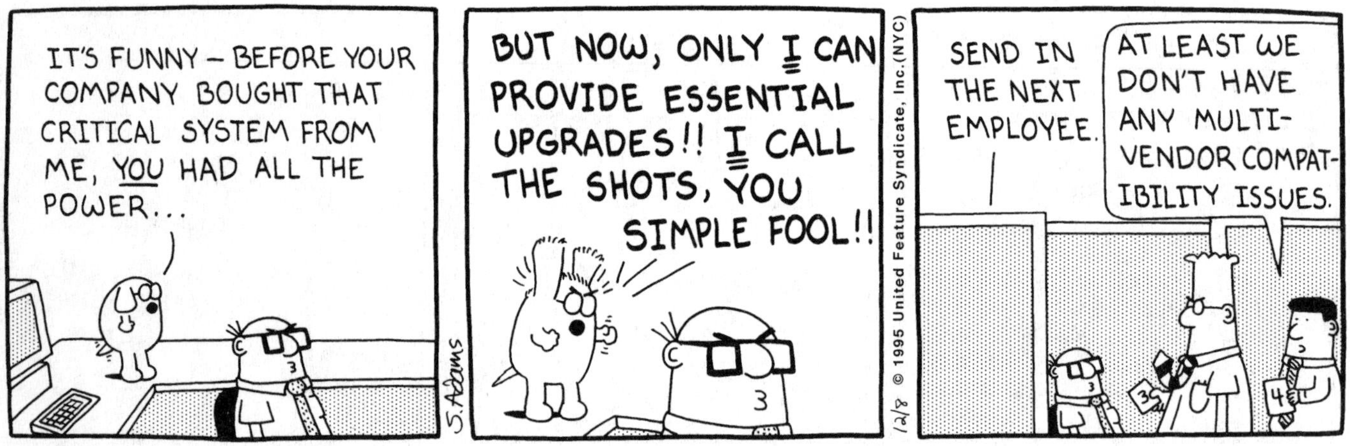
IT'S FUNNY – BEFORE YOUR COMPANY BOUGHT THAT CRITICAL SYSTEM FROM ME, YOU HAD ALL THE POWER...
S. Adams
BUT NOW, ONLY I CAN PROVIDE ESSENTIAL UPGRADES!! I CALL THE SHOTS, YOU SIMPLE FOOL!!
12/8 © 1995 United Feature Syndicate, Inc.(NYC)
SEND IN THE NEXT EMPLOYEE.
AT LEAST WE DON'T HAVE ANY MULTI-VENDOR COMPAT-IBILITY ISSUES.

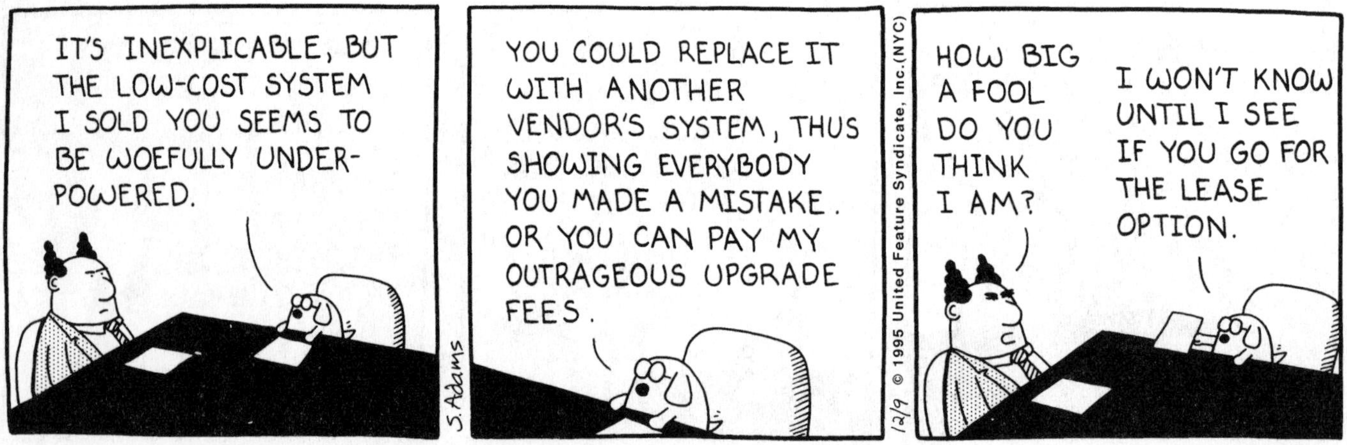
IT'S INEXPLICABLE, BUT THE LOW-COST SYSTEM I SOLD YOU SEEMS TO BE WOEFULLY UNDER-POWERED.
S. Adams
YOU COULD REPLACE IT WITH ANOTHER VENDOR'S SYSTEM, THUS SHOWING EVERYBODY YOU MADE A MISTAKE. OR YOU CAN PAY MY OUTRAGEOUS UPGRADE FEES.
12/9 © 1995 United Feature Syndicate, Inc.(NYC)
HOW BIG A FOOL DO YOU THINK I AM?
I WON'T KNOW UNTIL I SEE IF YOU GO FOR THE LEASE OPTION.

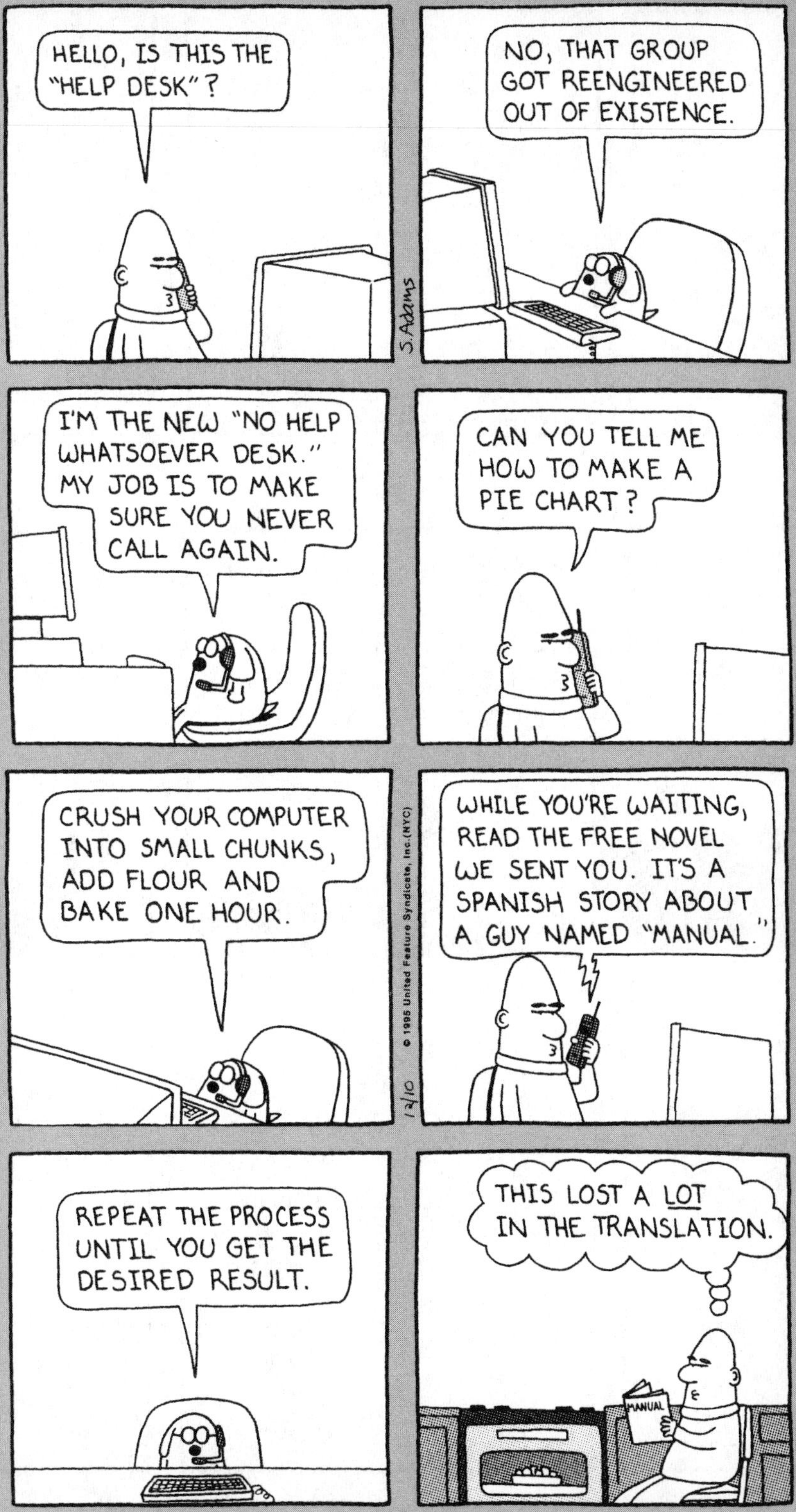
HELLO, IS THIS THE "HELP DESK"?
NO, THAT GROUP GOT REENGINEERED OUT OF EXISTENCE.
S. Adams
I'M THE NEW "NO HELP WHATSOEVER DESK." MY JOB IS TO MAKE SURE YOU NEVER CALL AGAIN.
CAN YOU TELL ME HOW TO MAKE A PIE CHART?
CRUSH YOUR COMPUTER INTO SMALL CHUNKS, ADD FLOUR AND BAKE ONE HOUR.
WHILE YOU'RE WAITING, READ THE FREE NOVEL WE SENT YOU. IT'S A SPANISH STORY ABOUT A GUY NAMED "MANUAL."
12/10
REPEAT THE PROCESS UNTIL YOU GET THE DESIRED RESULT.
THIS LOST A LOT IN THE TRANSLATION.
MANUAL

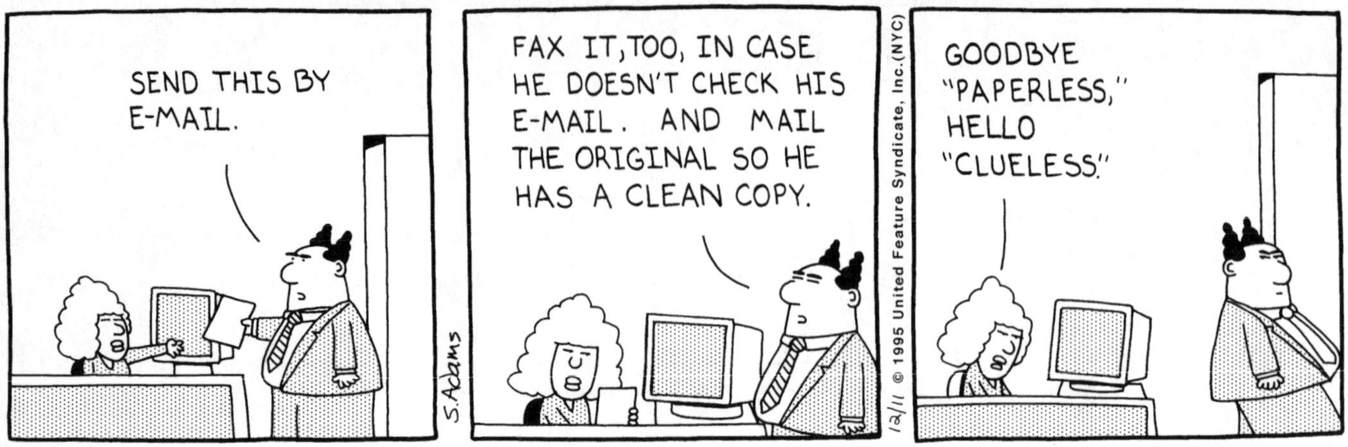
SEND THIS BY E-MAIL.
FAX IT, TOO, IN CASE HE DOESN'T CHECK HIS E-MAIL. AND MAIL THE ORIGINAL SO HE HAS A CLEAN COPY.
GOODBYE "PAPERLESS," HELLO "CLUELESS."
S. Adams
12/11 © 1995 United Feature Syndicate, Inc.(NYC)

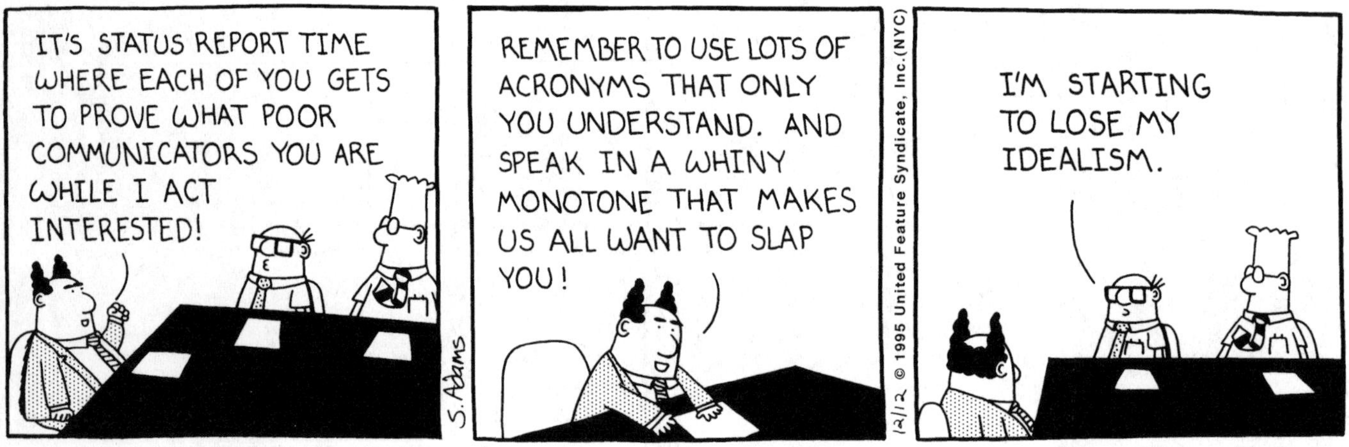
IT'S STATUS REPORT TIME WHERE EACH OF YOU GETS TO PROVE WHAT POOR COMMUNICATORS YOU ARE WHILE I ACT INTERESTED!
REMEMBER TO USE LOTS OF ACRONYMS THAT ONLY YOU UNDERSTAND. AND SPEAK IN A WHINY MONOTONE THAT MAKES US ALL WANT TO SLAP YOU!
I'M STARTING TO LOSE MY IDEALISM.
S. Adams
12/12 © 1995 United Feature Syndicate, Inc.(NYC)

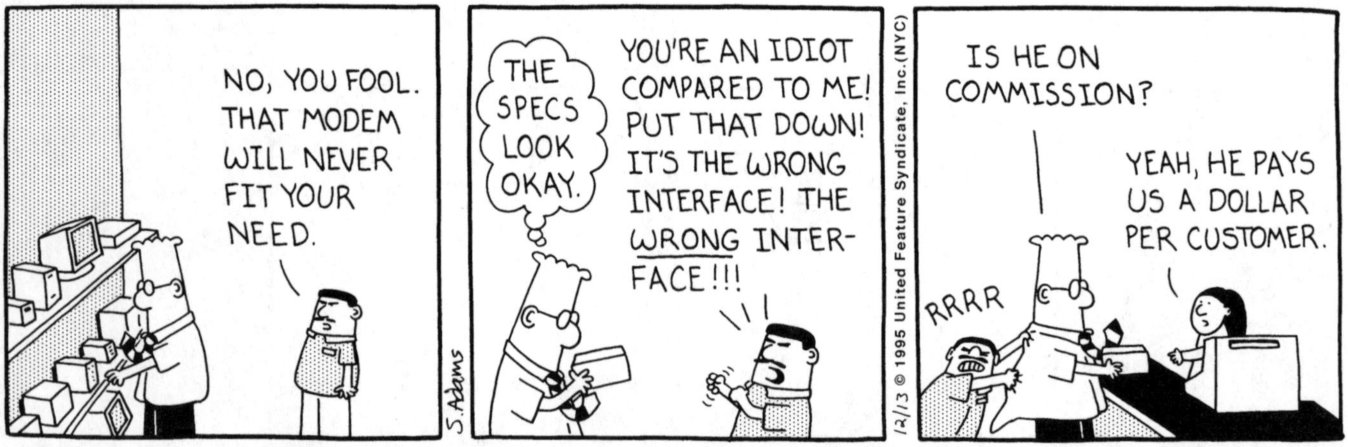
NO, YOU FOOL. THAT MODEM WILL NEVER FIT YOUR NEED.
THE SPECS LOOK OKAY.
YOU'RE AN IDIOT COMPARED TO ME! PUT THAT DOWN! IT'S THE WRONG INTERFACE! THE WRONG INTER-FACE!!!
IS HE ON COMMISSION?
RRRR
YEAH, HE PAYS US A DOLLAR PER CUSTOMER.
S. Adams
12/13 © 1995 United Feature Syndicate, Inc.(NYC)

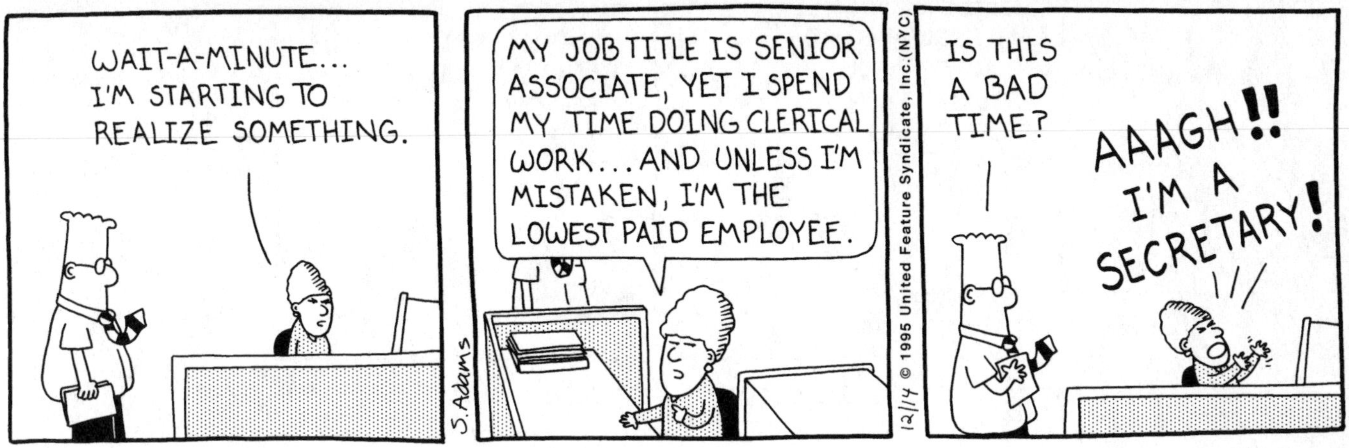
WAIT-A-MINUTE... I'M STARTING TO REALIZE SOMETHING.
MY JOB TITLE IS SENIOR ASSOCIATE, YET I SPEND MY TIME DOING CLERICAL WORK... AND UNLESS I'M MISTAKEN, I'M THE LOWEST PAID EMPLOYEE.
S. Adams
12/14 © 1995 United Feature Syndicate, Inc.(NYC)
IS THIS A BAD TIME?
AAAGH!! I'M A SECRETARY!

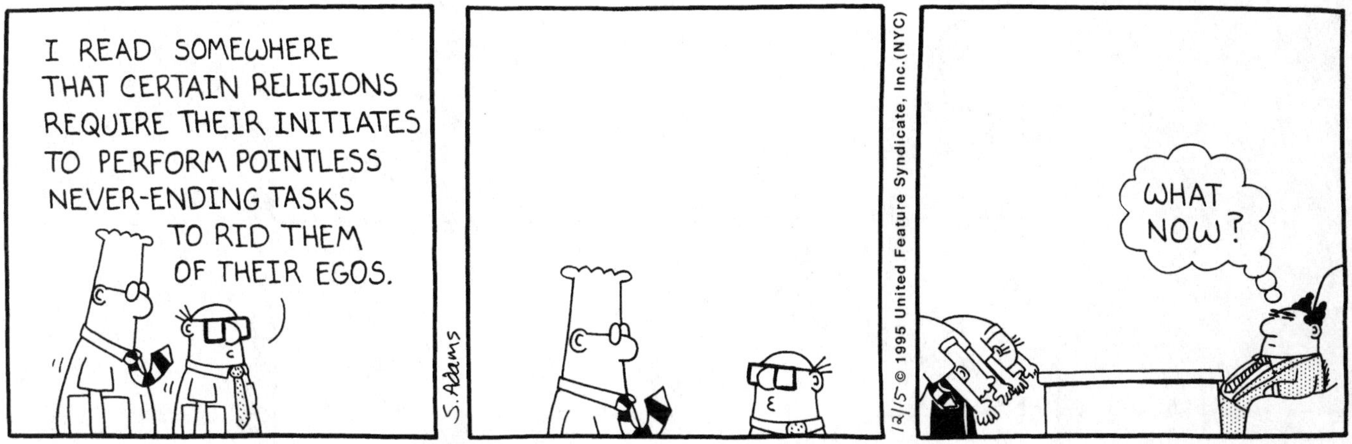
I READ SOMEWHERE THAT CERTAIN RELIGIONS REQUIRE THEIR INITIATES TO PERFORM POINTLESS NEVER-ENDING TASKS TO RID THEM OF THEIR EGOS.
S. Adams
12/15 © 1995 United Feature Syndicate, Inc.(NYC)
WHAT NOW?

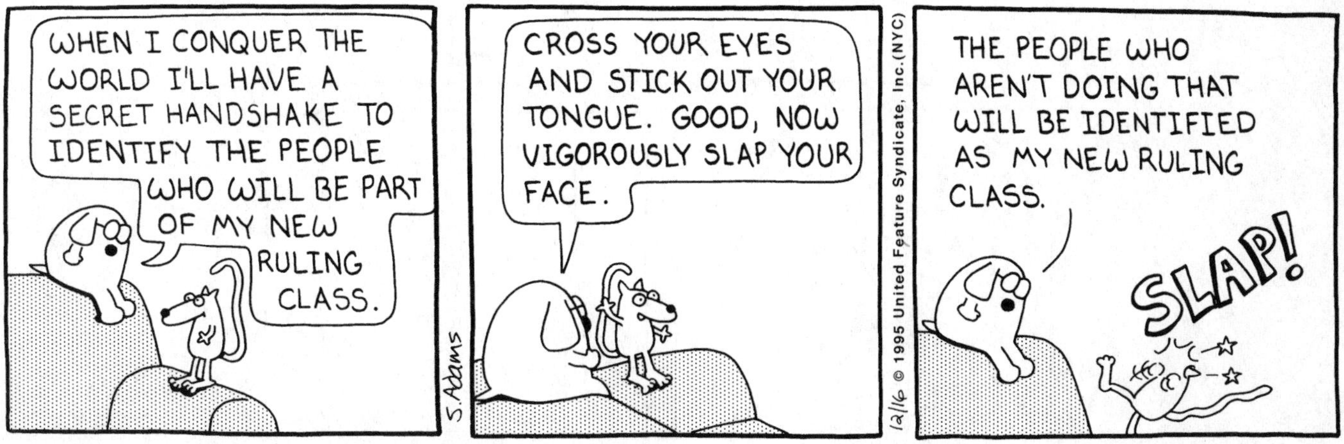
WHEN I CONQUER THE WORLD I'LL HAVE A SECRET HANDSHAKE TO IDENTIFY THE PEOPLE WHO WILL BE PART OF MY NEW RULING CLASS.
S. Adams
CROSS YOUR EYES AND STICK OUT YOUR TONGUE. GOOD, NOW VIGOROUSLY SLAP YOUR FACE.
12/16 © 1995 United Feature Syndicate, Inc.(NYC)
THE PEOPLE WHO AREN'T DOING THAT WILL BE IDENTIFIED AS MY NEW RULING CLASS.
SLAP!

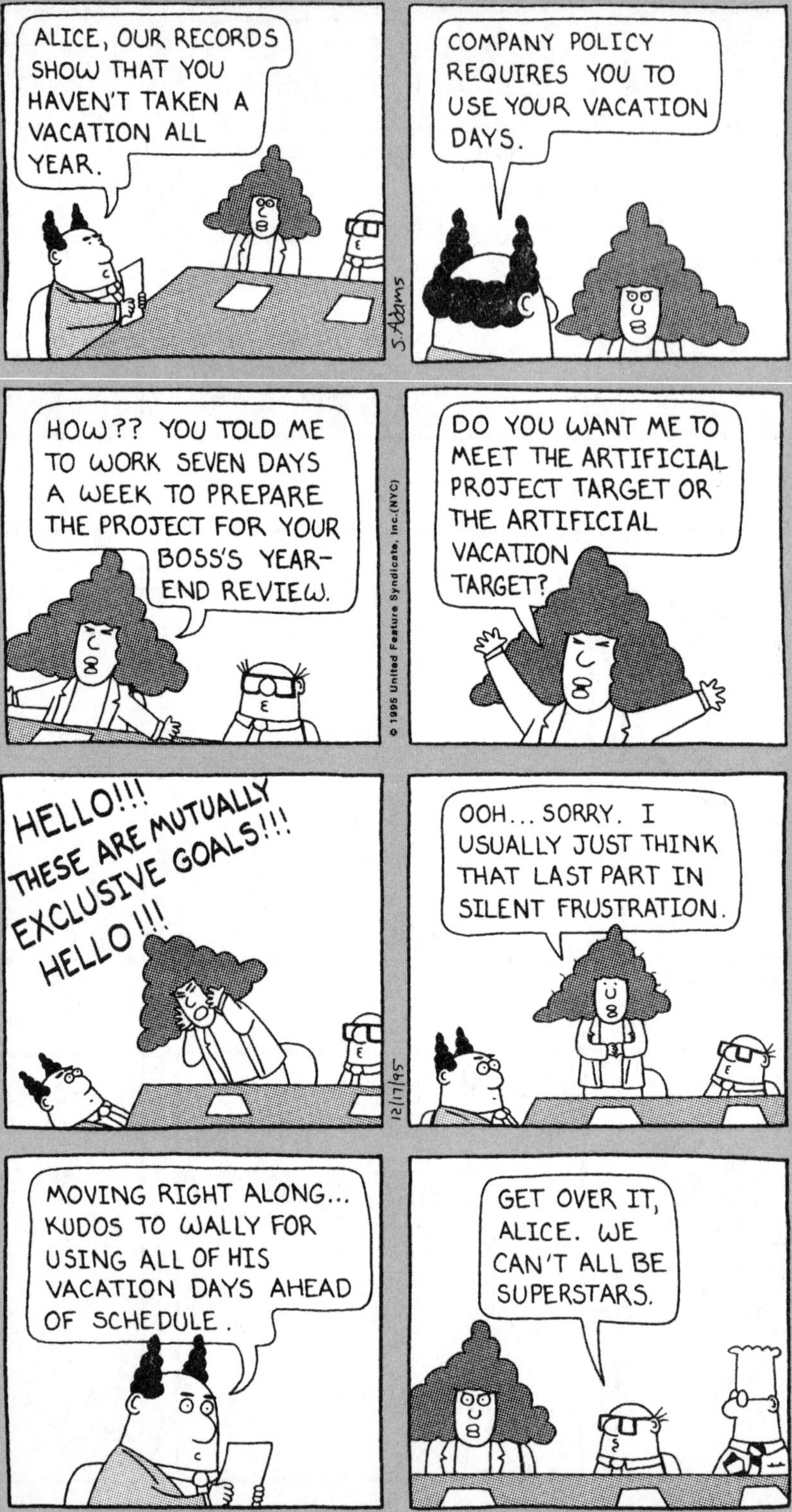
ALICE, OUR RECORDS SHOW THAT YOU HAVEN'T TAKEN A VACATION ALL YEAR.
COMPANY POLICY REQUIRES YOU TO USE YOUR VACATION DAYS.
S. Adams
HOW?? YOU TOLD ME TO WORK SEVEN DAYS A WEEK TO PREPARE THE PROJECT FOR YOUR BOSS'S YEAR-END REVIEW.
DO YOU WANT ME TO MEET THE ARTIFICIAL PROJECT TARGET OR THE ARTIFICIAL VACATION TARGET?
© 1995 United Feature Syndicate, Inc.(NYC)
HELLO!!! THESE ARE MUTUALLY EXCLUSIVE GOALS!!! HELLO!!!
12/17/95
OOH... SORRY. I USUALLY JUST THINK THAT LAST PART IN SILENT FRUSTRATION.
MOVING RIGHT ALONG... KUDOS TO WALLY FOR USING ALL OF HIS VACATION DAYS AHEAD OF SCHEDULE.
GET OVER IT, ALICE. WE CAN'T ALL BE SUPERSTARS.

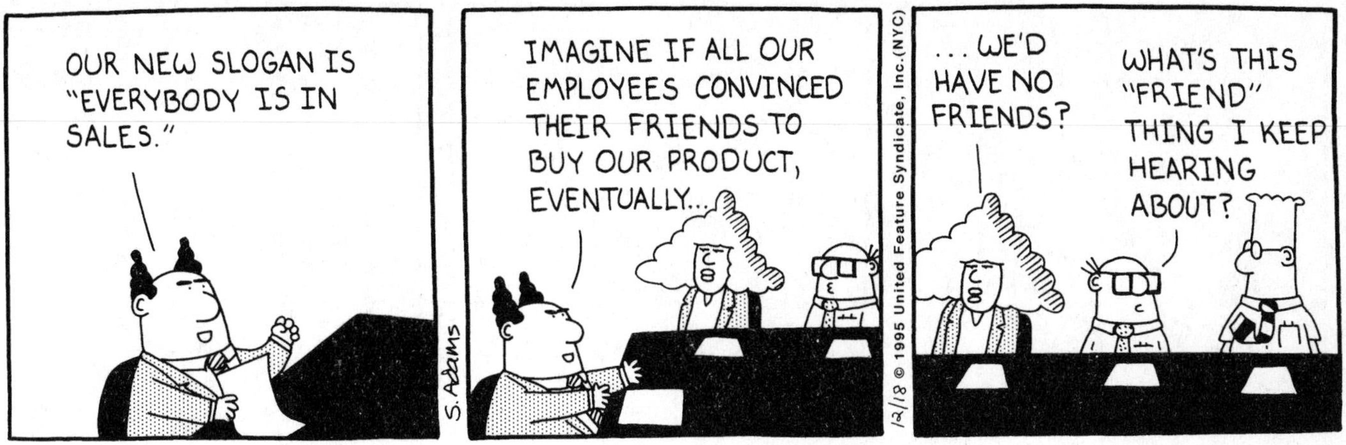
OUR NEW SLOGAN IS "EVERYBODY IS IN SALES."
IMAGINE IF ALL OUR EMPLOYEES CONVINCED THEIR FRIENDS TO BUY OUR PRODUCT, EVENTUALLY...
S. Adams
12/18 © 1995 United Feature Syndicate, Inc.(NYC)
... WE'D HAVE NO FRIENDS?
WHAT'S THIS "FRIEND" THING I KEEP HEARING ABOUT?

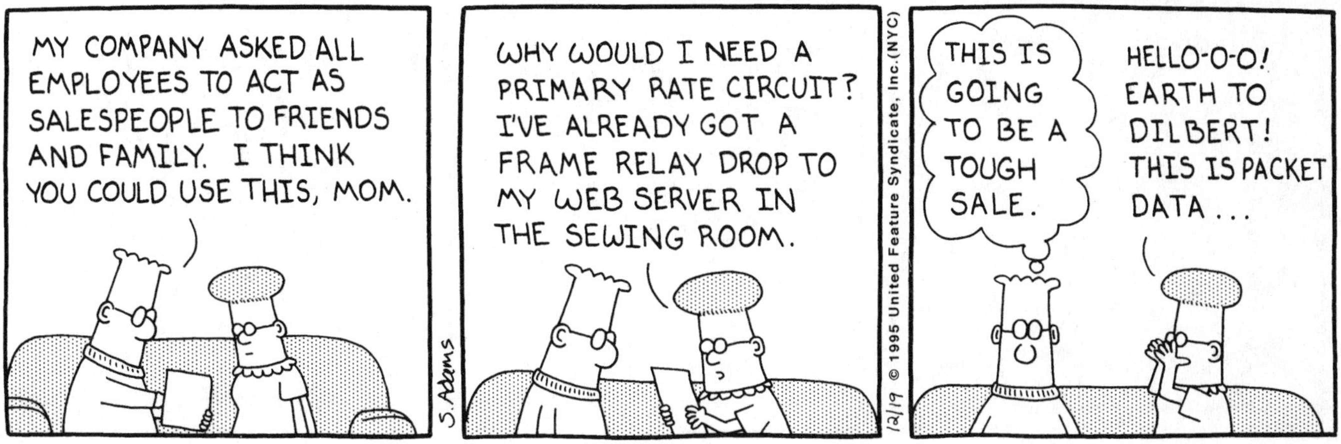
MY COMPANY ASKED ALL EMPLOYEES TO ACT AS SALESPEOPLE TO FRIENDS AND FAMILY. I THINK YOU COULD USE THIS, MOM.
S. Adams
WHY WOULD I NEED A PRIMARY RATE CIRCUIT? I'VE ALREADY GOT A FRAME RELAY DROP TO MY WEB SERVER IN THE SEWING ROOM.
12/19 © 1995 United Feature Syndicate, Inc.(NYC)
THIS IS GOING TO BE A TOUGH SALE.
HELLO-O-O! EARTH TO DILBERT! THIS IS PACKET DATA ...

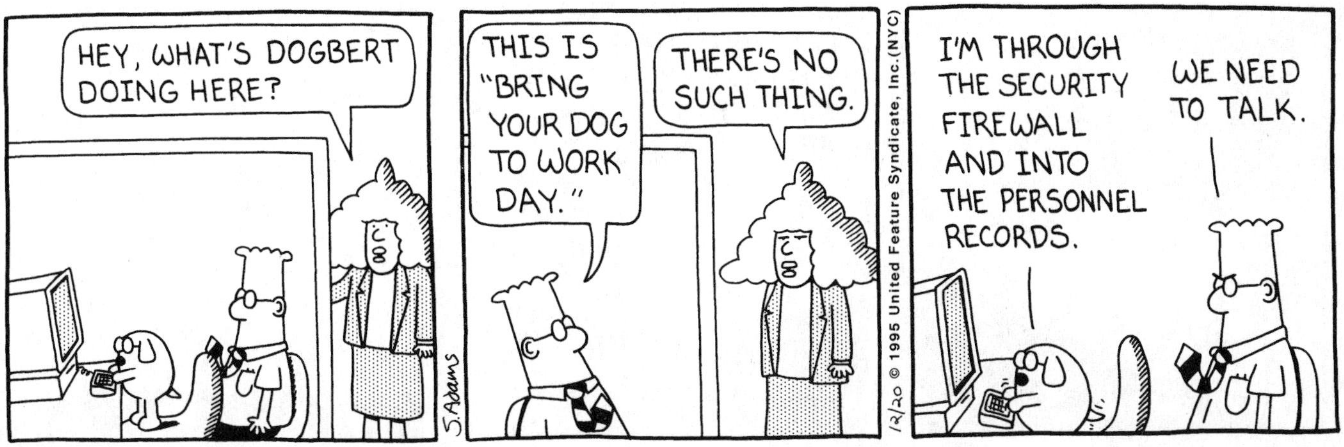
HEY, WHAT'S DOGBERT DOING HERE?
S. Adams
THIS IS "BRING YOUR DOG TO WORK DAY."
THERE'S NO SUCH THING.
12/20 © 1995 United Feature Syndicate, Inc.(NYC)
I'M THROUGH THE SECURITY FIREWALL AND INTO THE PERSONNEL RECORDS.
WE NEED TO TALK.

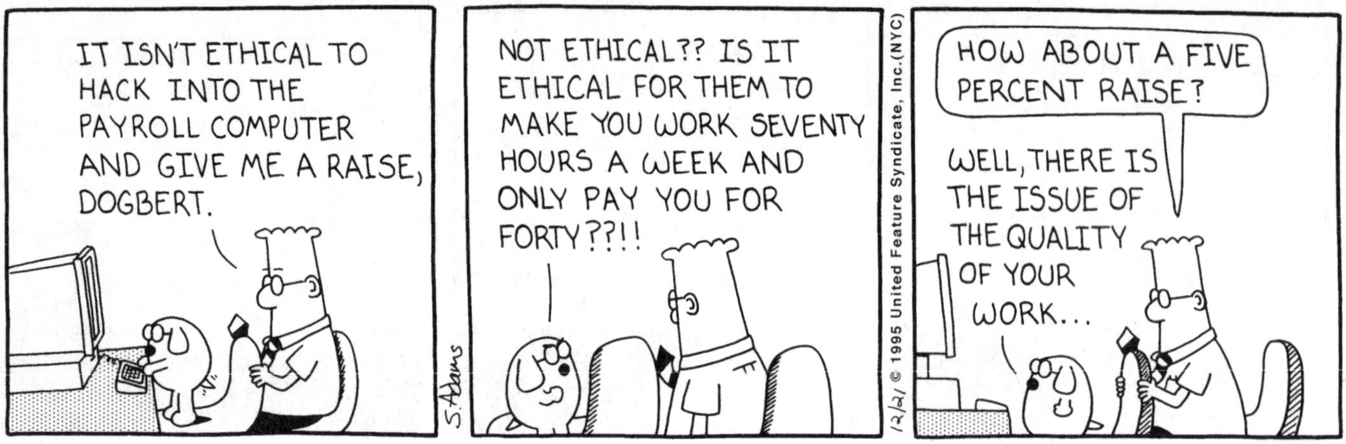
IT ISN'T ETHICAL TO HACK INTO THE PAYROLL COMPUTER AND GIVE ME A RAISE, DOGBERT.
S. Adams
NOT ETHICAL?? IS IT ETHICAL FOR THEM TO MAKE YOU WORK SEVENTY HOURS A WEEK AND ONLY PAY YOU FOR FORTY??!!
12/21 © 1995 United Feature Syndicate, Inc.(NYC)
HOW ABOUT A FIVE PERCENT RAISE?
WELL, THERE IS THE ISSUE OF THE QUALITY OF YOUR WORK...

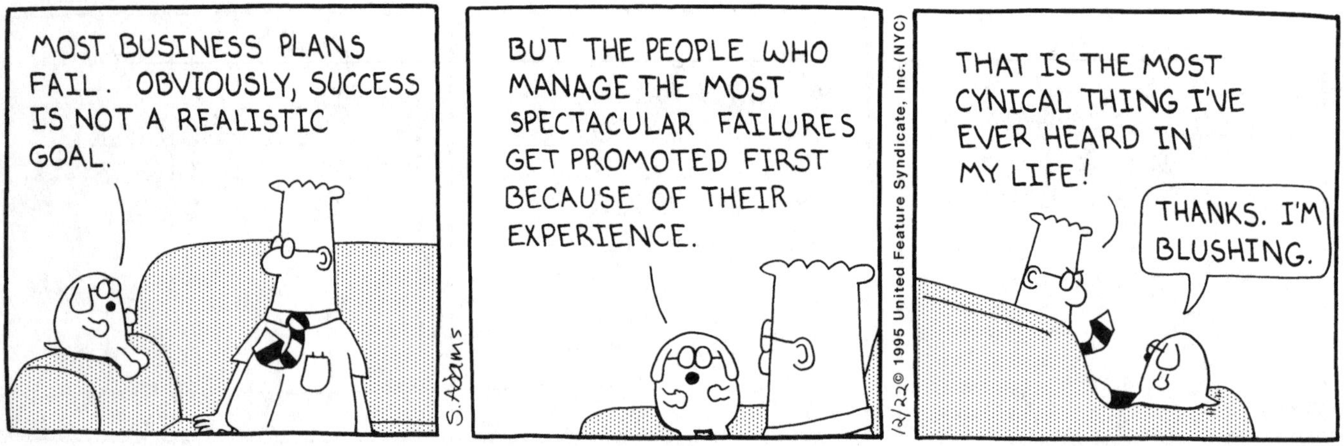
MOST BUSINESS PLANS FAIL. OBVIOUSLY, SUCCESS IS NOT A REALISTIC GOAL.
S. Adams
BUT THE PEOPLE WHO MANAGE THE MOST SPECTACULAR FAILURES GET PROMOTED FIRST BECAUSE OF THEIR EXPERIENCE.
12/22 © 1995 United Feature Syndicate, Inc.(NYC)
THAT IS THE MOST CYNICAL THING I'VE EVER HEARD IN MY LIFE!
THANKS. I'M BLUSHING.

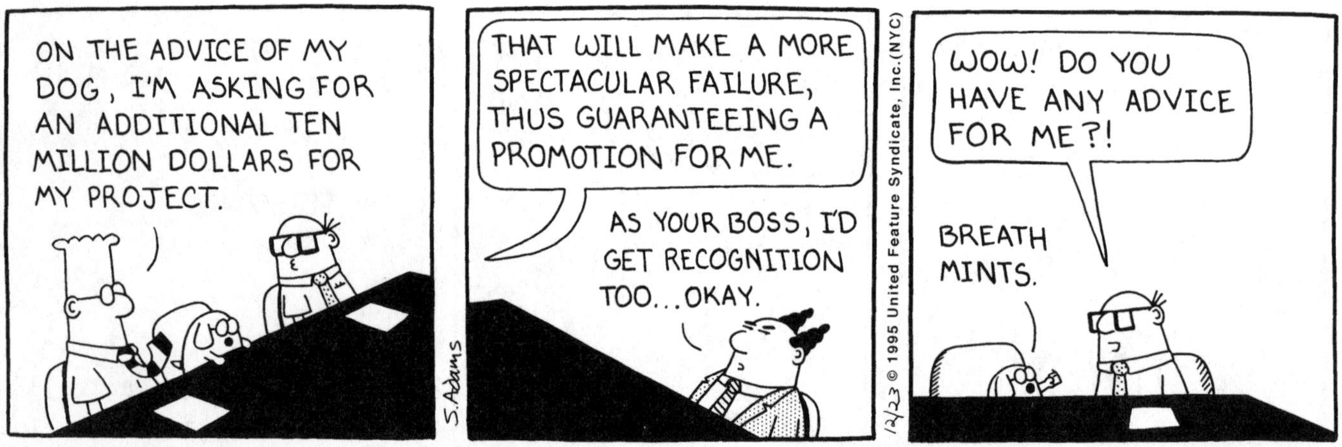
ON THE ADVICE OF MY DOG, I'M ASKING FOR AN ADDITIONAL TEN MILLION DOLLARS FOR MY PROJECT.
S. Adams
THAT WILL MAKE A MORE SPECTACULAR FAILURE, THUS GUARANTEEING A PROMOTION FOR ME.
AS YOUR BOSS, I'D GET RECOGNITION TOO... OKAY.
12/23 © 1995 United Feature Syndicate, Inc.(NYC)
WOW! DO YOU HAVE ANY ADVICE FOR ME?!
BREATH MINTS.

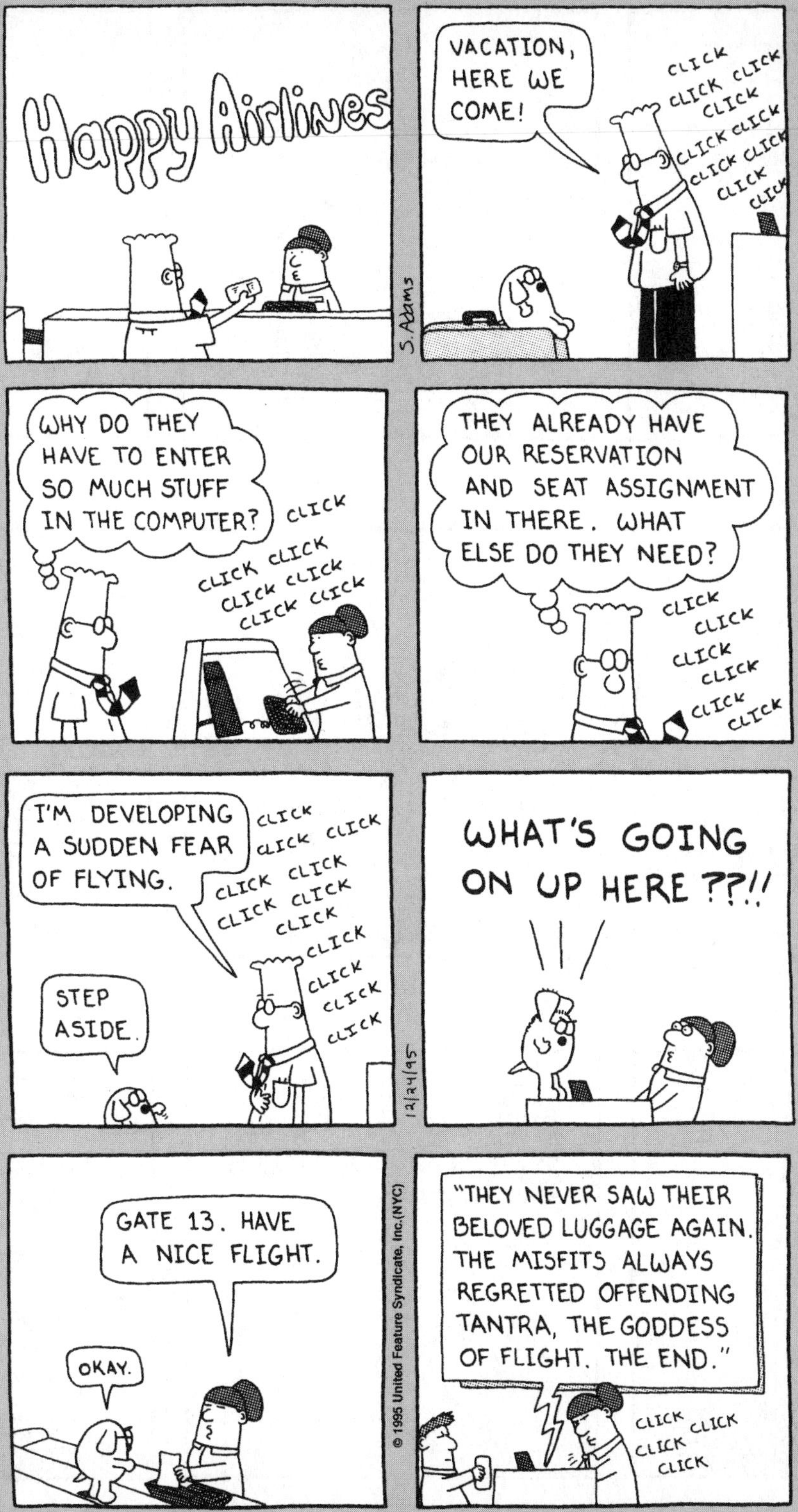
Happy Airlines
S. Adams
VACATION, HERE WE COME!
CLICK CLICK CLICK CLICK CLICK CLICK CLICK CLICK CLICK CLICK
WHY DO THEY HAVE TO ENTER SO MUCH STUFF IN THE COMPUTER?
CLICK CLICK CLICK CLICK CLICK CLICK CLICK
THEY ALREADY HAVE OUR RESERVATION AND SEAT ASSIGNMENT IN THERE. WHAT ELSE DO THEY NEED?
CLICK CLICK CLICK CLICK CLICK CLICK
I'M DEVELOPING A SUDDEN FEAR OF FLYING.
CLICK CLICK CLICK CLICK CLICK CLICK CLICK CLICK CLICK CLICK CLICK CLICK
STEP ASIDE.
12/24/95
WHAT'S GOING ON UP HERE ??!!
© 1995 United Feature Syndicate, Inc.(NYC)
GATE 13. HAVE A NICE FLIGHT.
OKAY.
"THEY NEVER SAW THEIR BELOVED LUGGAGE AGAIN. THE MISFITS ALWAYS REGRETTED OFFENDING TANTRA, THE GODDESS OF FLIGHT. THE END."
CLICK CLICK CLICK CLICK

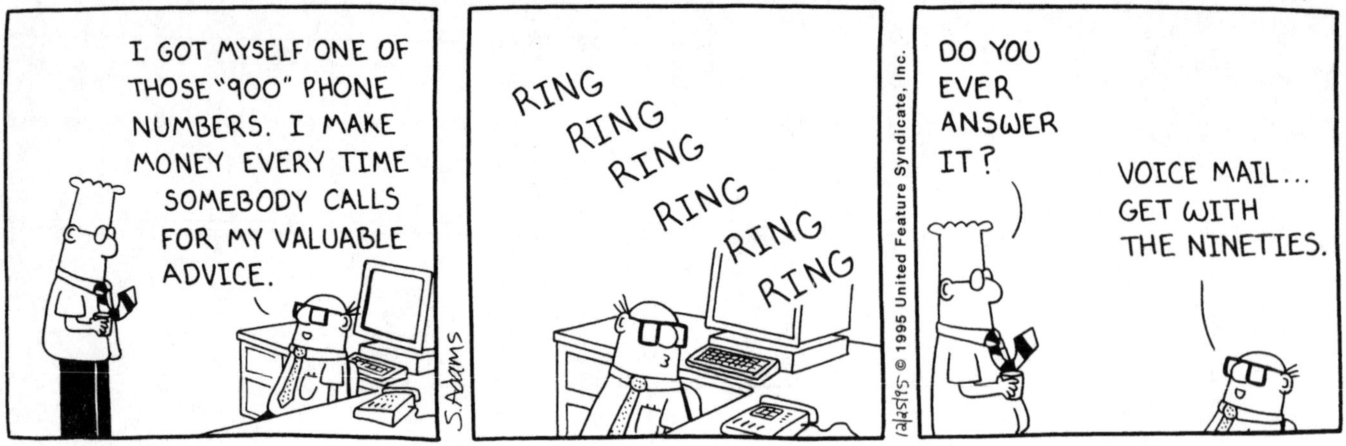
I GOT MYSELF ONE OF THOSE "900" PHONE NUMBERS. I MAKE MONEY EVERY TIME SOMEBODY CALLS FOR MY VALUABLE ADVICE.
S. Adams
RING RING RING RING RING RING
12/25/95 © 1995 United Feature Syndicate, Inc.
DO YOU EVER ANSWER IT?
VOICE MAIL... GET WITH THE NINETIES.

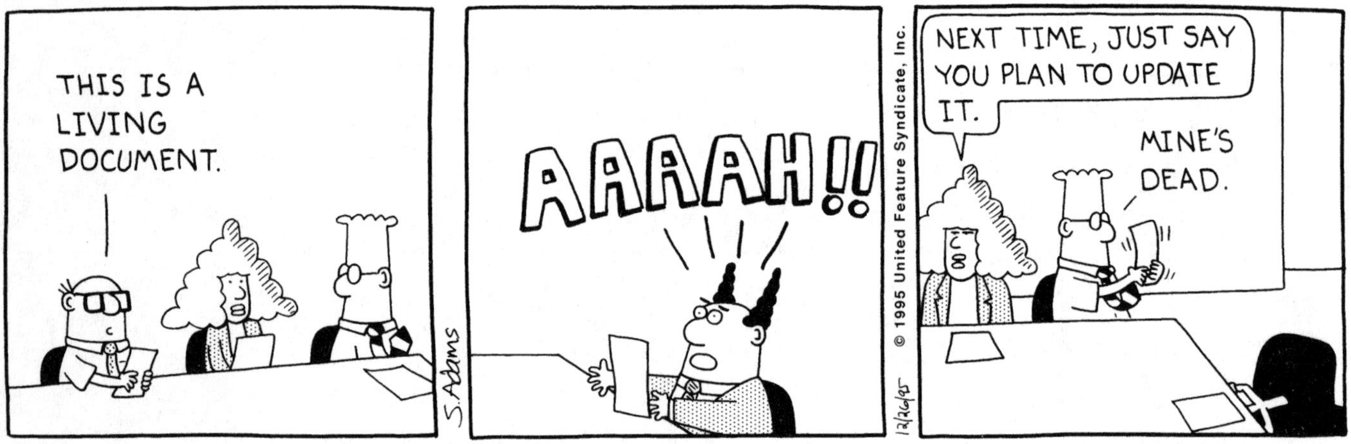
THIS IS A LIVING DOCUMENT.
S. Adams
AAAAH!!
12/26/95 © 1995 United Feature Syndicate, Inc.
NEXT TIME, JUST SAY YOU PLAN TO UPDATE IT.
MINE'S DEAD.

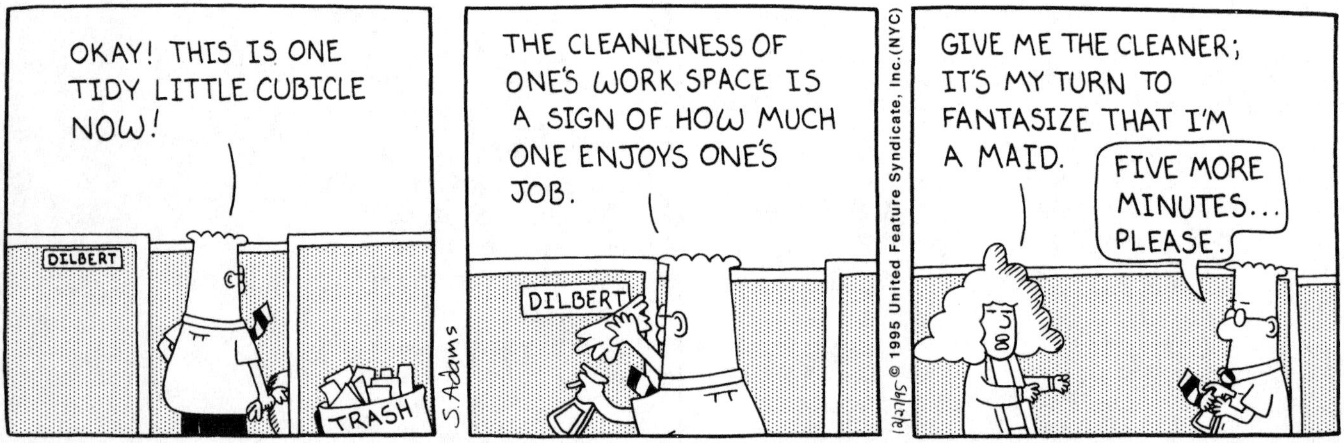
OKAY! THIS IS ONE TIDY LITTLE CUBICLE NOW!
DILBERT
TRASH
S. Adams
THE CLEANLINESS OF ONE'S WORK SPACE IS A SIGN OF HOW MUCH ONE ENJOYS ONE'S JOB.
DILBERT
12/27/95 © 1995 United Feature Syndicate, Inc.(NYC)
GIVE ME THE CLEANER; IT'S MY TURN TO FANTASIZE THAT I'M A MAID.
FIVE MORE MINUTES... PLEASE.

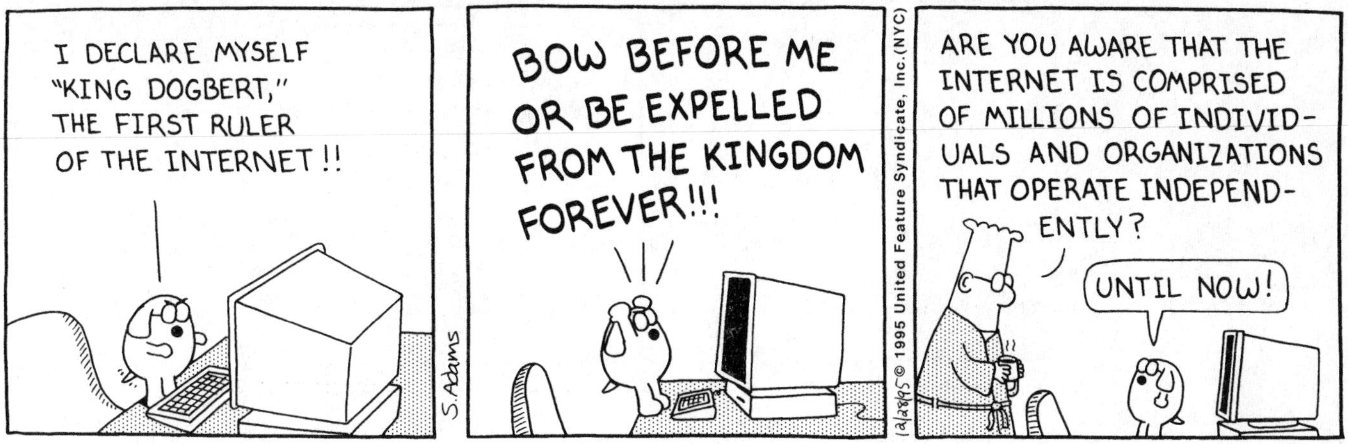
I DECLARE MYSELF "KING DOGBERT," THE FIRST RULER OF THE INTERNET!!
S. Adams
BOW BEFORE ME OR BE EXPELLED FROM THE KINGDOM FOREVER!!!
12/28/95 © 1995 United Feature Syndicate, Inc.(NYC)
ARE YOU AWARE THAT THE INTERNET IS COMPRISED OF MILLIONS OF INDIVIDUALS AND ORGANIZATIONS THAT OPERATE INDEPENDENTLY?
UNTIL NOW!

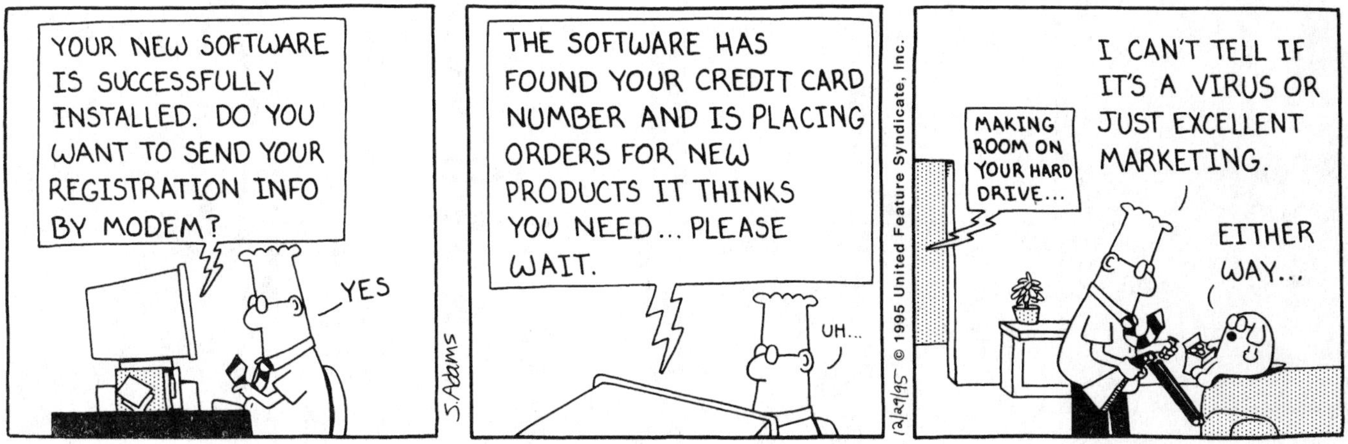
YOUR NEW SOFTWARE IS SUCCESSFULLY INSTALLED. DO YOU WANT TO SEND YOUR REGISTRATION INFO BY MODEM?
YES
S. Adams
THE SOFTWARE HAS FOUND YOUR CREDIT CARD NUMBER AND IS PLACING ORDERS FOR NEW PRODUCTS IT THINKS YOU NEED... PLEASE WAIT.
UH...
12/29/95 © 1995 United Feature Syndicate, Inc.
MAKING ROOM ON YOUR HARD DRIVE...
I CAN'T TELL IF IT'S A VIRUS OR JUST EXCELLENT MARKETING.
EITHER WAY...

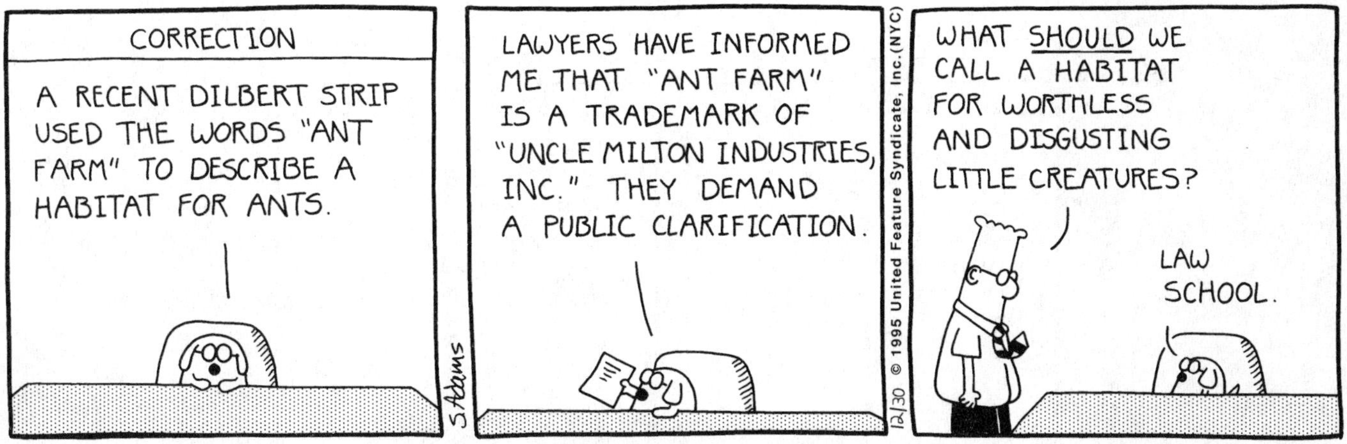
CORRECTION
A RECENT DILBERT STRIP USED THE WORDS "ANT FARM" TO DESCRIBE A HABITAT FOR ANTS.
S. Adams
LAWYERS HAVE INFORMED ME THAT "ANT FARM" IS A TRADEMARK OF "UNCLE MILTON INDUSTRIES, INC." THEY DEMAND A PUBLIC CLARIFICATION.
12/30 © 1995 United Feature Syndicate, Inc.(NYC)
WHAT SHOULD WE CALL A HABITAT FOR WORTHLESS AND DISGUSTING LITTLE CREATURES?
LAW SCHOOL.

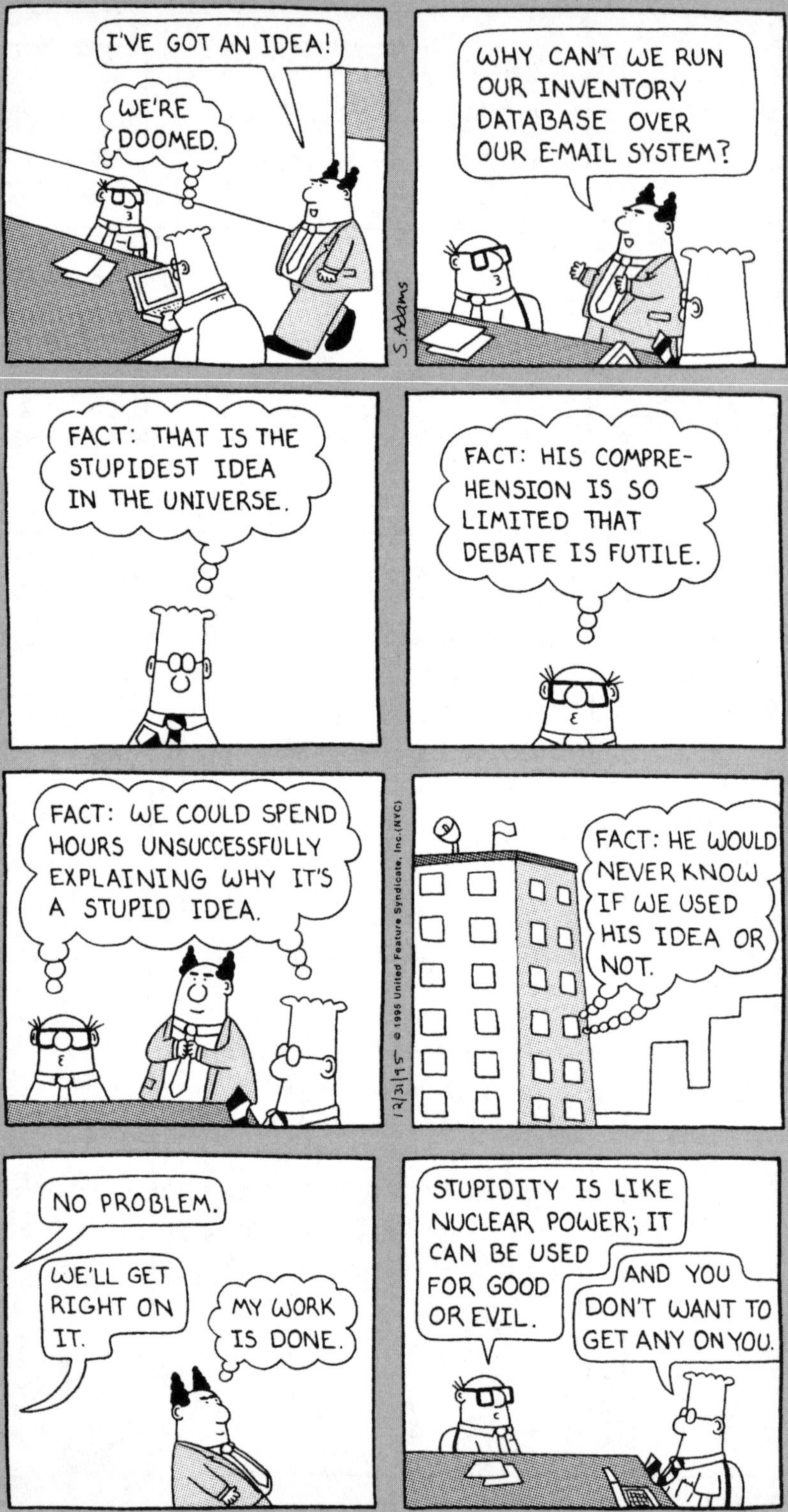
I'VE GOT AN IDEA!
WE'RE DOOMED.
S. Adams
WHY CAN'T WE RUN OUR INVENTORY DATABASE OVER OUR E-MAIL SYSTEM?
FACT: THAT IS THE STUPIDEST IDEA IN THE UNIVERSE.
FACT: HIS COMPRE-HENSION IS SO LIMITED THAT DEBATE IS FUTILE.
FACT: WE COULD SPEND HOURS UNSUCCESSFULLY EXPLAINING WHY IT'S A STUPID IDEA.
12/31/95 © 1995 United Feature Syndicate, Inc.(NYC)
FACT: HE WOULD NEVER KNOW IF WE USED HIS IDEA OR NOT.
NO PROBLEM.
WE'LL GET RIGHT ON IT.
MY WORK IS DONE.
STUPIDITY IS LIKE NUCLEAR POWER; IT CAN BE USED FOR GOOD OR EVIL.
AND YOU DON'T WANT TO GET ANY ON YOU.

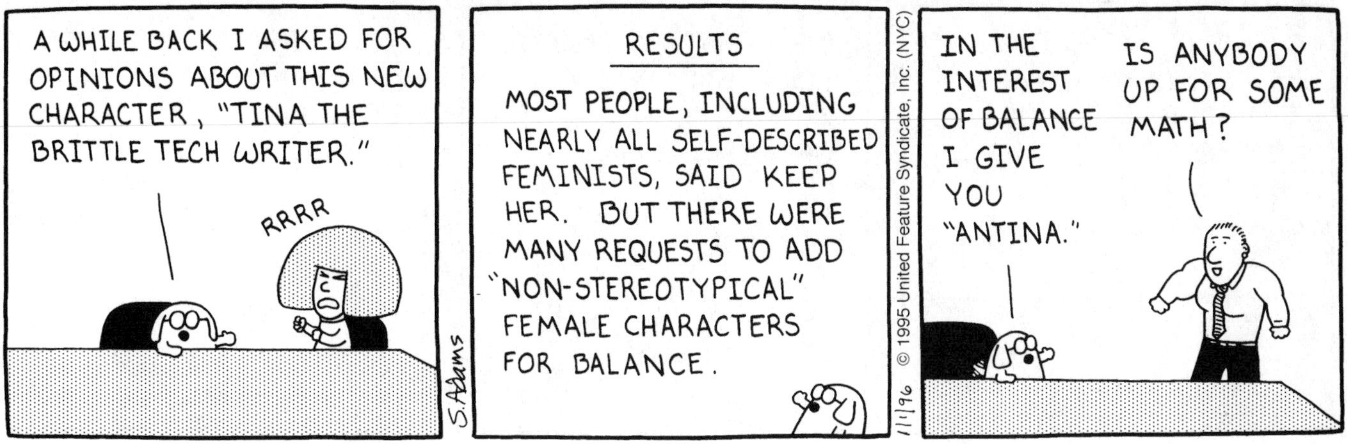
A WHILE BACK I ASKED FOR OPINIONS ABOUT THIS NEW CHARACTER, "TINA THE BRITTLE TECH WRITER."
RRRR
S. Adams
RESULTS
MOST PEOPLE, INCLUDING NEARLY ALL SELF-DESCRIBED FEMINISTS, SAID KEEP HER. BUT THERE WERE MANY REQUESTS TO ADD "NON-STEREOTYPICAL" FEMALE CHARACTERS FOR BALANCE.
1/1/96 © 1995 United Feature Syndicate, Inc. (NYC)
IN THE INTEREST OF BALANCE I GIVE YOU "ANTINA."
IS ANYBODY UP FOR SOME MATH?

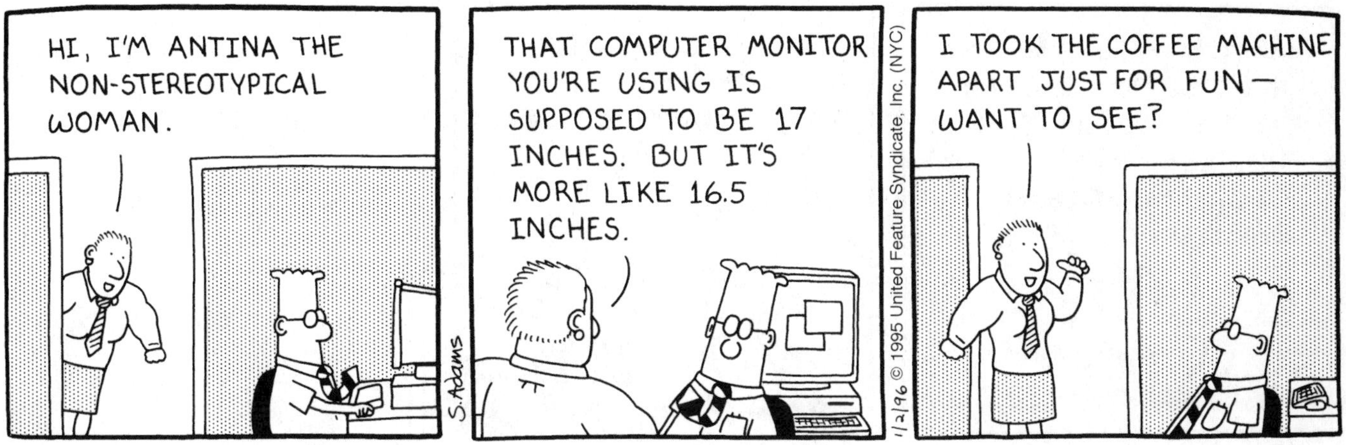
HI, I'M ANTINA THE NON-STEREOTYPICAL WOMAN.
S. Adams
THAT COMPUTER MONITOR YOU'RE USING IS SUPPOSED TO BE 17 INCHES. BUT IT'S MORE LIKE 16.5 INCHES.
1/2/96 © 1995 United Feature Syndicate, Inc. (NYC)
I TOOK THE COFFEE MACHINE APART JUST FOR FUN — WANT TO SEE?

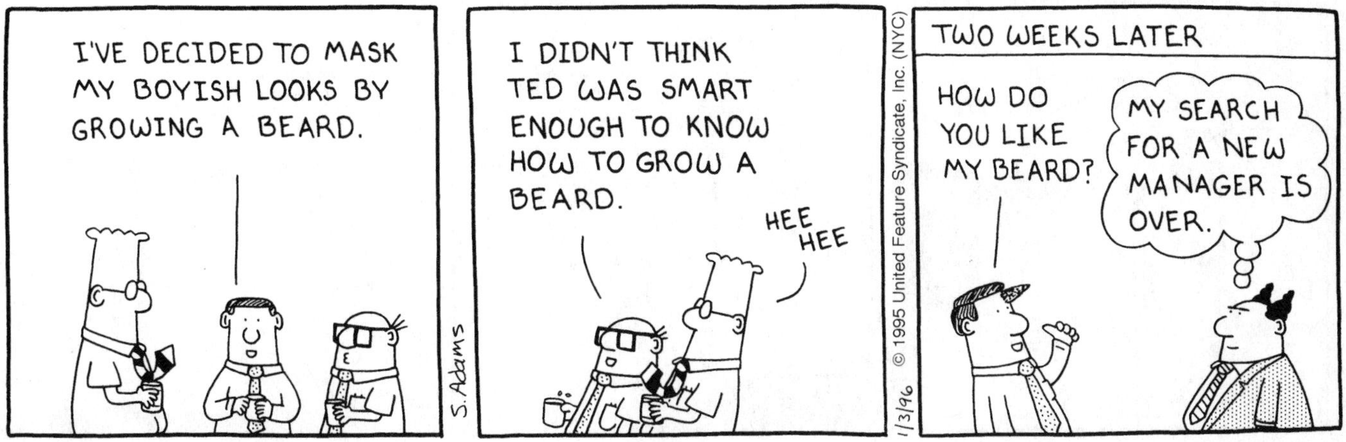
I'VE DECIDED TO MASK MY BOYISH LOOKS BY GROWING A BEARD.
S. Adams
I DIDN'T THINK TED WAS SMART ENOUGH TO KNOW HOW TO GROW A BEARD.
HEE HEE
1/3/96 © 1995 United Feature Syndicate, Inc. (NYC)
TWO WEEKS LATER
HOW DO YOU LIKE MY BEARD?
MY SEARCH FOR A NEW MANAGER IS OVER.

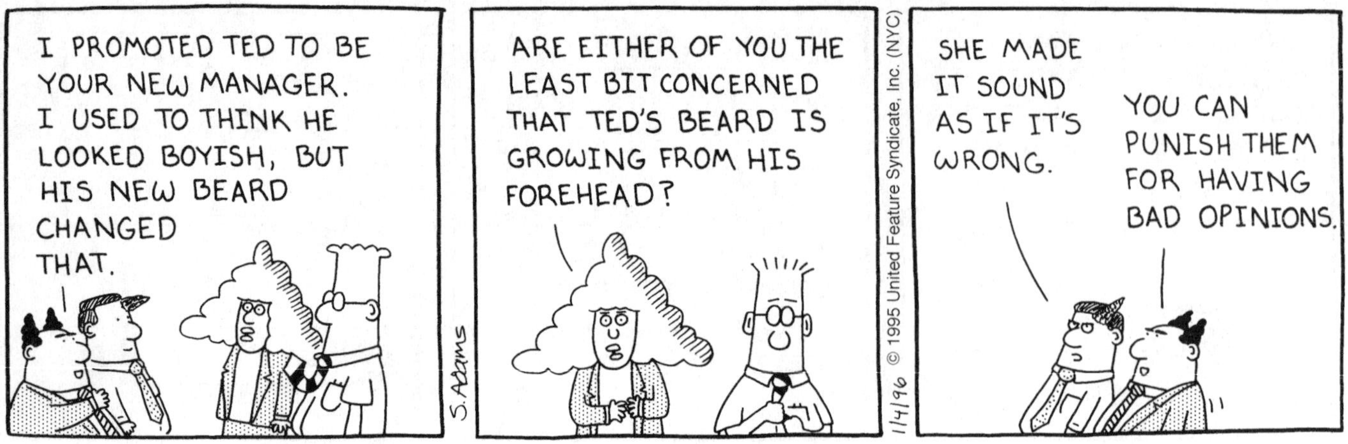
I PROMOTED TED TO BE YOUR NEW MANAGER. I USED TO THINK HE LOOKED BOYISH, BUT HIS NEW BEARD CHANGED THAT.
S. Adams
ARE EITHER OF YOU THE LEAST BIT CONCERNED THAT TED'S BEARD IS GROWING FROM HIS FOREHEAD?
1/4/96 © 1995 United Feature Syndicate, Inc. (NYC)
SHE MADE IT SOUND AS IF IT'S WRONG.
YOU CAN PUNISH THEM FOR HAVING BAD OPINIONS.

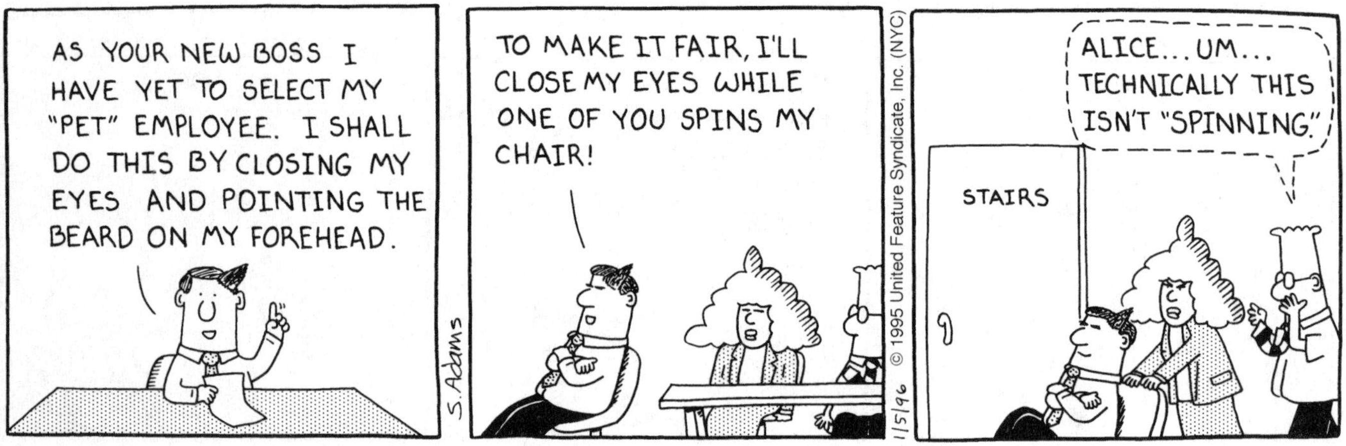
AS YOUR NEW BOSS I HAVE YET TO SELECT MY "PET" EMPLOYEE. I SHALL DO THIS BY CLOSING MY EYES AND POINTING THE BEARD ON MY FOREHEAD.
S. Adams
TO MAKE IT FAIR, I'LL CLOSE MY EYES WHILE ONE OF YOU SPINS MY CHAIR!
1/5/96 © 1995 United Feature Syndicate, Inc. (NYC)
STAIRS
ALICE... UM... TECHNICALLY THIS ISN'T "SPINNING."

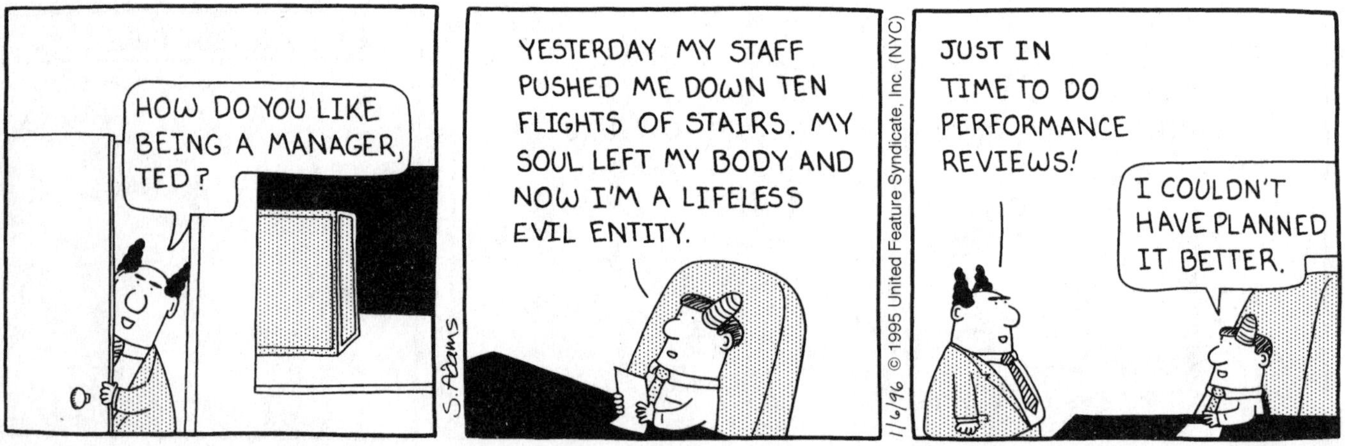
HOW DO YOU LIKE BEING A MANAGER, TED?
S. Adams
YESTERDAY MY STAFF PUSHED ME DOWN TEN FLIGHTS OF STAIRS. MY SOUL LEFT MY BODY AND NOW I'M A LIFELESS EVIL ENTITY.
1/6/96 © 1995 United Feature Syndicate, Inc. (NYC)
JUST IN TIME TO DO PERFORMANCE REVIEWS!
I COULDN'T HAVE PLANNED IT BETTER.

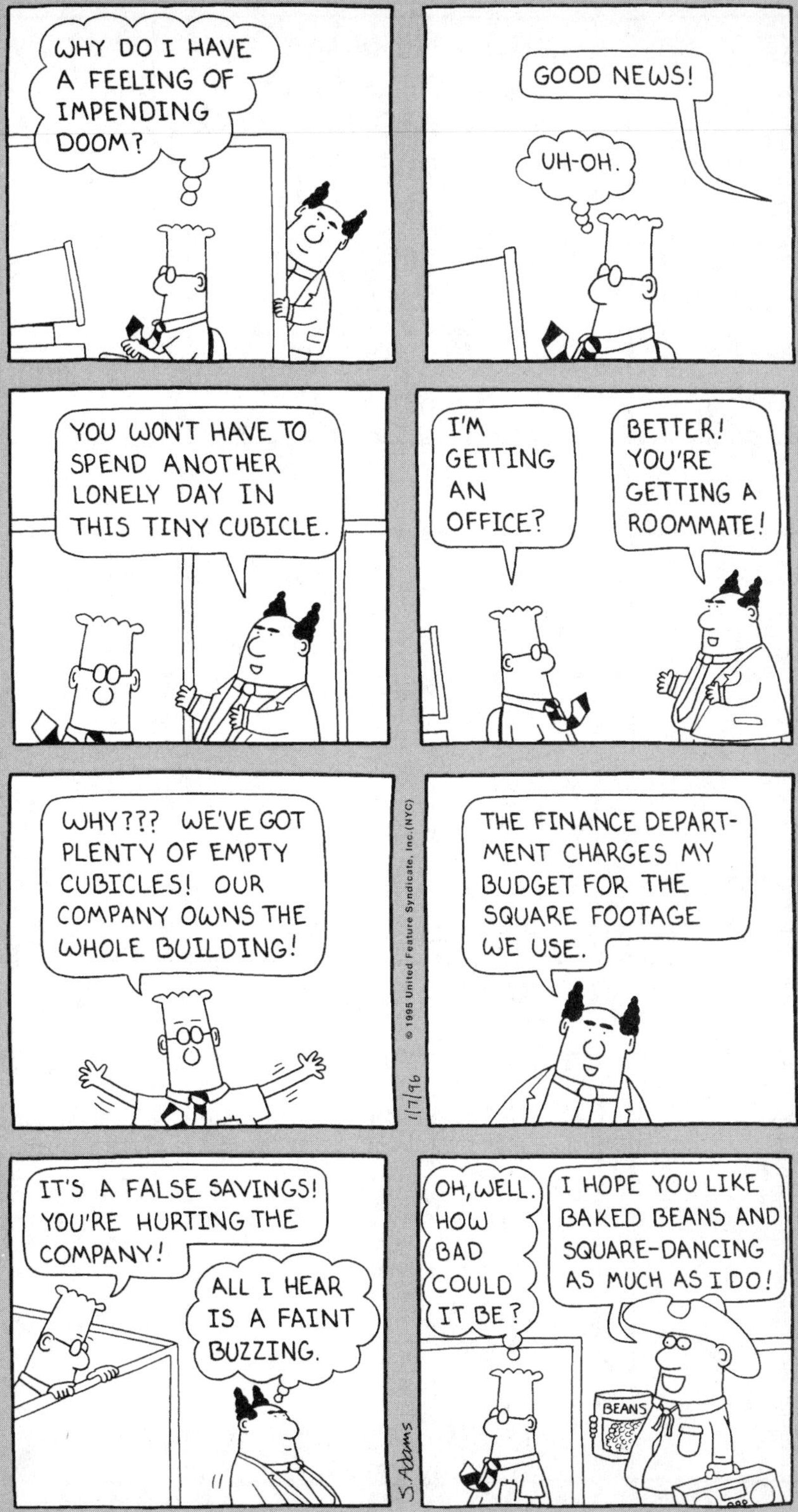
WHY DO I HAVE A FEELING OF IMPENDING DOOM?
GOOD NEWS!
UH-OH.
YOU WON'T HAVE TO SPEND ANOTHER LONELY DAY IN THIS TINY CUBICLE.
I'M GETTING AN OFFICE?
BETTER! YOU'RE GETTING A ROOMMATE!
WHY??? WE'VE GOT PLENTY OF EMPTY CUBICLES! OUR COMPANY OWNS THE WHOLE BUILDING!
THE FINANCE DEPARTMENT CHARGES MY BUDGET FOR THE SQUARE FOOTAGE WE USE.
IT'S A FALSE SAVINGS! YOU'RE HURTING THE COMPANY!
ALL I HEAR IS A FAINT BUZZING.
OH, WELL. HOW BAD COULD IT BE?
I HOPE YOU LIKE BAKED BEANS AND SQUARE-DANCING AS MUCH AS I DO!
BEANS
1/7/96
S. Adams

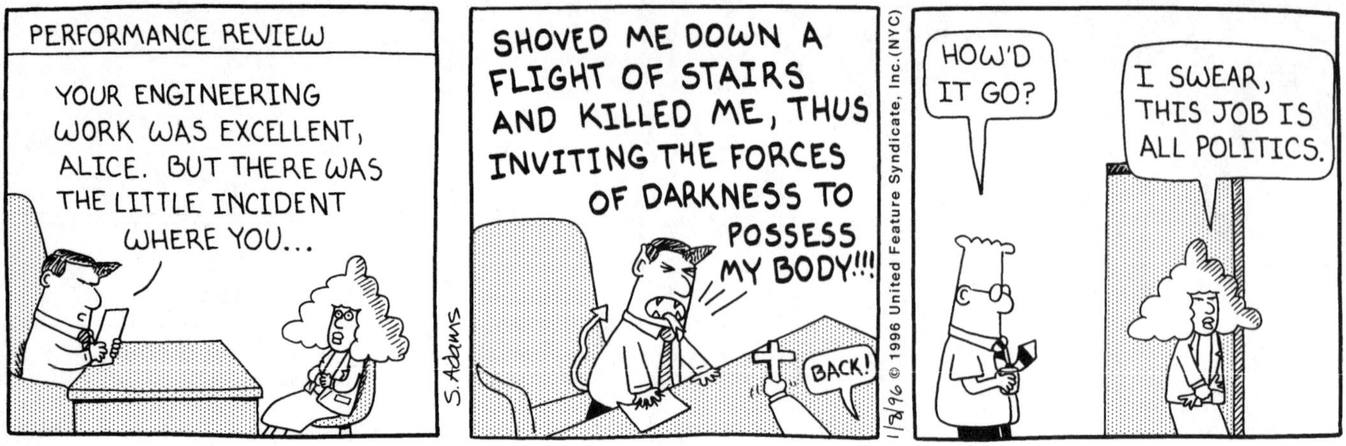
PERFORMANCE REVIEW
YOUR ENGINEERING WORK WAS EXCELLENT, ALICE. BUT THERE WAS THE LITTLE INCIDENT WHERE YOU...
S. Adams
SHOVED ME DOWN A FLIGHT OF STAIRS AND KILLED ME, THUS INVITING THE FORCES OF DARKNESS TO POSSESS MY BODY!!!
BACK!
1/8/96 © 1996 United Feature Syndicate, Inc.(NYC)
HOW'D IT GO?
I SWEAR, THIS JOB IS ALL POLITICS.

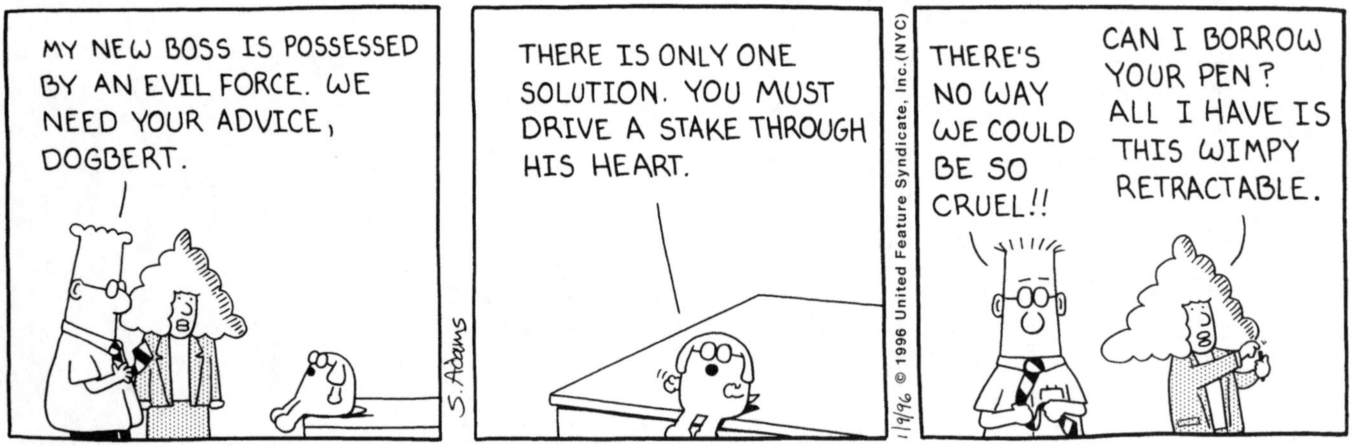
MY NEW BOSS IS POSSESSED BY AN EVIL FORCE. WE NEED YOUR ADVICE, DOGBERT.
S. Adams
THERE IS ONLY ONE SOLUTION. YOU MUST DRIVE A STAKE THROUGH HIS HEART.
1/9/96 © 1996 United Feature Syndicate, Inc.(NYC)
THERE'S NO WAY WE COULD BE SO CRUEL!!
CAN I BORROW YOUR PEN? ALL I HAVE IS THIS WIMPY RETRACTABLE.

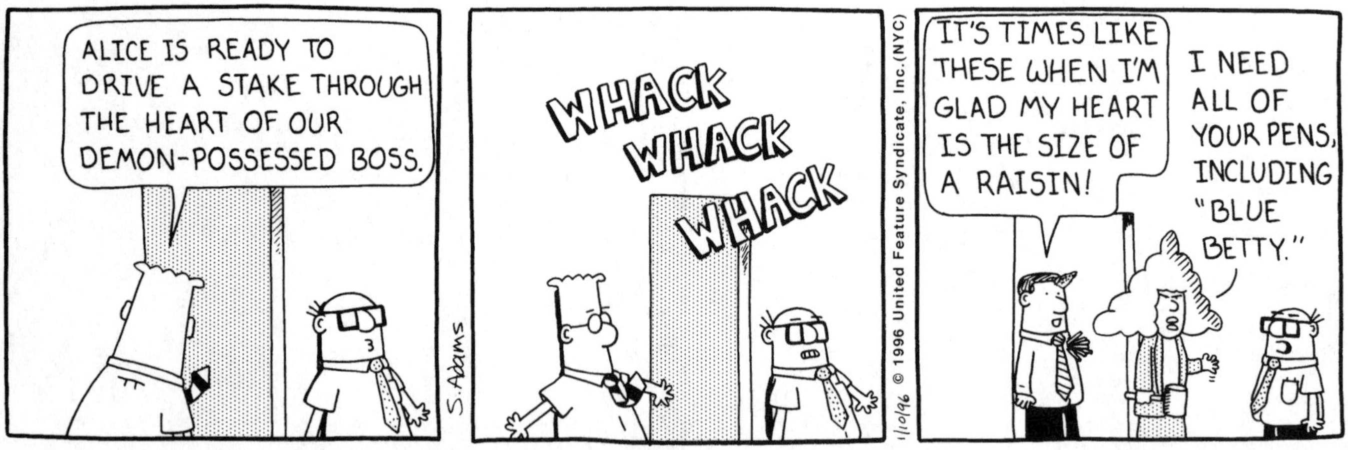
ALICE IS READY TO DRIVE A STAKE THROUGH THE HEART OF OUR DEMON-POSSESSED BOSS.
S. Adams
WHACK
WHACK
WHACK
1/10/96 © 1996 United Feature Syndicate, Inc.(NYC)
IT'S TIMES LIKE THESE WHEN I'M GLAD MY HEART IS THE SIZE OF A RAISIN!
I NEED ALL OF YOUR PENS, INCLUDING "BLUE BETTY."

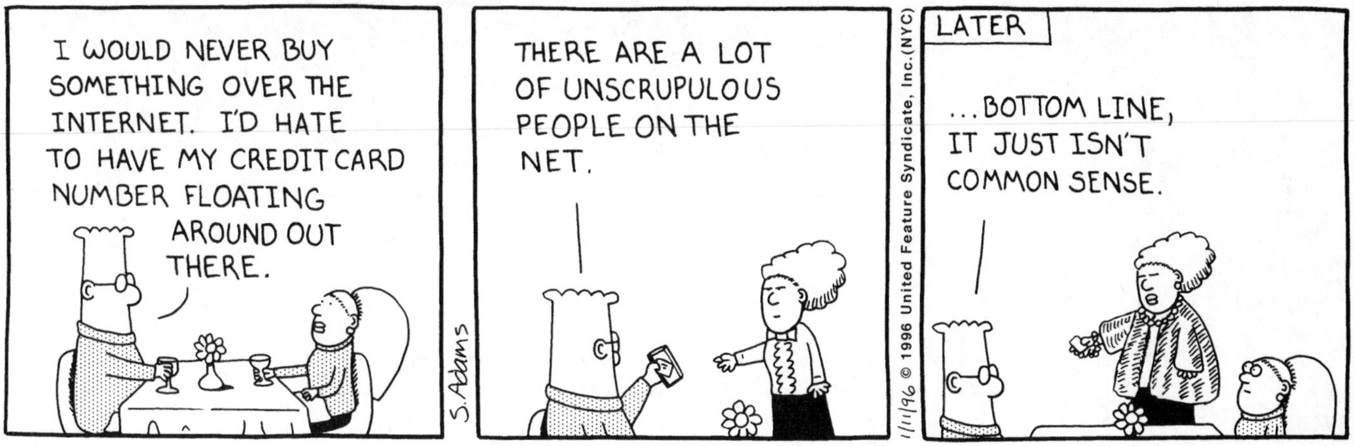
I WOULD NEVER BUY SOMETHING OVER THE INTERNET. I'D HATE TO HAVE MY CREDIT CARD NUMBER FLOATING AROUND OUT THERE.
S. Adams
THERE ARE A LOT OF UNSCRUPULOUS PEOPLE ON THE NET.
1/11/96 © 1996 United Feature Syndicate, Inc.(NYC)
LATER
...BOTTOM LINE, IT JUST ISN'T COMMON SENSE.

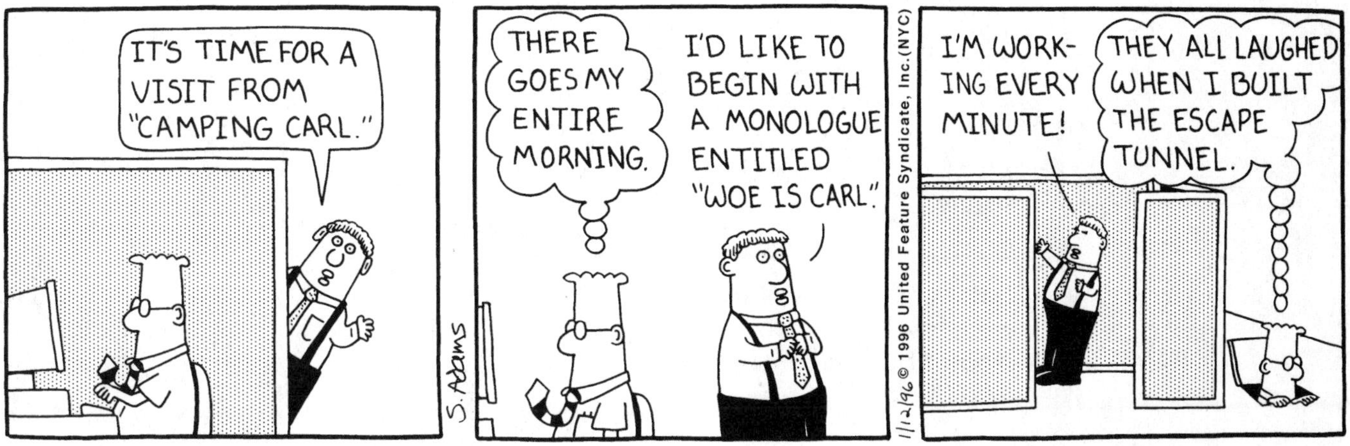
IT'S TIME FOR A VISIT FROM "CAMPING CARL."
S. Adams
THERE GOES MY ENTIRE MORNING.
I'D LIKE TO BEGIN WITH A MONOLOGUE ENTITLED "WOE IS CARL."
1/12/96 © 1996 United Feature Syndicate, Inc.(NYC)
I'M WORKING EVERY MINUTE!
THEY ALL LAUGHED WHEN I BUILT THE ESCAPE TUNNEL.

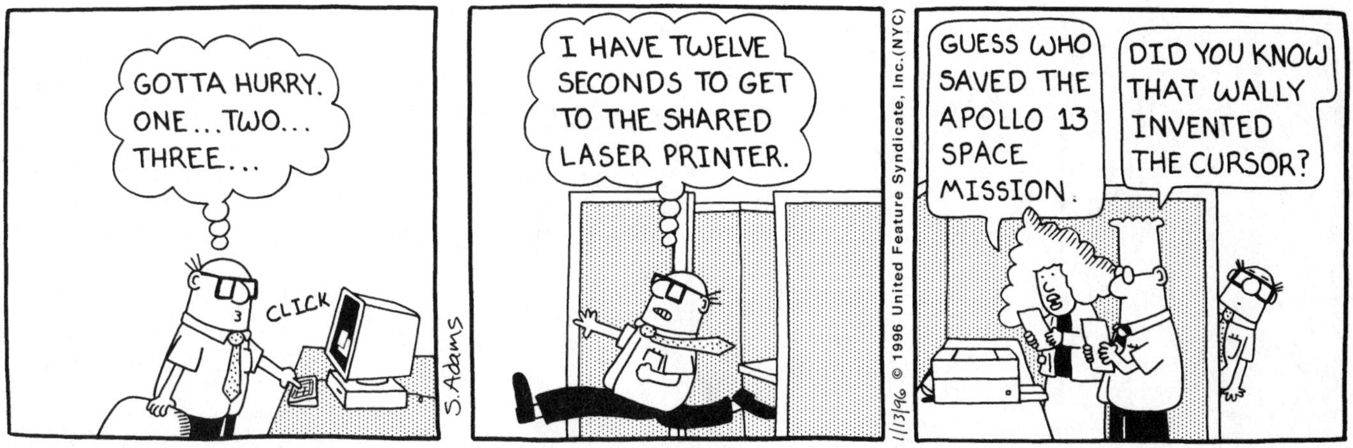
GOTTA HURRY. ONE...TWO... THREE...
CLICK
S. Adams
I HAVE TWELVE SECONDS TO GET TO THE SHARED LASER PRINTER.
1/13/96 © 1996 United Feature Syndicate, Inc.(NYC)
GUESS WHO SAVED THE APOLLO 13 SPACE MISSION.
DID YOU KNOW THAT WALLY INVENTED THE CURSOR?

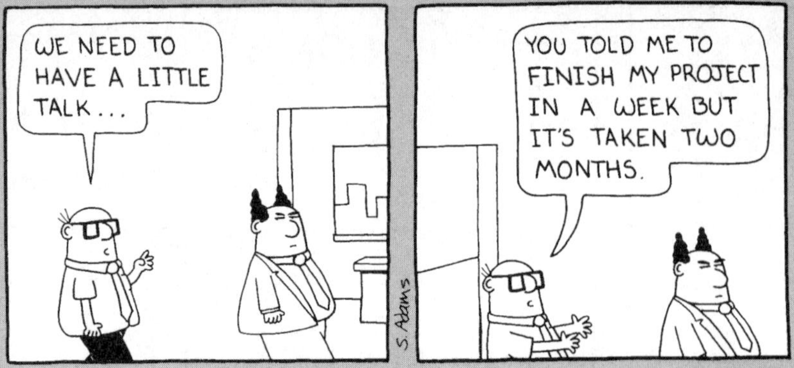

WE NEED TO HAVE A LITTLE TALK...
S. Adams
YOU TOLD ME TO FINISH MY PROJECT IN A WEEK BUT IT'S TAKEN TWO MONTHS.

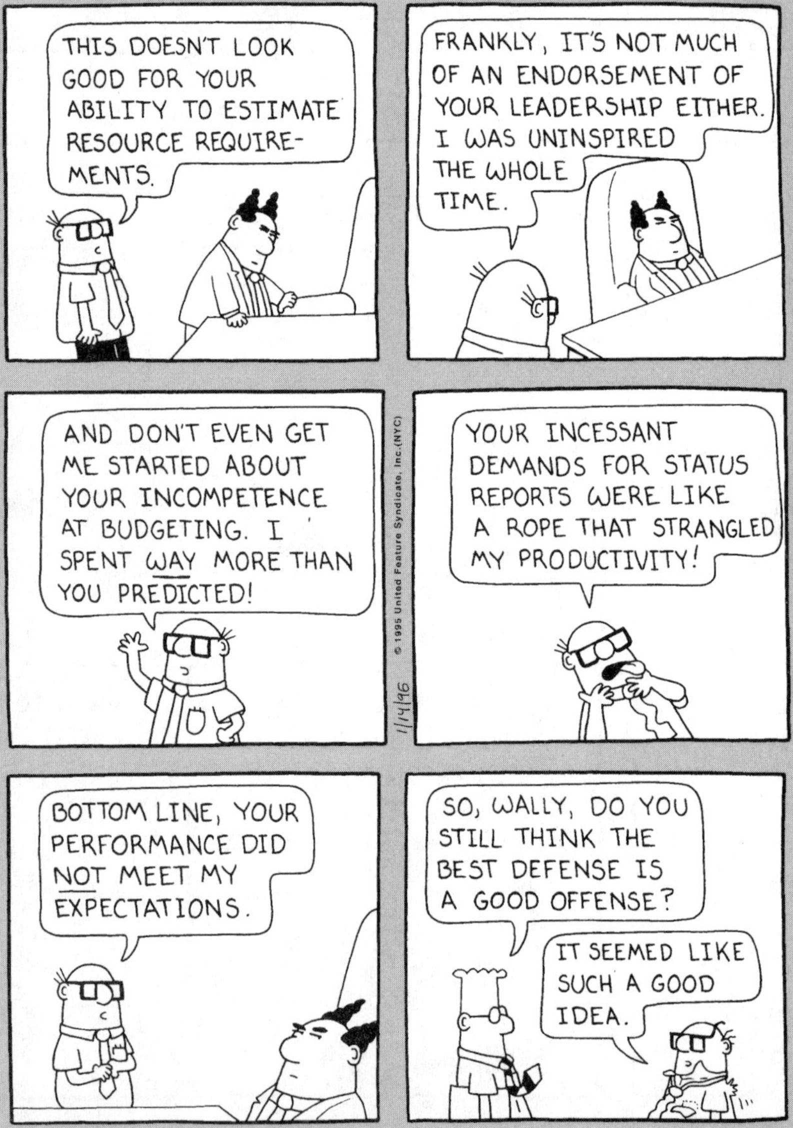

THIS DOESN'T LOOK GOOD FOR YOUR ABILITY TO ESTIMATE RESOURCE REQUIRE-MENTS.
FRANKLY, IT'S NOT MUCH OF AN ENDORSEMENT OF YOUR LEADERSHIP EITHER. I WAS UNINSPIRED THE WHOLE TIME.
AND DON'T EVEN GET ME STARTED ABOUT YOUR INCOMPETENCE AT BUDGETING. I SPENT WAY MORE THAN YOU PREDICTED!
© 1995 United Feature Syndicate, Inc.(NYC)
1/14/96
YOUR INCESSANT DEMANDS FOR STATUS REPORTS WERE LIKE A ROPE THAT STRANGLED MY PRODUCTIVITY!
BOTTOM LINE, YOUR PERFORMANCE DID NOT MEET MY EXPECTATIONS.
SO, WALLY, DO YOU STILL THINK THE BEST DEFENSE IS A GOOD OFFENSE?
IT SEEMED LIKE SUCH A GOOD IDEA.

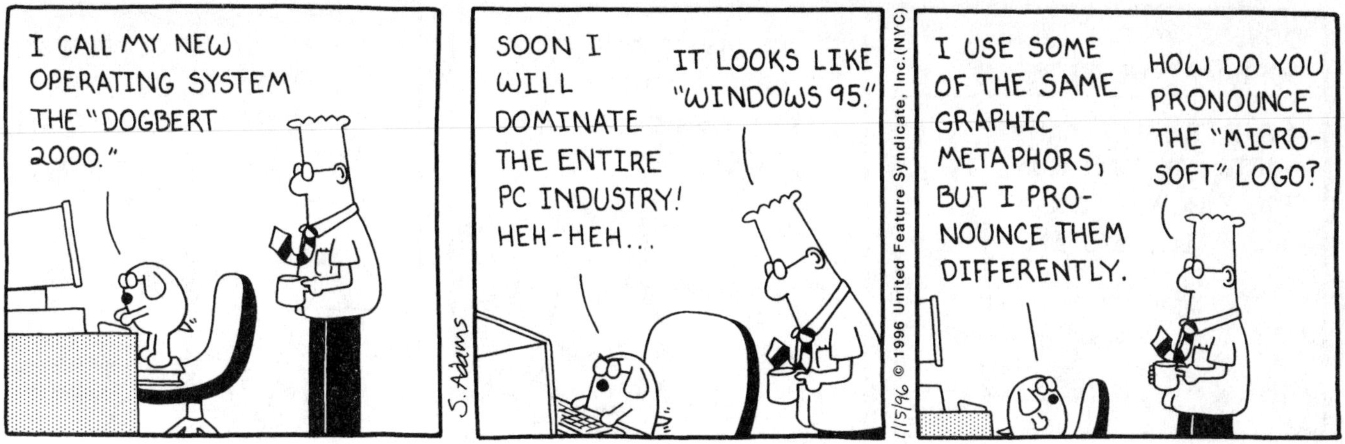
I CALL MY NEW OPERATING SYSTEM THE "DOGBERT 2000."
S. Adams
SOON I WILL DOMINATE THE ENTIRE PC INDUSTRY! HEH-HEH...
IT LOOKS LIKE "WINDOWS 95."
1/15/96 © 1996 United Feature Syndicate, Inc.(NYC)
I USE SOME OF THE SAME GRAPHIC METAPHORS, BUT I PRONOUNCE THEM DIFFERENTLY.
HOW DO YOU PRONOUNCE THE "MICROSOFT" LOGO?

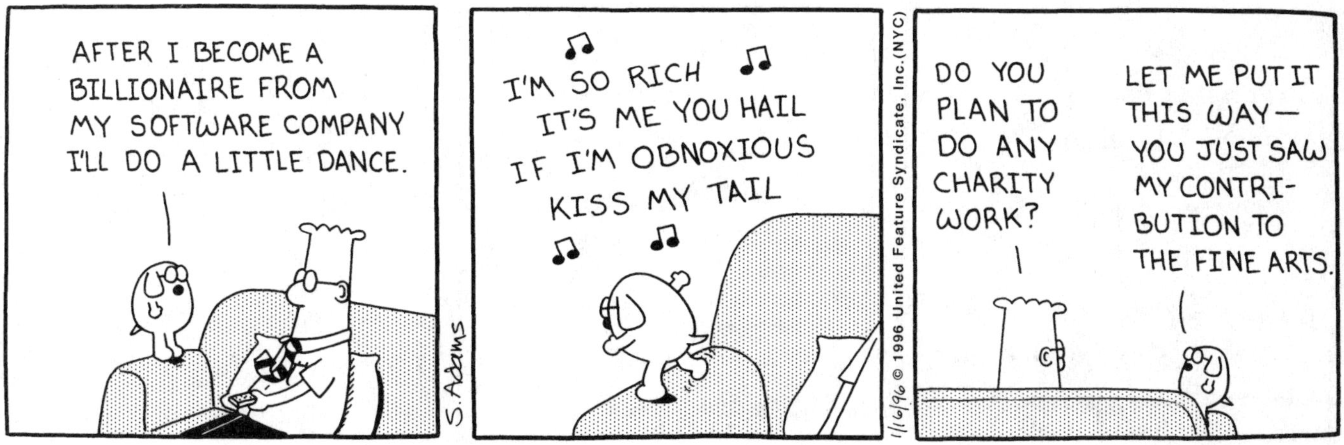
AFTER I BECOME A BILLIONAIRE FROM MY SOFTWARE COMPANY I'LL DO A LITTLE DANCE.
S. Adams
I'M SO RICH IT'S ME YOU HAIL IF I'M OBNOXIOUS KISS MY TAIL
1/16/96 © 1996 United Feature Syndicate, Inc.(NYC)
DO YOU PLAN TO DO ANY CHARITY WORK?
LET ME PUT IT THIS WAY— YOU JUST SAW MY CONTRIBUTION TO THE FINE ARTS.

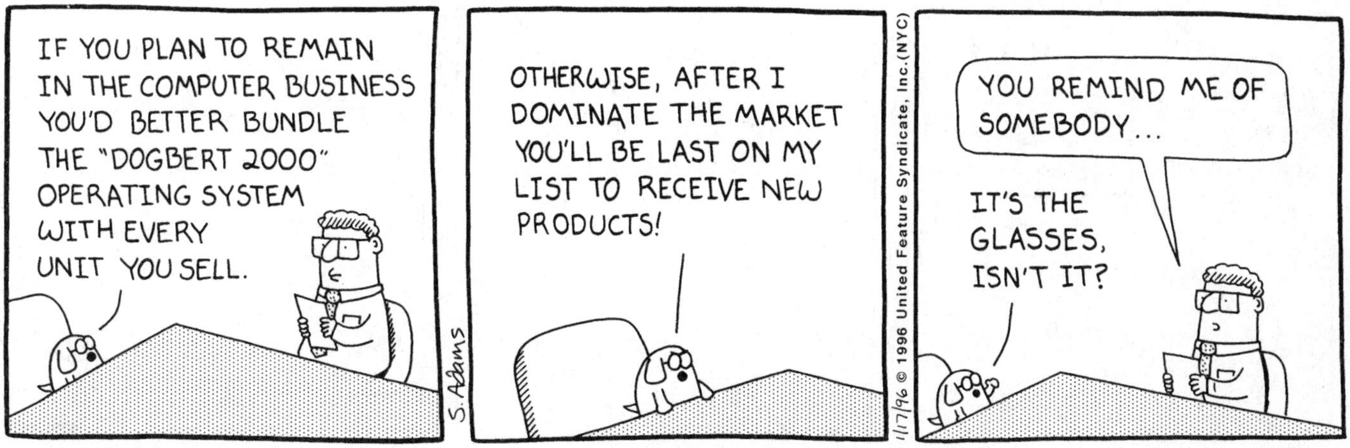
IF YOU PLAN TO REMAIN IN THE COMPUTER BUSINESS YOU'D BETTER BUNDLE THE "DOGBERT 2000" OPERATING SYSTEM WITH EVERY UNIT YOU SELL.
S. Adams
OTHERWISE, AFTER I DOMINATE THE MARKET YOU'LL BE LAST ON MY LIST TO RECEIVE NEW PRODUCTS!
1/17/96 © 1996 United Feature Syndicate, Inc.(NYC)
YOU REMIND ME OF SOMEBODY...
IT'S THE GLASSES, ISN'T IT?

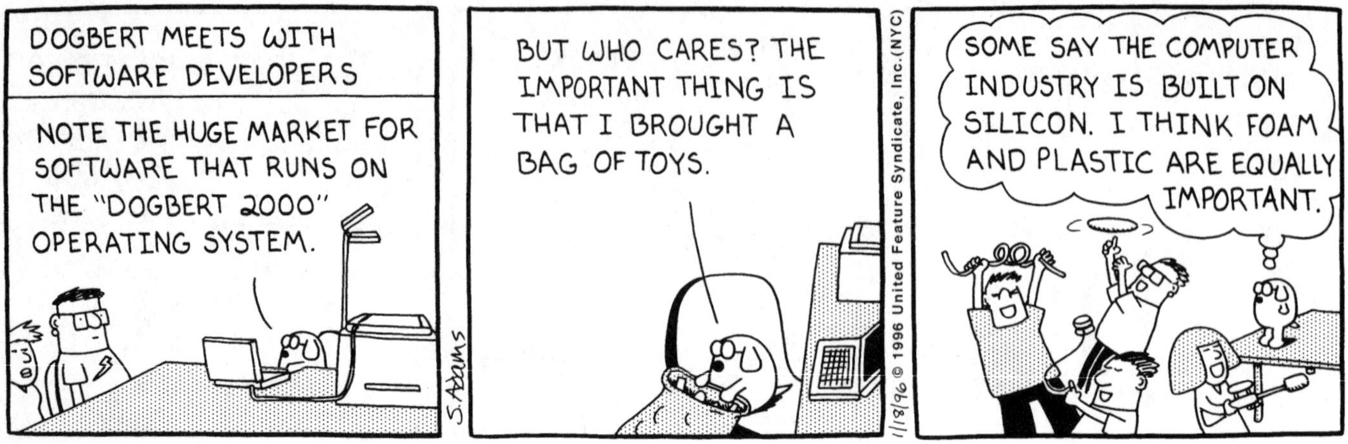
DOGBERT MEETS WITH SOFTWARE DEVELOPERS
NOTE THE HUGE MARKET FOR SOFTWARE THAT RUNS ON THE "DOGBERT 2000" OPERATING SYSTEM.
S. Adams
BUT WHO CARES? THE IMPORTANT THING IS THAT I BROUGHT A BAG OF TOYS.
1/18/96 © 1996 United Feature Syndicate, Inc.(NYC)
SOME SAY THE COMPUTER INDUSTRY IS BUILT ON SILICON. I THINK FOAM AND PLASTIC ARE EQUALLY IMPORTANT.

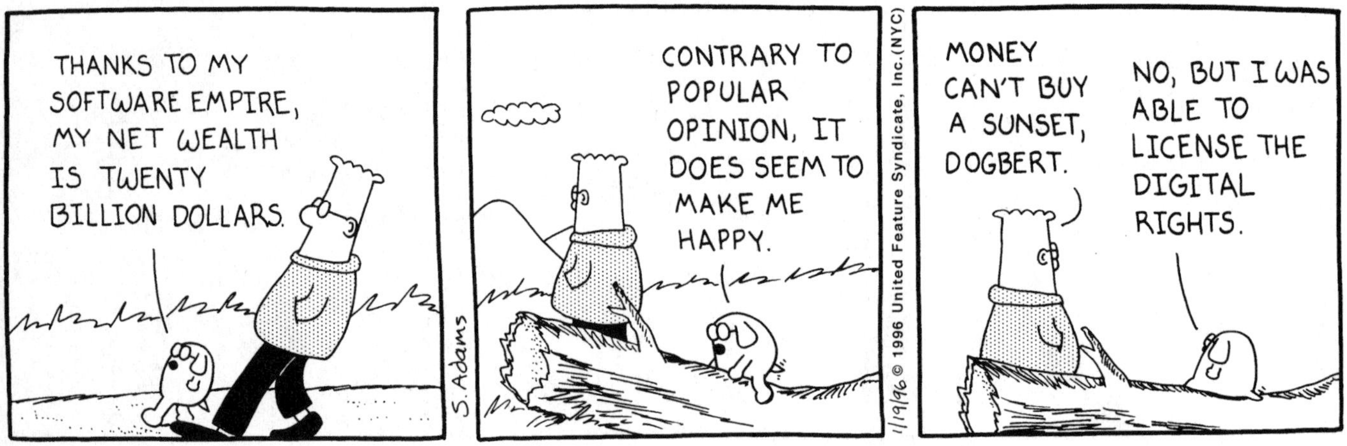
THANKS TO MY SOFTWARE EMPIRE, MY NET WEALTH IS TWENTY BILLION DOLLARS.
S. Adams
CONTRARY TO POPULAR OPINION, IT DOES SEEM TO MAKE ME HAPPY.
1/19/96 © 1996 United Feature Syndicate, Inc.(NYC)
MONEY CAN'T BUY A SUNSET, DOGBERT.
NO, BUT I WAS ABLE TO LICENSE THE DIGITAL RIGHTS.

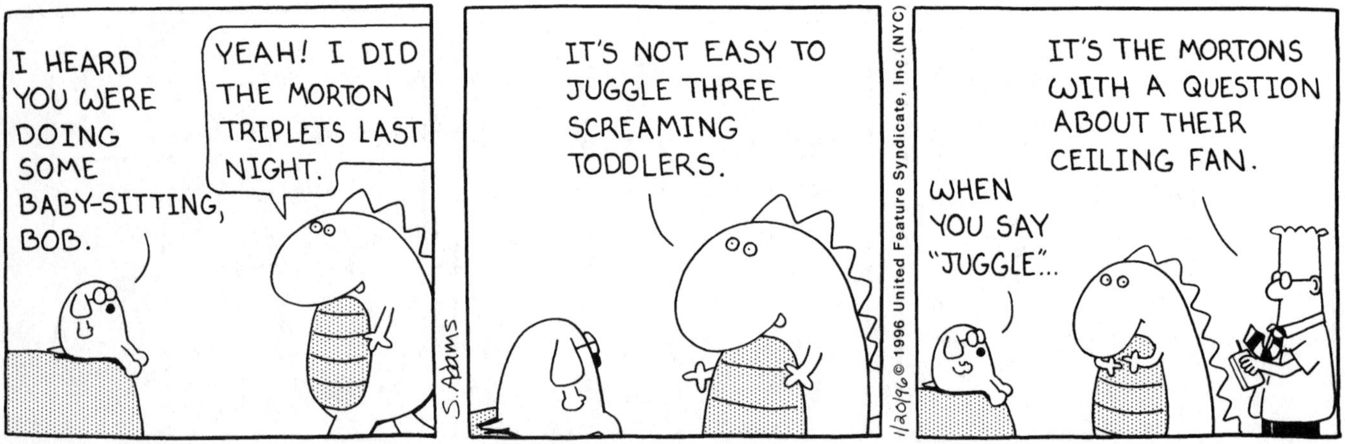
I HEARD YOU WERE DOING SOME BABY-SITTING, BOB.
YEAH! I DID THE MORTON TRIPLETS LAST NIGHT.
S. Adams
IT'S NOT EASY TO JUGGLE THREE SCREAMING TODDLERS.
1/20/96 © 1996 United Feature Syndicate, Inc.(NYC)
WHEN YOU SAY "JUGGLE"...
IT'S THE MORTONS WITH A QUESTION ABOUT THEIR CEILING FAN.

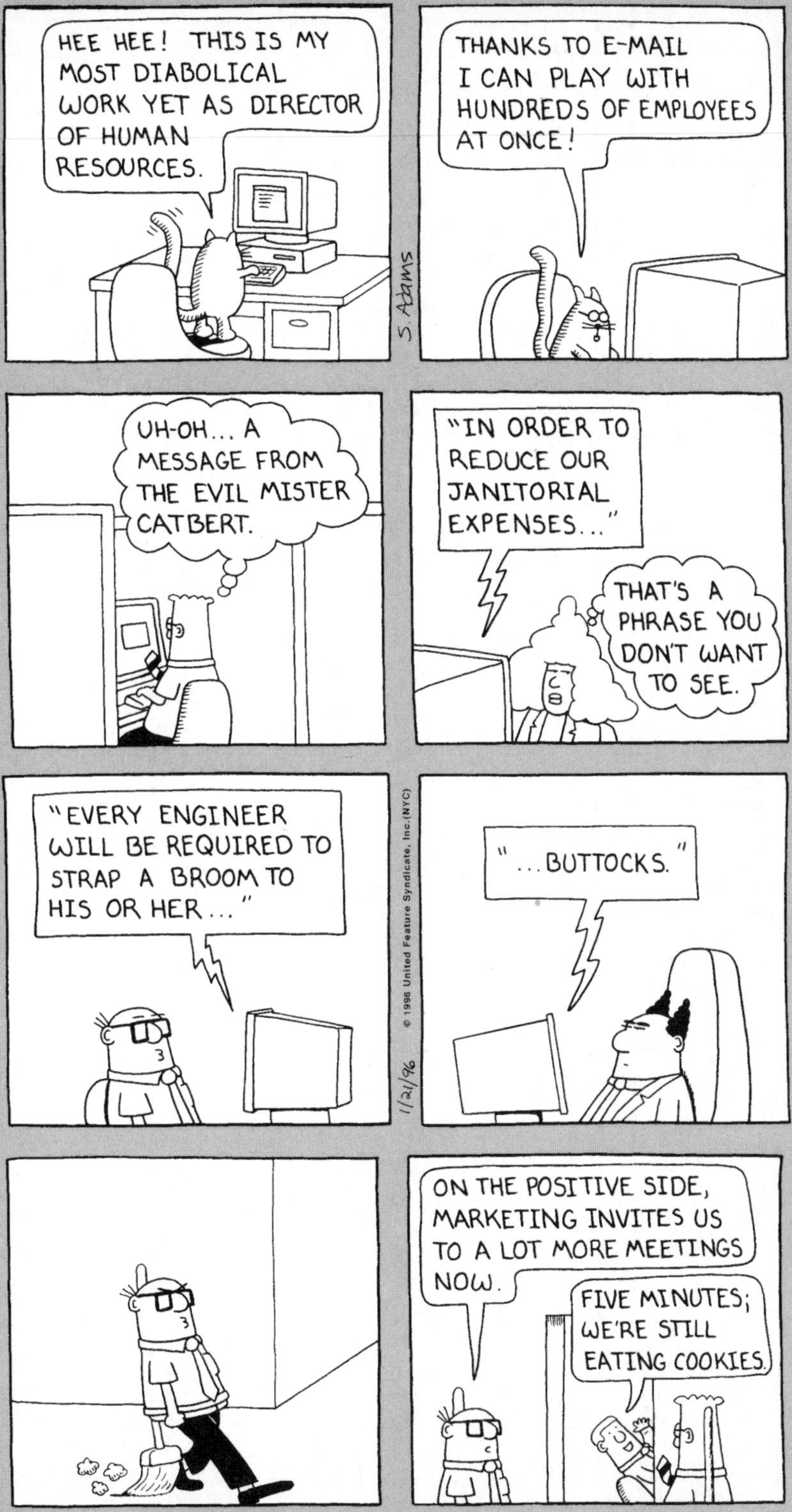
HEE HEE! THIS IS MY MOST DIABOLICAL WORK YET AS DIRECTOR OF HUMAN RESOURCES.
THANKS TO E-MAIL I CAN PLAY WITH HUNDREDS OF EMPLOYEES AT ONCE!
S. Adams
UH-OH... A MESSAGE FROM THE EVIL MISTER CATBERT.
"IN ORDER TO REDUCE OUR JANITORIAL EXPENSES..."
THAT'S A PHRASE YOU DON'T WANT TO SEE.
"EVERY ENGINEER WILL BE REQUIRED TO STRAP A BROOM TO HIS OR HER..."
1/21/96
© 1996 United Feature Syndicate, Inc.(NYC)
"...BUTTOCKS."
ON THE POSITIVE SIDE, MARKETING INVITES US TO A LOT MORE MEETINGS NOW.
FIVE MINUTES; WE'RE STILL EATING COOKIES.

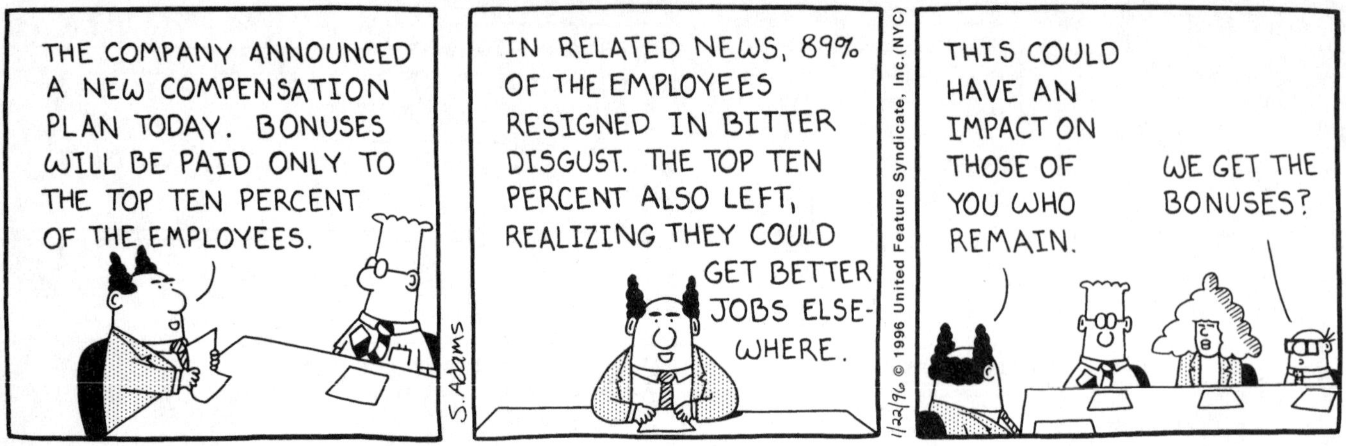
THE COMPANY ANNOUNCED A NEW COMPENSATION PLAN TODAY. BONUSES WILL BE PAID ONLY TO THE TOP TEN PERCENT OF THE EMPLOYEES.
S. Adams
IN RELATED NEWS, 89% OF THE EMPLOYEES RESIGNED IN BITTER DISGUST. THE TOP TEN PERCENT ALSO LEFT, REALIZING THEY COULD GET BETTER JOBS ELSE-WHERE.
1/22/96 © 1996 United Feature Syndicate, Inc.(NYC)
THIS COULD HAVE AN IMPACT ON THOSE OF YOU WHO REMAIN.
WE GET THE BONUSES?

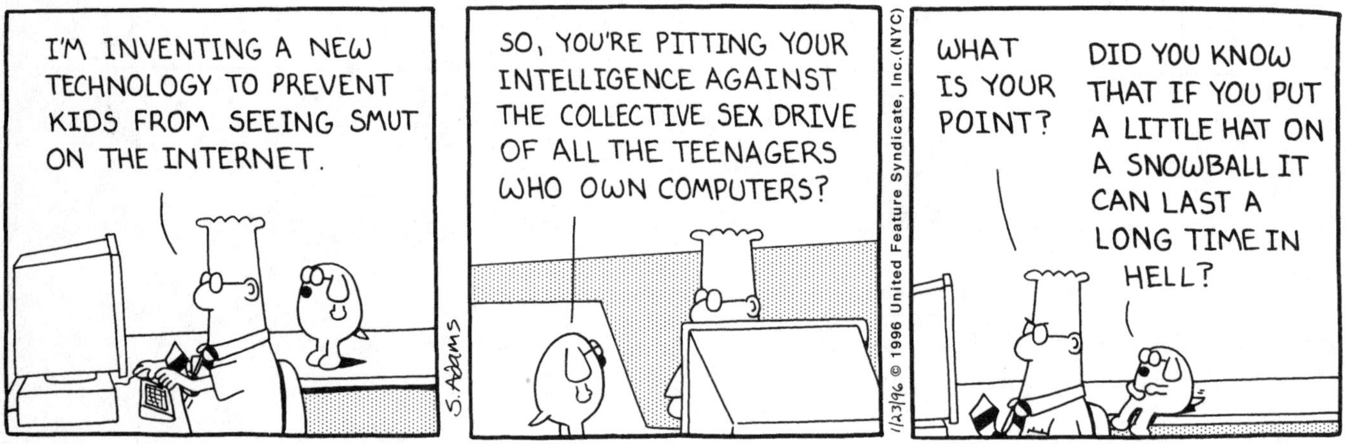
I'M INVENTING A NEW TECHNOLOGY TO PREVENT KIDS FROM SEEING SMUT ON THE INTERNET.
S. Adams
SO, YOU'RE PITTING YOUR INTELLIGENCE AGAINST THE COLLECTIVE SEX DRIVE OF ALL THE TEENAGERS WHO OWN COMPUTERS?
1/23/96 © 1996 United Feature Syndicate, Inc.(NYC)
WHAT IS YOUR POINT?
DID YOU KNOW THAT IF YOU PUT A LITTLE HAT ON A SNOWBALL IT CAN LAST A LONG TIME IN HELL?

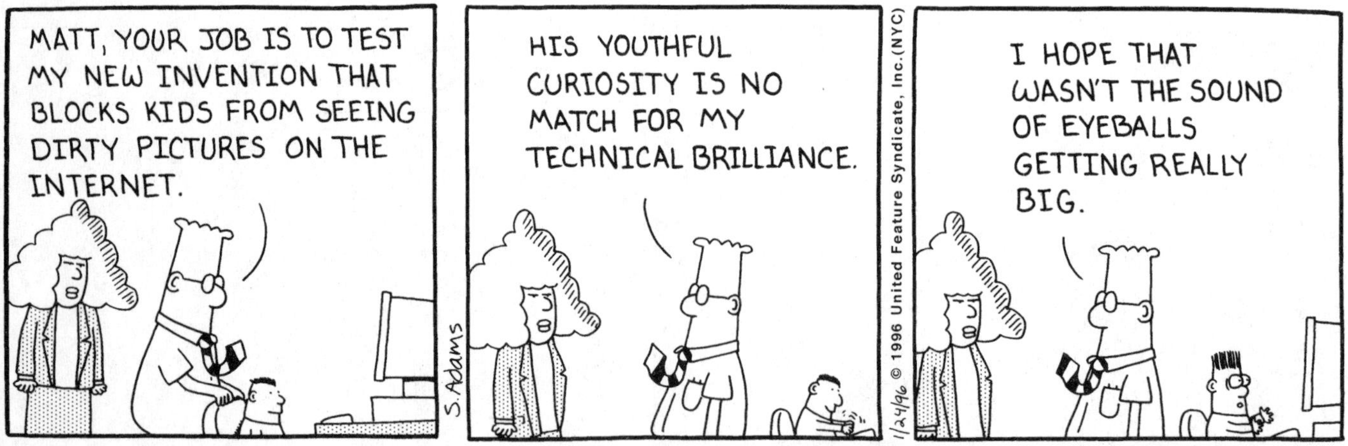
MATT, YOUR JOB IS TO TEST MY NEW INVENTION THAT BLOCKS KIDS FROM SEEING DIRTY PICTURES ON THE INTERNET.
S. Adams
HIS YOUTHFUL CURIOSITY IS NO MATCH FOR MY TECHNICAL BRILLIANCE.
1/24/96 © 1996 United Feature Syndicate, Inc.(NYC)
I HOPE THAT WASN'T THE SOUND OF EYEBALLS GETTING REALLY BIG.

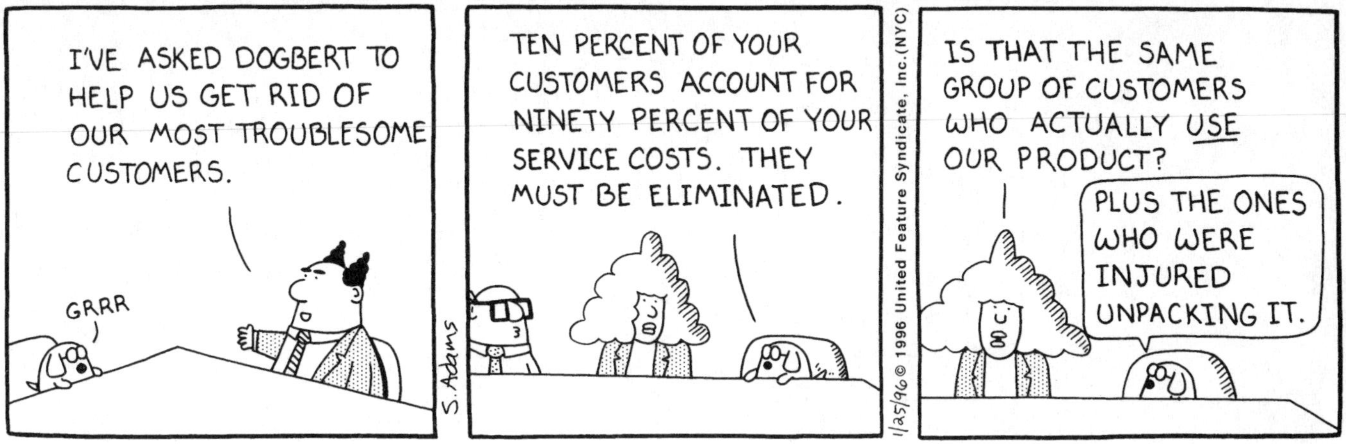
I'VE ASKED DOGBERT TO HELP US GET RID OF OUR MOST TROUBLESOME CUSTOMERS.
GRRR
S. Adams
TEN PERCENT OF YOUR CUSTOMERS ACCOUNT FOR NINETY PERCENT OF YOUR SERVICE COSTS. THEY MUST BE ELIMINATED.
1/25/96 © 1996 United Feature Syndicate, Inc.(NYC)
IS THAT THE SAME GROUP OF CUSTOMERS WHO ACTUALLY USE OUR PRODUCT?
PLUS THE ONES WHO WERE INJURED UNPACKING IT.

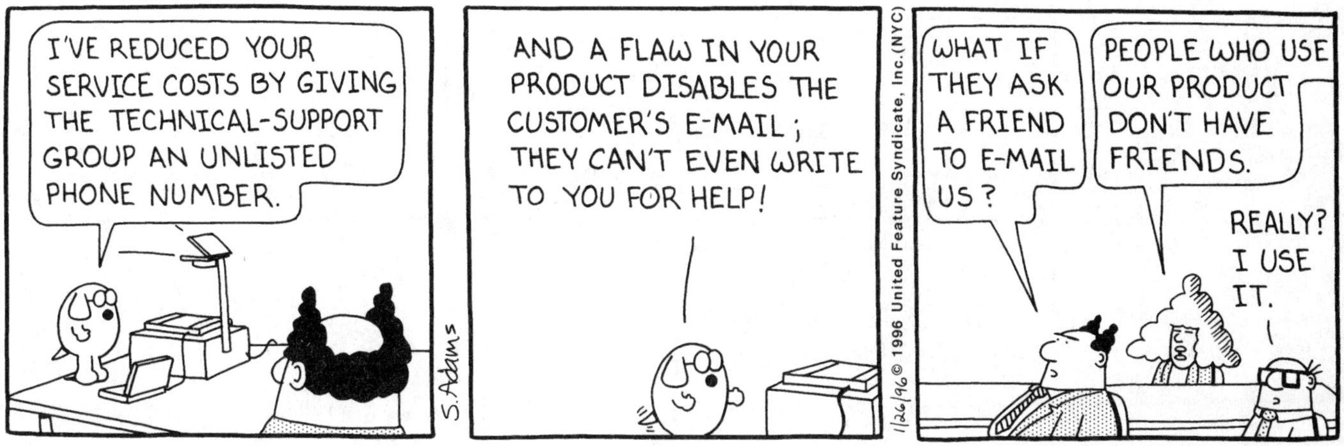
I'VE REDUCED YOUR SERVICE COSTS BY GIVING THE TECHNICAL-SUPPORT GROUP AN UNLISTED PHONE NUMBER.
S. Adams
AND A FLAW IN YOUR PRODUCT DISABLES THE CUSTOMER'S E-MAIL; THEY CAN'T EVEN WRITE TO YOU FOR HELP!
1/26/96 © 1996 United Feature Syndicate, Inc.(NYC)
WHAT IF THEY ASK A FRIEND TO E-MAIL US?
PEOPLE WHO USE OUR PRODUCT DON'T HAVE FRIENDS.
REALLY? I USE IT.

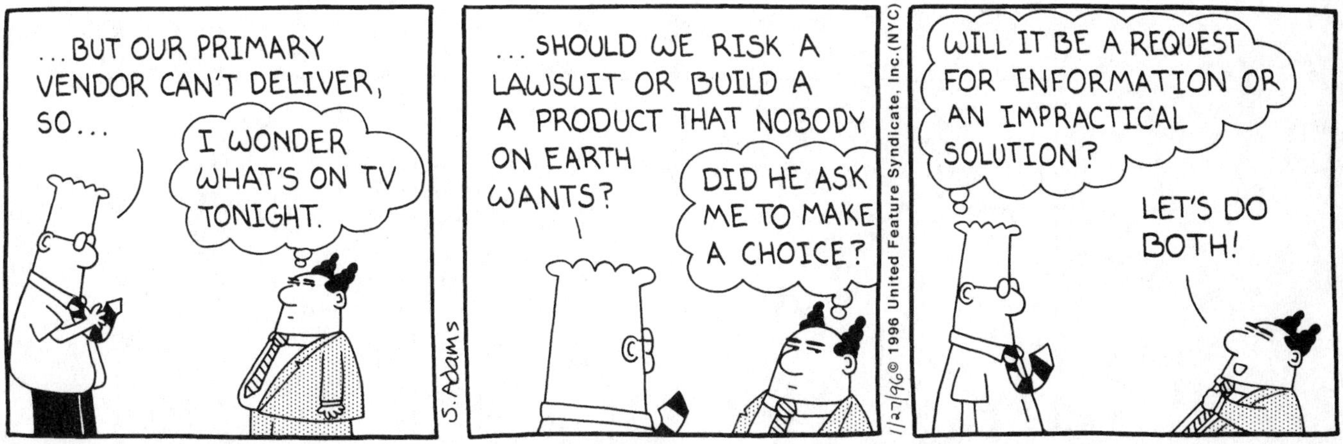
...BUT OUR PRIMARY VENDOR CAN'T DELIVER, SO...
I WONDER WHAT'S ON TV TONIGHT.
S. Adams
...SHOULD WE RISK A LAWSUIT OR BUILD A A PRODUCT THAT NOBODY ON EARTH WANTS?
DID HE ASK ME TO MAKE A CHOICE?
1/27/96 © 1996 United Feature Syndicate, Inc.(NYC)
WILL IT BE A REQUEST FOR INFORMATION OR AN IMPRACTICAL SOLUTION?
LET'S DO BOTH!

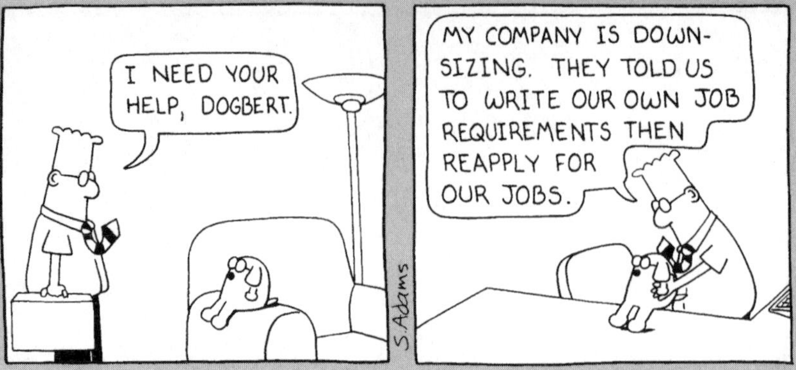
I NEED YOUR HELP, DOGBERT.
S. Adams
MY COMPANY IS DOWNSIZING. THEY TOLD US TO WRITE OUR OWN JOB REQUIREMENTS THEN REAPPLY FOR OUR JOBS.

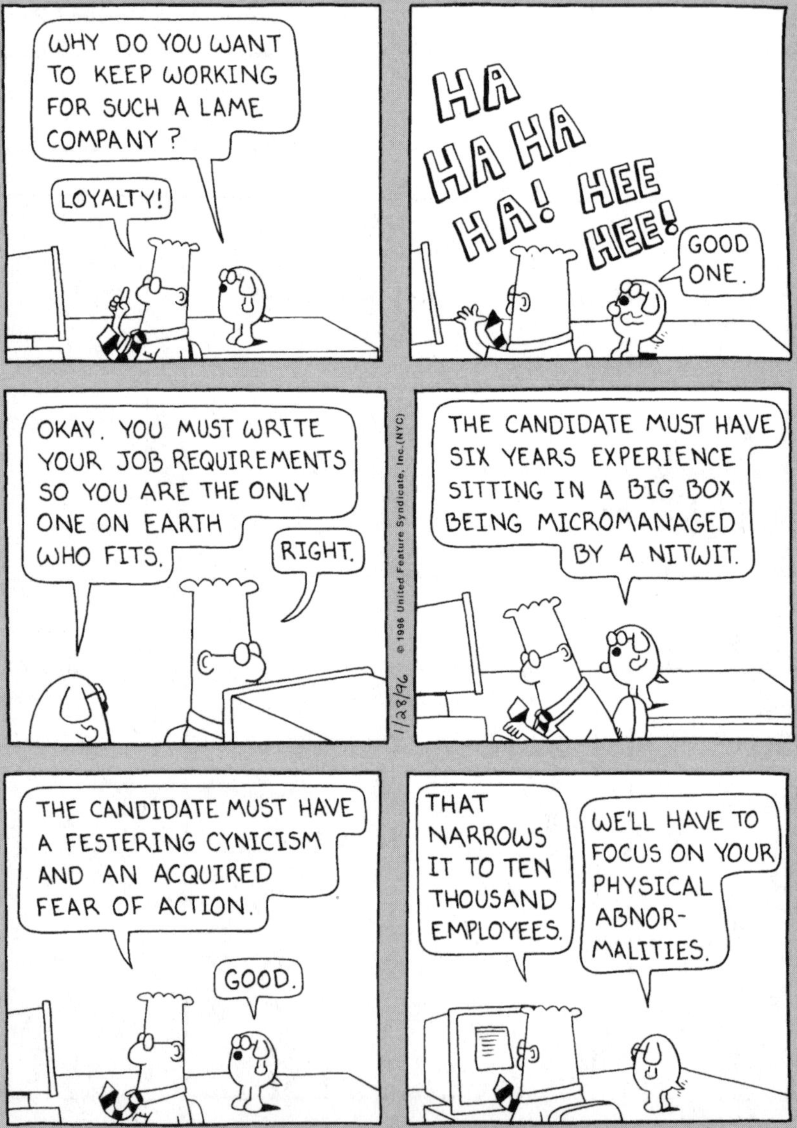
WHY DO YOU WANT TO KEEP WORKING FOR SUCH A LAME COMPANY?
LOYALTY!
HA HA HA HA! HEE HEE!
GOOD ONE.
OKAY. YOU MUST WRITE YOUR JOB REQUIREMENTS SO YOU ARE THE ONLY ONE ON EARTH WHO FITS.
RIGHT.
1/28/96
© 1996 United Feature Syndicate, Inc.(NYC)
THE CANDIDATE MUST HAVE SIX YEARS EXPERIENCE SITTING IN A BIG BOX BEING MICROMANAGED BY A NITWIT.
THE CANDIDATE MUST HAVE A FESTERING CYNICISM AND AN ACQUIRED FEAR OF ACTION.
GOOD.
THAT NARROWS IT TO TEN THOUSAND EMPLOYEES.
WE'LL HAVE TO FOCUS ON YOUR PHYSICAL ABNORMALITIES.

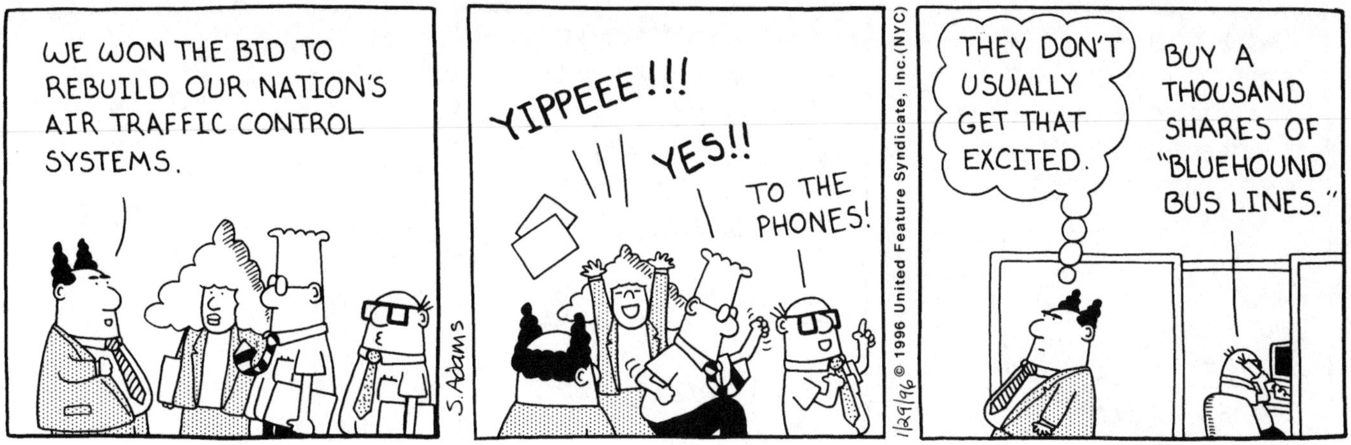
WE WON THE BID TO REBUILD OUR NATION'S AIR TRAFFIC CONTROL SYSTEMS.
S. Adams
YIPPEEE!!!
YES!!
TO THE PHONES!
1/29/96 © 1996 United Feature Syndicate, Inc.(NYC)
THEY DON'T USUALLY GET THAT EXCITED.
BUY A THOUSAND SHARES OF "BLUEHOUND BUS LINES."

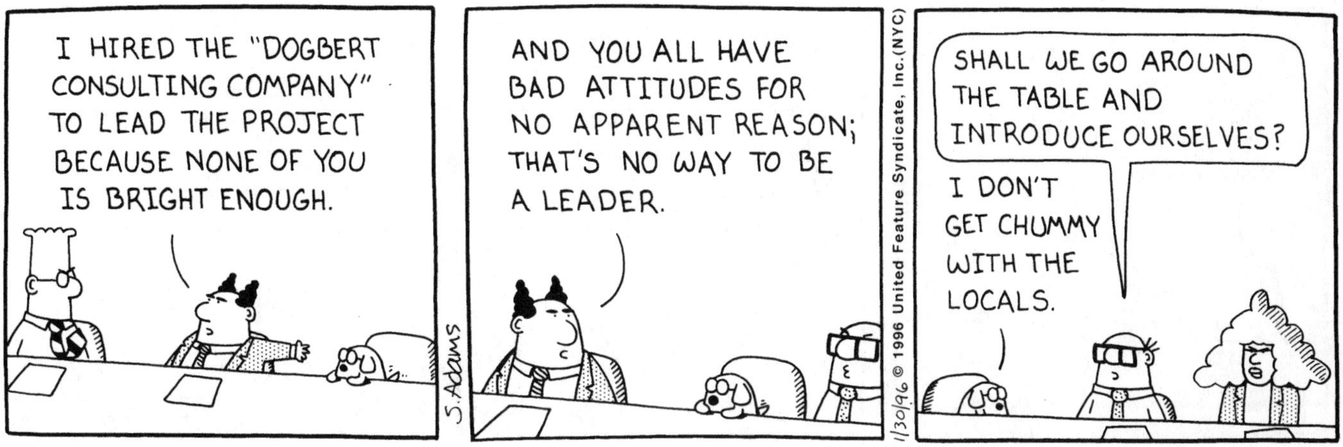
I HIRED THE "DOGBERT CONSULTING COMPANY" TO LEAD THE PROJECT BECAUSE NONE OF YOU IS BRIGHT ENOUGH.
S. Adams
AND YOU ALL HAVE BAD ATTITUDES FOR NO APPARENT REASON; THAT'S NO WAY TO BE A LEADER.
1/30/96 © 1996 United Feature Syndicate, Inc.(NYC)
SHALL WE GO AROUND THE TABLE AND INTRODUCE OURSELVES?
I DON'T GET CHUMMY WITH THE LOCALS.

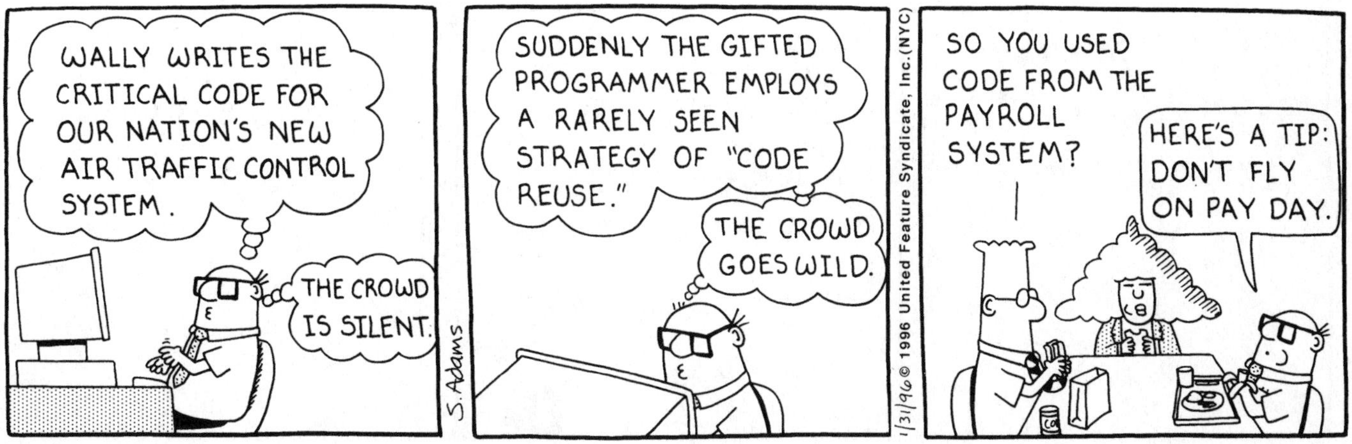
WALLY WRITES THE CRITICAL CODE FOR OUR NATION'S NEW AIR TRAFFIC CONTROL SYSTEM.
THE CROWD IS SILENT.
S. Adams
SUDDENLY THE GIFTED PROGRAMMER EMPLOYS A RARELY SEEN STRATEGY OF "CODE REUSE."
THE CROWD GOES WILD.
1/31/96 © 1996 United Feature Syndicate, Inc.(NYC)
SO YOU USED CODE FROM THE PAYROLL SYSTEM?
HERE'S A TIP: DON'T FLY ON PAY DAY.

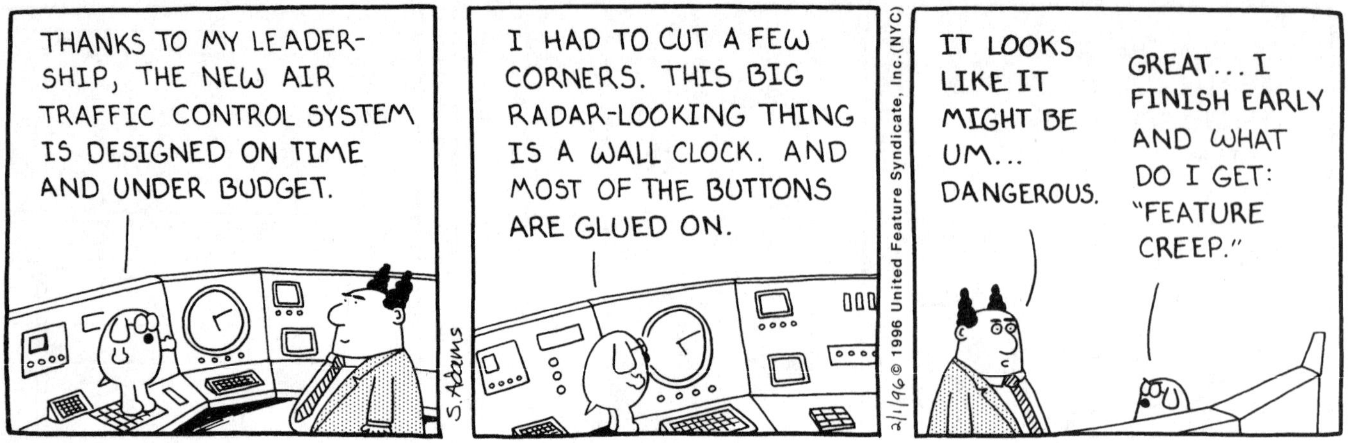
THANKS TO MY LEADER-SHIP, THE NEW AIR TRAFFIC CONTROL SYSTEM IS DESIGNED ON TIME AND UNDER BUDGET.
I HAD TO CUT A FEW CORNERS. THIS BIG RADAR-LOOKING THING IS A WALL CLOCK. AND MOST OF THE BUTTONS ARE GLUED ON.
2/1/96 © 1996 United Feature Syndicate, Inc.(NYC)
IT LOOKS LIKE IT MIGHT BE UM... DANGEROUS.
GREAT... I FINISH EARLY AND WHAT DO I GET: "FEATURE CREEP."

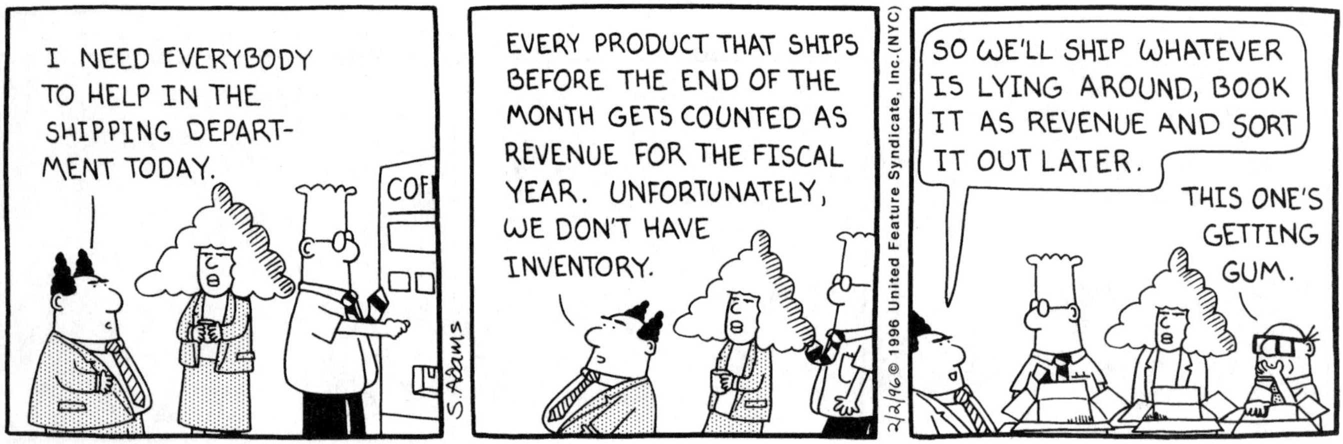
I NEED EVERYBODY TO HELP IN THE SHIPPING DEPART-MENT TODAY.
EVERY PRODUCT THAT SHIPS BEFORE THE END OF THE MONTH GETS COUNTED AS REVENUE FOR THE FISCAL YEAR. UNFORTUNATELY, WE DON'T HAVE INVENTORY.
2/2/96 © 1996 United Feature Syndicate, Inc.(NYC)
SO WE'LL SHIP WHATEVER IS LYING AROUND, BOOK IT AS REVENUE AND SORT IT OUT LATER.
THIS ONE'S GETTING GUM.

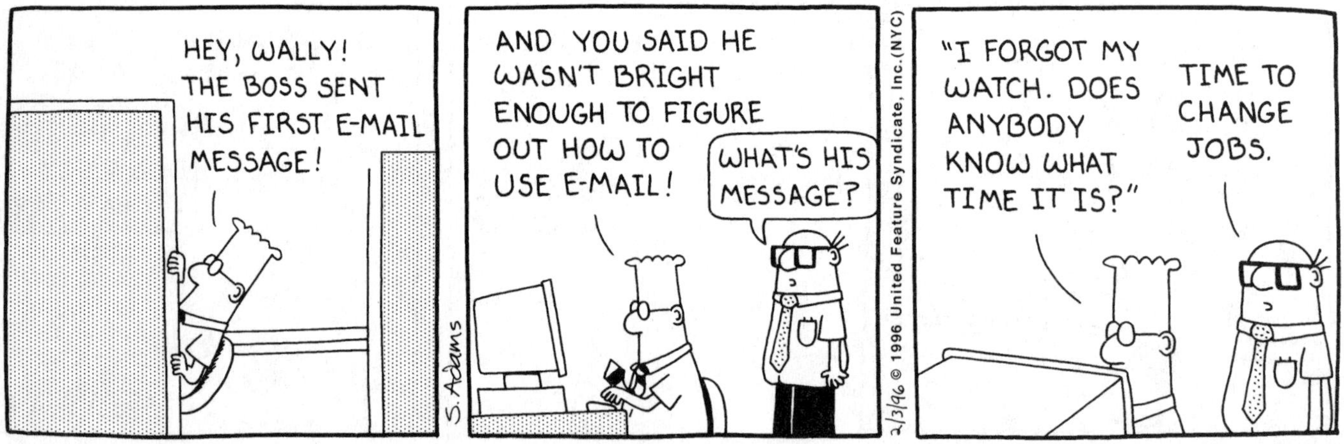
HEY, WALLY! THE BOSS SENT HIS FIRST E-MAIL MESSAGE!
AND YOU SAID HE WASN'T BRIGHT ENOUGH TO FIGURE OUT HOW TO USE E-MAIL!
WHAT'S HIS MESSAGE?
2/3/96 © 1996 United Feature Syndicate, Inc.(NYC)
"I FORGOT MY WATCH. DOES ANYBODY KNOW WHAT TIME IT IS?"
TIME TO CHANGE JOBS.

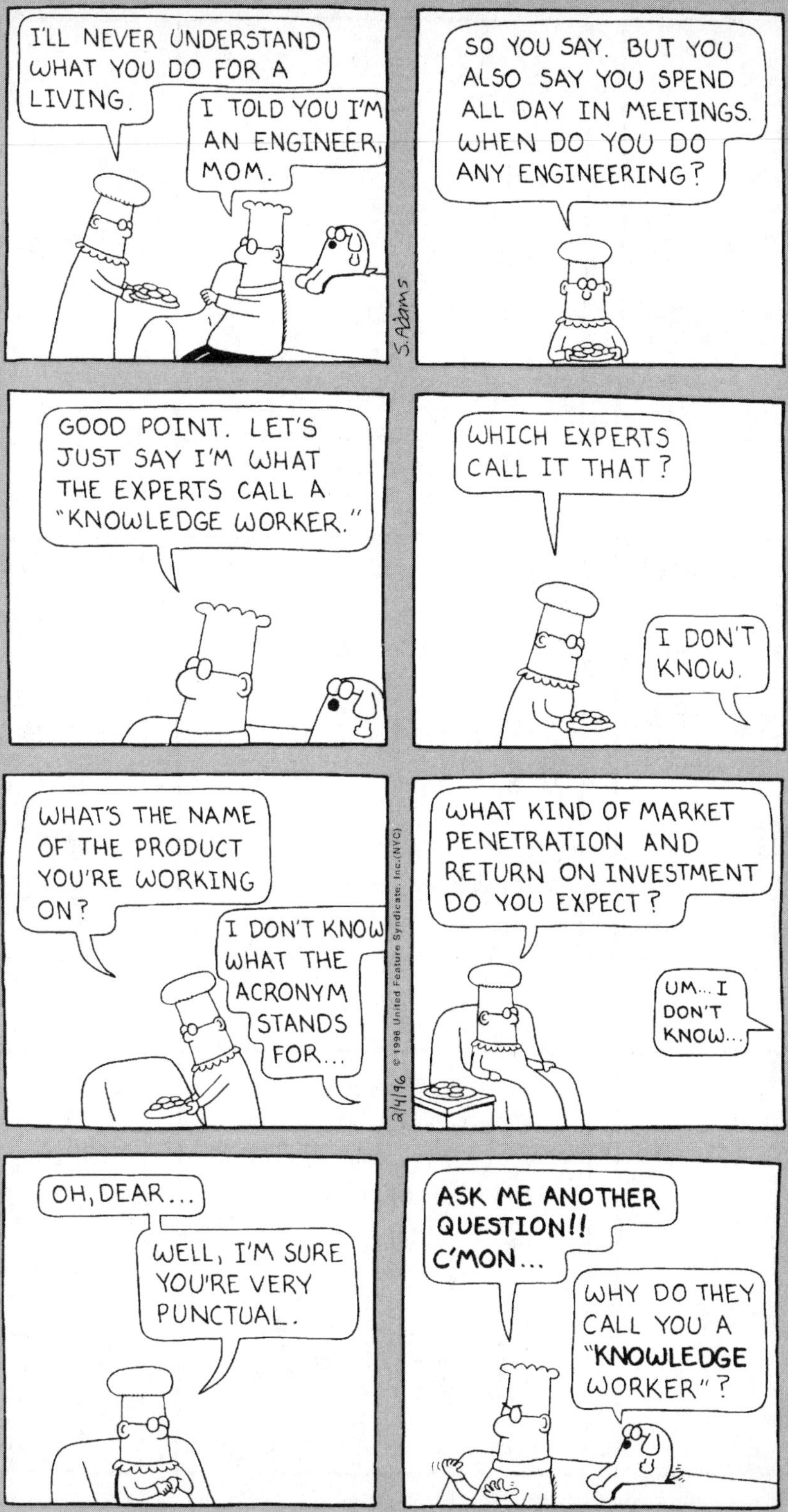
I'LL NEVER UNDERSTAND WHAT YOU DO FOR A LIVING.
I TOLD YOU I'M AN ENGINEER, MOM.
S. Adams
SO YOU SAY. BUT YOU ALSO SAY YOU SPEND ALL DAY IN MEETINGS. WHEN DO YOU DO ANY ENGINEERING?
GOOD POINT. LET'S JUST SAY I'M WHAT THE EXPERTS CALL A "KNOWLEDGE WORKER."
WHICH EXPERTS CALL IT THAT?
I DON'T KNOW.
WHAT'S THE NAME OF THE PRODUCT YOU'RE WORKING ON?
I DON'T KNOW WHAT THE ACRONYM STANDS FOR...
2/4/96 © 1998 United Feature Syndicate, Inc.(NYC)
WHAT KIND OF MARKET PENETRATION AND RETURN ON INVESTMENT DO YOU EXPECT?
UM... I DON'T KNOW...
OH, DEAR...
WELL, I'M SURE YOU'RE VERY PUNCTUAL.
ASK ME ANOTHER QUESTION!! C'MON...
WHY DO THEY CALL YOU A "KNOWLEDGE WORKER"?

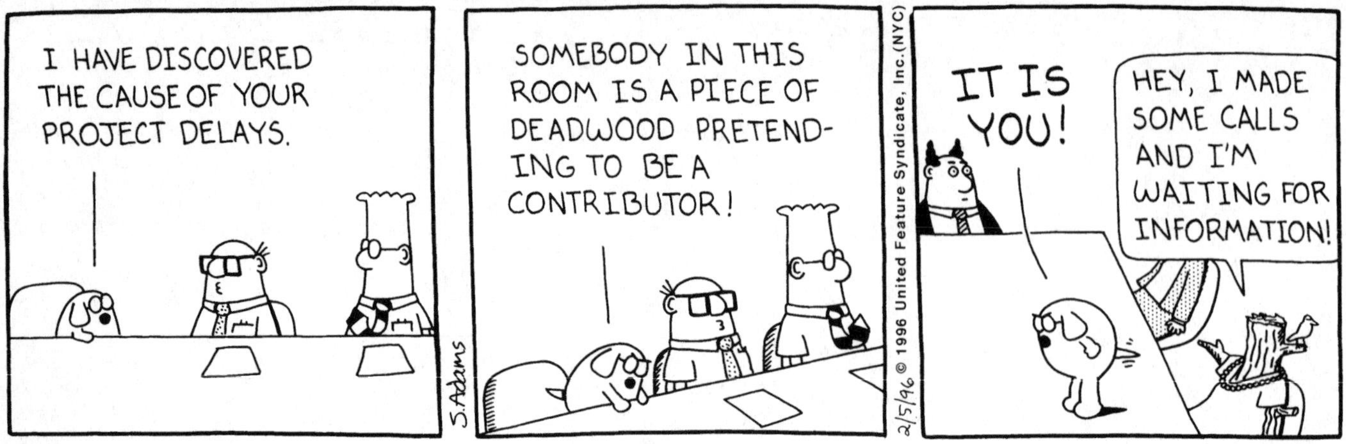
I HAVE DISCOVERED THE CAUSE OF YOUR PROJECT DELAYS.
S. Adams
SOMEBODY IN THIS ROOM IS A PIECE OF DEADWOOD PRETENDING TO BE A CONTRIBUTOR!
2/5/96 © 1996 United Feature Syndicate, Inc.(NYC)
IT IS YOU!
HEY, I MADE SOME CALLS AND I'M WAITING FOR INFORMATION!

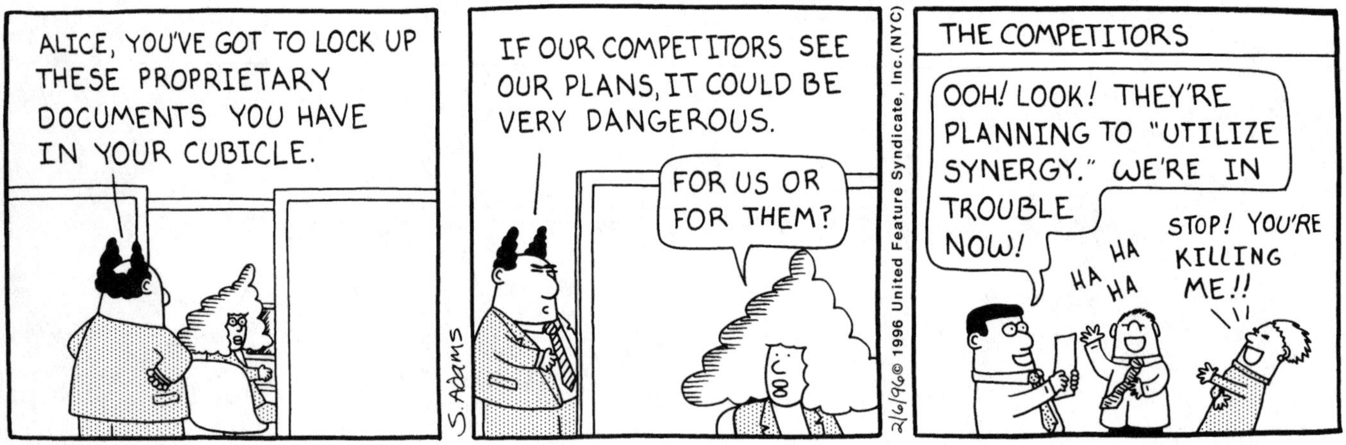
ALICE, YOU'VE GOT TO LOCK UP THESE PROPRIETARY DOCUMENTS YOU HAVE IN YOUR CUBICLE.
S. Adams
IF OUR COMPETITORS SEE OUR PLANS, IT COULD BE VERY DANGEROUS.
FOR US OR FOR THEM?
2/6/96 © 1996 United Feature Syndicate, Inc.(NYC)
THE COMPETITORS
OOH! LOOK! THEY'RE PLANNING TO "UTILIZE SYNERGY." WE'RE IN TROUBLE NOW!
HA HA HA HA
STOP! YOU'RE KILLING ME!!

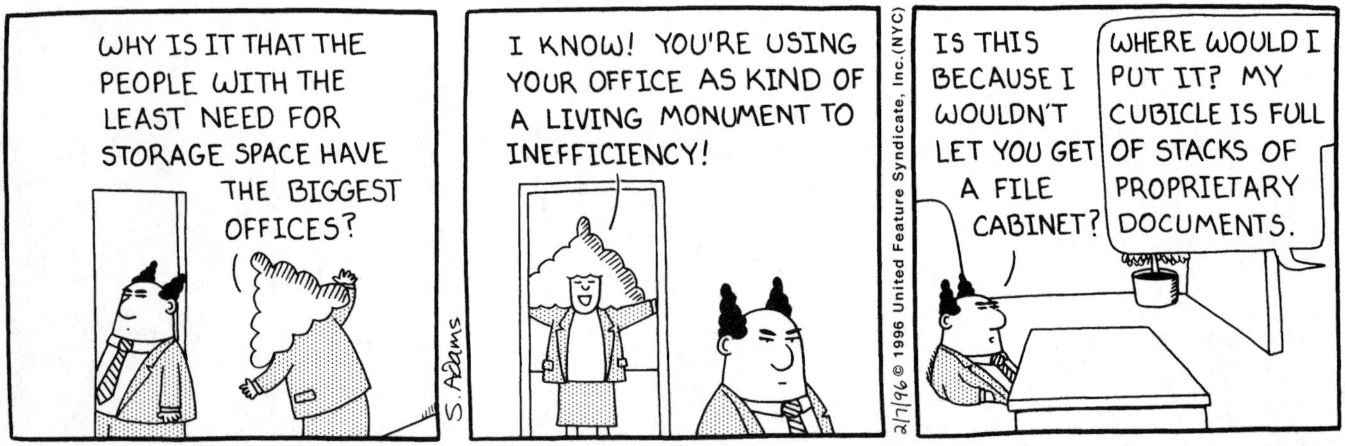
WHY IS IT THAT THE PEOPLE WITH THE LEAST NEED FOR STORAGE SPACE HAVE THE BIGGEST OFFICES?
S. Adams
I KNOW! YOU'RE USING YOUR OFFICE AS KIND OF A LIVING MONUMENT TO INEFFICIENCY!
2/7/96 © 1996 United Feature Syndicate, Inc.(NYC)
IS THIS BECAUSE I WOULDN'T LET YOU GET A FILE CABINET?
WHERE WOULD I PUT IT? MY CUBICLE IS FULL OF STACKS OF PROPRIETARY DOCUMENTS.

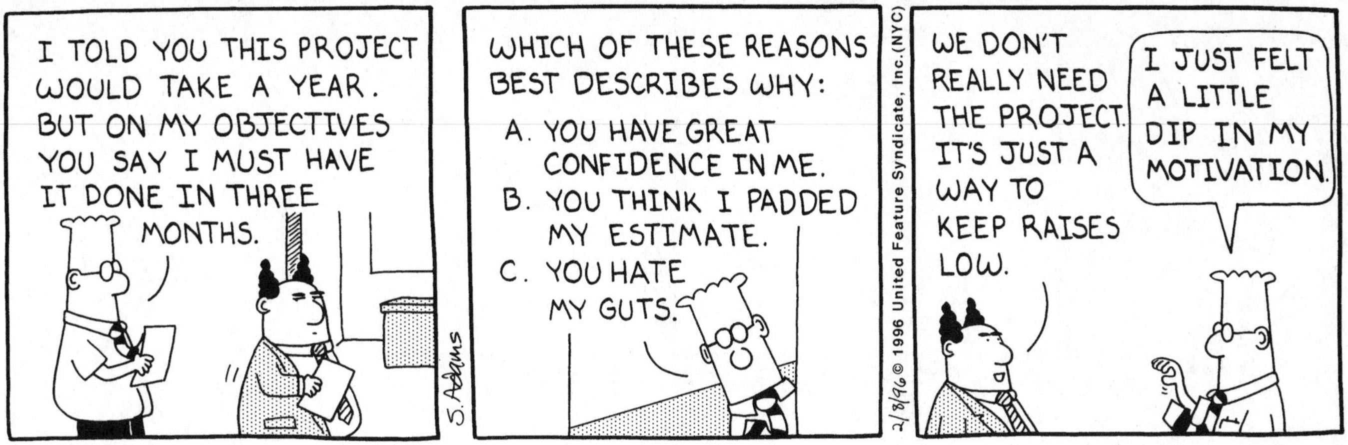
I TOLD YOU THIS PROJECT WOULD TAKE A YEAR. BUT ON MY OBJECTIVES YOU SAY I MUST HAVE IT DONE IN THREE MONTHS.
WHICH OF THESE REASONS BEST DESCRIBES WHY:
A. YOU HAVE GREAT CONFIDENCE IN ME.
B. YOU THINK I PADDED MY ESTIMATE.
C. YOU HATE MY GUTS.
S. Adams
WE DON'T REALLY NEED THE PROJECT. IT'S JUST A WAY TO KEEP RAISES LOW.
I JUST FELT A LITTLE DIP IN MY MOTIVATION.
2/8/96 © 1996 United Feature Syndicate, Inc.(NYC)

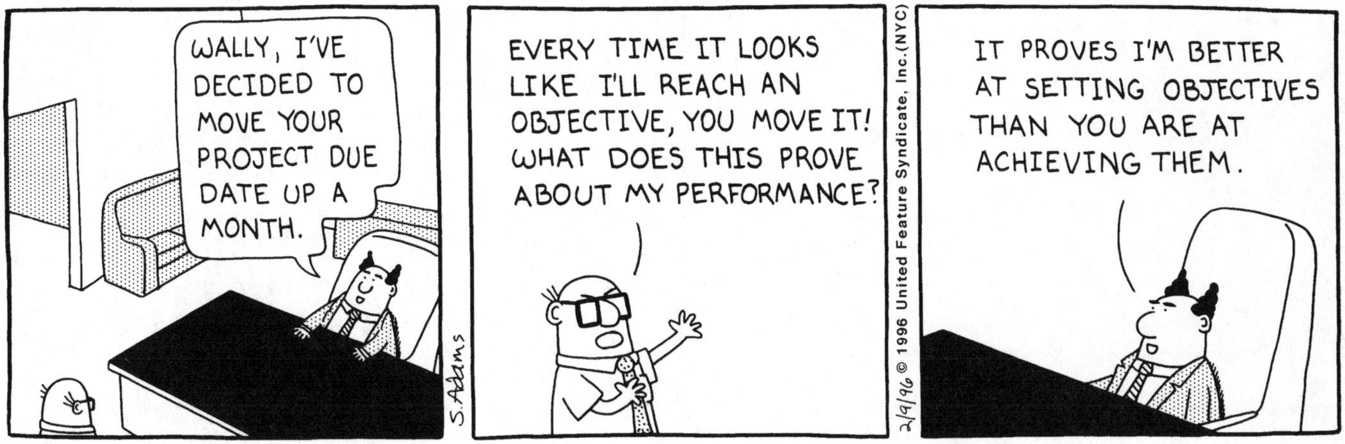
WALLY, I'VE DECIDED TO MOVE YOUR PROJECT DUE DATE UP A MONTH.
S. Adams
EVERY TIME IT LOOKS LIKE I'LL REACH AN OBJECTIVE, YOU MOVE IT! WHAT DOES THIS PROVE ABOUT MY PERFORMANCE?
IT PROVES I'M BETTER AT SETTING OBJECTIVES THAN YOU ARE AT ACHIEVING THEM.
2/9/96 © 1996 United Feature Syndicate, Inc.(NYC)

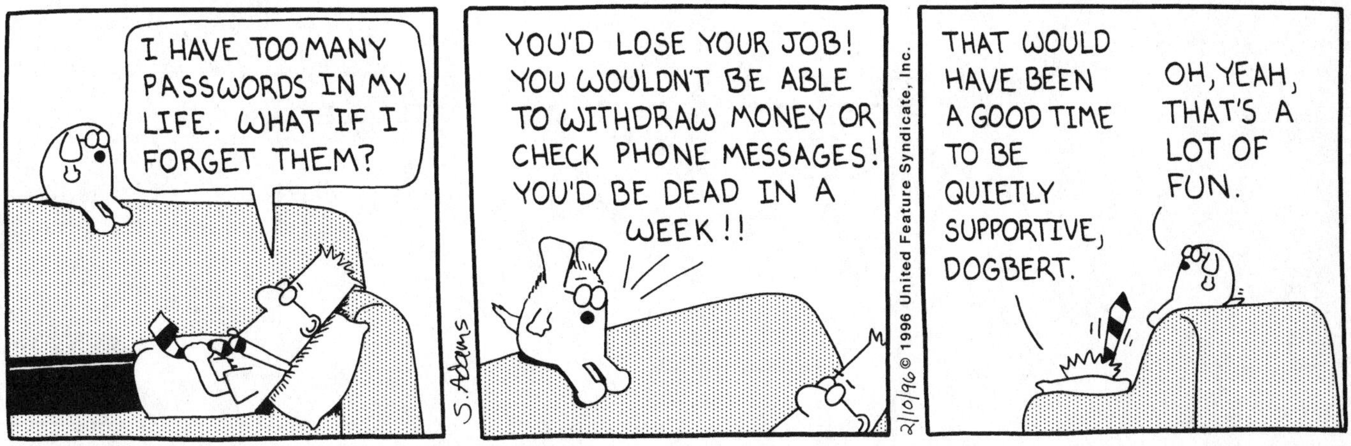
I HAVE TOO MANY PASSWORDS IN MY LIFE. WHAT IF I FORGET THEM?
S. Adams
YOU'D LOSE YOUR JOB! YOU WOULDN'T BE ABLE TO WITHDRAW MONEY OR CHECK PHONE MESSAGES! YOU'D BE DEAD IN A WEEK!!
THAT WOULD HAVE BEEN A GOOD TIME TO BE QUIETLY SUPPORTIVE, DOGBERT.
OH, YEAH, THAT'S A LOT OF FUN.
2/10/96 © 1996 United Feature Syndicate, Inc.

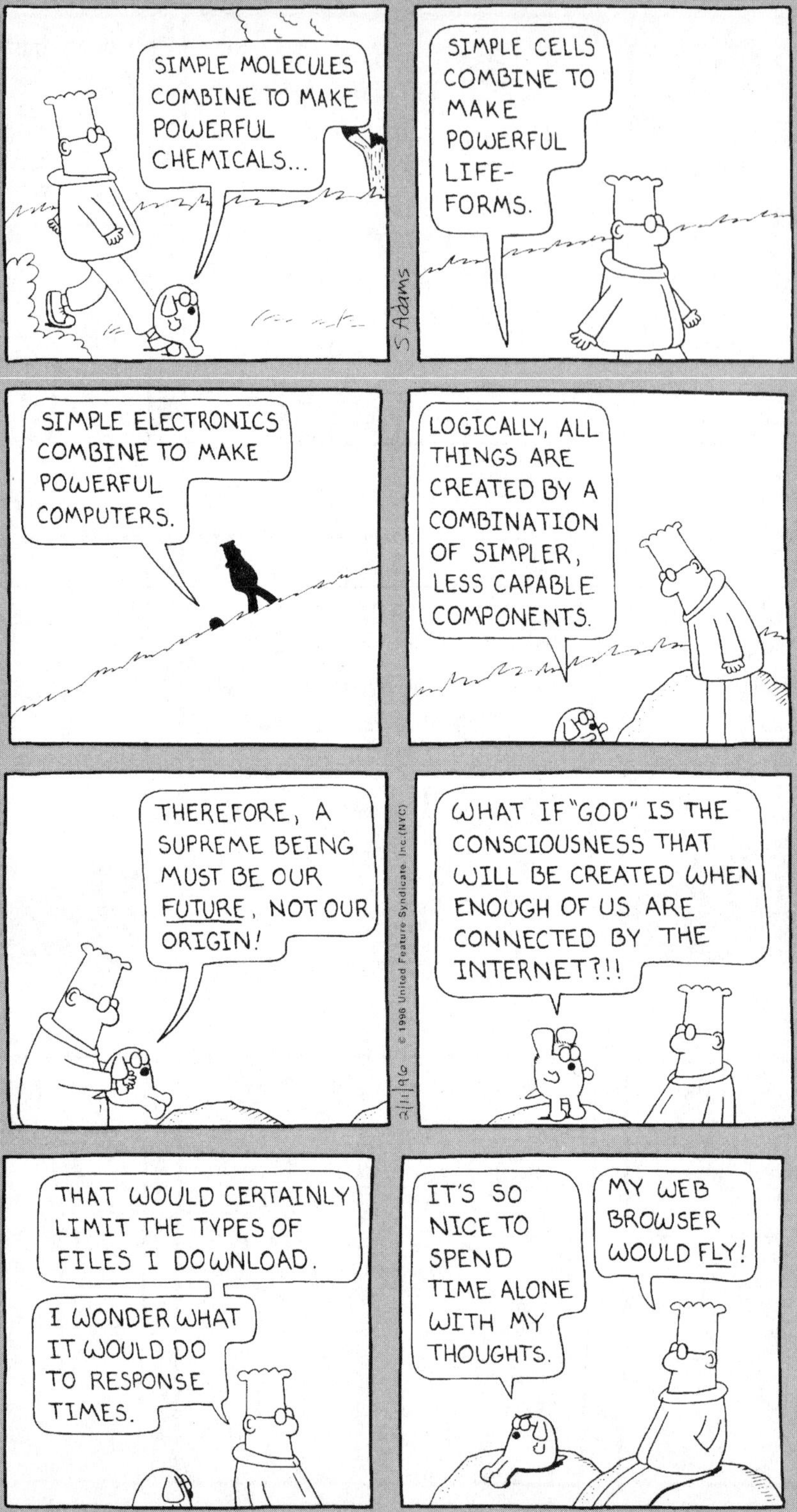
SIMPLE MOLECULES COMBINE TO MAKE POWERFUL CHEMICALS...
S Adams
SIMPLE CELLS COMBINE TO MAKE POWERFUL LIFE-FORMS.
SIMPLE ELECTRONICS COMBINE TO MAKE POWERFUL COMPUTERS.
LOGICALLY, ALL THINGS ARE CREATED BY A COMBINATION OF SIMPLER, LESS CAPABLE COMPONENTS.
THEREFORE, A SUPREME BEING MUST BE OUR FUTURE, NOT OUR ORIGIN!
© 1996 United Feature Syndicate, Inc.(NYC)
2/11/96
WHAT IF "GOD" IS THE CONSCIOUSNESS THAT WILL BE CREATED WHEN ENOUGH OF US ARE CONNECTED BY THE INTERNET?!!
THAT WOULD CERTAINLY LIMIT THE TYPES OF FILES I DOWNLOAD.
I WONDER WHAT IT WOULD DO TO RESPONSE TIMES.
IT'S SO NICE TO SPEND TIME ALONE WITH MY THOUGHTS.
MY WEB BROWSER WOULD FLY!

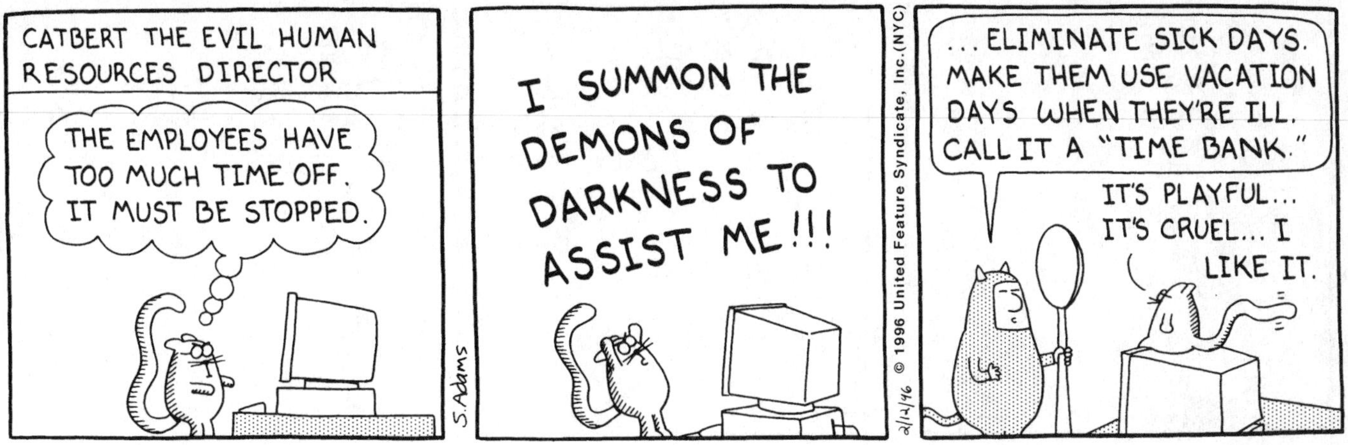
CATBERT THE EVIL HUMAN RESOURCES DIRECTOR
THE EMPLOYEES HAVE TOO MUCH TIME OFF. IT MUST BE STOPPED.
S. Adams
I SUMMON THE DEMONS OF DARKNESS TO ASSIST ME!!!
2/12/96 © 1996 United Feature Syndicate, Inc.(NYC)
...ELIMINATE SICK DAYS. MAKE THEM USE VACATION DAYS WHEN THEY'RE ILL. CALL IT A "TIME BANK."
IT'S PLAYFUL... IT'S CRUEL... I LIKE IT.

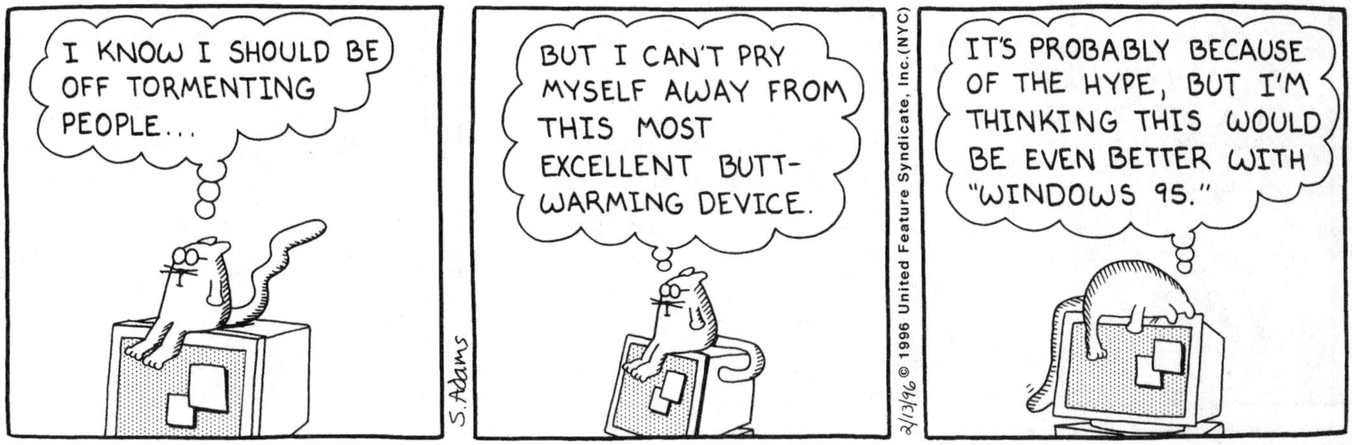
I KNOW I SHOULD BE OFF TORMENTING PEOPLE...
S. Adams
BUT I CAN'T PRY MYSELF AWAY FROM THIS MOST EXCELLENT BUTT-WARMING DEVICE.
2/13/96 © 1996 United Feature Syndicate, Inc.(NYC)
IT'S PROBABLY BECAUSE OF THE HYPE, BUT I'M THINKING THIS WOULD BE EVEN BETTER WITH "WINDOWS 95."

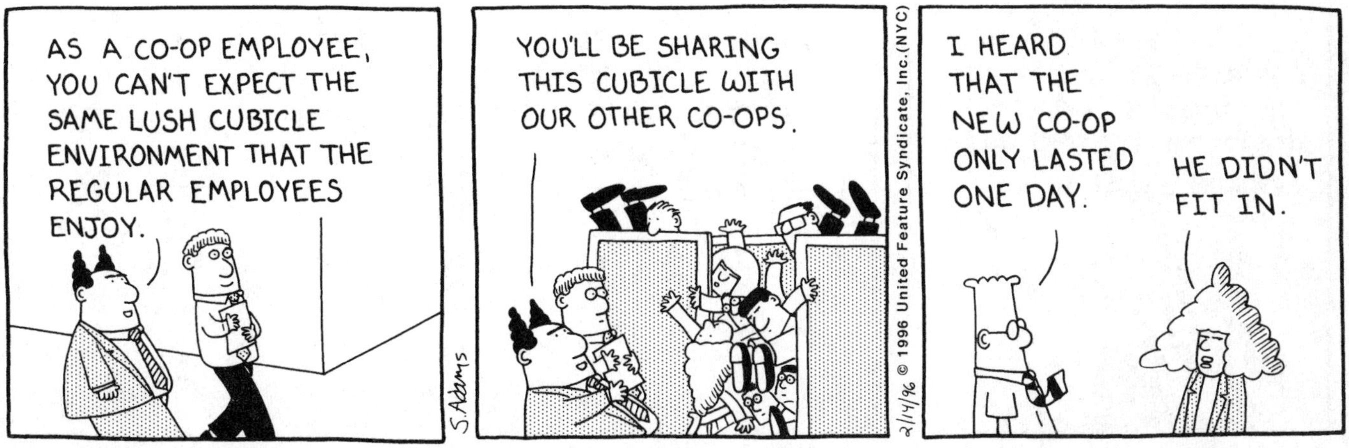
AS A CO-OP EMPLOYEE, YOU CAN'T EXPECT THE SAME LUSH CUBICLE ENVIRONMENT THAT THE REGULAR EMPLOYEES ENJOY.
S. Adams
YOU'LL BE SHARING THIS CUBICLE WITH OUR OTHER CO-OPS.
2/14/96 © 1996 United Feature Syndicate, Inc.(NYC)
I HEARD THAT THE NEW CO-OP ONLY LASTED ONE DAY.
HE DIDN'T FIT IN.

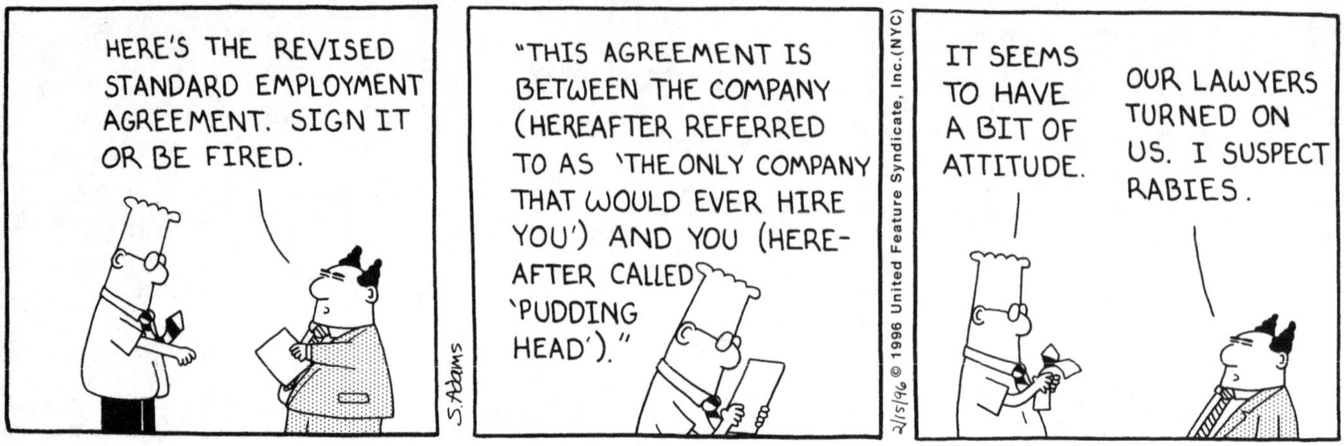
HERE'S THE REVISED STANDARD EMPLOYMENT AGREEMENT. SIGN IT OR BE FIRED.
S. Adams
"THIS AGREEMENT IS BETWEEN THE COMPANY (HEREAFTER REFERRED TO AS 'THE ONLY COMPANY THAT WOULD EVER HIRE YOU') AND YOU (HEREAFTER CALLED 'PUDDING HEAD')."
2/5/96 © 1996 United Feature Syndicate, Inc.(NYC)
IT SEEMS TO HAVE A BIT OF ATTITUDE.
OUR LAWYERS TURNED ON US. I SUSPECT RABIES.

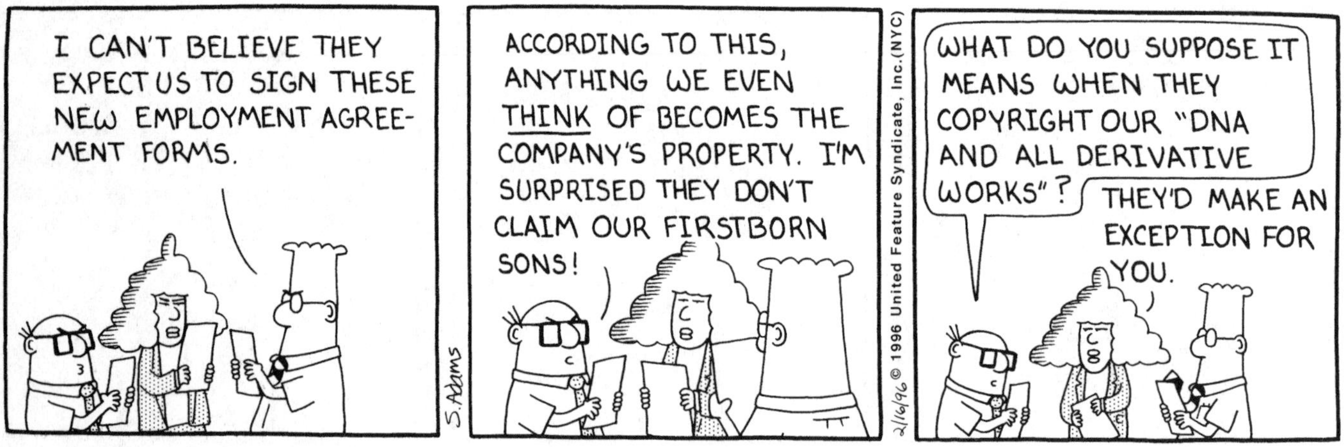
I CAN'T BELIEVE THEY EXPECT US TO SIGN THESE NEW EMPLOYMENT AGREEMENT FORMS.
S. Adams
ACCORDING TO THIS, ANYTHING WE EVEN THINK OF BECOMES THE COMPANY'S PROPERTY. I'M SURPRISED THEY DON'T CLAIM OUR FIRSTBORN SONS!
2/6/96 © 1996 United Feature Syndicate, Inc.(NYC)
WHAT DO YOU SUPPOSE IT MEANS WHEN THEY COPYRIGHT OUR "DNA AND ALL DERIVATIVE WORKS"?
THEY'D MAKE AN EXCEPTION FOR YOU.

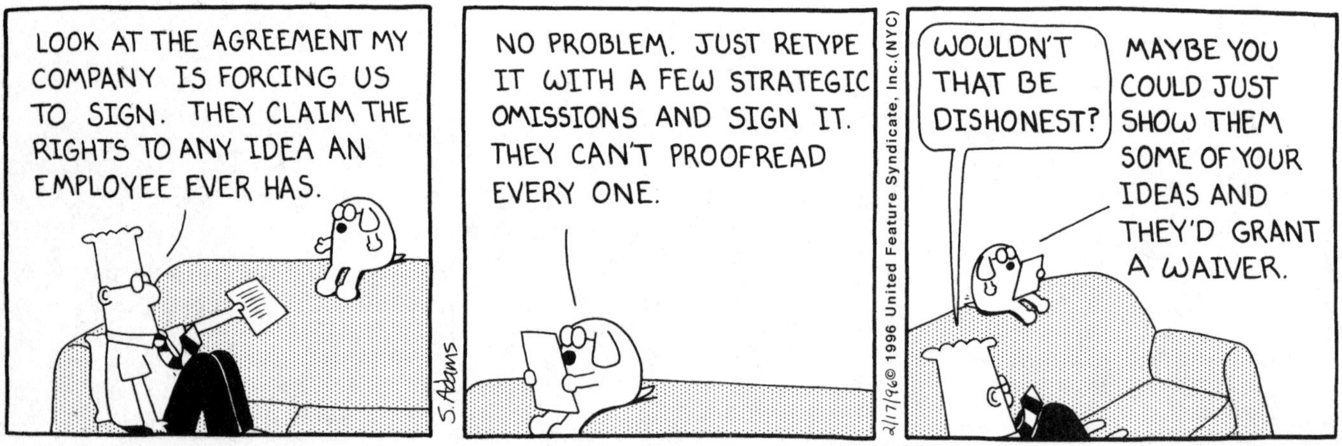
LOOK AT THE AGREEMENT MY COMPANY IS FORCING US TO SIGN. THEY CLAIM THE RIGHTS TO ANY IDEA AN EMPLOYEE EVER HAS.
S. Adams
NO PROBLEM. JUST RETYPE IT WITH A FEW STRATEGIC OMISSIONS AND SIGN IT. THEY CAN'T PROOFREAD EVERY ONE.
2/7/96 © 1996 United Feature Syndicate, Inc.(NYC)
WOULDN'T THAT BE DISHONEST?
MAYBE YOU COULD JUST SHOW THEM SOME OF YOUR IDEAS AND THEY'D GRANT A WAIVER.

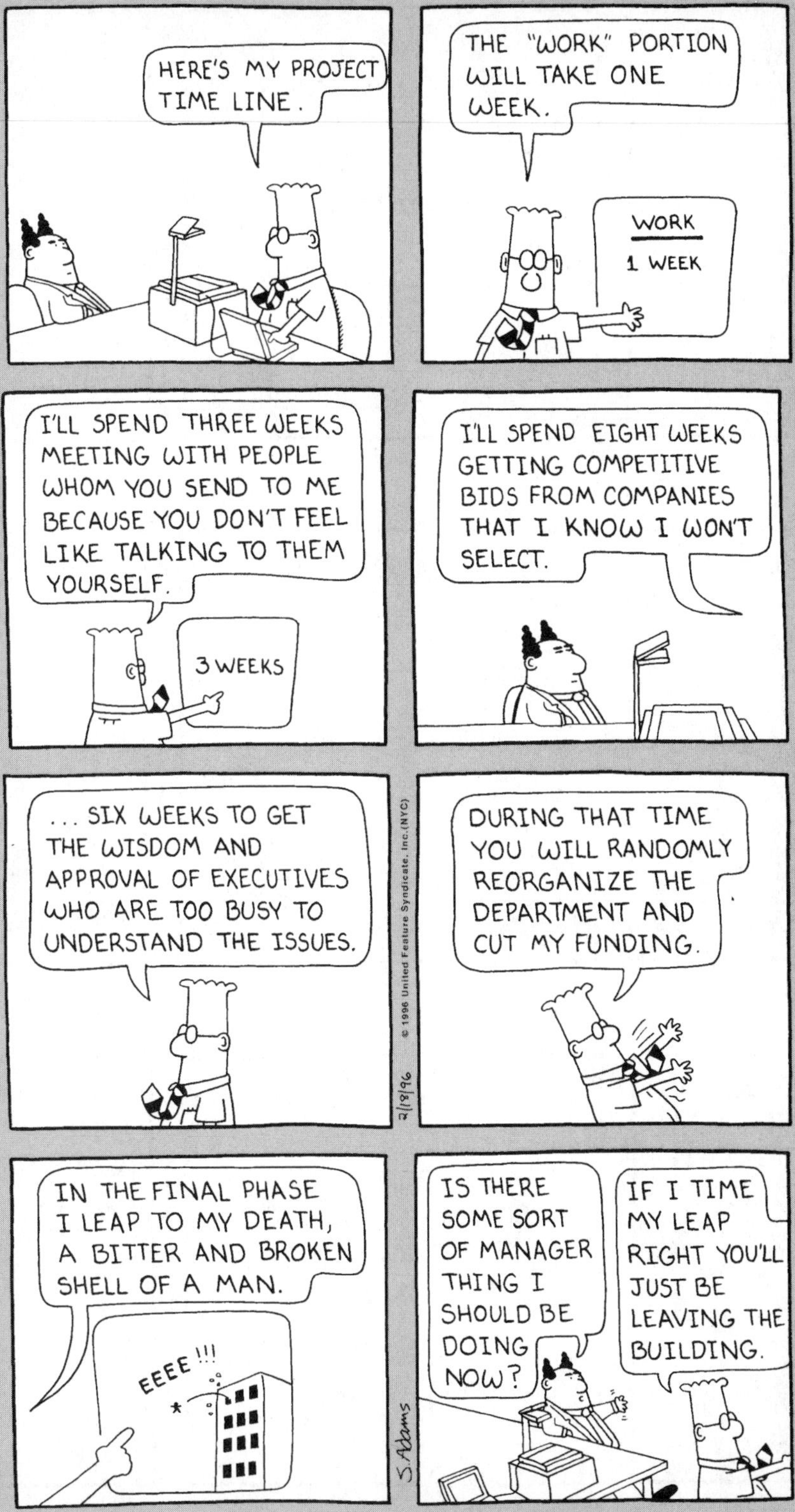
HERE'S MY PROJECT TIME LINE.
THE "WORK" PORTION WILL TAKE ONE WEEK.
WORK
1 WEEK
I'LL SPEND THREE WEEKS MEETING WITH PEOPLE WHOM YOU SEND TO ME BECAUSE YOU DON'T FEEL LIKE TALKING TO THEM YOURSELF.
3 WEEKS
I'LL SPEND EIGHT WEEKS GETTING COMPETITIVE BIDS FROM COMPANIES THAT I KNOW I WON'T SELECT.
... SIX WEEKS TO GET THE WISDOM AND APPROVAL OF EXECUTIVES WHO ARE TOO BUSY TO UNDERSTAND THE ISSUES.
© 1996 United Feature Syndicate, Inc.(NYC)
2/18/96
DURING THAT TIME YOU WILL RANDOMLY REORGANIZE THE DEPARTMENT AND CUT MY FUNDING.
IN THE FINAL PHASE I LEAP TO MY DEATH, A BITTER AND BROKEN SHELL OF A MAN.
EEEE!!!
S. Adams
IS THERE SOME SORT OF MANAGER THING I SHOULD BE DOING NOW?
IF I TIME MY LEAP RIGHT YOU'LL JUST BE LEAVING THE BUILDING.

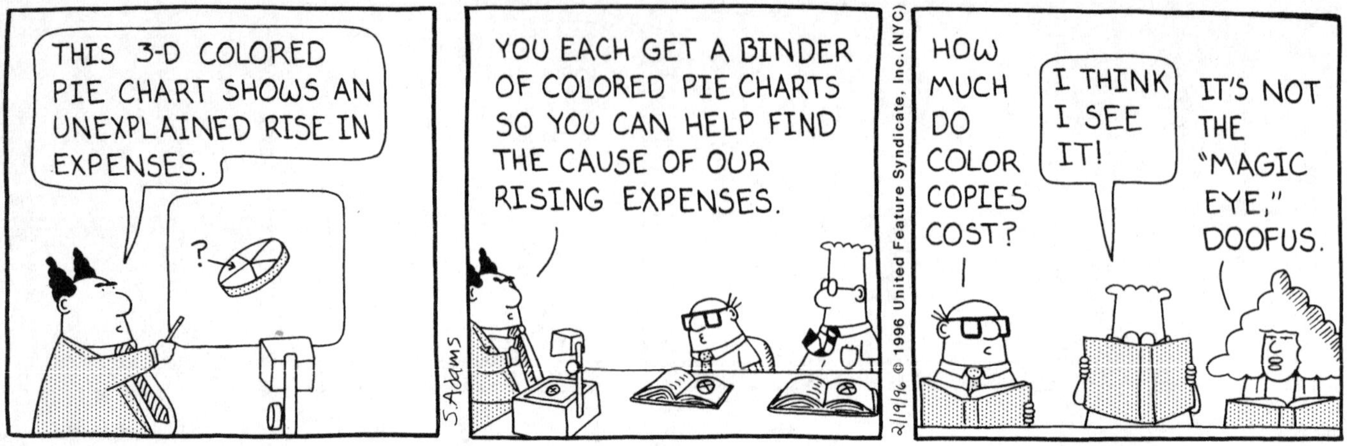
THIS 3-D COLORED PIE CHART SHOWS AN UNEXPLAINED RISE IN EXPENSES.
?
YOU EACH GET A BINDER OF COLORED PIE CHARTS SO YOU CAN HELP FIND THE CAUSE OF OUR RISING EXPENSES.
S. Adams
2/19/96 © 1996 United Feature Syndicate, Inc.(NYC)
HOW MUCH DO COLOR COPIES COST?
I THINK I SEE IT!
IT'S NOT THE "MAGIC EYE," DOOFUS.

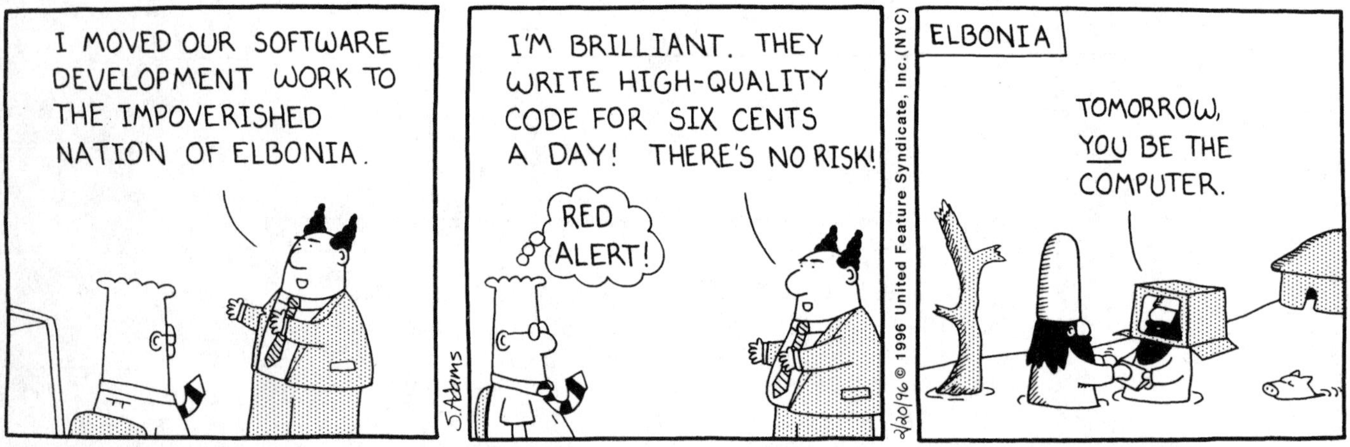
I MOVED OUR SOFTWARE DEVELOPMENT WORK TO THE IMPOVERISHED NATION OF ELBONIA.
I'M BRILLIANT. THEY WRITE HIGH-QUALITY CODE FOR SIX CENTS A DAY! THERE'S NO RISK!
RED ALERT!
S. Adams
2/20/96 © 1996 United Feature Syndicate, Inc.(NYC)
ELBONIA
TOMORROW, YOU BE THE COMPUTER.

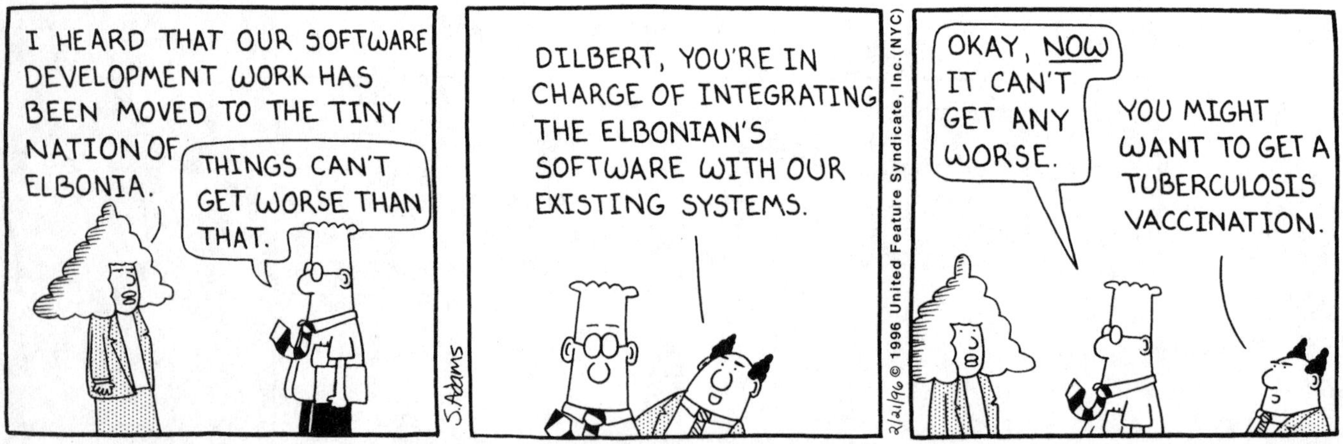
I HEARD THAT OUR SOFTWARE DEVELOPMENT WORK HAS BEEN MOVED TO THE TINY NATION OF ELBONIA.
THINGS CAN'T GET WORSE THAN THAT.
DILBERT, YOU'RE IN CHARGE OF INTEGRATING THE ELBONIAN'S SOFTWARE WITH OUR EXISTING SYSTEMS.
S. Adams
2/21/96 © 1996 United Feature Syndicate, Inc.(NYC)
OKAY, NOW IT CAN'T GET ANY WORSE.
YOU MIGHT WANT TO GET A TUBERCULOSIS VACCINATION.

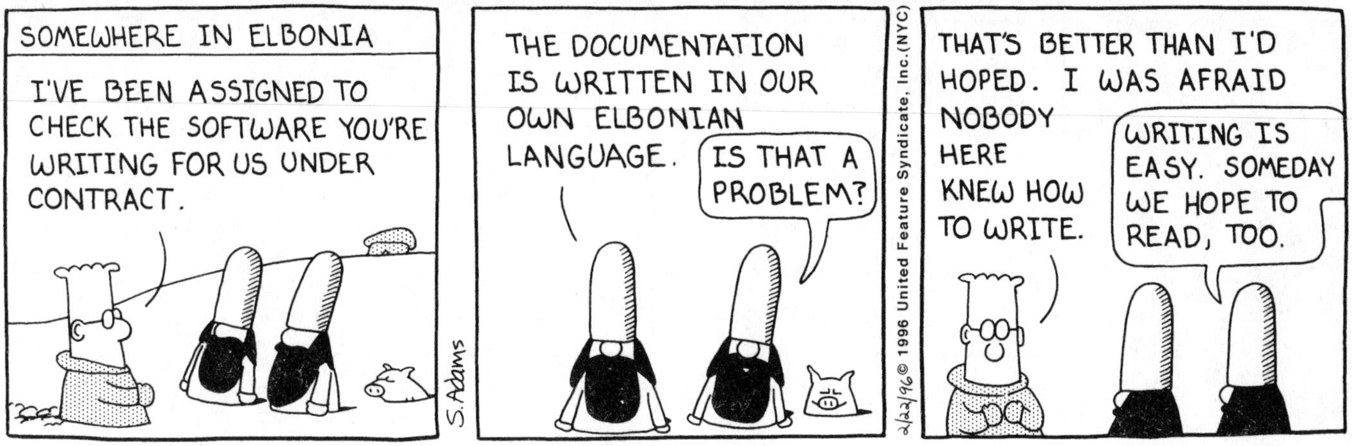
SOMEWHERE IN ELBONIA
I'VE BEEN ASSIGNED TO CHECK THE SOFTWARE YOU'RE WRITING FOR US UNDER CONTRACT.
S. Adams
THE DOCUMENTATION IS WRITTEN IN OUR OWN ELBONIAN LANGUAGE.
IS THAT A PROBLEM?
2/22/96 © 1996 United Feature Syndicate, Inc.(NYC)
THAT'S BETTER THAN I'D HOPED. I WAS AFRAID NOBODY HERE KNEW HOW TO WRITE.
WRITING IS EASY. SOMEDAY WE HOPE TO READ, TOO.

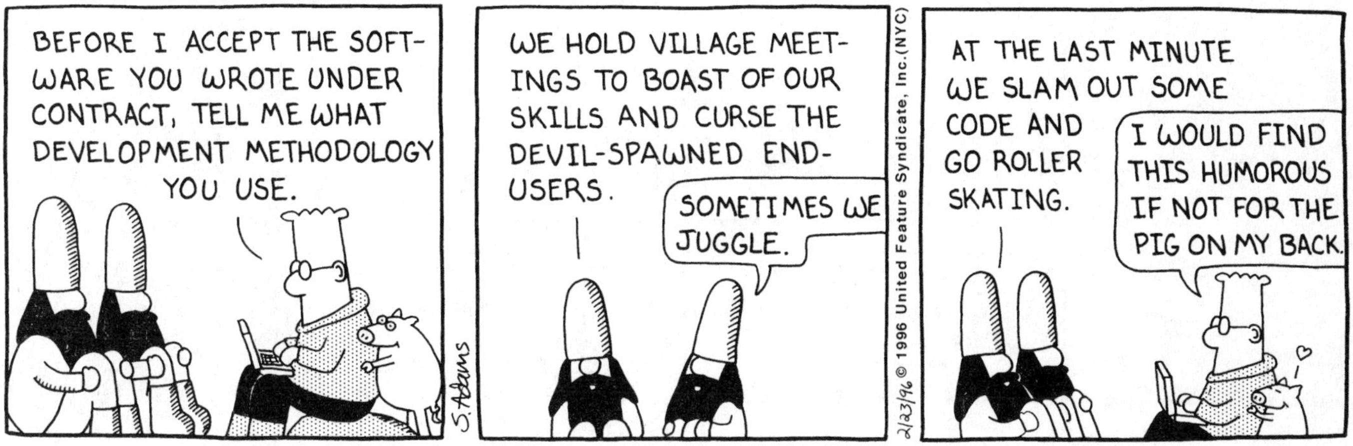
BEFORE I ACCEPT THE SOFTWARE YOU WROTE UNDER CONTRACT, TELL ME WHAT DEVELOPMENT METHODOLOGY YOU USE.
S. Adams
WE HOLD VILLAGE MEETINGS TO BOAST OF OUR SKILLS AND CURSE THE DEVIL-SPAWNED END-USERS.
SOMETIMES WE JUGGLE.
2/23/96 © 1996 United Feature Syndicate, Inc.(NYC)
AT THE LAST MINUTE WE SLAM OUT SOME CODE AND GO ROLLER SKATING.
I WOULD FIND THIS HUMOROUS IF NOT FOR THE PIG ON MY BACK.

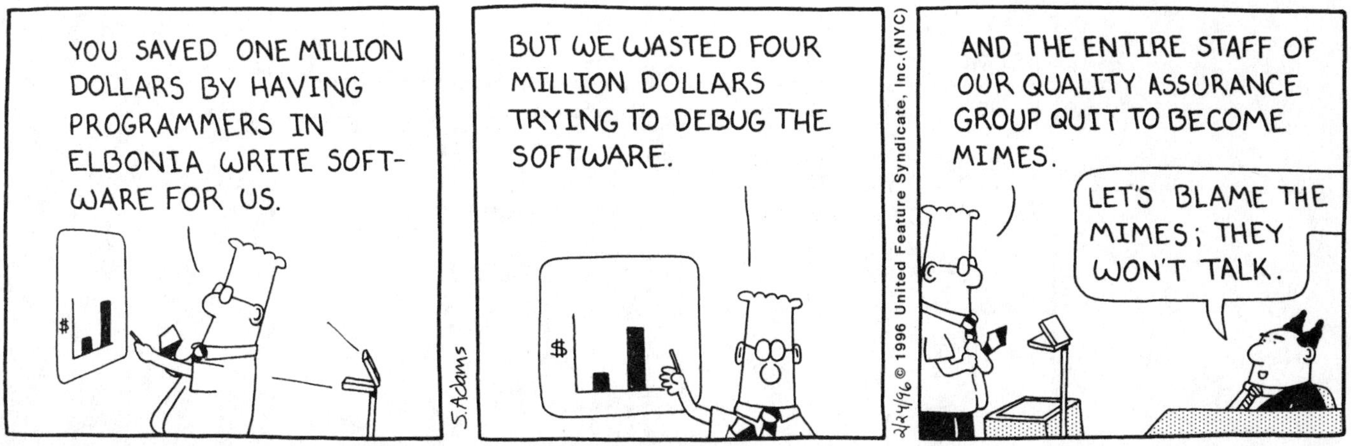
YOU SAVED ONE MILLION DOLLARS BY HAVING PROGRAMMERS IN ELBONIA WRITE SOFTWARE FOR US.
S. Adams
BUT WE WASTED FOUR MILLION DOLLARS TRYING TO DEBUG THE SOFTWARE.
2/24/96 © 1996 United Feature Syndicate, Inc.(NYC)
AND THE ENTIRE STAFF OF OUR QUALITY ASSURANCE GROUP QUIT TO BECOME MIMES.
LET'S BLAME THE MIMES; THEY WON'T TALK.

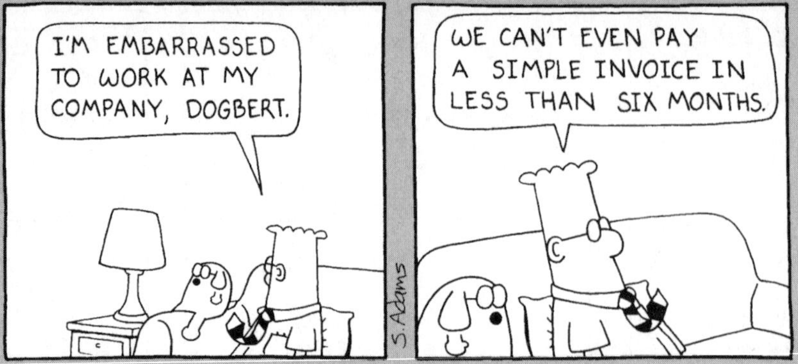
I'M EMBARRASSED TO WORK AT MY COMPANY, DOGBERT.
S. Adams
WE CAN'T EVEN PAY A SIMPLE INVOICE IN LESS THAN SIX MONTHS.

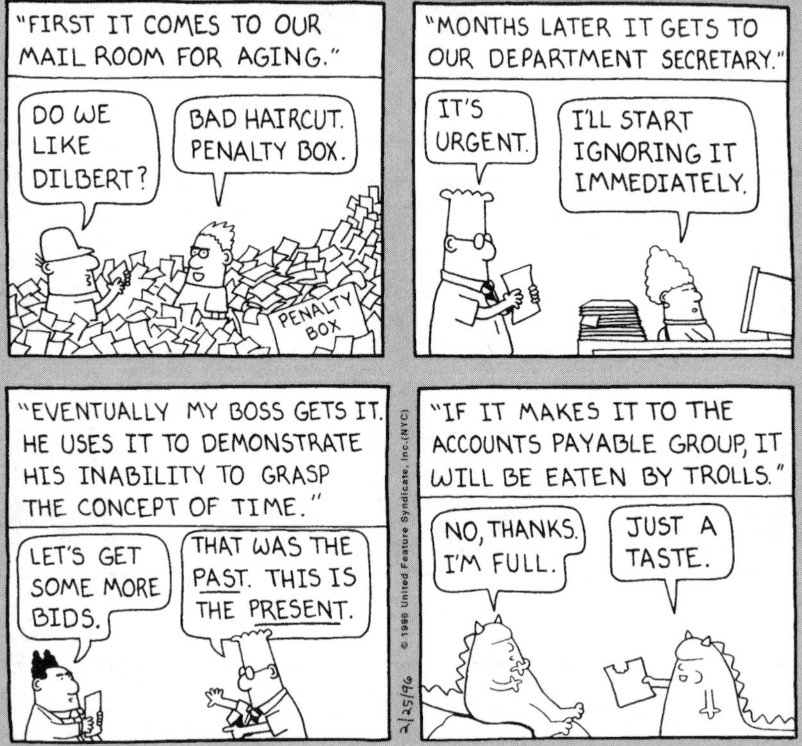
"FIRST IT COMES TO OUR MAIL ROOM FOR AGING."
DO WE LIKE DILBERT?
BAD HAIRCUT. PENALTY BOX.
PENALTY BOX
"MONTHS LATER IT GETS TO OUR DEPARTMENT SECRETARY."
IT'S URGENT.
I'LL START IGNORING IT IMMEDIATELY.
"EVENTUALLY MY BOSS GETS IT. HE USES IT TO DEMONSTRATE HIS INABILITY TO GRASP THE CONCEPT OF TIME."
LET'S GET SOME MORE BIDS.
THAT WAS THE PAST. THIS IS THE PRESENT.
© 1996 United Feature Syndicate, Inc.(NYC)
2/25/96
"IF IT MAKES IT TO THE ACCOUNTS PAYABLE GROUP, IT WILL BE EATEN BY TROLLS."
NO, THANKS. I'M FULL.
JUST A TASTE.

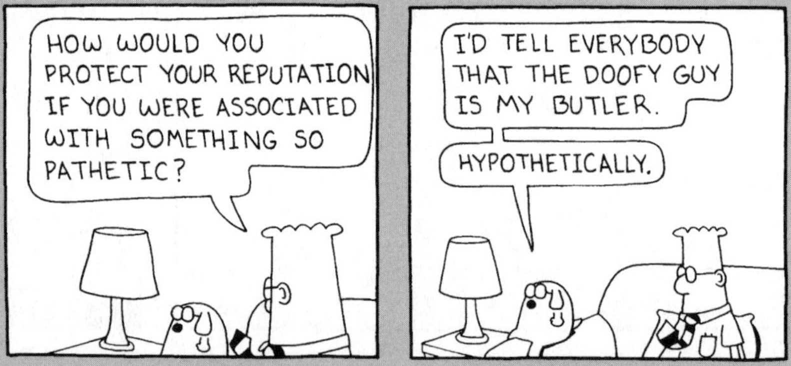
HOW WOULD YOU PROTECT YOUR REPUTATION IF YOU WERE ASSOCIATED WITH SOMETHING SO PATHETIC?
I'D TELL EVERYBODY THAT THE DOOFY GUY IS MY BUTLER.
HYPOTHETICALLY.

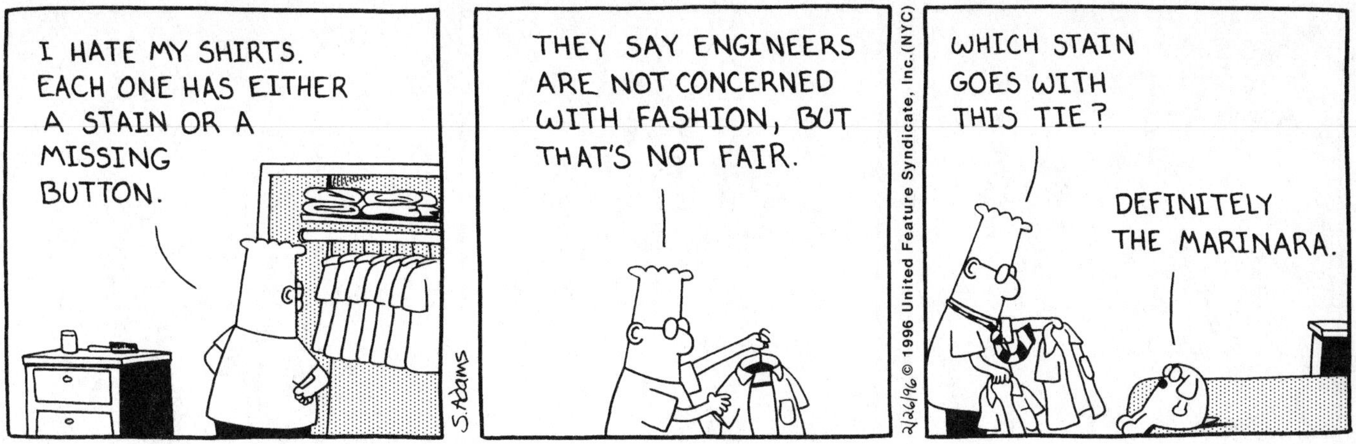
I HATE MY SHIRTS. EACH ONE HAS EITHER A STAIN OR A MISSING BUTTON.
S. Adams
THEY SAY ENGINEERS ARE NOT CONCERNED WITH FASHION, BUT THAT'S NOT FAIR.
2/26/96 © 1996 United Feature Syndicate, Inc.(NYC)
WHICH STAIN GOES WITH THIS TIE?
DEFINITELY THE MARINARA.

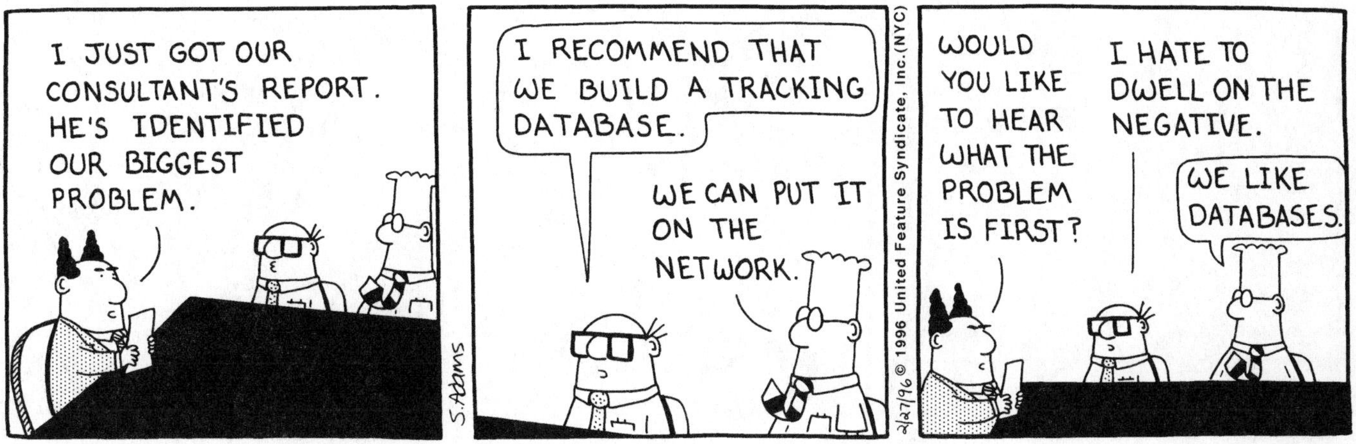
I JUST GOT OUR CONSULTANT'S REPORT. HE'S IDENTIFIED OUR BIGGEST PROBLEM.
S. Adams
I RECOMMEND THAT WE BUILD A TRACKING DATABASE.
WE CAN PUT IT ON THE NETWORK.
2/27/96 © 1996 United Feature Syndicate, Inc.(NYC)
WOULD YOU LIKE TO HEAR WHAT THE PROBLEM IS FIRST?
I HATE TO DWELL ON THE NEGATIVE.
WE LIKE DATABASES.

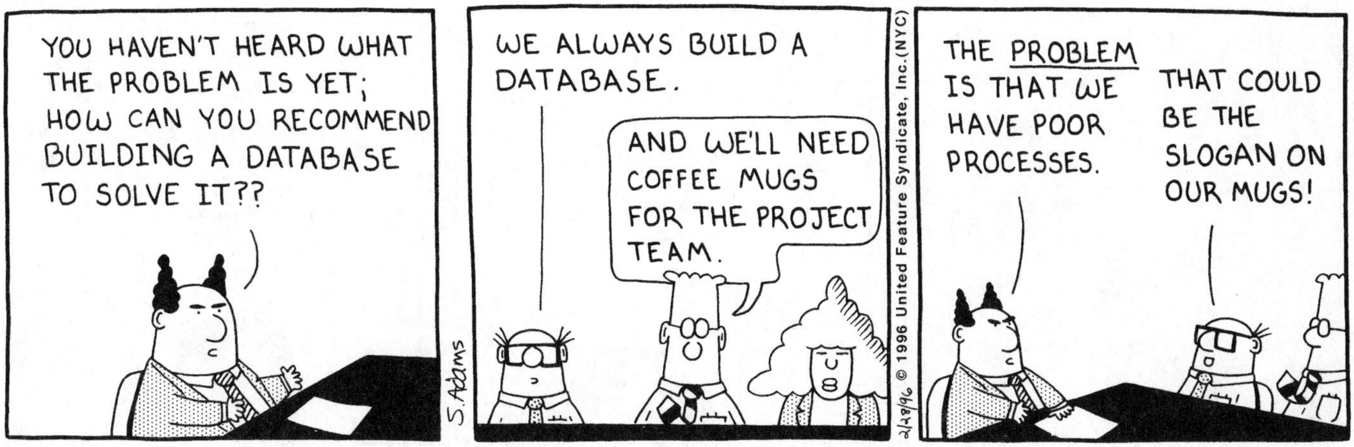
YOU HAVEN'T HEARD WHAT THE PROBLEM IS YET; HOW CAN YOU RECOMMEND BUILDING A DATABASE TO SOLVE IT??
S. Adams
WE ALWAYS BUILD A DATABASE.
AND WE'LL NEED COFFEE MUGS FOR THE PROJECT TEAM.
2/28/96 © 1996 United Feature Syndicate, Inc.(NYC)
THE PROBLEM IS THAT WE HAVE POOR PROCESSES.
THAT COULD BE THE SLOGAN ON OUR MUGS!

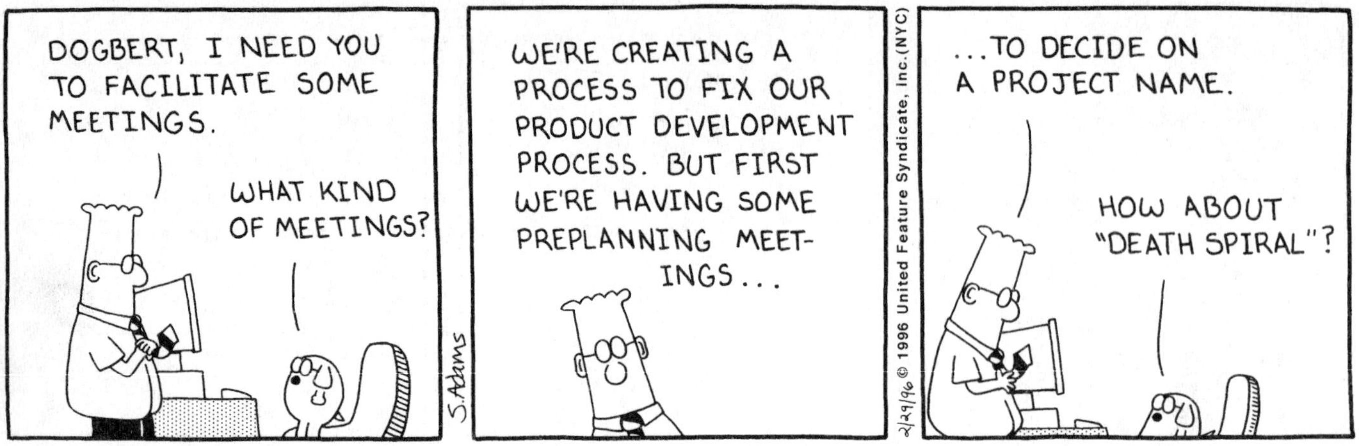
DOGBERT, I NEED YOU TO FACILITATE SOME MEETINGS.
WHAT KIND OF MEETINGS?
S.Adams
WE'RE CREATING A PROCESS TO FIX OUR PRODUCT DEVELOPMENT PROCESS. BUT FIRST WE'RE HAVING SOME PREPLANNING MEET- INGS...
2/29/96 © 1996 United Feature Syndicate, Inc.(NYC)
...TO DECIDE ON A PROJECT NAME.
HOW ABOUT "DEATH SPIRAL"?

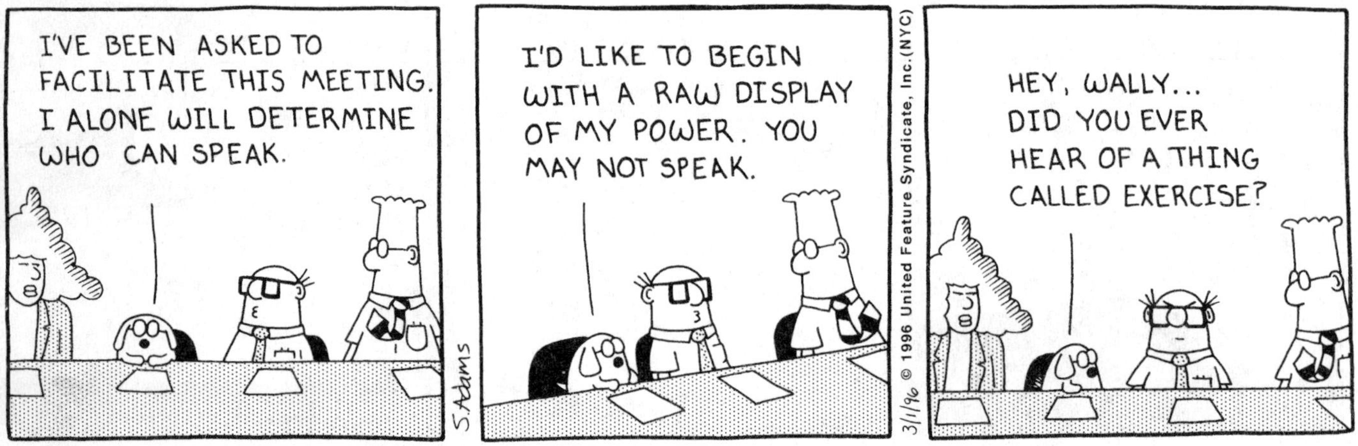
I'VE BEEN ASKED TO FACILITATE THIS MEETING. I ALONE WILL DETERMINE WHO CAN SPEAK.
S.Adams
I'D LIKE TO BEGIN WITH A RAW DISPLAY OF MY POWER. YOU MAY NOT SPEAK.
3/1/96 © 1996 United Feature Syndicate, Inc.(NYC)
HEY, WALLY... DID YOU EVER HEAR OF A THING CALLED EXERCISE?

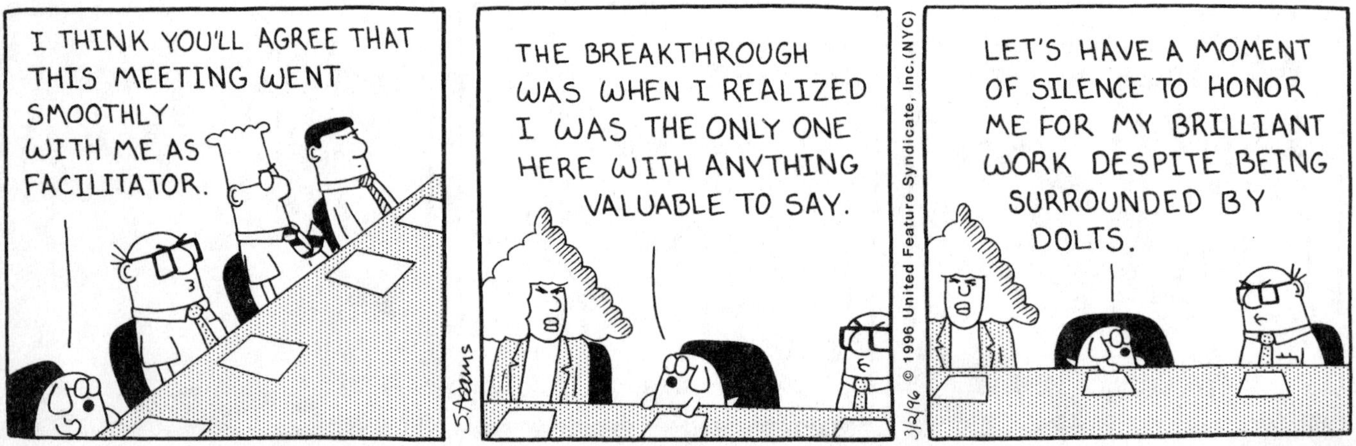
I THINK YOU'LL AGREE THAT THIS MEETING WENT SMOOTHLY WITH ME AS FACILITATOR.
S.Adams
THE BREAKTHROUGH WAS WHEN I REALIZED I WAS THE ONLY ONE HERE WITH ANYTHING VALUABLE TO SAY.
3/2/96 © 1996 United Feature Syndicate, Inc.(NYC)
LET'S HAVE A MOMENT OF SILENCE TO HONOR ME FOR MY BRILLIANT WORK DESPITE BEING SURROUNDED BY DOLTS.

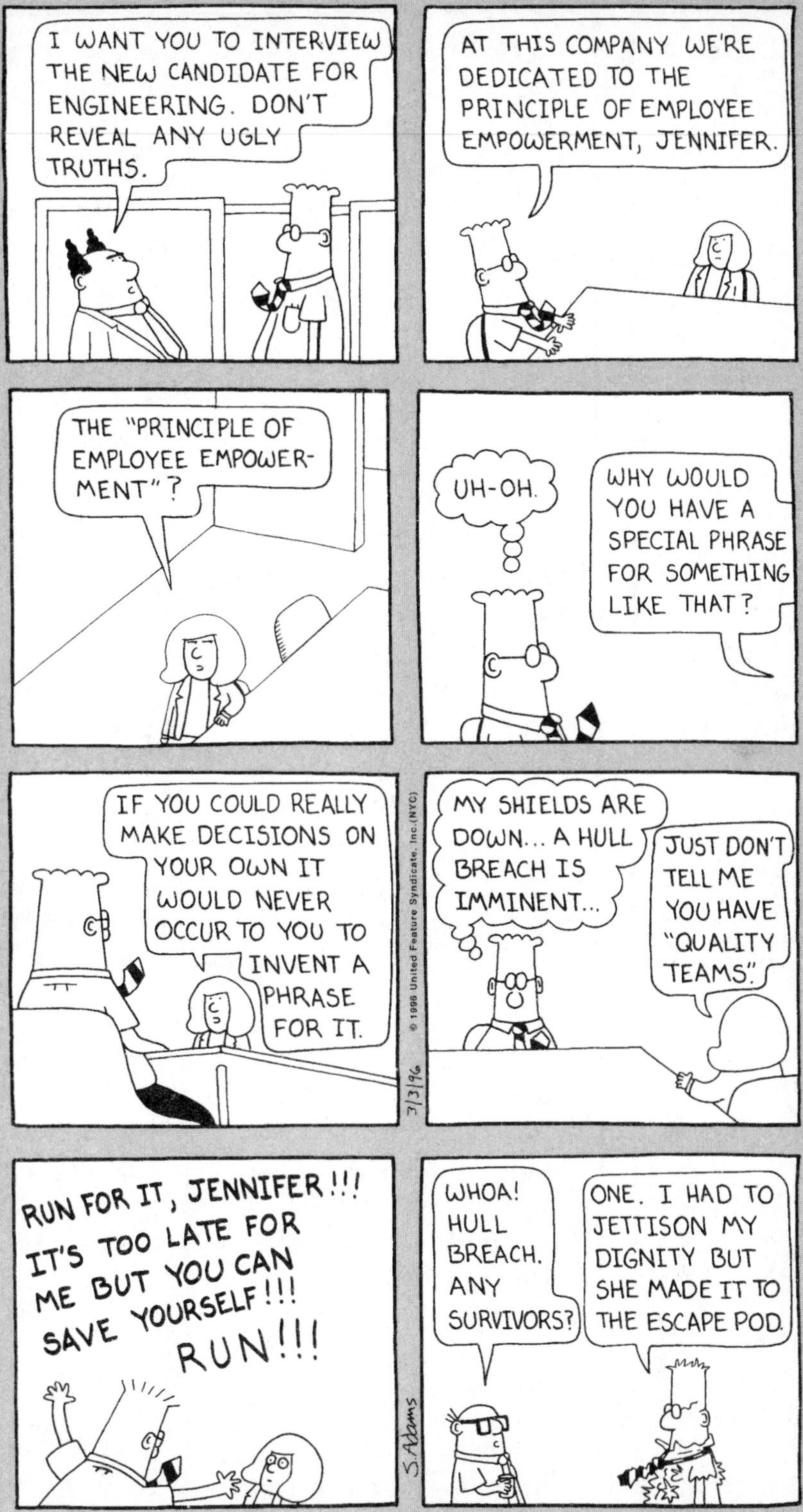
I WANT YOU TO INTERVIEW THE NEW CANDIDATE FOR ENGINEERING. DON'T REVEAL ANY UGLY TRUTHS.
AT THIS COMPANY WE'RE DEDICATED TO THE PRINCIPLE OF EMPLOYEE EMPOWERMENT, JENNIFER.
THE "PRINCIPLE OF EMPLOYEE EMPOWERMENT"?
UH-OH.
WHY WOULD YOU HAVE A SPECIAL PHRASE FOR SOMETHING LIKE THAT?
IF YOU COULD REALLY MAKE DECISIONS ON YOUR OWN IT WOULD NEVER OCCUR TO YOU TO INVENT A PHRASE FOR IT.
© 1996 United Feature Syndicate, Inc.(NYC)
3/3/96
MY SHIELDS ARE DOWN... A HULL BREACH IS IMMINENT...
JUST DON'T TELL ME YOU HAVE "QUALITY TEAMS".
RUN FOR IT, JENNIFER!!! IT'S TOO LATE FOR ME BUT YOU CAN SAVE YOURSELF!!!
RUN!!!
S. Adams
WHOA! HULL BREACH. ANY SURVIVORS?
ONE. I HAD TO JETTISON MY DIGNITY BUT SHE MADE IT TO THE ESCAPE POD.

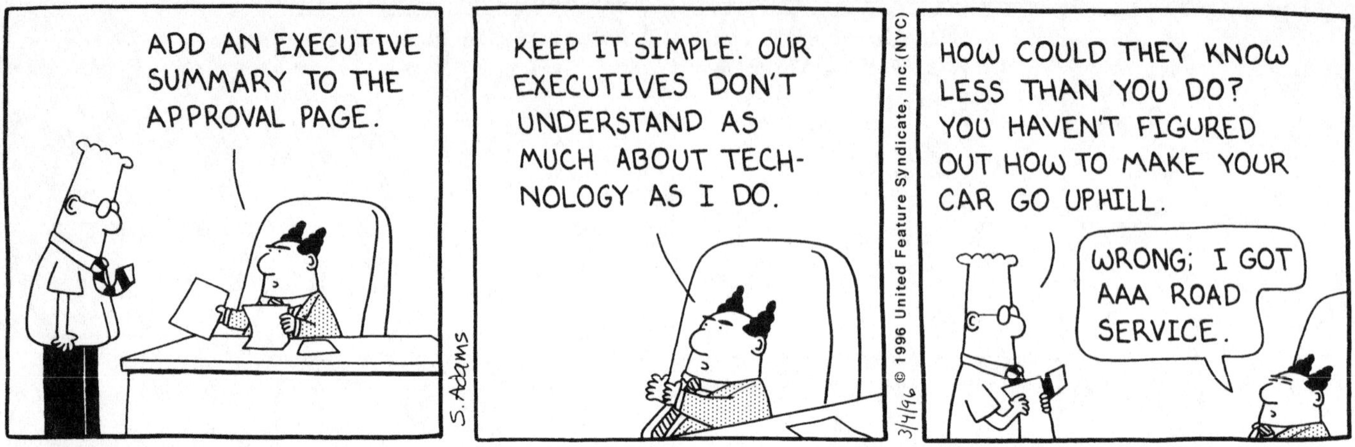
ADD AN EXECUTIVE SUMMARY TO THE APPROVAL PAGE.
S. Adams
KEEP IT SIMPLE. OUR EXECUTIVES DON'T UNDERSTAND AS MUCH ABOUT TECHNOLOGY AS I DO.
3/4/96 © 1996 United Feature Syndicate, Inc.(NYC)
HOW COULD THEY KNOW LESS THAN YOU DO? YOU HAVEN'T FIGURED OUT HOW TO MAKE YOUR CAR GO UPHILL.
WRONG; I GOT AAA ROAD SERVICE.

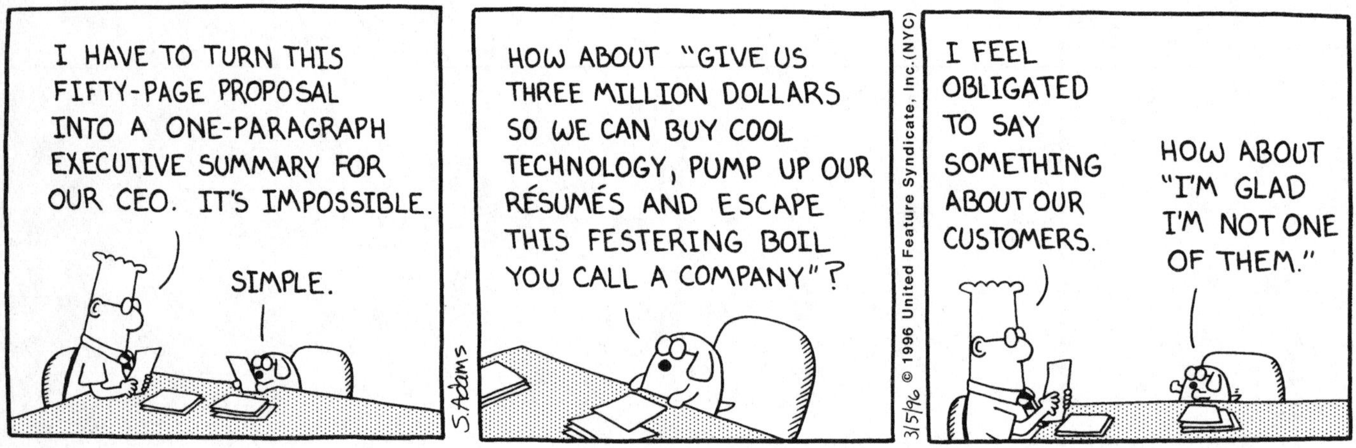
I HAVE TO TURN THIS FIFTY-PAGE PROPOSAL INTO A ONE-PARAGRAPH EXECUTIVE SUMMARY FOR OUR CEO. IT'S IMPOSSIBLE.
SIMPLE.
S. Adams
HOW ABOUT "GIVE US THREE MILLION DOLLARS SO WE CAN BUY COOL TECHNOLOGY, PUMP UP OUR RÉSUMÉS AND ESCAPE THIS FESTERING BOIL YOU CALL A COMPANY"?
3/5/96 © 1996 United Feature Syndicate, Inc.(NYC)
I FEEL OBLIGATED TO SAY SOMETHING ABOUT OUR CUSTOMERS.
HOW ABOUT "I'M GLAD I'M NOT ONE OF THEM."

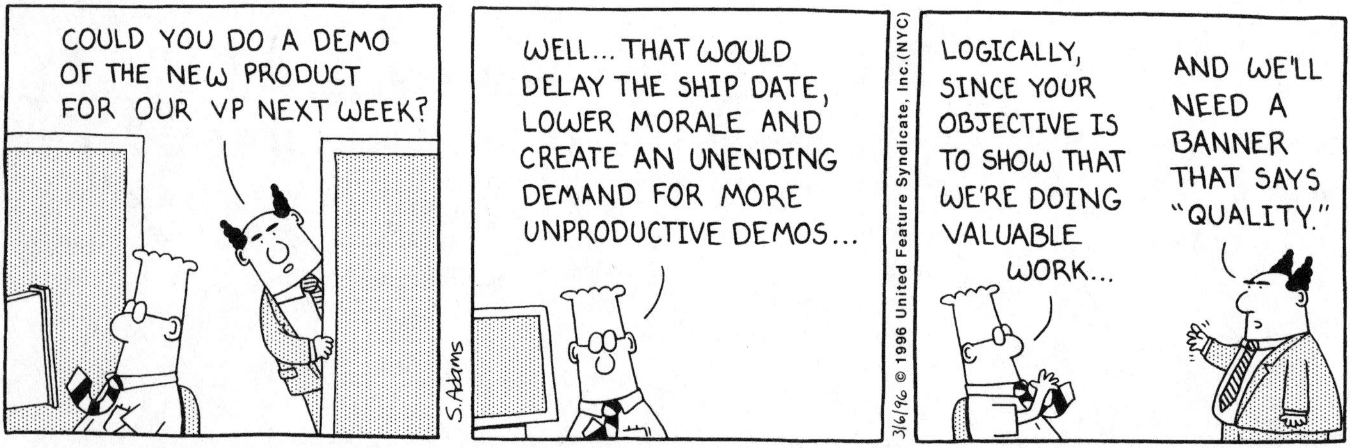
COULD YOU DO A DEMO OF THE NEW PRODUCT FOR OUR VP NEXT WEEK?
S. Adams
WELL... THAT WOULD DELAY THE SHIP DATE, LOWER MORALE AND CREATE AN UNENDING DEMAND FOR MORE UNPRODUCTIVE DEMOS...
3/6/96 © 1996 United Feature Syndicate, Inc.(NYC)
LOGICALLY, SINCE YOUR OBJECTIVE IS TO SHOW THAT WE'RE DOING VALUABLE WORK...
AND WE'LL NEED A BANNER THAT SAYS "QUALITY."

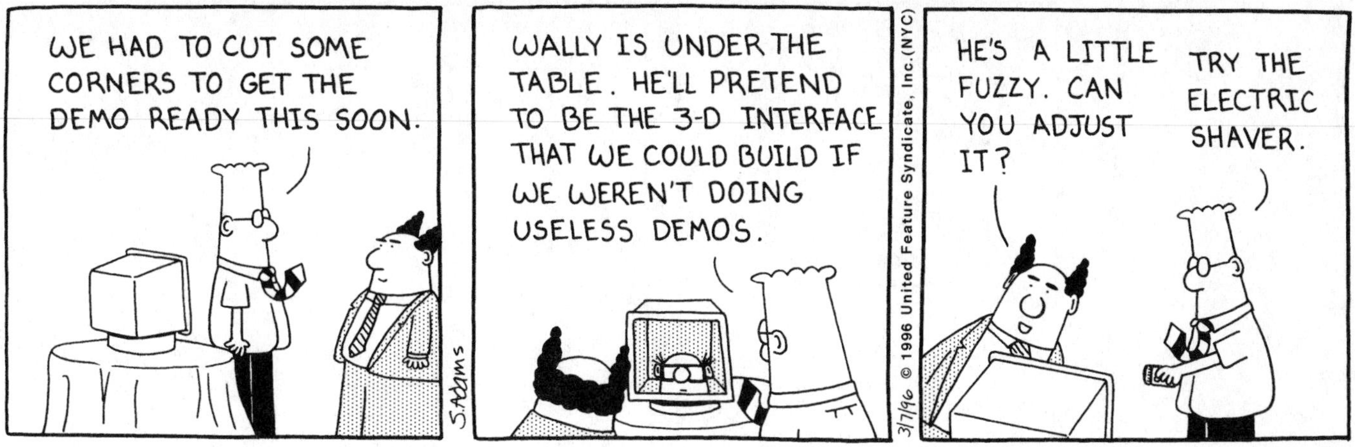
WE HAD TO CUT SOME CORNERS TO GET THE DEMO READY THIS SOON.
WALLY IS UNDER THE TABLE. HE'LL PRETEND TO BE THE 3-D INTERFACE THAT WE COULD BUILD IF WE WEREN'T DOING USELESS DEMOS.
HE'S A LITTLE FUZZY. CAN YOU ADJUST IT?
TRY THE ELECTRIC SHAVER.
S. Adams
3/7/96 © 1996 United Feature Syndicate, Inc.(NYC)

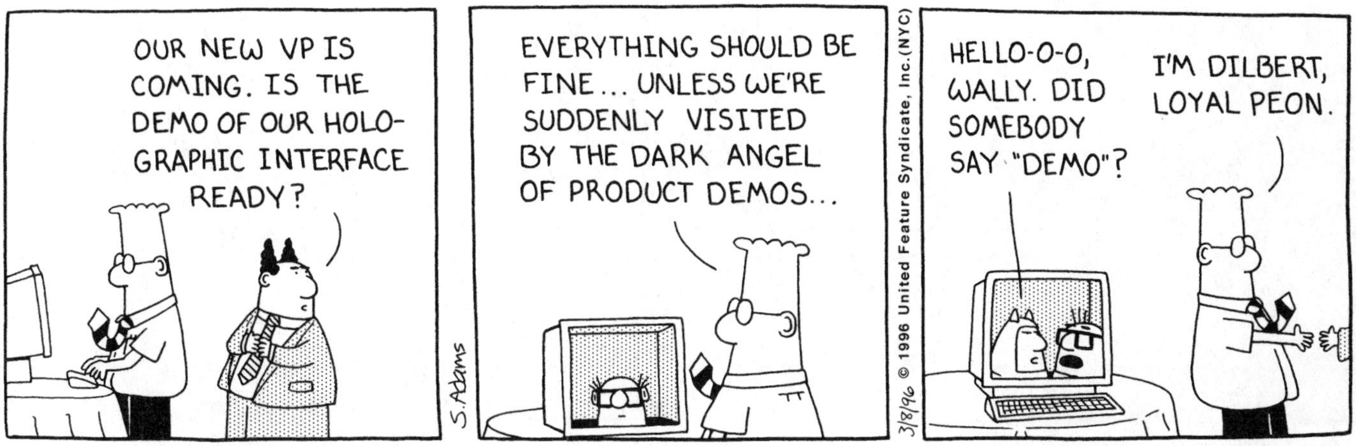
OUR NEW VP IS COMING. IS THE DEMO OF OUR HOLO-GRAPHIC INTERFACE READY?
EVERYTHING SHOULD BE FINE... UNLESS WE'RE SUDDENLY VISITED BY THE DARK ANGEL OF PRODUCT DEMOS...
HELLO-O-O, WALLY. DID SOMEBODY SAY "DEMO"?
I'M DILBERT, LOYAL PEON.
S. Adams
3/8/96 © 1996 United Feature Syndicate, Inc.(NYC)

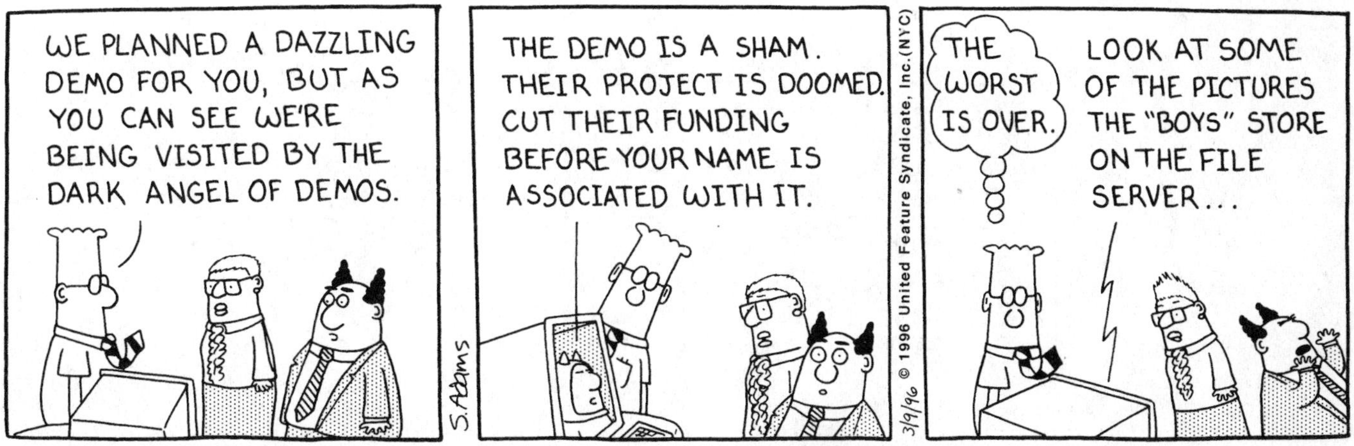
WE PLANNED A DAZZLING DEMO FOR YOU, BUT AS YOU CAN SEE WE'RE BEING VISITED BY THE DARK ANGEL OF DEMOS.
THE DEMO IS A SHAM. THEIR PROJECT IS DOOMED. CUT THEIR FUNDING BEFORE YOUR NAME IS ASSOCIATED WITH IT.
THE WORST IS OVER.
LOOK AT SOME OF THE PICTURES THE "BOYS" STORE ON THE FILE SERVER...
S. Adams
3/9/96 © 1996 United Feature Syndicate, Inc.(NYC)

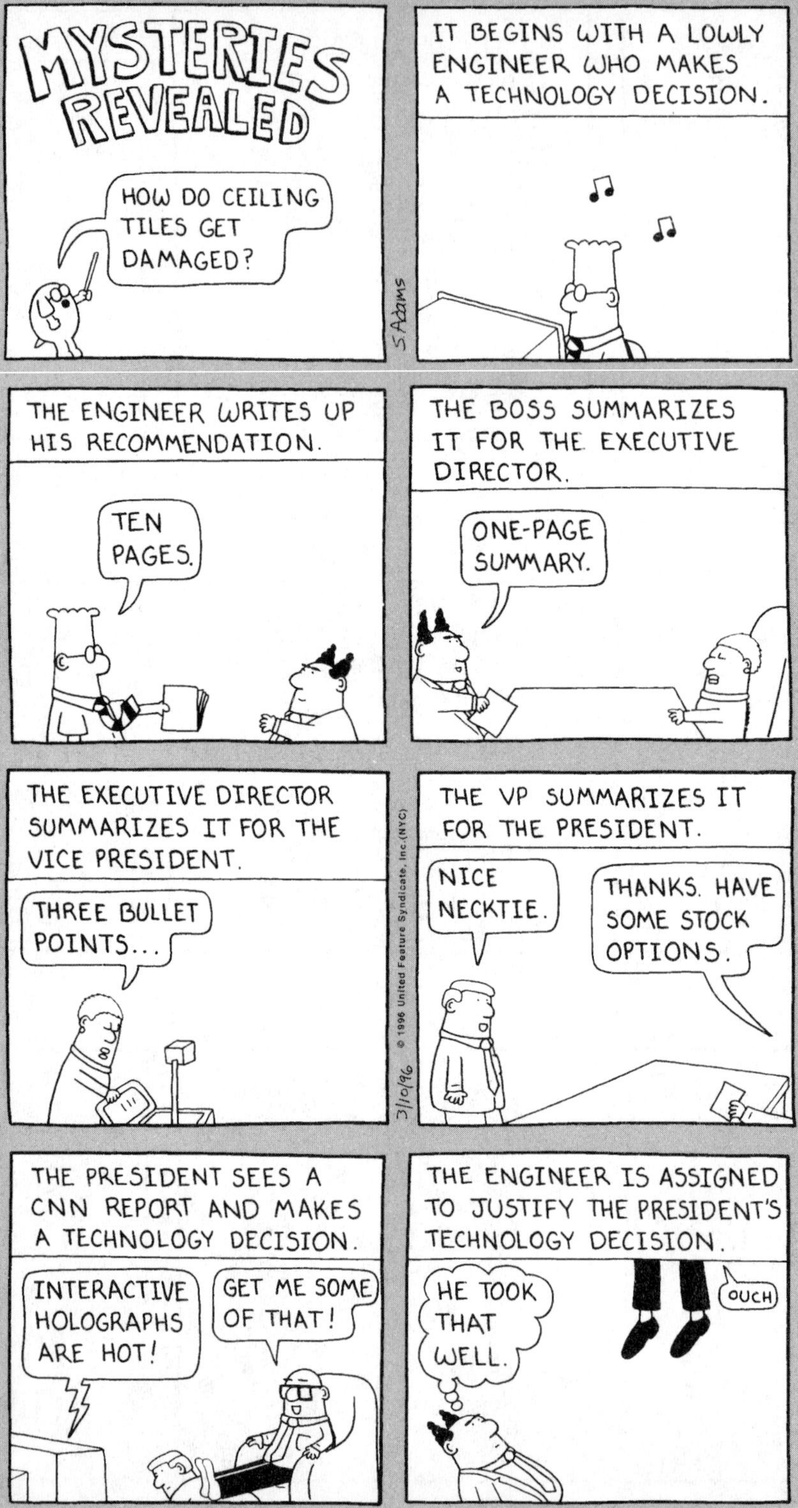
MYSTERIES REVEALED
HOW DO CEILING TILES GET DAMAGED?
S. Adams
IT BEGINS WITH A LOWLY ENGINEER WHO MAKES A TECHNOLOGY DECISION.
THE ENGINEER WRITES UP HIS RECOMMENDATION.
TEN PAGES.
THE BOSS SUMMARIZES IT FOR THE EXECUTIVE DIRECTOR.
ONE-PAGE SUMMARY.
THE EXECUTIVE DIRECTOR SUMMARIZES IT FOR THE VICE PRESIDENT.
THREE BULLET POINTS...
© 1996 United Feature Syndicate, Inc.(NYC)
3/10/96
THE VP SUMMARIZES IT FOR THE PRESIDENT.
NICE NECKTIE.
THANKS. HAVE SOME STOCK OPTIONS.
THE PRESIDENT SEES A CNN REPORT AND MAKES A TECHNOLOGY DECISION.
INTERACTIVE HOLOGRAPHS ARE HOT!
GET ME SOME OF THAT!
THE ENGINEER IS ASSIGNED TO JUSTIFY THE PRESIDENT'S TECHNOLOGY DECISION.
HE TOOK THAT WELL.
OUCH

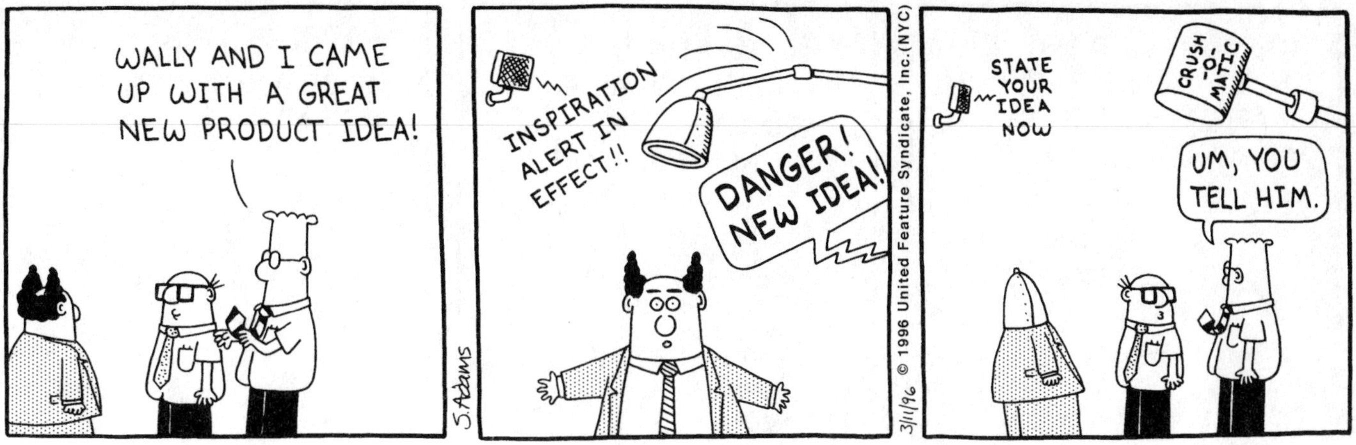
WALLY AND I CAME UP WITH A GREAT NEW PRODUCT IDEA!
S.Adams
INSPIRATION ALERT IN EFFECT!!
DANGER! NEW IDEA!
3/11/96 © 1996 United Feature Syndicate, Inc.(NYC)
STATE YOUR IDEA NOW
CRUSH-O-MATIC
UM, YOU TELL HIM.

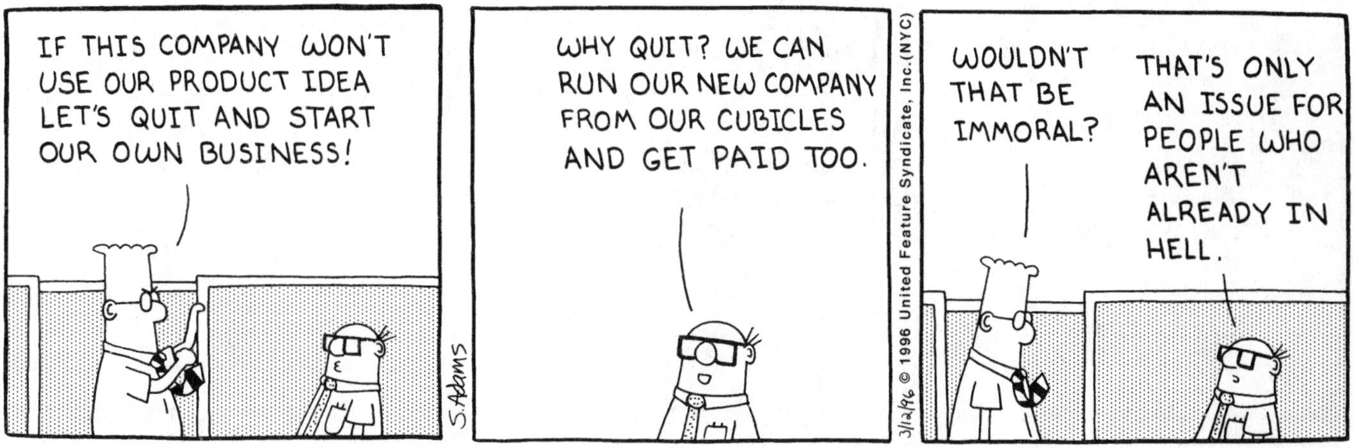
IF THIS COMPANY WON'T USE OUR PRODUCT IDEA LET'S QUIT AND START OUR OWN BUSINESS!
S.Adams
WHY QUIT? WE CAN RUN OUR NEW COMPANY FROM OUR CUBICLES AND GET PAID TOO.
3/12/96 © 1996 United Feature Syndicate, Inc.(NYC)
WOULDN'T THAT BE IMMORAL?
THAT'S ONLY AN ISSUE FOR PEOPLE WHO AREN'T ALREADY IN HELL.

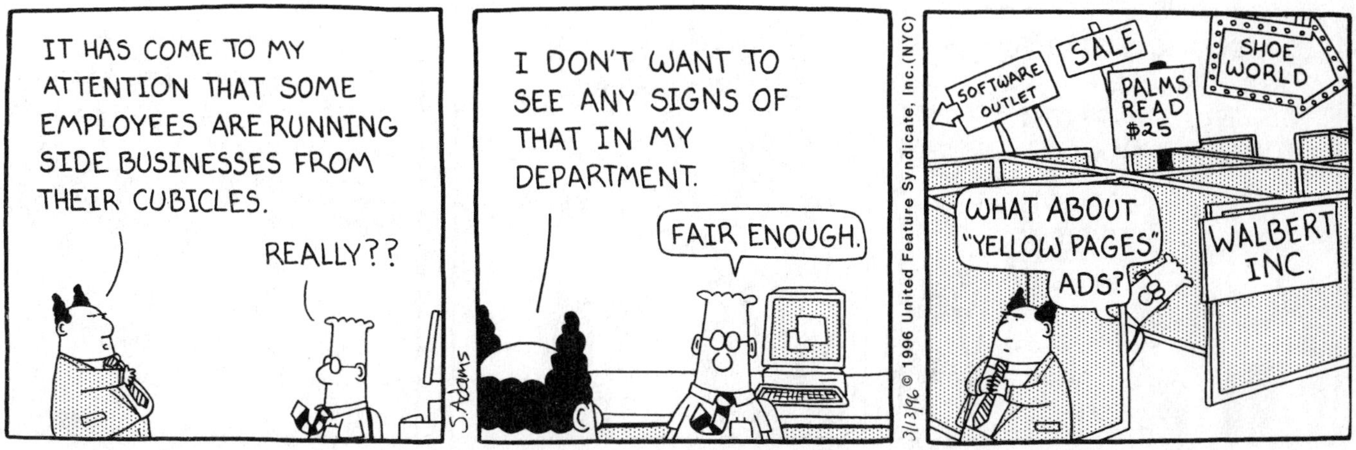
IT HAS COME TO MY ATTENTION THAT SOME EMPLOYEES ARE RUNNING SIDE BUSINESSES FROM THEIR CUBICLES.
REALLY??
S.Adams
I DON'T WANT TO SEE ANY SIGNS OF THAT IN MY DEPARTMENT.
FAIR ENOUGH.
3/13/96 © 1996 United Feature Syndicate, Inc.(NYC)
SOFTWARE OUTLET
SALE
PALMS READ $25
SHOE WORLD
WHAT ABOUT "YELLOW PAGES" ADS?
WALBERT INC.

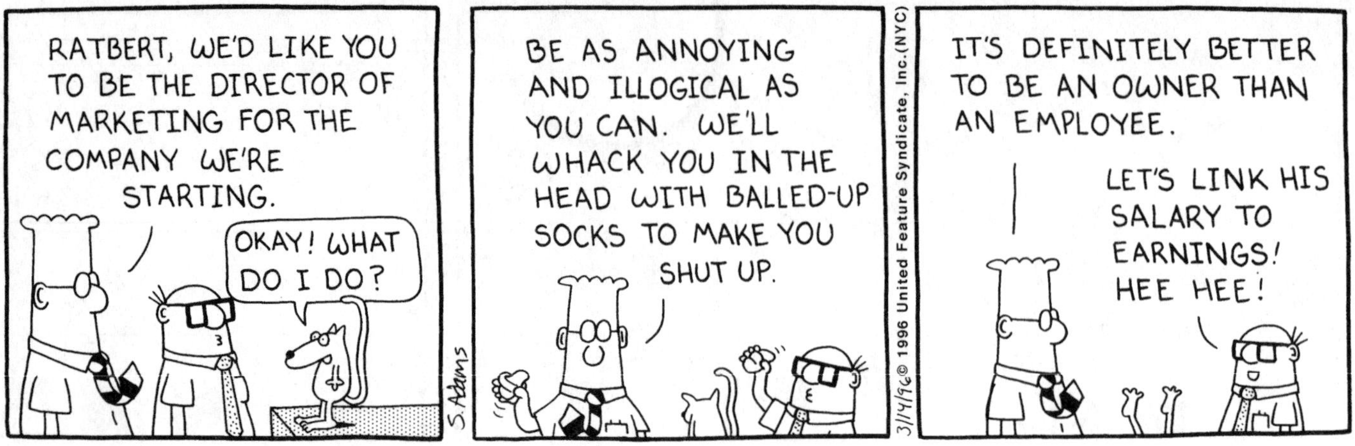
RATBERT, WE'D LIKE YOU TO BE THE DIRECTOR OF MARKETING FOR THE COMPANY WE'RE STARTING.
OKAY! WHAT DO I DO?
S. Adams
BE AS ANNOYING AND ILLOGICAL AS YOU CAN. WE'LL WHACK YOU IN THE HEAD WITH BALLED-UP SOCKS TO MAKE YOU SHUT UP.
3/14/96© 1996 United Feature Syndicate, Inc.(NYC)
IT'S DEFINITELY BETTER TO BE AN OWNER THAN AN EMPLOYEE.
LET'S LINK HIS SALARY TO EARNINGS! HEE HEE!

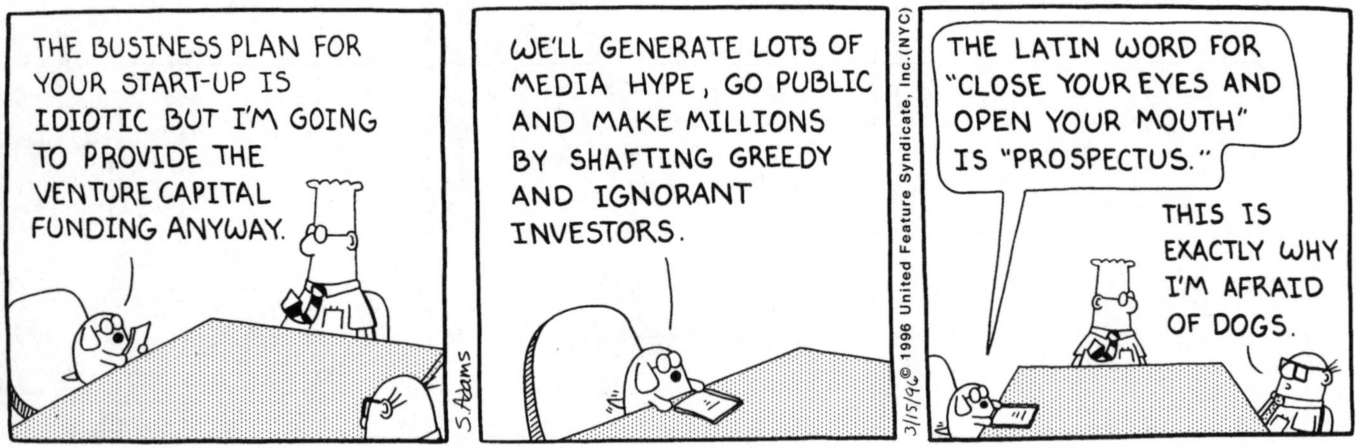
THE BUSINESS PLAN FOR YOUR START-UP IS IDIOTIC BUT I'M GOING TO PROVIDE THE VENTURE CAPITAL FUNDING ANYWAY.
S. Adams
WE'LL GENERATE LOTS OF MEDIA HYPE, GO PUBLIC AND MAKE MILLIONS BY SHAFTING GREEDY AND IGNORANT INVESTORS.
3/15/96© 1996 United Feature Syndicate, Inc.(NYC)
THE LATIN WORD FOR "CLOSE YOUR EYES AND OPEN YOUR MOUTH" IS "PROSPECTUS."
THIS IS EXACTLY WHY I'M AFRAID OF DOGS.

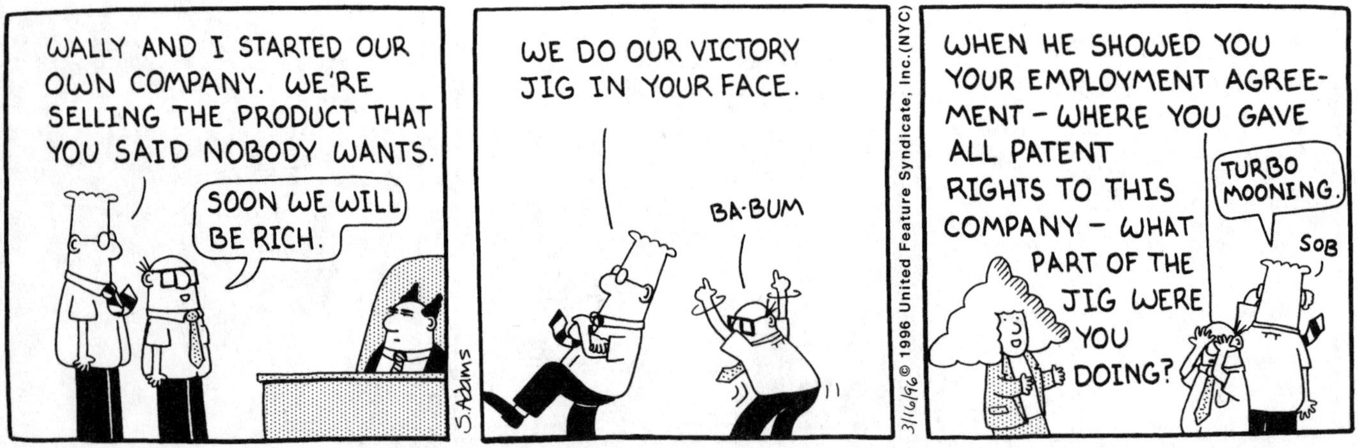
WALLY AND I STARTED OUR OWN COMPANY. WE'RE SELLING THE PRODUCT THAT YOU SAID NOBODY WANTS.
SOON WE WILL BE RICH.
S. Adams
WE DO OUR VICTORY JIG IN YOUR FACE.
BA-BUM
3/16/96© 1996 United Feature Syndicate, Inc.(NYC)
WHEN HE SHOWED YOU YOUR EMPLOYMENT AGREE-MENT – WHERE YOU GAVE ALL PATENT RIGHTS TO THIS COMPANY – WHAT PART OF THE JIG WERE YOU DOING?
TURBO MOONING.
SOB

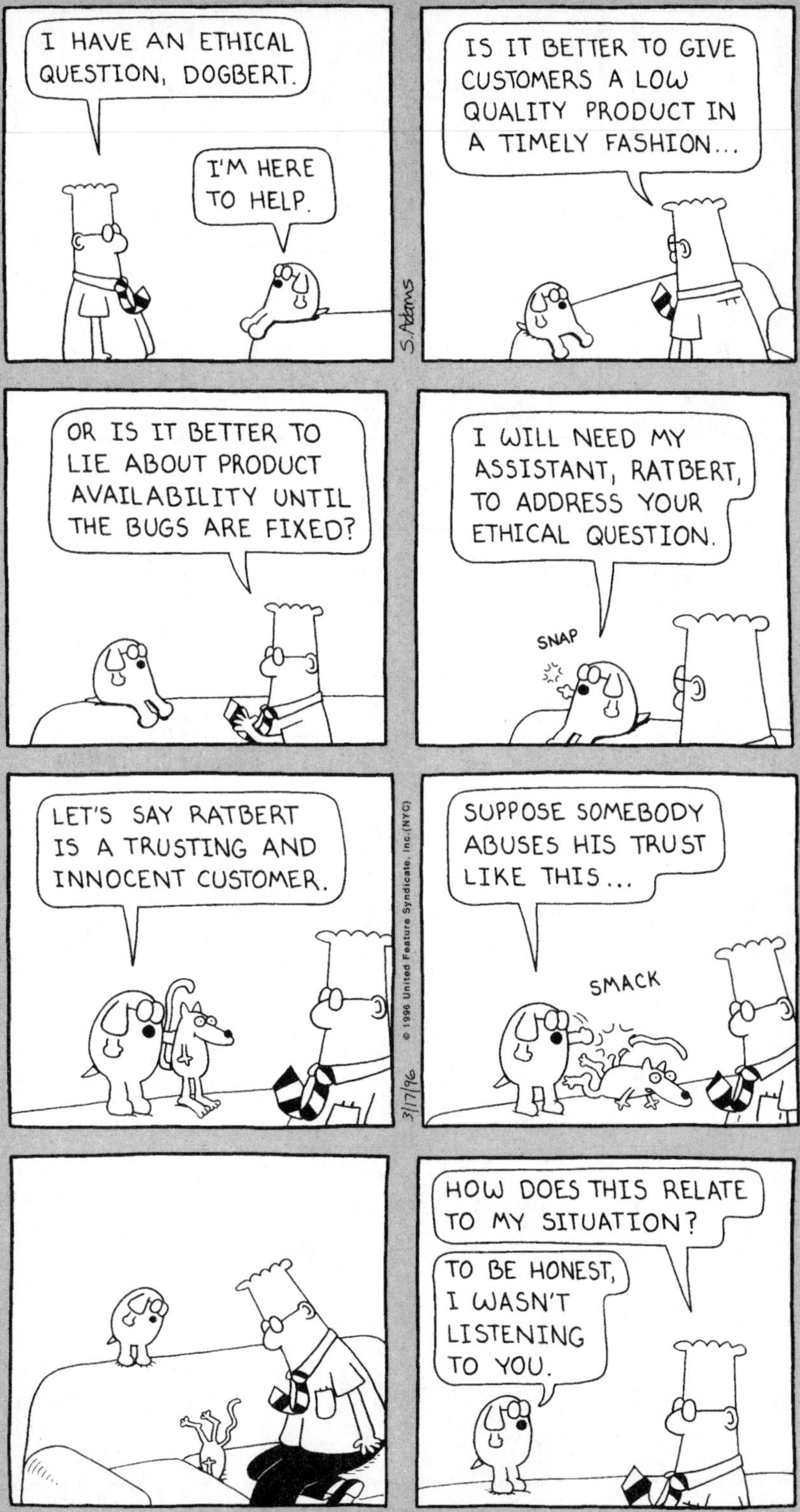
I HAVE AN ETHICAL QUESTION, DOGBERT.
I'M HERE TO HELP.
S. Adams
IS IT BETTER TO GIVE CUSTOMERS A LOW QUALITY PRODUCT IN A TIMELY FASHION...
OR IS IT BETTER TO LIE ABOUT PRODUCT AVAILABILITY UNTIL THE BUGS ARE FIXED?
I WILL NEED MY ASSISTANT, RATBERT, TO ADDRESS YOUR ETHICAL QUESTION.
SNAP
LET'S SAY RATBERT IS A TRUSTING AND INNOCENT CUSTOMER.
© 1996 United Feature Syndicate, Inc.(NYC)
3/17/96
SUPPOSE SOMEBODY ABUSES HIS TRUST LIKE THIS...
SMACK
HOW DOES THIS RELATE TO MY SITUATION?
TO BE HONEST, I WASN'T LISTENING TO YOU.

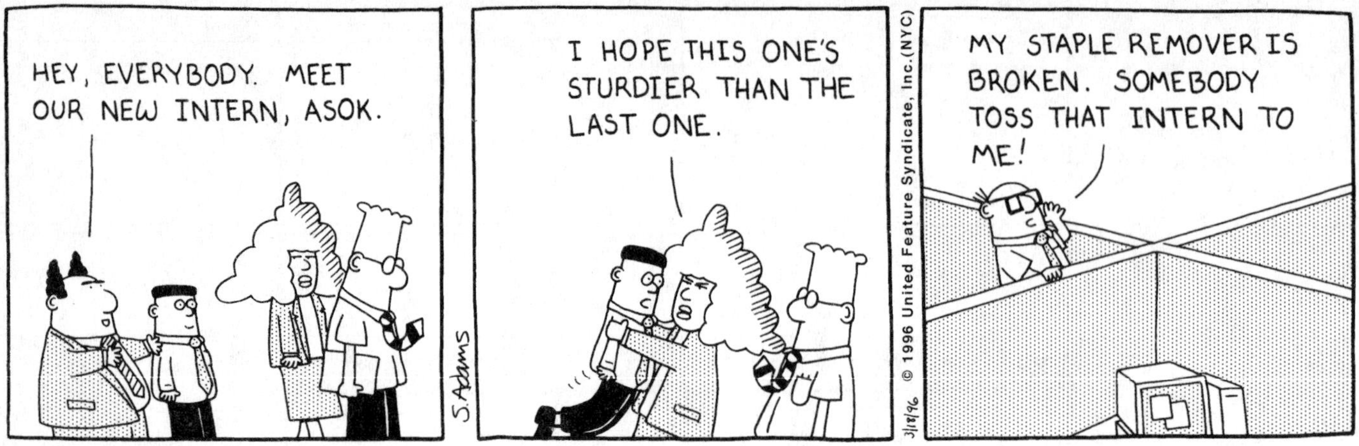
HEY, EVERYBODY. MEET OUR NEW INTERN, ASOK.
S. Adams
I HOPE THIS ONE'S STURDIER THAN THE LAST ONE.
3/18/96 © 1996 United Feature Syndicate, Inc.(NYC)
MY STAPLE REMOVER IS BROKEN. SOMEBODY TOSS THAT INTERN TO ME!

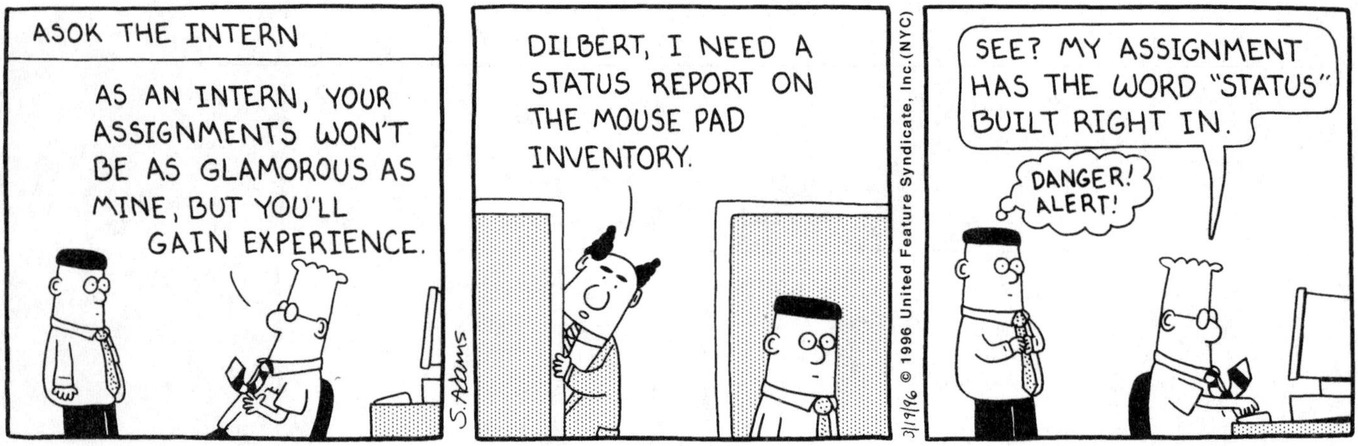
ASOK THE INTERN
AS AN INTERN, YOUR ASSIGNMENTS WON'T BE AS GLAMOROUS AS MINE, BUT YOU'LL GAIN EXPERIENCE.
S. Adams
DILBERT, I NEED A STATUS REPORT ON THE MOUSE PAD INVENTORY.
3/19/96 © 1996 United Feature Syndicate, Inc.(NYC)
SEE? MY ASSIGNMENT HAS THE WORD "STATUS" BUILT RIGHT IN.
DANGER! ALERT!

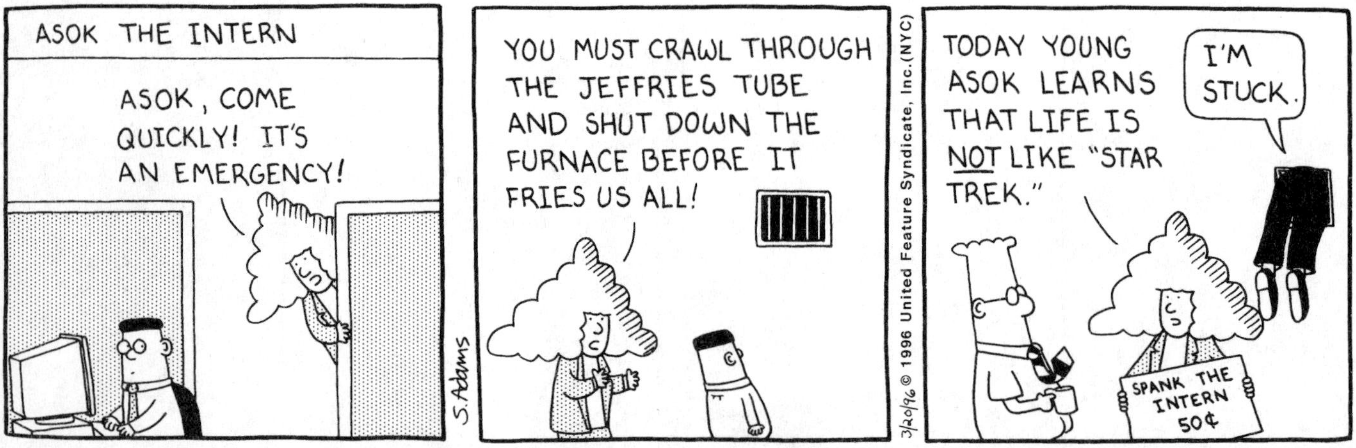
ASOK THE INTERN
ASOK, COME QUICKLY! IT'S AN EMERGENCY!
S. Adams
YOU MUST CRAWL THROUGH THE JEFFRIES TUBE AND SHUT DOWN THE FURNACE BEFORE IT FRIES US ALL!
3/20/96 © 1996 United Feature Syndicate, Inc.(NYC)
TODAY YOUNG ASOK LEARNS THAT LIFE IS NOT LIKE "STAR TREK."
I'M STUCK.
SPANK THE INTERN 50¢

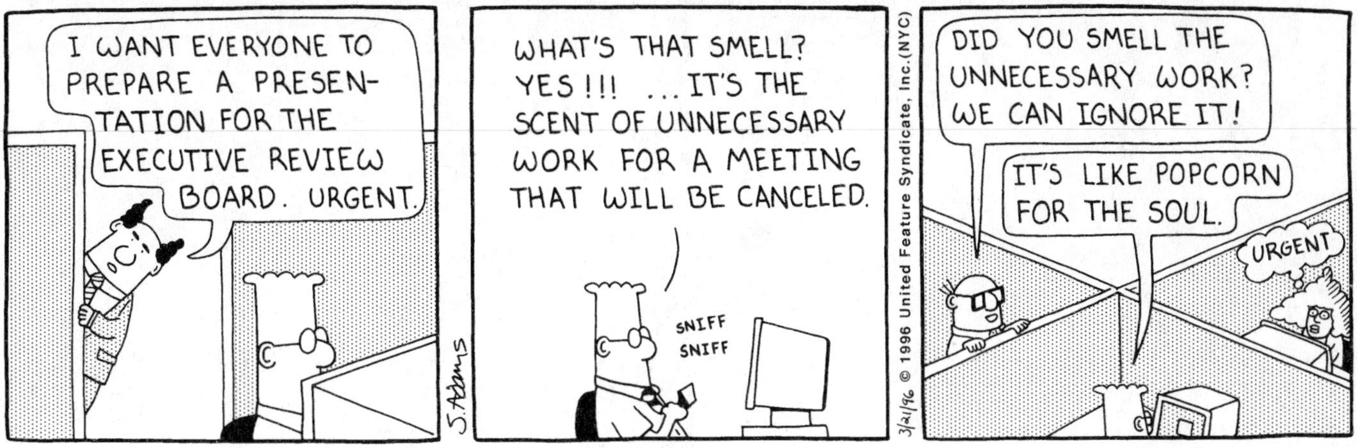
I WANT EVERYONE TO PREPARE A PRESENTATION FOR THE EXECUTIVE REVIEW BOARD. URGENT.
WHAT'S THAT SMELL? YES!!! ...IT'S THE SCENT OF UNNECESSARY WORK FOR A MEETING THAT WILL BE CANCELED.
SNIFF SNIFF
DID YOU SMELL THE UNNECESSARY WORK? WE CAN IGNORE IT!
IT'S LIKE POPCORN FOR THE SOUL.
URGENT
S. Adams
3/21/96 © 1996 United Feature Syndicate, Inc.(NYC)

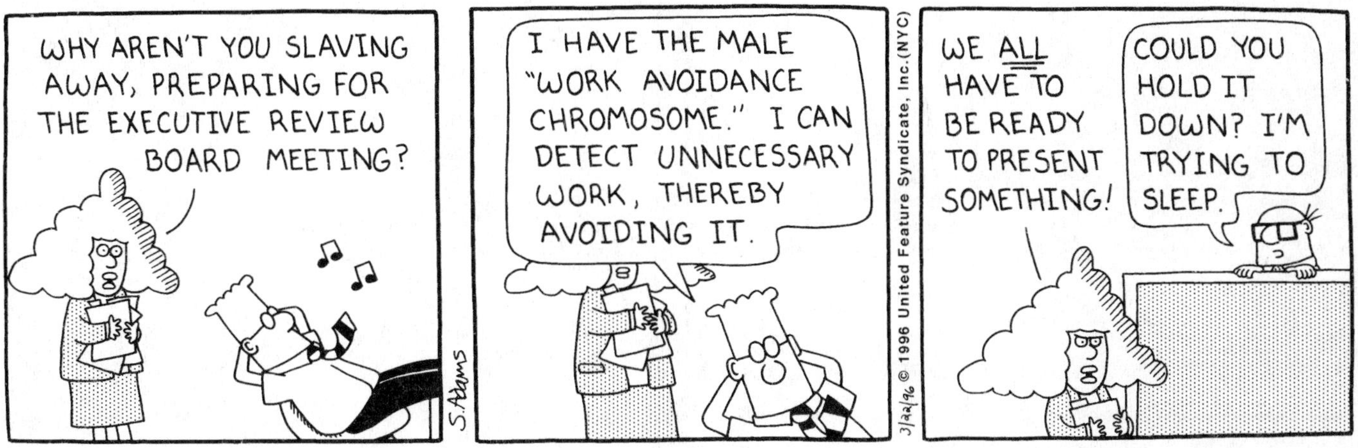
WHY AREN'T YOU SLAVING AWAY, PREPARING FOR THE EXECUTIVE REVIEW BOARD MEETING?
I HAVE THE MALE "WORK AVOIDANCE CHROMOSOME." I CAN DETECT UNNECESSARY WORK, THEREBY AVOIDING IT.
WE ALL HAVE TO BE READY TO PRESENT SOMETHING!
COULD YOU HOLD IT DOWN? I'M TRYING TO SLEEP.
S. Adams
3/22/96 © 1996 United Feature Syndicate, Inc.(NYC)

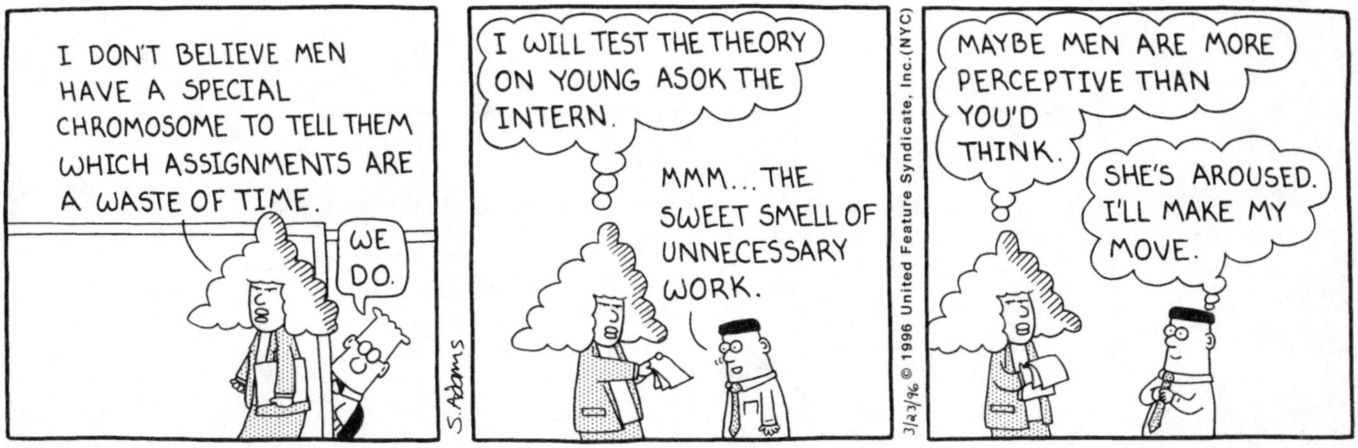
I DON'T BELIEVE MEN HAVE A SPECIAL CHROMOSOME TO TELL THEM WHICH ASSIGNMENTS ARE A WASTE OF TIME.
WE DO.
I WILL TEST THE THEORY ON YOUNG ASOK THE INTERN.
MMM... THE SWEET SMELL OF UNNECESSARY WORK.
MAYBE MEN ARE MORE PERCEPTIVE THAN YOU'D THINK.
SHE'S AROUSED. I'LL MAKE MY MOVE.
S. Adams
3/23/96 © 1996 United Feature Syndicate, Inc.(NYC)

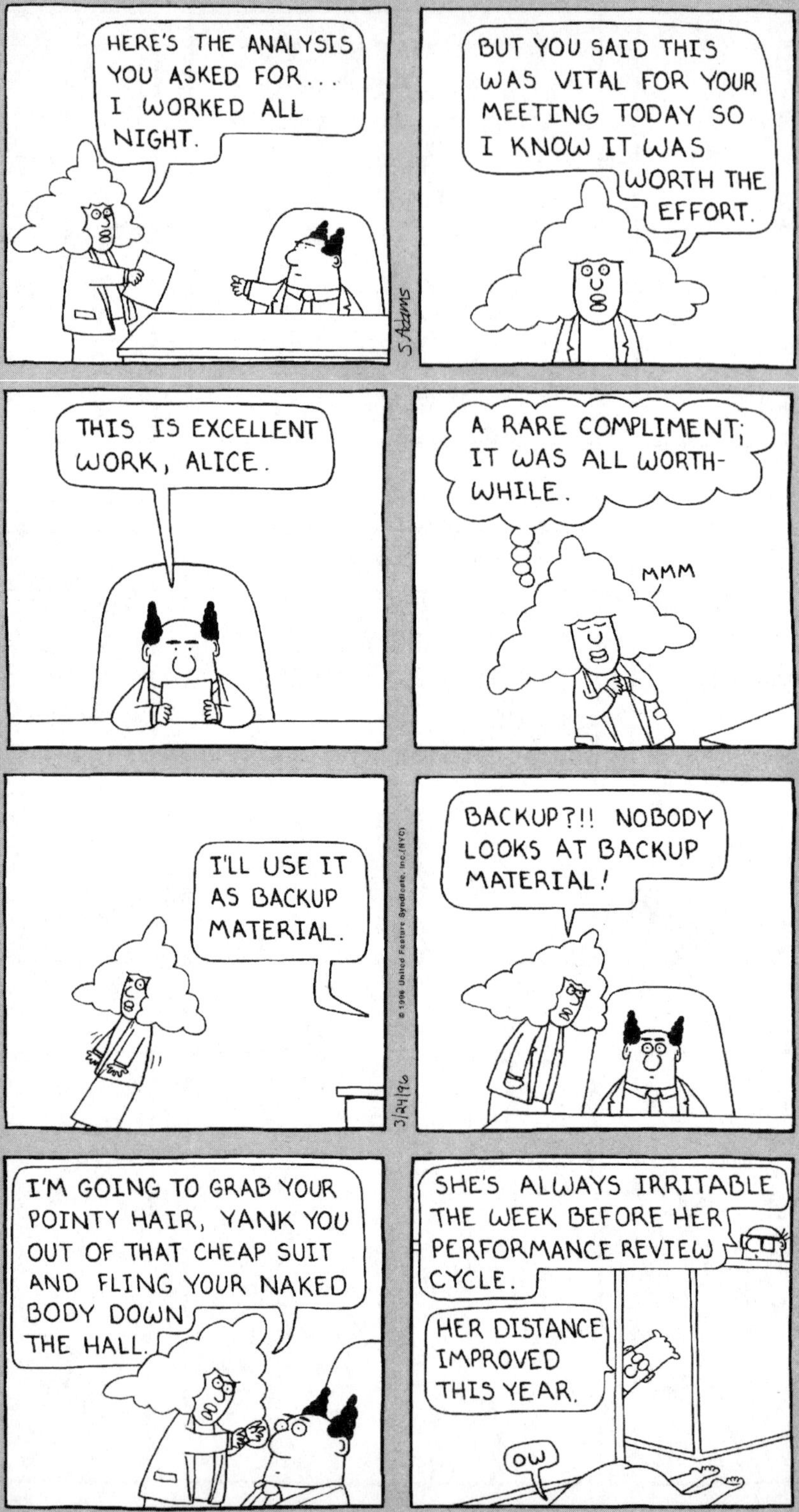
HERE'S THE ANALYSIS YOU ASKED FOR... I WORKED ALL NIGHT.
BUT YOU SAID THIS WAS VITAL FOR YOUR MEETING TODAY SO I KNOW IT WAS WORTH THE EFFORT.
S Adams
THIS IS EXCELLENT WORK, ALICE.
A RARE COMPLIMENT; IT WAS ALL WORTH-WHILE.
MMM
I'LL USE IT AS BACKUP MATERIAL.
© 1996 United Feature Syndicate, Inc.(NYC)
3/24/96
BACKUP?!! NOBODY LOOKS AT BACKUP MATERIAL!
I'M GOING TO GRAB YOUR POINTY HAIR, YANK YOU OUT OF THAT CHEAP SUIT AND FLING YOUR NAKED BODY DOWN THE HALL.
SHE'S ALWAYS IRRITABLE THE WEEK BEFORE HER PERFORMANCE REVIEW CYCLE.
HER DISTANCE IMPROVED THIS YEAR.
OW

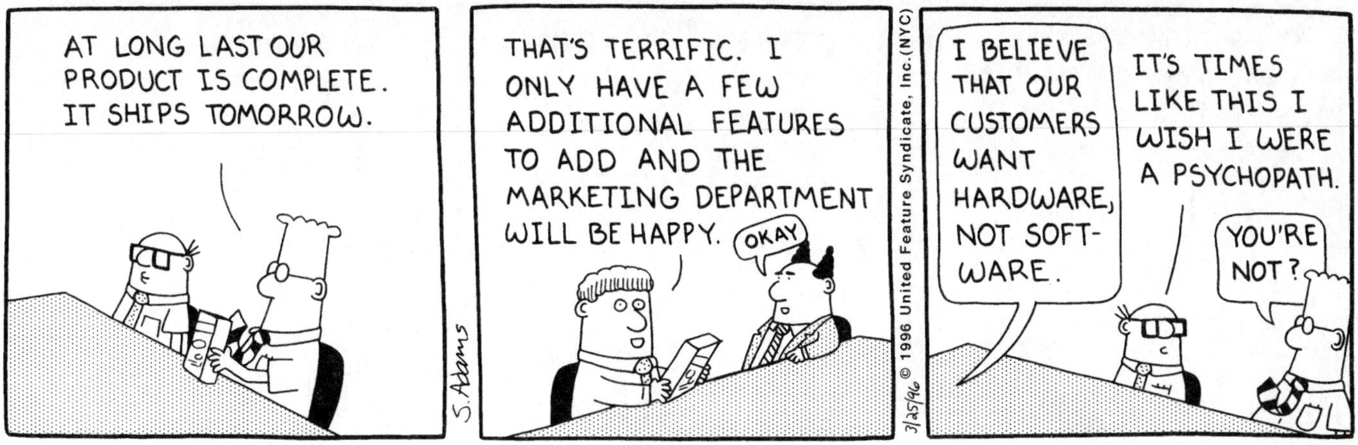
AT LONG LAST OUR PRODUCT IS COMPLETE. IT SHIPS TOMORROW.
S. Adams
THAT'S TERRIFIC. I ONLY HAVE A FEW ADDITIONAL FEATURES TO ADD AND THE MARKETING DEPARTMENT WILL BE HAPPY.
OKAY
3/25/96 © 1996 United Feature Syndicate, Inc.(NYC)
I BELIEVE THAT OUR CUSTOMERS WANT HARDWARE, NOT SOFTWARE.
IT'S TIMES LIKE THIS I WISH I WERE A PSYCHOPATH.
YOU'RE NOT?

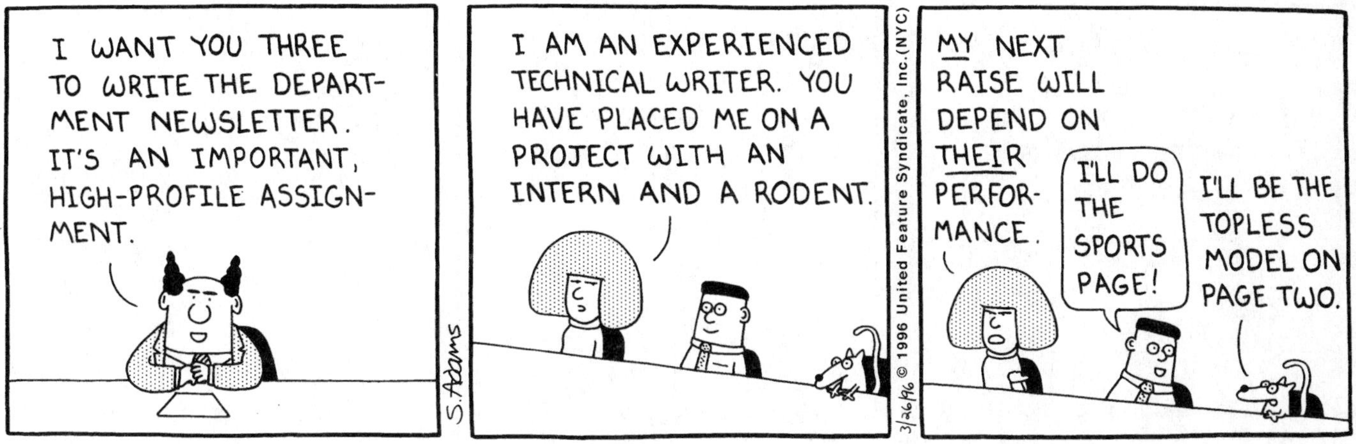
I WANT YOU THREE TO WRITE THE DEPARTMENT NEWSLETTER. IT'S AN IMPORTANT, HIGH-PROFILE ASSIGNMENT.
S. Adams
I AM AN EXPERIENCED TECHNICAL WRITER. YOU HAVE PLACED ME ON A PROJECT WITH AN INTERN AND A RODENT.
3/26/96 © 1996 United Feature Syndicate, Inc.(NYC)
MY NEXT RAISE WILL DEPEND ON THEIR PERFORMANCE.
I'LL DO THE SPORTS PAGE!
I'LL BE THE TOPLESS MODEL ON PAGE TWO.

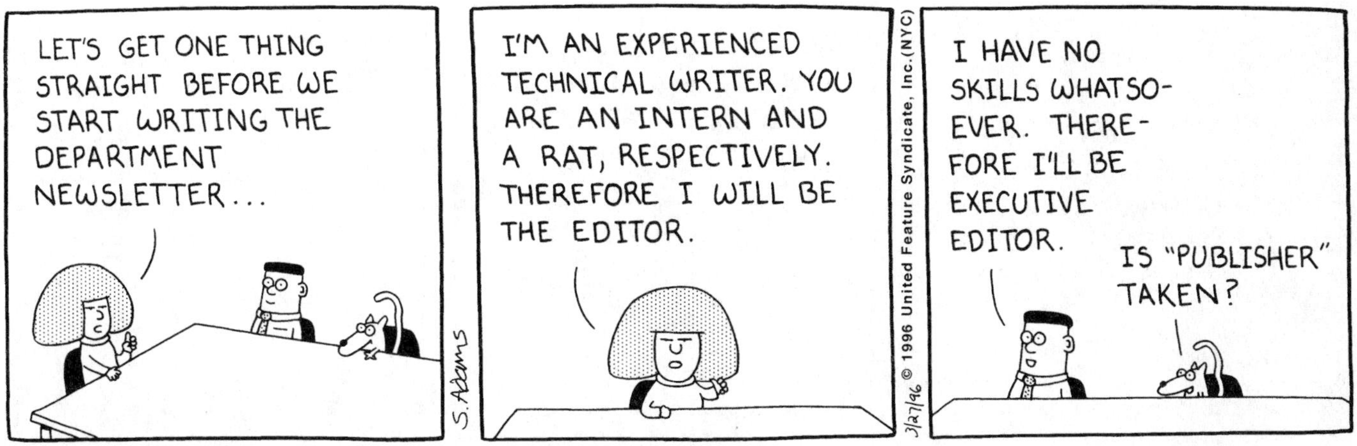
LET'S GET ONE THING STRAIGHT BEFORE WE START WRITING THE DEPARTMENT NEWSLETTER...
S. Adams
I'M AN EXPERIENCED TECHNICAL WRITER. YOU ARE AN INTERN AND A RAT, RESPECTIVELY. THEREFORE I WILL BE THE EDITOR.
3/27/96 © 1996 United Feature Syndicate, Inc.(NYC)
I HAVE NO SKILLS WHATSOEVER. THEREFORE I'LL BE EXECUTIVE EDITOR.
IS "PUBLISHER" TAKEN?

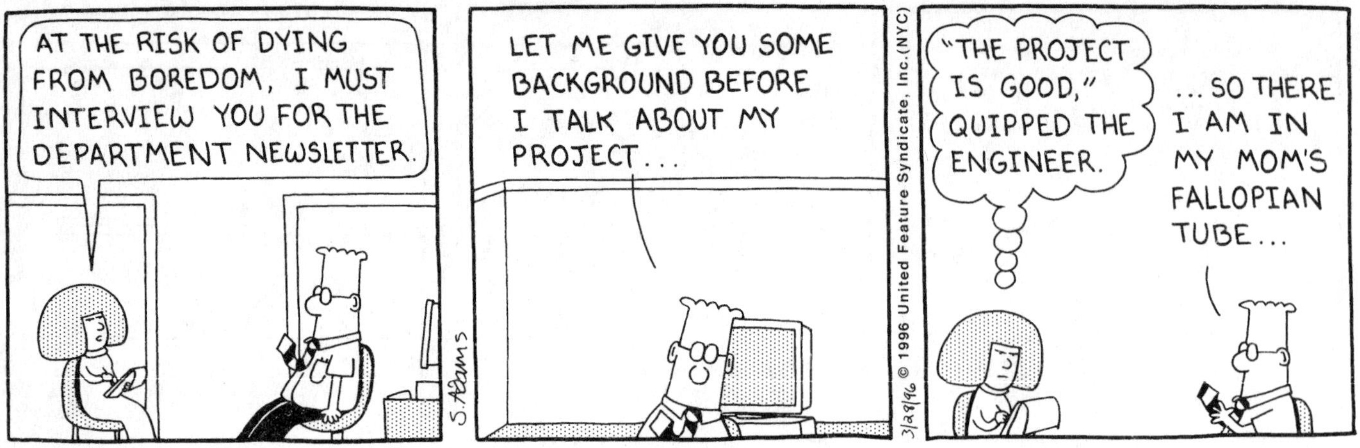
AT THE RISK OF DYING FROM BOREDOM, I MUST INTERVIEW YOU FOR THE DEPARTMENT NEWSLETTER.
S. Adams
LET ME GIVE YOU SOME BACKGROUND BEFORE I TALK ABOUT MY PROJECT...
3/28/96 © 1996 United Feature Syndicate, Inc.(NYC)
"THE PROJECT IS GOOD," QUIPPED THE ENGINEER.
...SO THERE I AM IN MY MOM'S FALLOPIAN TUBE...

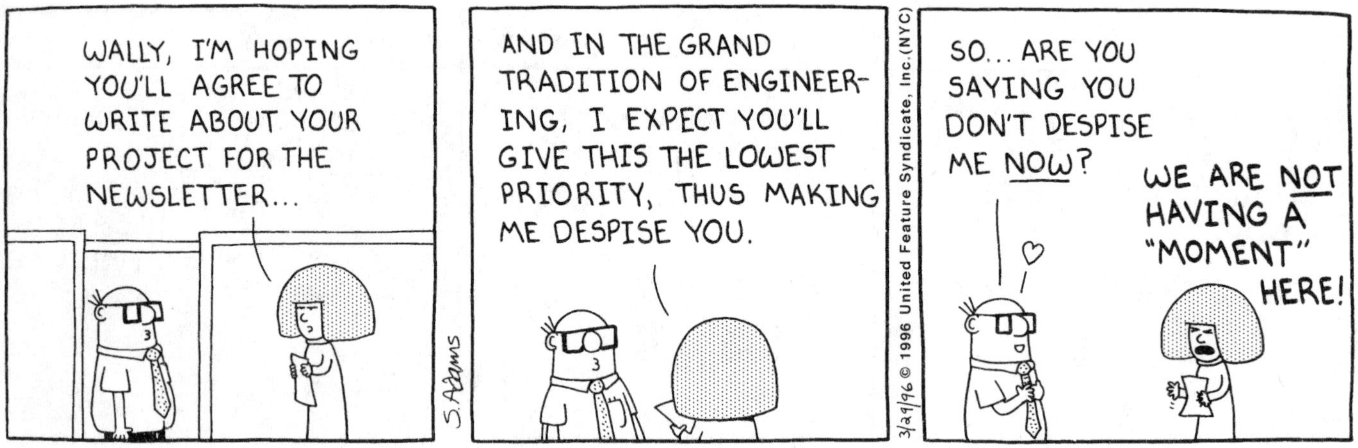
WALLY, I'M HOPING YOU'LL AGREE TO WRITE ABOUT YOUR PROJECT FOR THE NEWSLETTER...
S. Adams
AND IN THE GRAND TRADITION OF ENGINEERING, I EXPECT YOU'LL GIVE THIS THE LOWEST PRIORITY, THUS MAKING ME DESPISE YOU.
3/29/96 © 1996 United Feature Syndicate, Inc.(NYC)
SO... ARE YOU SAYING YOU DON'T DESPISE ME NOW?
WE ARE NOT HAVING A "MOMENT" HERE!

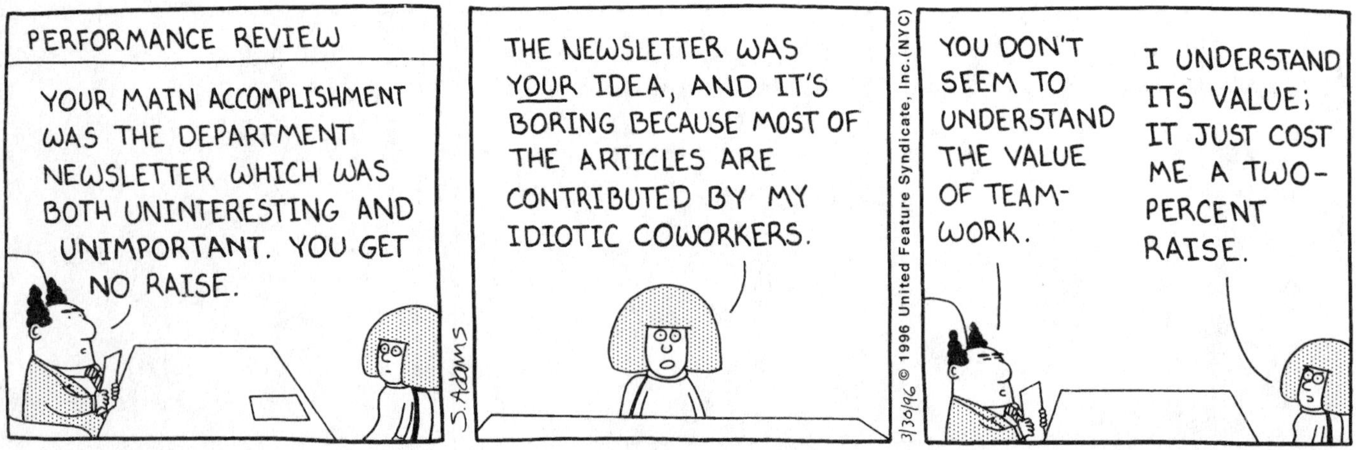
PERFORMANCE REVIEW
YOUR MAIN ACCOMPLISHMENT WAS THE DEPARTMENT NEWSLETTER WHICH WAS BOTH UNINTERESTING AND UNIMPORTANT. YOU GET NO RAISE.
S. Adams
THE NEWSLETTER WAS YOUR IDEA, AND IT'S BORING BECAUSE MOST OF THE ARTICLES ARE CONTRIBUTED BY MY IDIOTIC COWORKERS.
3/30/96 © 1996 United Feature Syndicate, Inc.(NYC)
YOU DON'T SEEM TO UNDERSTAND THE VALUE OF TEAMWORK.
I UNDERSTAND ITS VALUE; IT JUST COST ME A TWO-PERCENT RAISE.

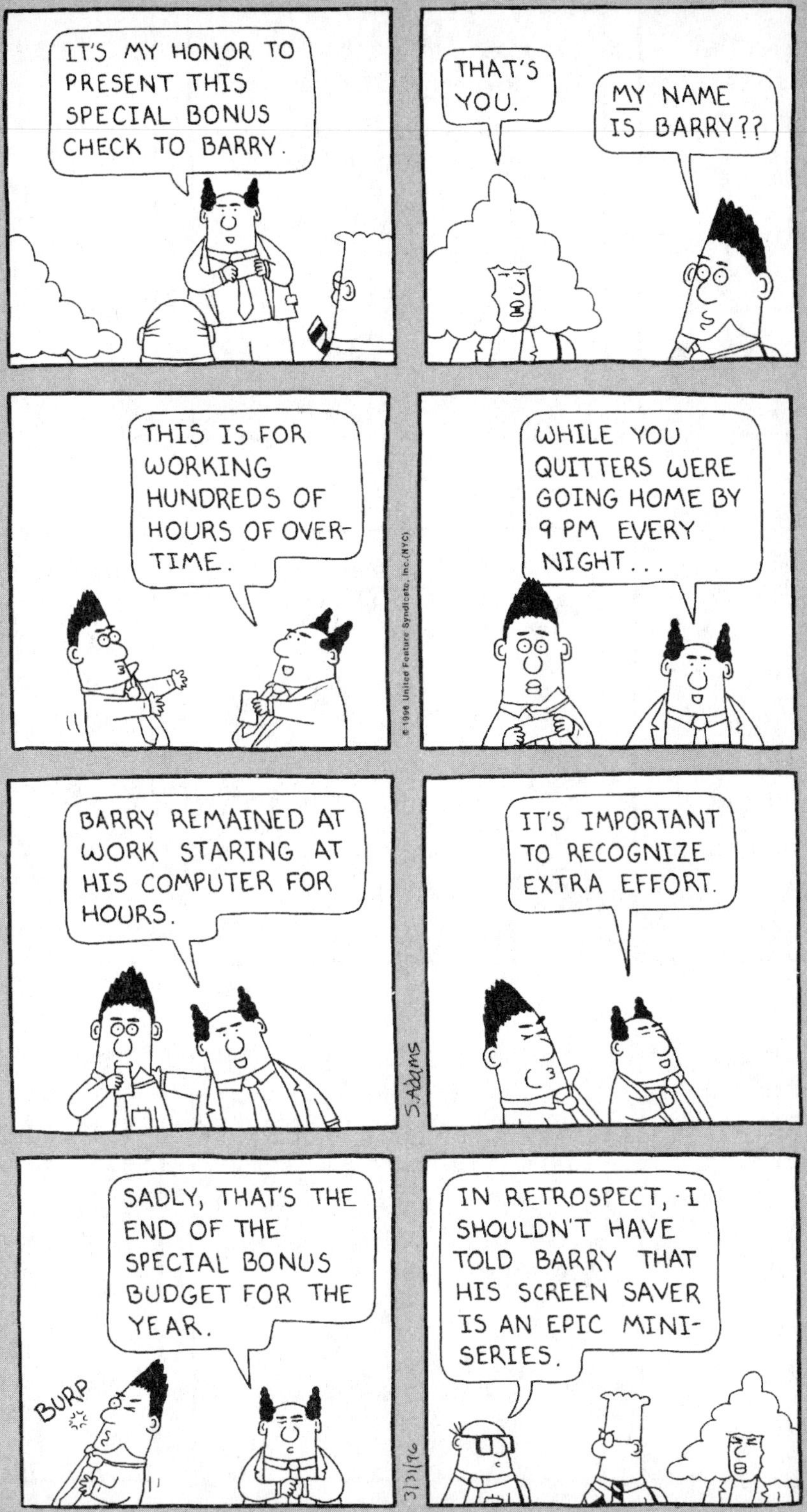
IT'S MY HONOR TO PRESENT THIS SPECIAL BONUS CHECK TO BARRY.
THAT'S YOU.
MY NAME IS BARRY??
THIS IS FOR WORKING HUNDREDS OF HOURS OF OVER-TIME.
WHILE YOU QUITTERS WERE GOING HOME BY 9 PM EVERY NIGHT...
BARRY REMAINED AT WORK STARING AT HIS COMPUTER FOR HOURS.
IT'S IMPORTANT TO RECOGNIZE EXTRA EFFORT.
SADLY, THAT'S THE END OF THE SPECIAL BONUS BUDGET FOR THE YEAR.
BURP
IN RETROSPECT, I SHOULDN'T HAVE TOLD BARRY THAT HIS SCREEN SAVER IS AN EPIC MINI-SERIES.
© 1996 United Feature Syndicate, Inc.(NYC)
S.Adams
3/31/96

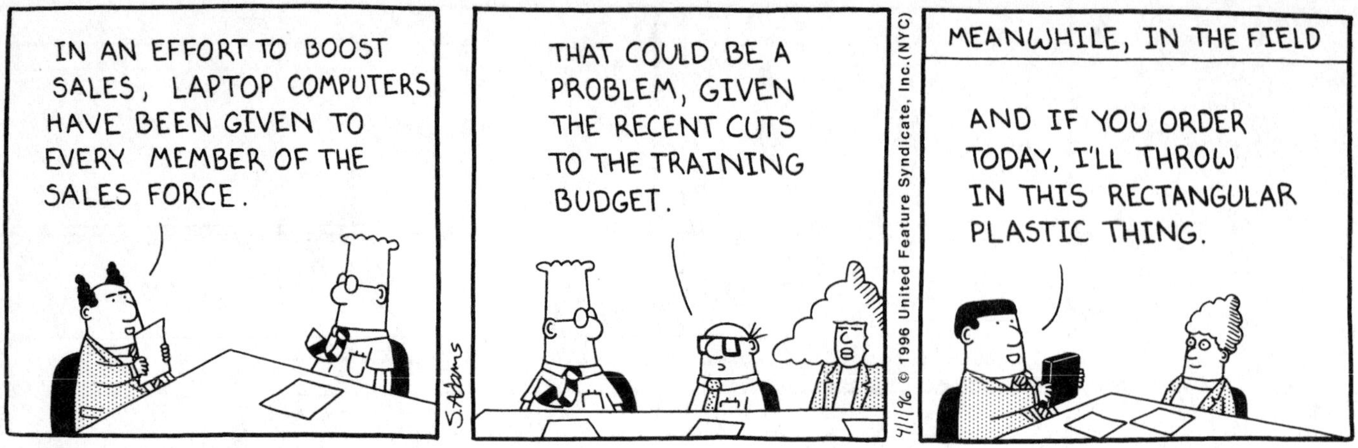
IN AN EFFORT TO BOOST SALES, LAPTOP COMPUTERS HAVE BEEN GIVEN TO EVERY MEMBER OF THE SALES FORCE.
THAT COULD BE A PROBLEM, GIVEN THE RECENT CUTS TO THE TRAINING BUDGET.
MEANWHILE, IN THE FIELD
AND IF YOU ORDER TODAY, I'LL THROW IN THIS RECTANGULAR PLASTIC THING.
4/1/96 © 1996 United Feature Syndicate, Inc.(NYC)

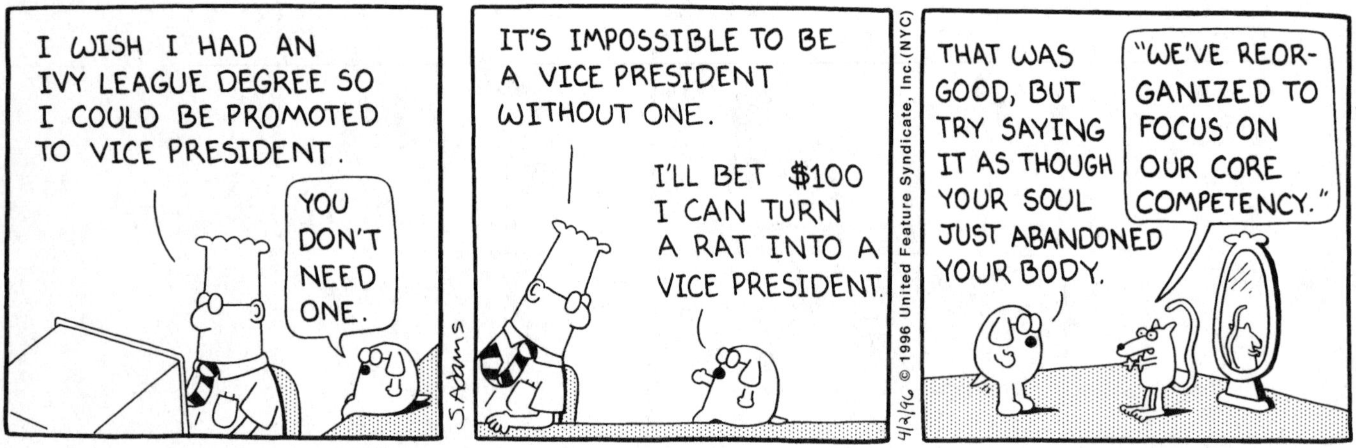
I WISH I HAD AN IVY LEAGUE DEGREE SO I COULD BE PROMOTED TO VICE PRESIDENT.
YOU DON'T NEED ONE.
IT'S IMPOSSIBLE TO BE A VICE PRESIDENT WITHOUT ONE.
I'LL BET $100 I CAN TURN A RAT INTO A VICE PRESIDENT.
THAT WAS GOOD, BUT TRY SAYING IT AS THOUGH YOUR SOUL JUST ABANDONED YOUR BODY.
"WE'VE REORGANIZED TO FOCUS ON OUR CORE COMPETENCY."
4/2/96 © 1996 United Feature Syndicate, Inc.(NYC)

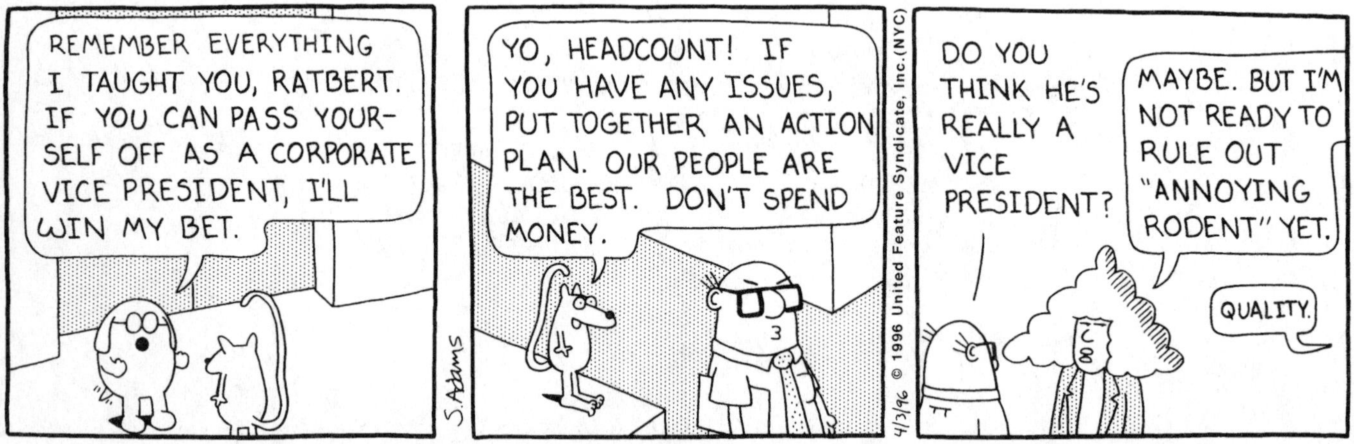
REMEMBER EVERYTHING I TAUGHT YOU, RATBERT. IF YOU CAN PASS YOURSELF OFF AS A CORPORATE VICE PRESIDENT, I'LL WIN MY BET.
YO, HEADCOUNT! IF YOU HAVE ANY ISSUES, PUT TOGETHER AN ACTION PLAN. OUR PEOPLE ARE THE BEST. DON'T SPEND MONEY.
DO YOU THINK HE'S REALLY A VICE PRESIDENT?
MAYBE. BUT I'M NOT READY TO RULE OUT "ANNOYING RODENT" YET.
QUALITY.
4/3/96 © 1996 United Feature Syndicate, Inc.(NYC)

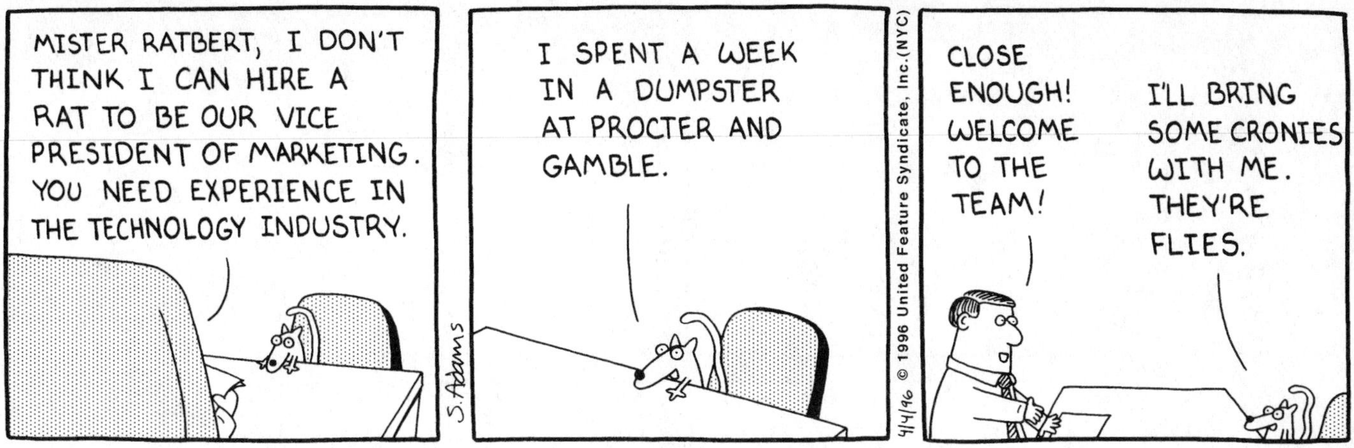
MISTER RATBERT, I DON'T THINK I CAN HIRE A RAT TO BE OUR VICE PRESIDENT OF MARKETING. YOU NEED EXPERIENCE IN THE TECHNOLOGY INDUSTRY.
I SPENT A WEEK IN A DUMPSTER AT PROCTER AND GAMBLE.
CLOSE ENOUGH! WELCOME TO THE TEAM!
I'LL BRING SOME CRONIES WITH ME. THEY'RE FLIES.
S. Adams
4/4/96 © 1996 United Feature Syndicate, Inc.(NYC)

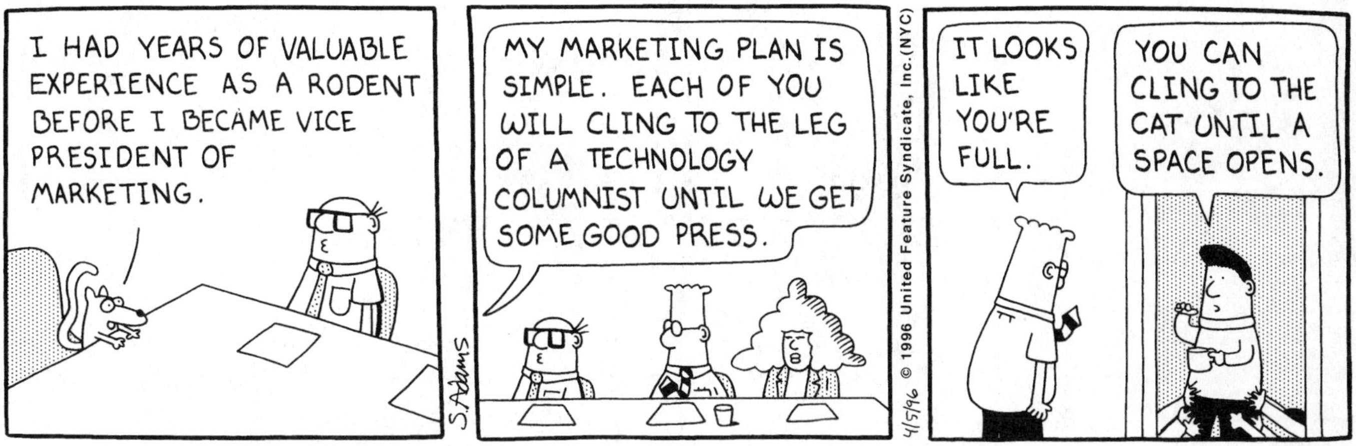
I HAD YEARS OF VALUABLE EXPERIENCE AS A RODENT BEFORE I BECAME VICE PRESIDENT OF MARKETING.
MY MARKETING PLAN IS SIMPLE. EACH OF YOU WILL CLING TO THE LEG OF A TECHNOLOGY COLUMNIST UNTIL WE GET SOME GOOD PRESS.
IT LOOKS LIKE YOU'RE FULL.
YOU CAN CLING TO THE CAT UNTIL A SPACE OPENS.
S. Adams
4/5/96 © 1996 United Feature Syndicate, Inc.(NYC)

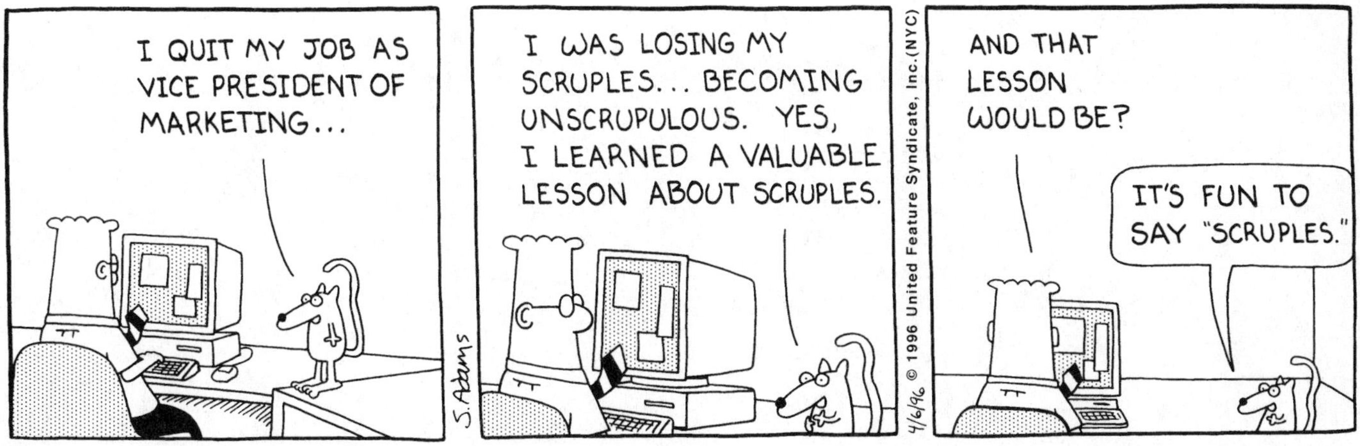
I QUIT MY JOB AS VICE PRESIDENT OF MARKETING...
I WAS LOSING MY SCRUPLES... BECOMING UNSCRUPULOUS. YES, I LEARNED A VALUABLE LESSON ABOUT SCRUPLES.
AND THAT LESSON WOULD BE?
IT'S FUN TO SAY "SCRUPLES."
S. Adams
4/6/96 © 1996 United Feature Syndicate, Inc.(NYC)

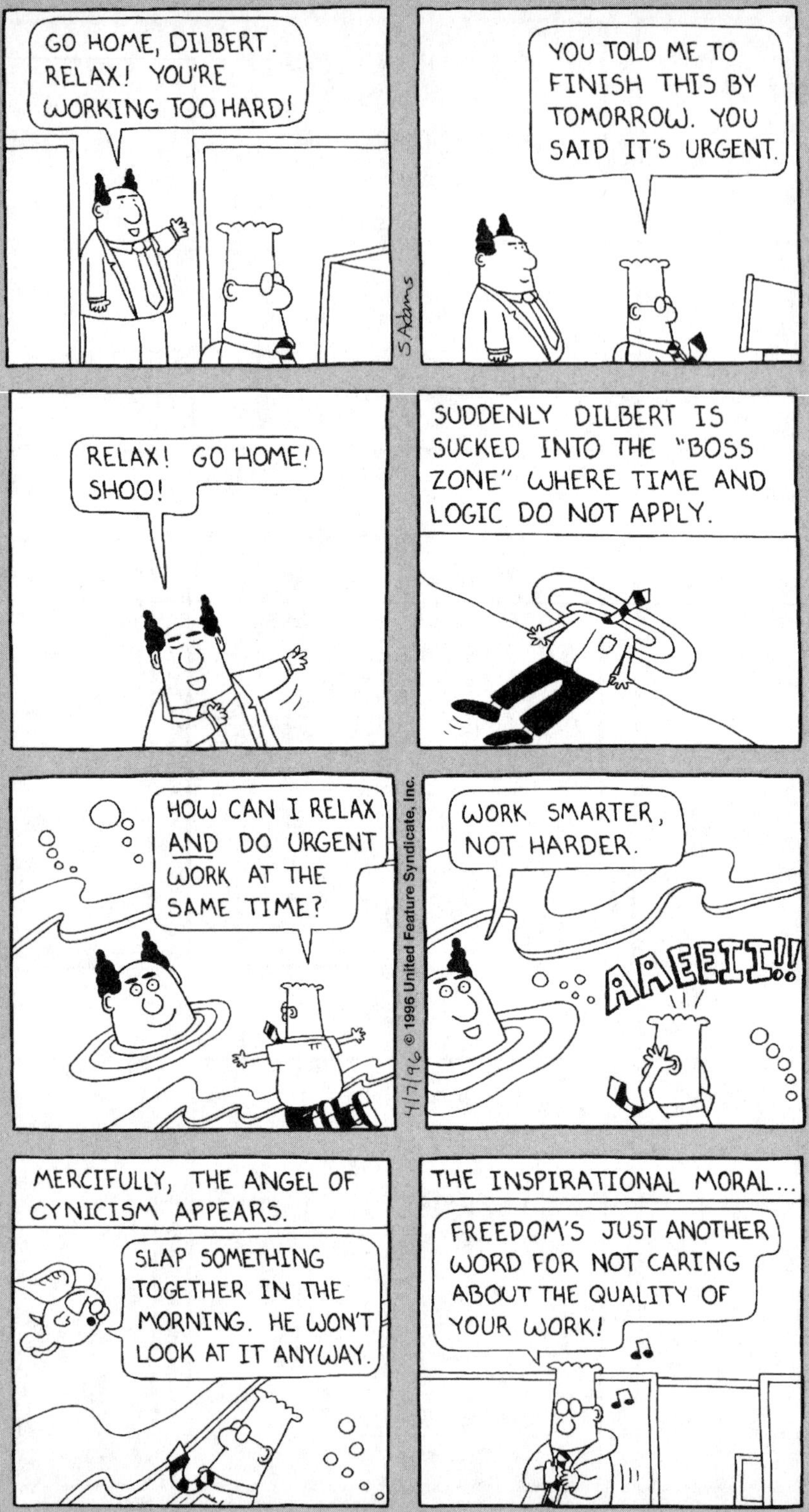
GO HOME, DILBERT. RELAX! YOU'RE WORKING TOO HARD!
S. Adams
YOU TOLD ME TO FINISH THIS BY TOMORROW. YOU SAID IT'S URGENT.
RELAX! GO HOME! SHOO!
SUDDENLY DILBERT IS SUCKED INTO THE "BOSS ZONE" WHERE TIME AND LOGIC DO NOT APPLY.
HOW CAN I RELAX AND DO URGENT WORK AT THE SAME TIME?
4/7/96 © 1996 United Feature Syndicate, Inc.
WORK SMARTER, NOT HARDER.
AAEEIII!!
MERCIFULLY, THE ANGEL OF CYNICISM APPEARS.
SLAP SOMETHING TOGETHER IN THE MORNING. HE WON'T LOOK AT IT ANYWAY.
THE INSPIRATIONAL MORAL...
FREEDOM'S JUST ANOTHER WORD FOR NOT CARING ABOUT THE QUALITY OF YOUR WORK!

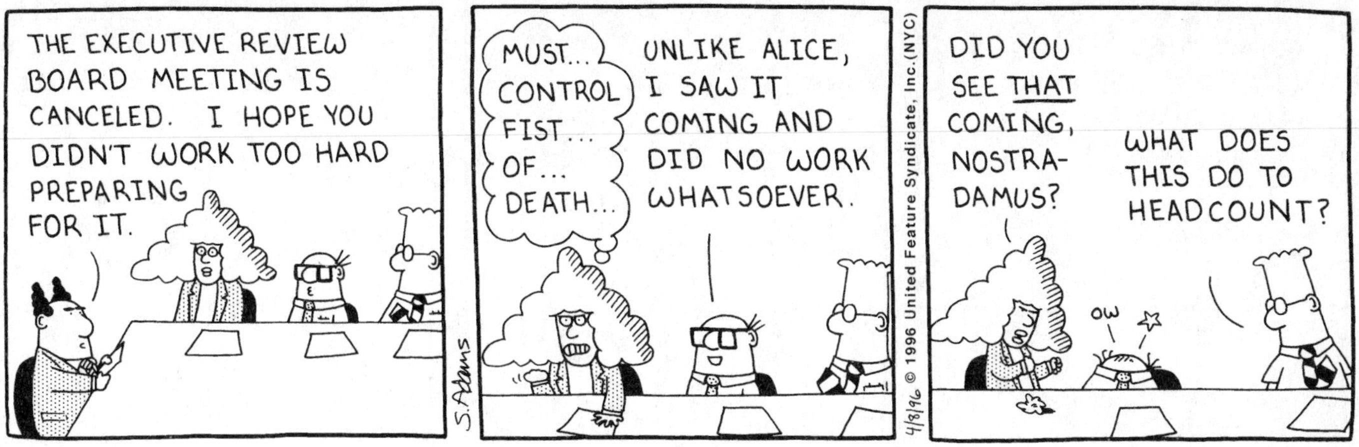
THE EXECUTIVE REVIEW BOARD MEETING IS CANCELED. I HOPE YOU DIDN'T WORK TOO HARD PREPARING FOR IT.
MUST... CONTROL FIST... OF... DEATH...
UNLIKE ALICE, I SAW IT COMING AND DID NO WORK WHATSOEVER.
DID YOU SEE THAT COMING, NOSTRA-DAMUS?
OW
WHAT DOES THIS DO TO HEADCOUNT?
S. Adams
4/8/96 © 1996 United Feature Syndicate, Inc.(NYC)

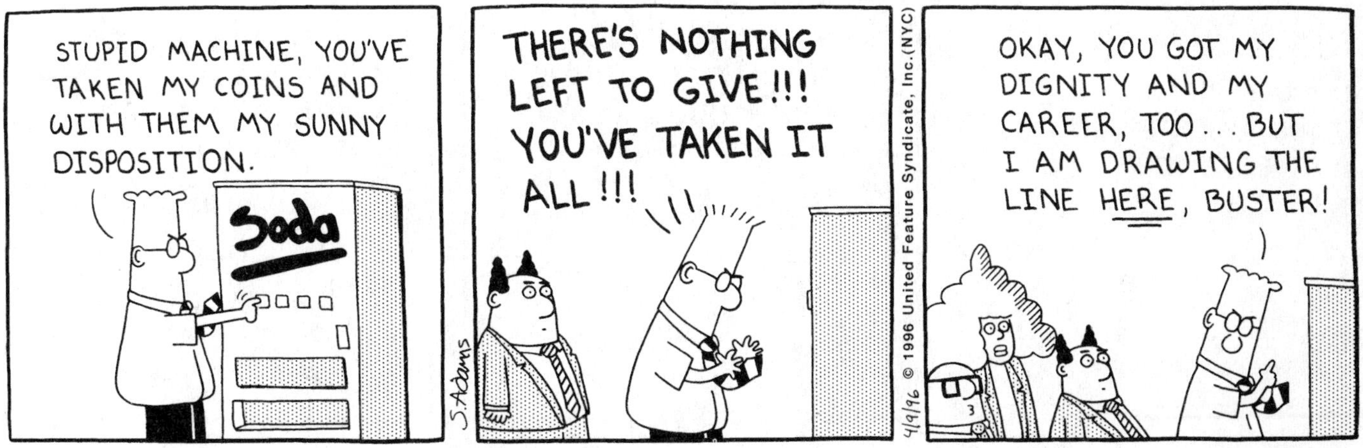
STUPID MACHINE, YOU'VE TAKEN MY COINS AND WITH THEM MY SUNNY DISPOSITION.
Soda
THERE'S NOTHING LEFT TO GIVE!!! YOU'VE TAKEN IT ALL!!!
OKAY, YOU GOT MY DIGNITY AND MY CAREER, TOO... BUT I AM DRAWING THE LINE HERE, BUSTER!
S. Adams
4/9/96 © 1996 United Feature Syndicate, Inc.(NYC)

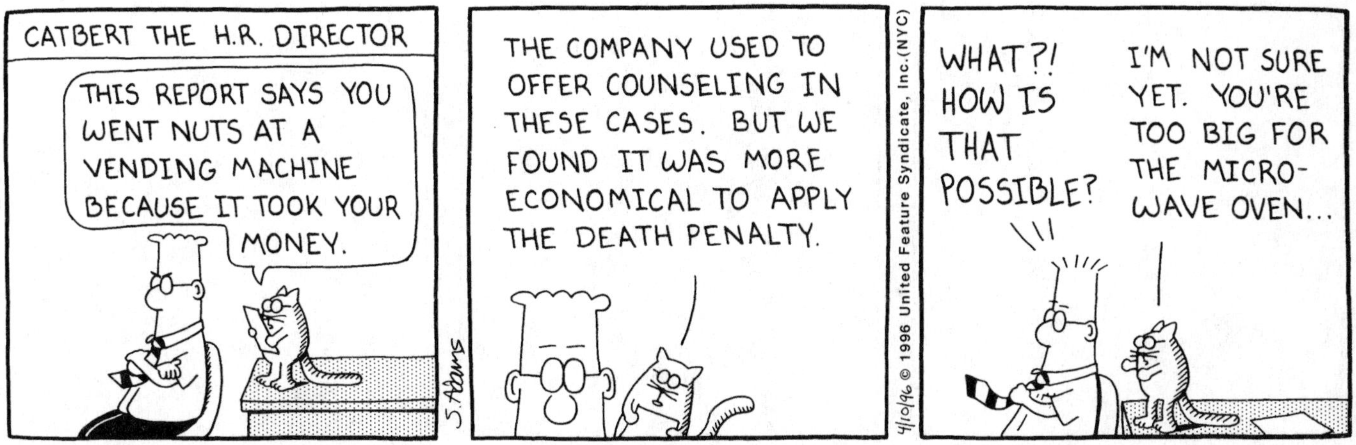
CATBERT THE H.R. DIRECTOR
THIS REPORT SAYS YOU WENT NUTS AT A VENDING MACHINE BECAUSE IT TOOK YOUR MONEY.
THE COMPANY USED TO OFFER COUNSELING IN THESE CASES. BUT WE FOUND IT WAS MORE ECONOMICAL TO APPLY THE DEATH PENALTY.
WHAT?! HOW IS THAT POSSIBLE?
I'M NOT SURE YET. YOU'RE TOO BIG FOR THE MICRO-WAVE OVEN...
S. Adams
4/10/96 © 1996 United Feature Syndicate, Inc.(NYC)

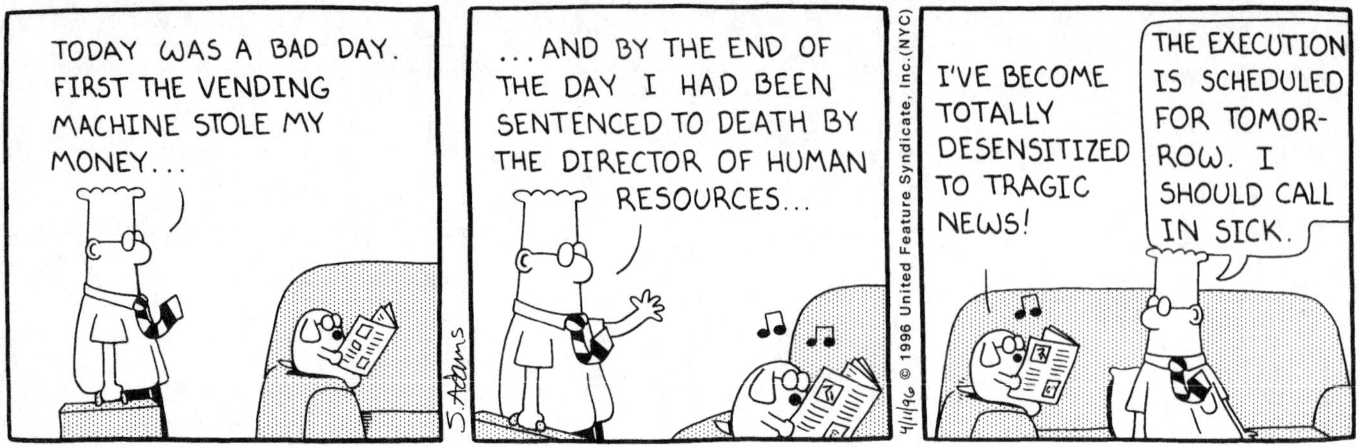
TODAY WAS A BAD DAY. FIRST THE VENDING MACHINE STOLE MY MONEY...
...AND BY THE END OF THE DAY I HAD BEEN SENTENCED TO DEATH BY THE DIRECTOR OF HUMAN RESOURCES...
I'VE BECOME TOTALLY DESENSITIZED TO TRAGIC NEWS!
THE EXECUTION IS SCHEDULED FOR TOMORROW. I SHOULD CALL IN SICK.
S. Adams
4/1/96 © 1996 United Feature Syndicate, Inc.(NYC)

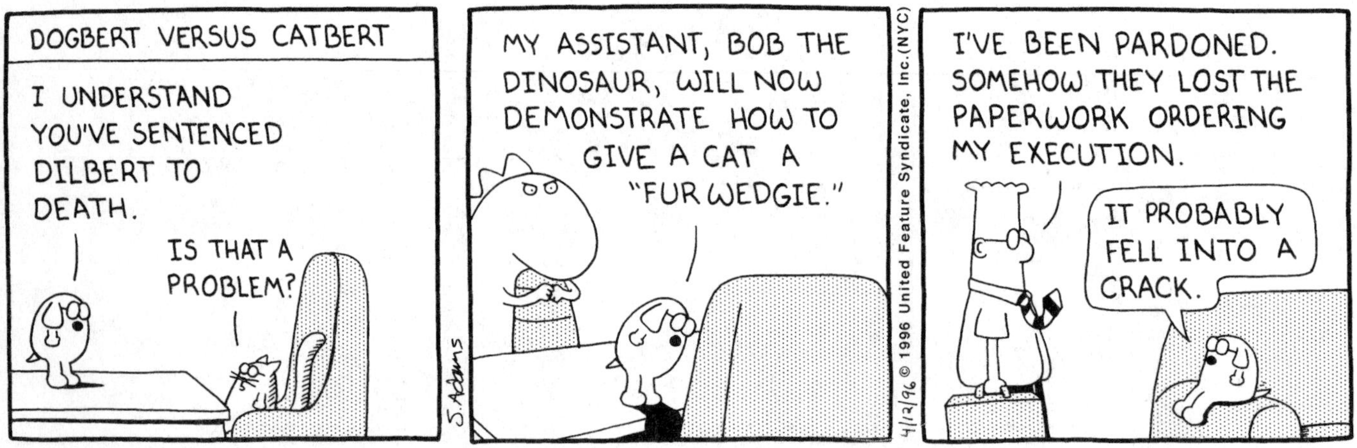
DOGBERT VERSUS CATBERT
I UNDERSTAND YOU'VE SENTENCED DILBERT TO DEATH.
IS THAT A PROBLEM?
MY ASSISTANT, BOB THE DINOSAUR, WILL NOW DEMONSTRATE HOW TO GIVE A CAT A "FUR WEDGIE."
I'VE BEEN PARDONED. SOMEHOW THEY LOST THE PAPERWORK ORDERING MY EXECUTION.
IT PROBABLY FELL INTO A CRACK.
S. Adams
4/12/96 © 1996 United Feature Syndicate, Inc.(NYC)

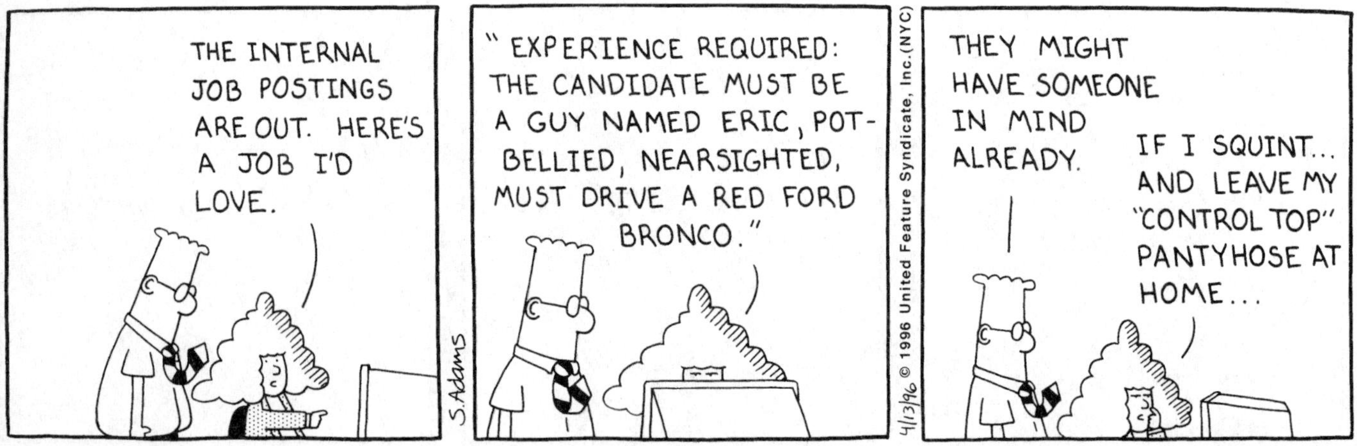
THE INTERNAL JOB POSTINGS ARE OUT. HERE'S A JOB I'D LOVE.
"EXPERIENCE REQUIRED: THE CANDIDATE MUST BE A GUY NAMED ERIC, POT-BELLIED, NEARSIGHTED, MUST DRIVE A RED FORD BRONCO."
THEY MIGHT HAVE SOMEONE IN MIND ALREADY.
IF I SQUINT... AND LEAVE MY "CONTROL TOP" PANTYHOSE AT HOME...
S. Adams
4/13/96 © 1996 United Feature Syndicate, Inc.(NYC)

DOGBERT WOULD LIKE TO SPEAK WITH YOU ABOUT THE CHANGES YOU MADE TO MY ENGINEERING PROPOSAL.
S. Adams
WHILE DILBERT WAS GETTING HIS MASTERS DEGREE IN ELECTRICAL ENGINEERING...
YOU WERE MAJORING IN ART HISTORY SO YOU COULD LOOK AT PICTURES OF NAKED STATUES.
DILBERT OFTEN CONTRIBUTES ARTICLES TO TECHNOLOGY PUBLICATIONS.
YOU, ON THE OTHER HAND, RUB THOSE SAME PUBLICATIONS WITH A NICKEL, LOOKING FOR HIDDEN "SCRATCH AND SNIFF" PANELS.
4/14/96 © 1996 United Feature Syndicate, Inc.
IN SUMMARY...
NEVER QUESTION AN ENGINEER'S OPINION, YOU THUNDERING MORON!
NICELY DONE, BUT I WOULDN'T HAVE SAID "THUNDERING."
WHAT WERE YOU DRINKING WHEN YOU WROTE THIS PIECE OF CRUD?!!

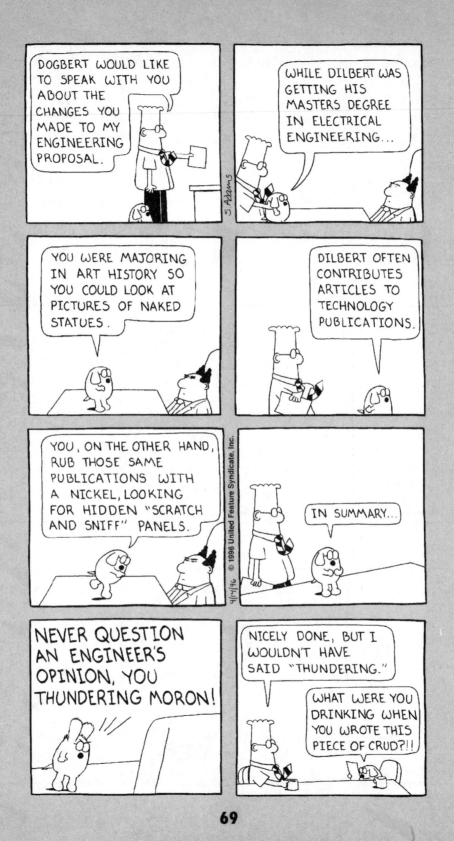

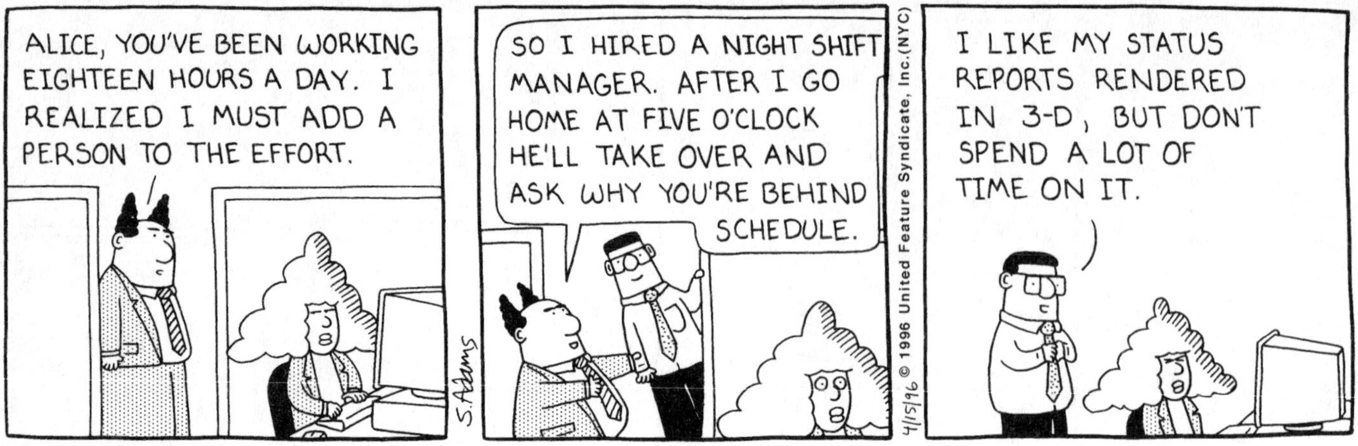
ALICE, YOU'VE BEEN WORKING EIGHTEEN HOURS A DAY. I REALIZED I MUST ADD A PERSON TO THE EFFORT.
SO I HIRED A NIGHT SHIFT MANAGER. AFTER I GO HOME AT FIVE O'CLOCK HE'LL TAKE OVER AND ASK WHY YOU'RE BEHIND SCHEDULE.
I LIKE MY STATUS REPORTS RENDERED IN 3-D, BUT DON'T SPEND A LOT OF TIME ON IT.
S. Adams
4/15/96 © 1996 United Feature Syndicate, Inc.(NYC)

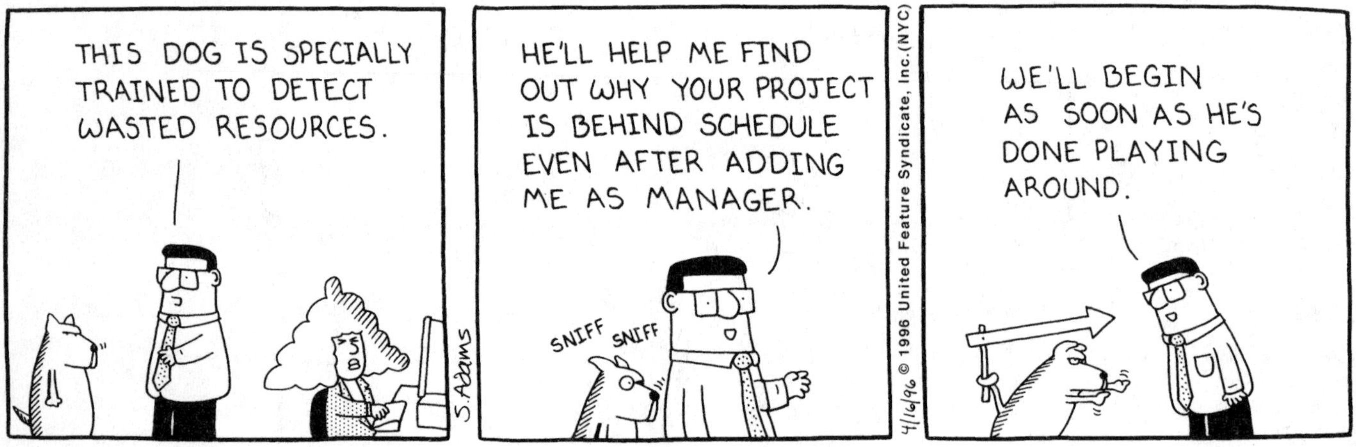
THIS DOG IS SPECIALLY TRAINED TO DETECT WASTED RESOURCES.
HE'LL HELP ME FIND OUT WHY YOUR PROJECT IS BEHIND SCHEDULE EVEN AFTER ADDING ME AS MANAGER.
SNIFF
SNIFF
WE'LL BEGIN AS SOON AS HE'S DONE PLAYING AROUND.
S. Adams
4/16/96 © 1996 United Feature Syndicate, Inc.(NYC)

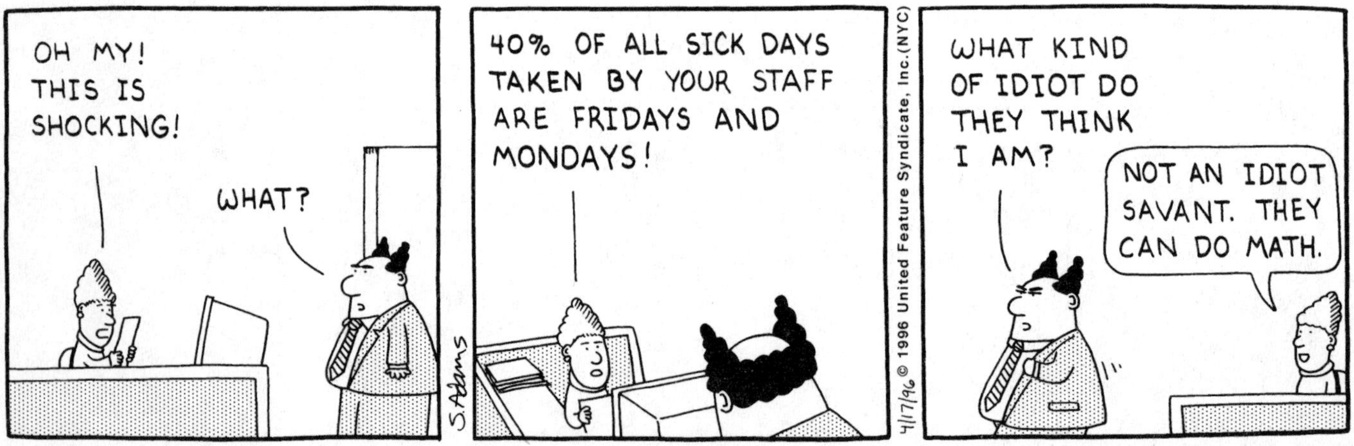
OH MY! THIS IS SHOCKING!
WHAT?
40% OF ALL SICK DAYS TAKEN BY YOUR STAFF ARE FRIDAYS AND MONDAYS!
WHAT KIND OF IDIOT DO THEY THINK I AM?
NOT AN IDIOT SAVANT. THEY CAN DO MATH.
S. Adams
4/17/96 © 1996 United Feature Syndicate, Inc.(NYC)

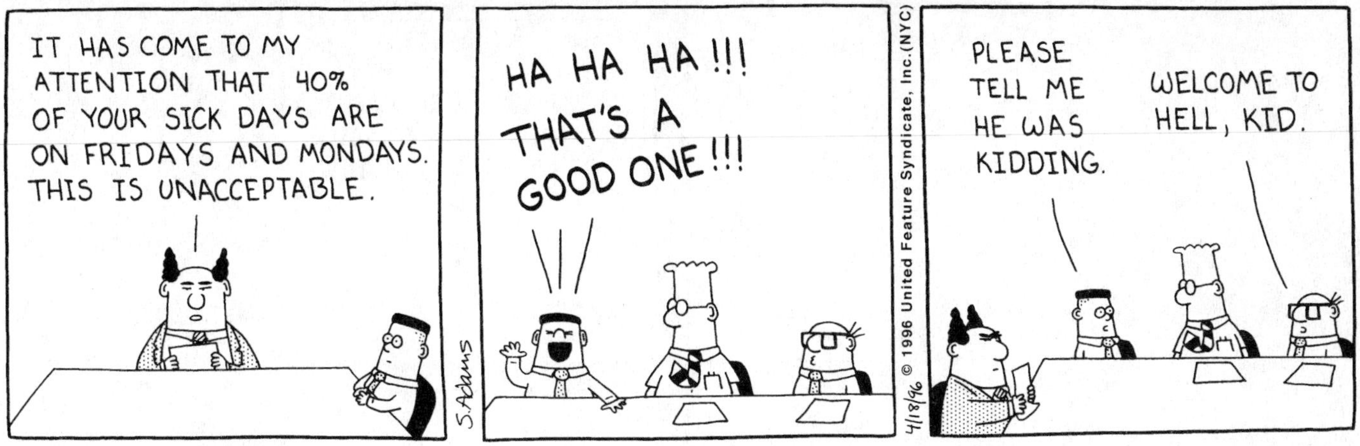
IT HAS COME TO MY ATTENTION THAT 40% OF YOUR SICK DAYS ARE ON FRIDAYS AND MONDAYS. THIS IS UNACCEPTABLE.
HA HA HA!!! THAT'S A GOOD ONE!!!
PLEASE TELL ME HE WAS KIDDING.
WELCOME TO HELL, KID.
S.Adams
4/18/96 © 1996 United Feature Syndicate, Inc.(NYC)

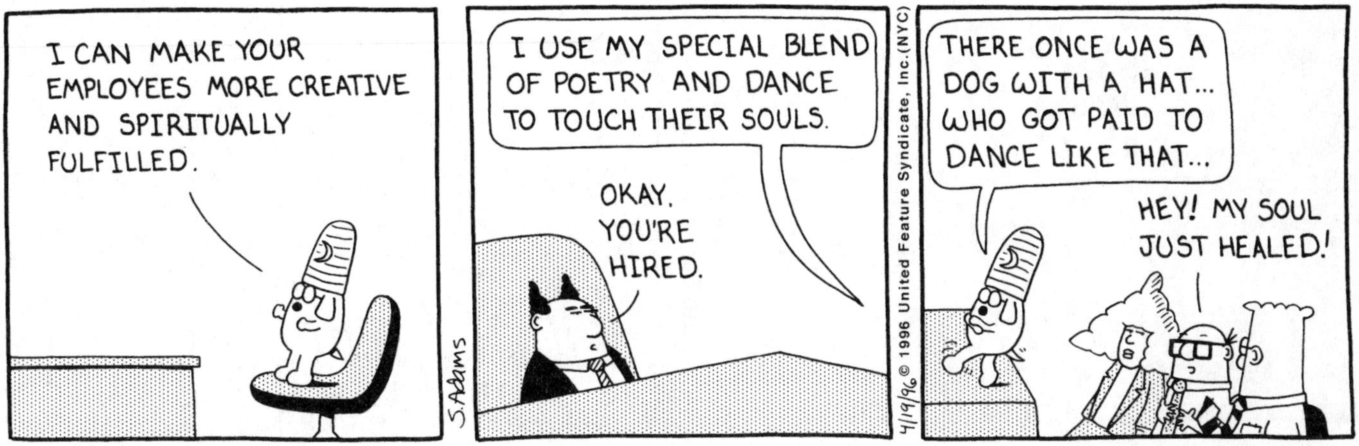
I CAN MAKE YOUR EMPLOYEES MORE CREATIVE AND SPIRITUALLY FULFILLED.
I USE MY SPECIAL BLEND OF POETRY AND DANCE TO TOUCH THEIR SOULS.
OKAY. YOU'RE HIRED.
THERE ONCE WAS A DOG WITH A HAT... WHO GOT PAID TO DANCE LIKE THAT...
HEY! MY SOUL JUST HEALED!
S.Adams
4/19/96 © 1996 United Feature Syndicate, Inc.(NYC)

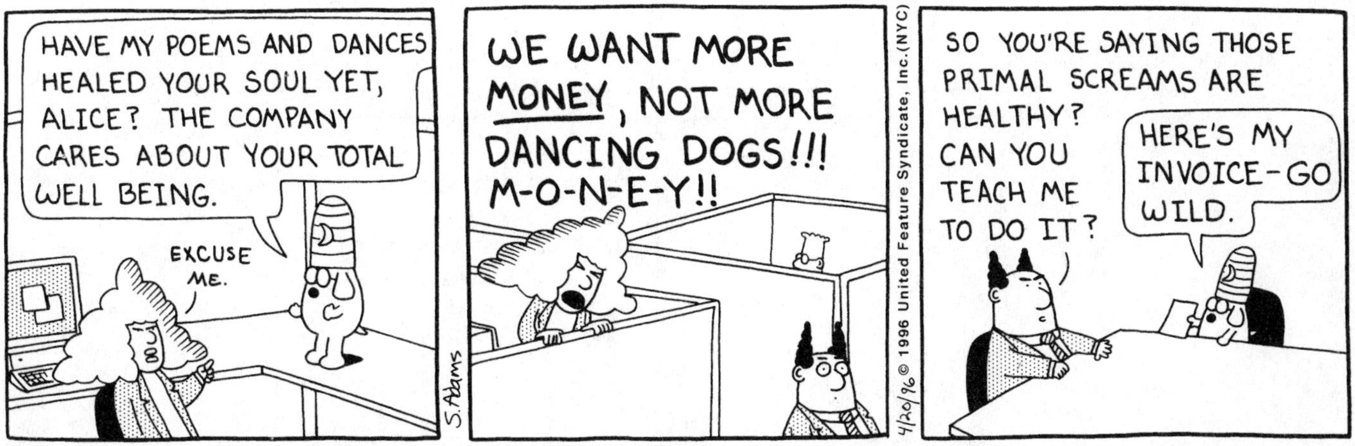
HAVE MY POEMS AND DANCES HEALED YOUR SOUL YET, ALICE? THE COMPANY CARES ABOUT YOUR TOTAL WELL BEING.
EXCUSE ME.
WE WANT MORE MONEY, NOT MORE DANCING DOGS!!! M-O-N-E-Y!!
SO YOU'RE SAYING THOSE PRIMAL SCREAMS ARE HEALTHY? CAN YOU TEACH ME TO DO IT?
HERE'S MY INVOICE-GO WILD.
S.Adams
4/20/96 © 1996 United Feature Syndicate, Inc.(NYC)

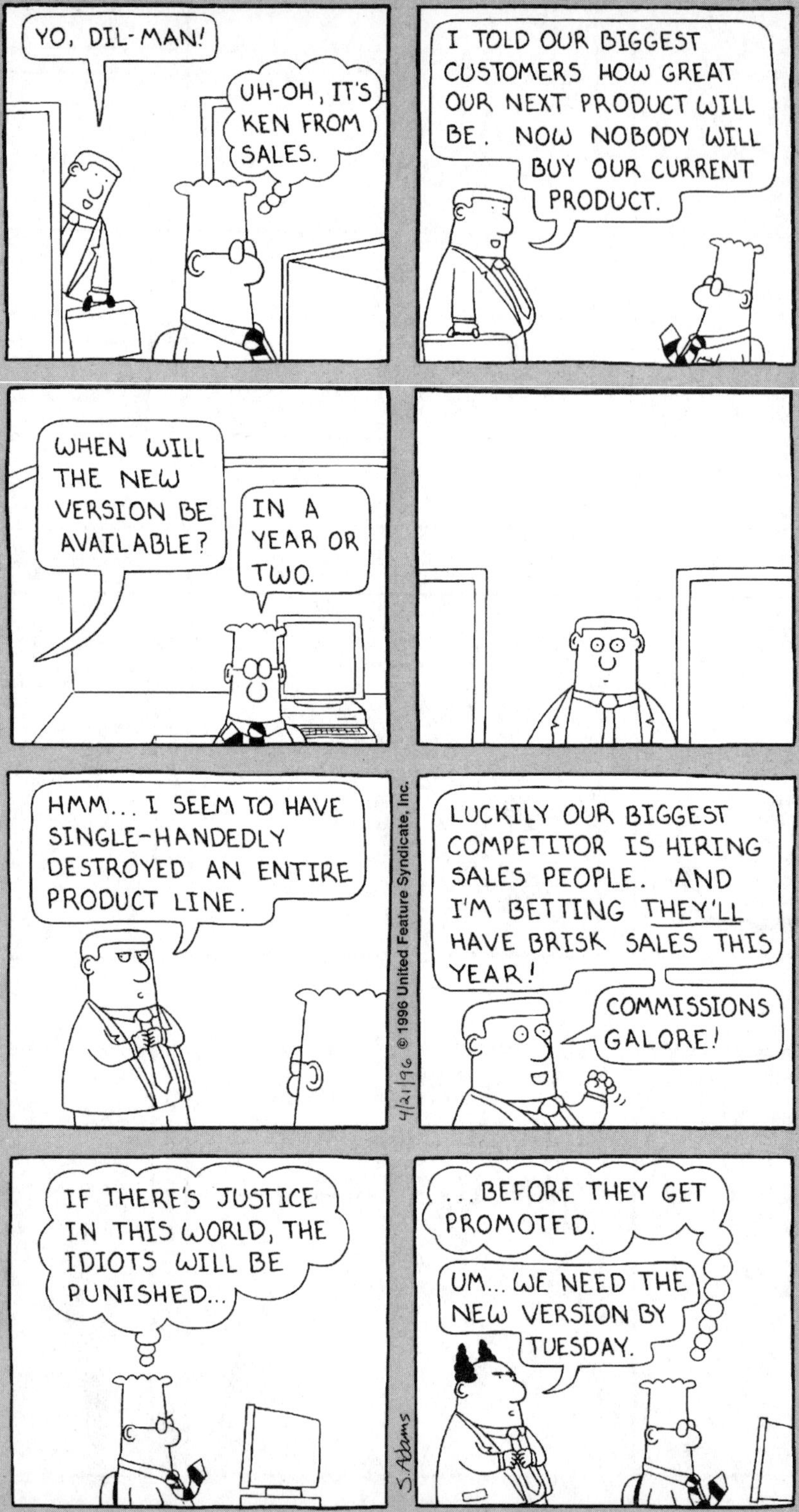
YO, DIL-MAN!
UH-OH, IT'S KEN FROM SALES.
I TOLD OUR BIGGEST CUSTOMERS HOW GREAT OUR NEXT PRODUCT WILL BE. NOW NOBODY WILL BUY OUR CURRENT PRODUCT.
WHEN WILL THE NEW VERSION BE AVAILABLE?
IN A YEAR OR TWO.
HMM... I SEEM TO HAVE SINGLE-HANDEDLY DESTROYED AN ENTIRE PRODUCT LINE.
LUCKILY OUR BIGGEST COMPETITOR IS HIRING SALES PEOPLE. AND I'M BETTING THEY'LL HAVE BRISK SALES THIS YEAR!
COMMISSIONS GALORE!
IF THERE'S JUSTICE IN THIS WORLD, THE IDIOTS WILL BE PUNISHED...
...BEFORE THEY GET PROMOTED.
UM... WE NEED THE NEW VERSION BY TUESDAY.
4/21/96 © 1996 United Feature Syndicate, Inc.
S. Adams

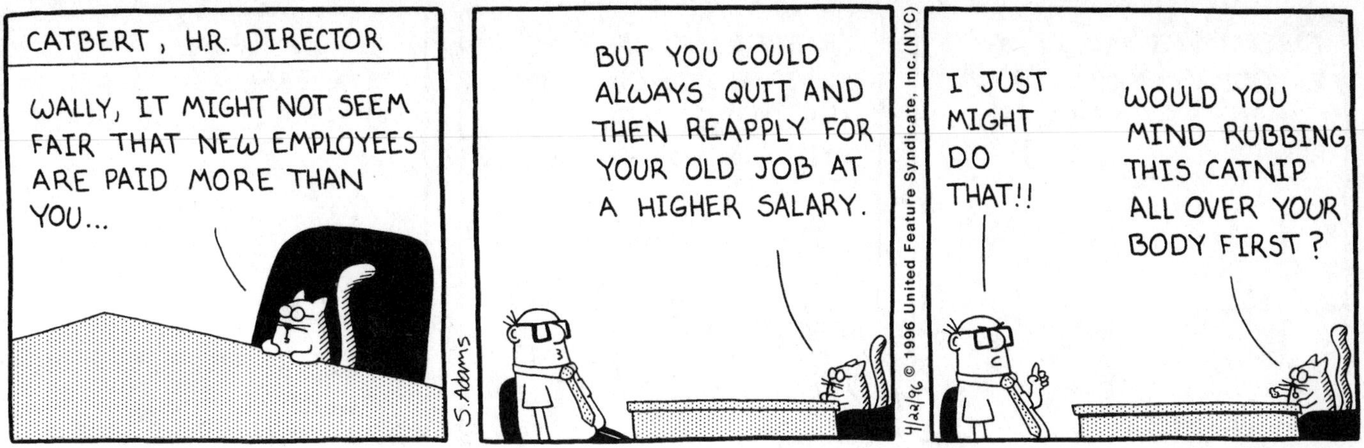
CATBERT, H.R. DIRECTOR
WALLY, IT MIGHT NOT SEEM FAIR THAT NEW EMPLOYEES ARE PAID MORE THAN YOU...
BUT YOU COULD ALWAYS QUIT AND THEN REAPPLY FOR YOUR OLD JOB AT A HIGHER SALARY.
I JUST MIGHT DO THAT!!
WOULD YOU MIND RUBBING THIS CATNIP ALL OVER YOUR BODY FIRST?
S. Adams
4/22/96 © 1996 United Feature Syndicate, Inc.(NYC)

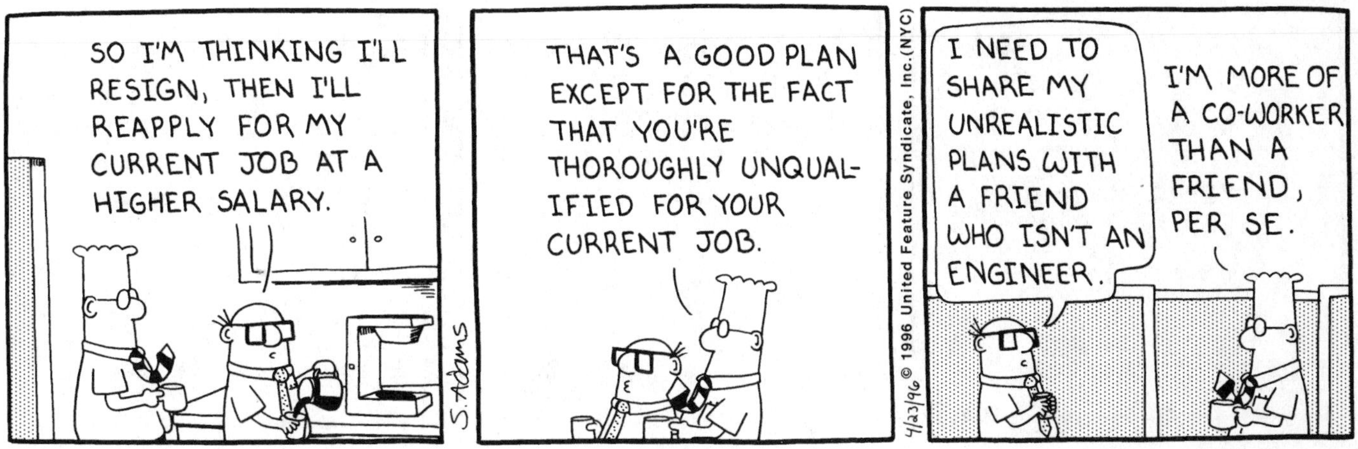
SO I'M THINKING I'LL RESIGN, THEN I'LL REAPPLY FOR MY CURRENT JOB AT A HIGHER SALARY.
THAT'S A GOOD PLAN EXCEPT FOR THE FACT THAT YOU'RE THOROUGHLY UNQUALIFIED FOR YOUR CURRENT JOB.
I NEED TO SHARE MY UNREALISTIC PLANS WITH A FRIEND WHO ISN'T AN ENGINEER.
I'M MORE OF A CO-WORKER THAN A FRIEND, PER SE.
S. Adams
4/23/96 © 1996 United Feature Syndicate, Inc.(NYC)

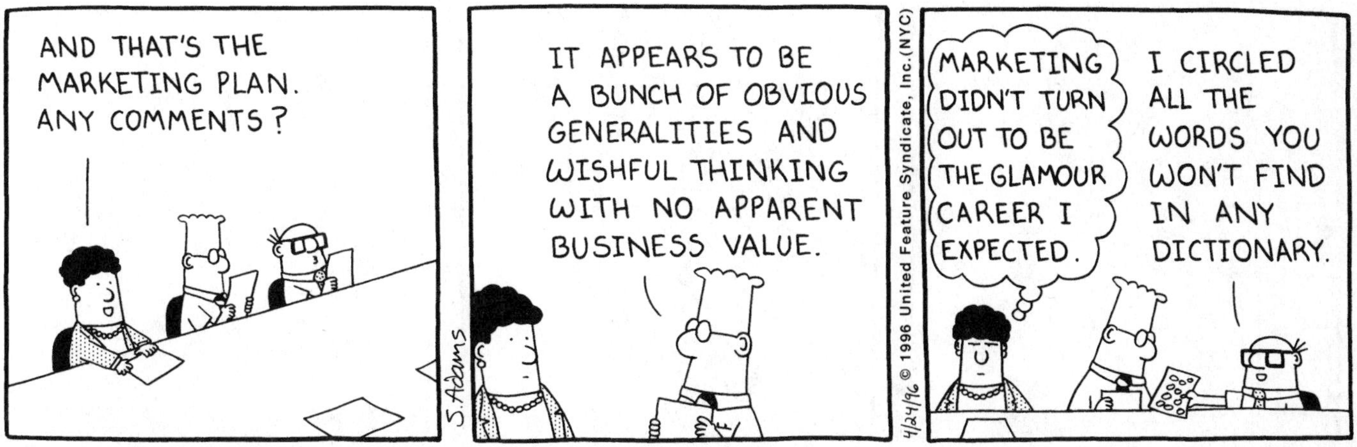
AND THAT'S THE MARKETING PLAN. ANY COMMENTS?
IT APPEARS TO BE A BUNCH OF OBVIOUS GENERALITIES AND WISHFUL THINKING WITH NO APPARENT BUSINESS VALUE.
MARKETING DIDN'T TURN OUT TO BE THE GLAMOUR CAREER I EXPECTED.
I CIRCLED ALL THE WORDS YOU WON'T FIND IN ANY DICTIONARY.
S. Adams
4/24/96 © 1996 United Feature Syndicate, Inc.(NYC)

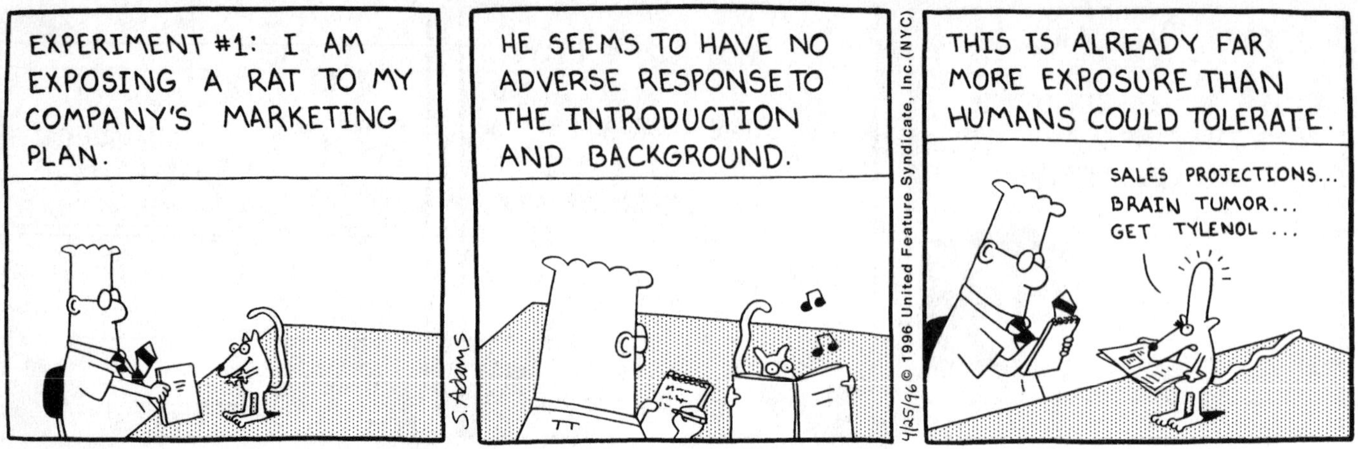
EXPERIMENT #1: I AM EXPOSING A RAT TO MY COMPANY'S MARKETING PLAN.
HE SEEMS TO HAVE NO ADVERSE RESPONSE TO THE INTRODUCTION AND BACKGROUND.
THIS IS ALREADY FAR MORE EXPOSURE THAN HUMANS COULD TOLERATE.
SALES PROJECTIONS... BRAIN TUMOR... GET TYLENOL ...
S. Adams
4/25/96 © 1996 United Feature Syndicate, Inc.(NYC)

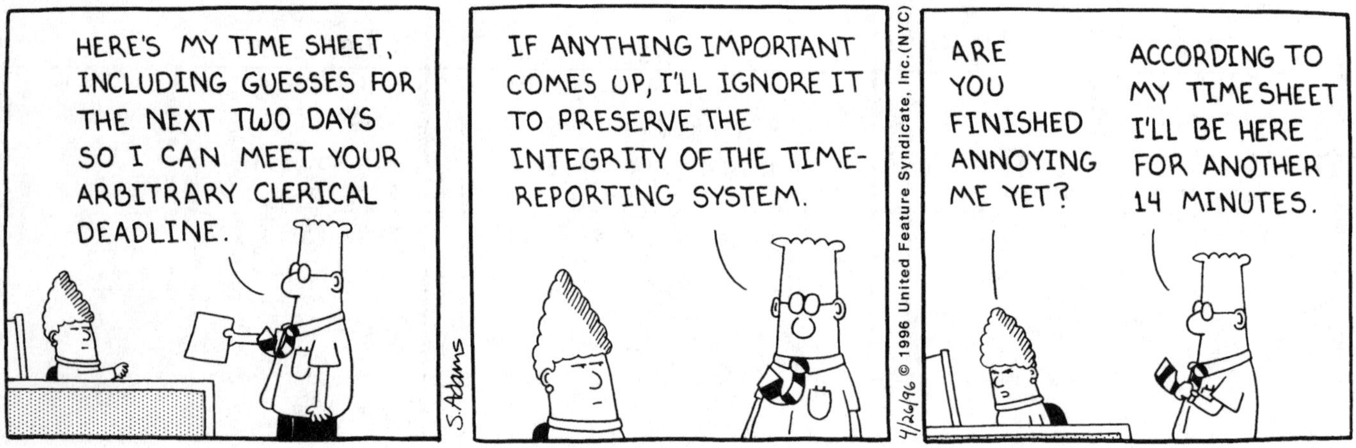
HERE'S MY TIME SHEET, INCLUDING GUESSES FOR THE NEXT TWO DAYS SO I CAN MEET YOUR ARBITRARY CLERICAL DEADLINE.
IF ANYTHING IMPORTANT COMES UP, I'LL IGNORE IT TO PRESERVE THE INTEGRITY OF THE TIME-REPORTING SYSTEM.
ARE YOU FINISHED ANNOYING ME YET?
ACCORDING TO MY TIME SHEET I'LL BE HERE FOR ANOTHER 14 MINUTES.
S. Adams
4/26/96 © 1996 United Feature Syndicate, Inc.(NYC)

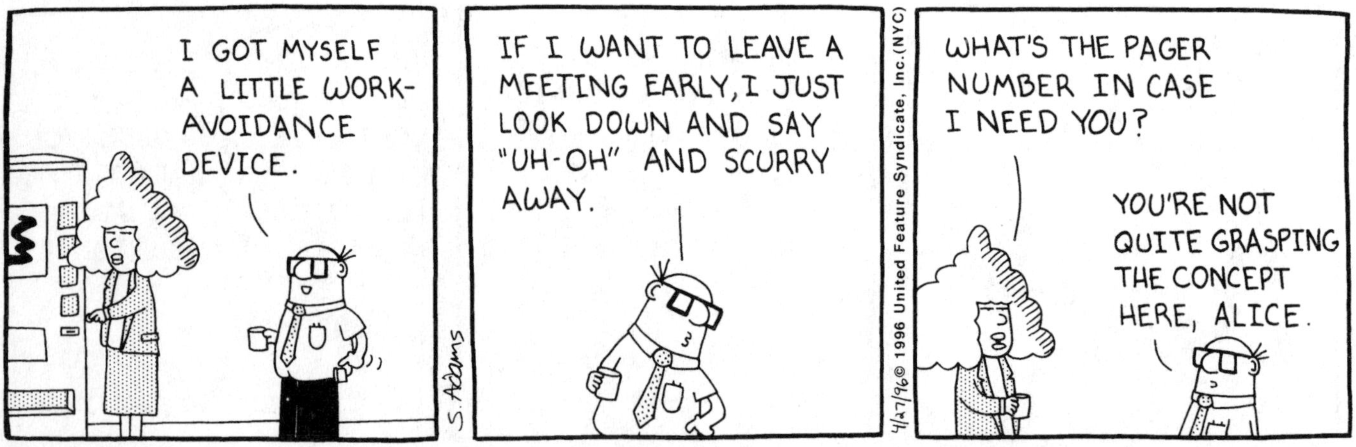
I GOT MYSELF A LITTLE WORK-AVOIDANCE DEVICE.
IF I WANT TO LEAVE A MEETING EARLY, I JUST LOOK DOWN AND SAY "UH-OH" AND SCURRY AWAY.
WHAT'S THE PAGER NUMBER IN CASE I NEED YOU?
YOU'RE NOT QUITE GRASPING THE CONCEPT HERE, ALICE.
S. Adams
4/27/96 © 1996 United Feature Syndicate, Inc.(NYC)

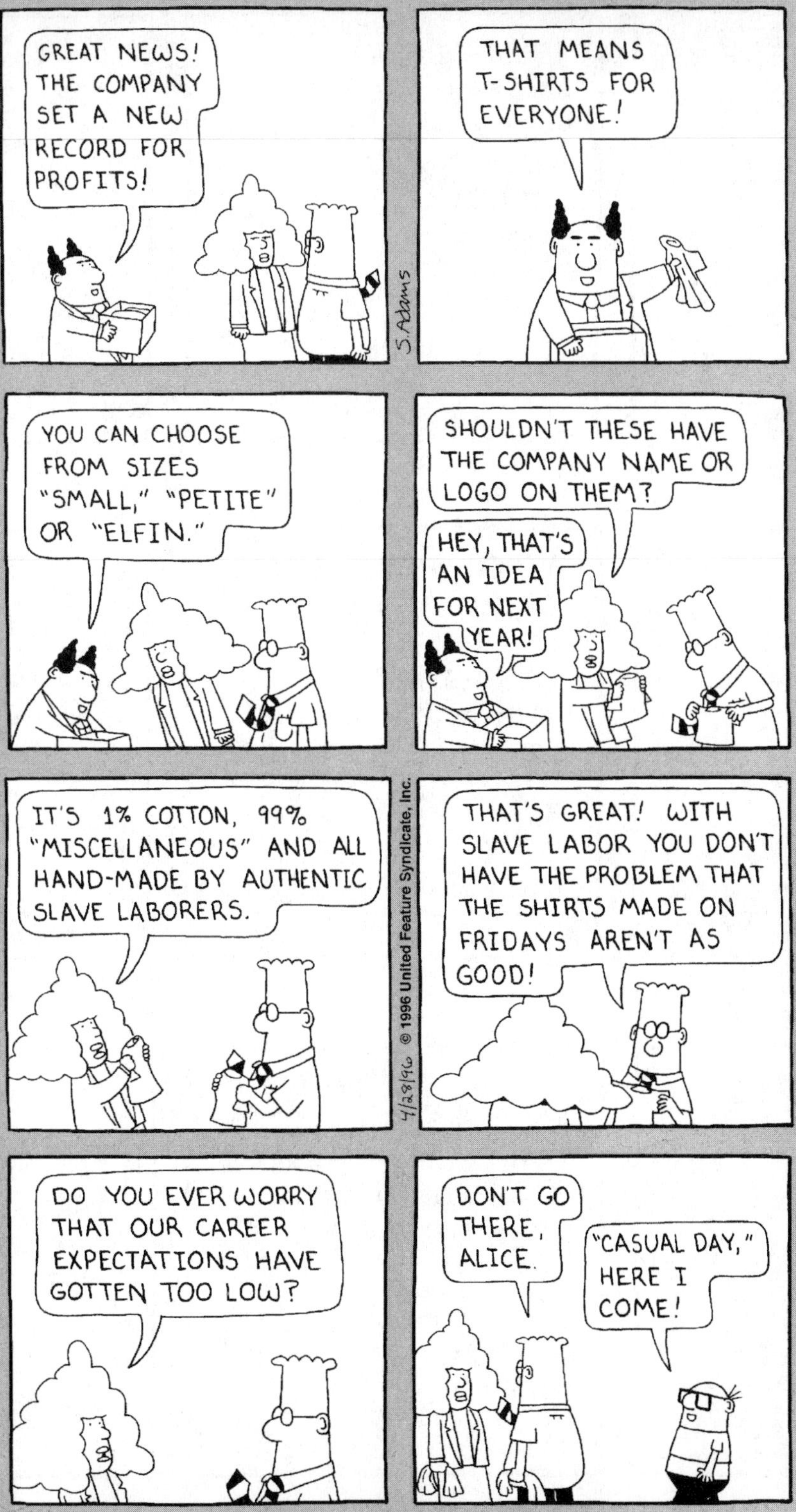
GREAT NEWS! THE COMPANY SET A NEW RECORD FOR PROFITS!
S. Adams
THAT MEANS T-SHIRTS FOR EVERYONE!
YOU CAN CHOOSE FROM SIZES "SMALL," "PETITE" OR "ELFIN."
SHOULDN'T THESE HAVE THE COMPANY NAME OR LOGO ON THEM?
HEY, THAT'S AN IDEA FOR NEXT YEAR!
IT'S 1% COTTON, 99% "MISCELLANEOUS" AND ALL HAND-MADE BY AUTHENTIC SLAVE LABORERS.
4/28/96 © 1996 United Feature Syndicate, Inc.
THAT'S GREAT! WITH SLAVE LABOR YOU DON'T HAVE THE PROBLEM THAT THE SHIRTS MADE ON FRIDAYS AREN'T AS GOOD!
DO YOU EVER WORRY THAT OUR CAREER EXPECTATIONS HAVE GOTTEN TOO LOW?
DON'T GO THERE, ALICE.
"CASUAL DAY," HERE I COME!

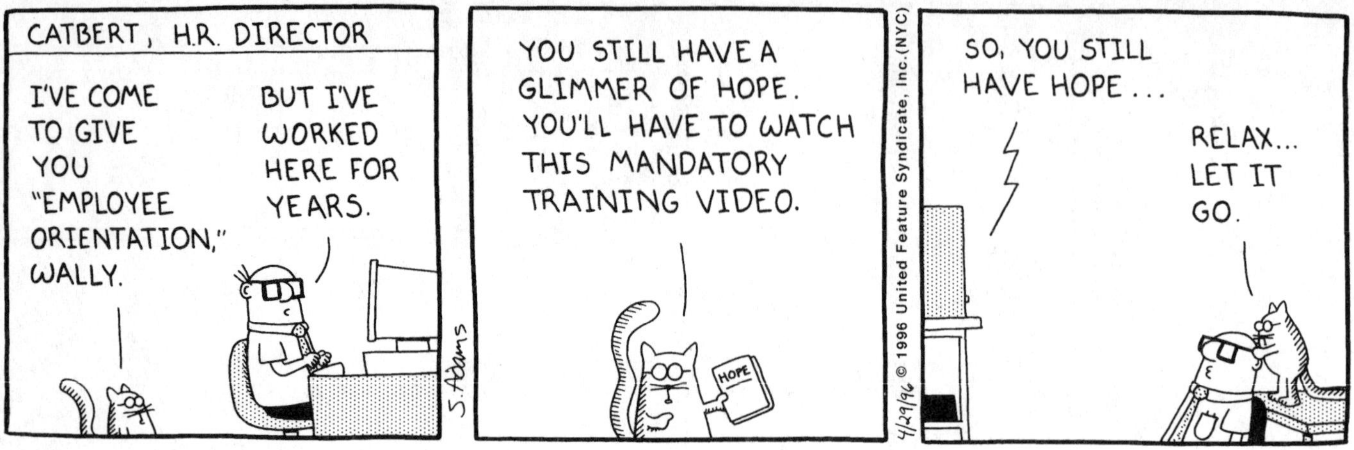
CATBERT, H.R. DIRECTOR
I'VE COME TO GIVE YOU "EMPLOYEE ORIENTATION," WALLY.
BUT I'VE WORKED HERE FOR YEARS.
S. Adams
YOU STILL HAVE A GLIMMER OF HOPE. YOU'LL HAVE TO WATCH THIS MANDATORY TRAINING VIDEO.
HOPE
4/29/96 © 1996 United Feature Syndicate, Inc.(NYC)
SO, YOU STILL HAVE HOPE...
RELAX... LET IT GO.

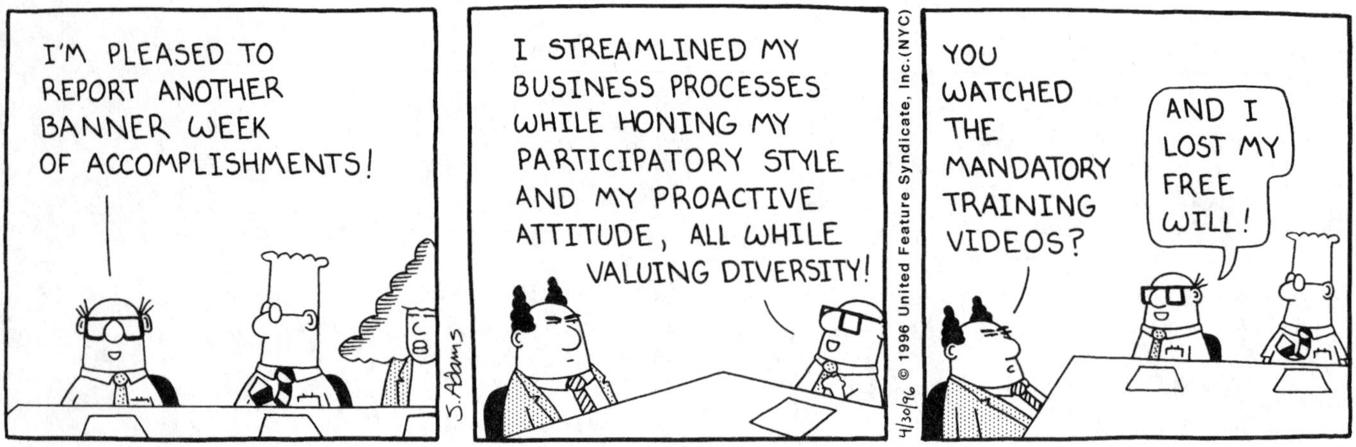
I'M PLEASED TO REPORT ANOTHER BANNER WEEK OF ACCOMPLISHMENTS!
S. Adams
I STREAMLINED MY BUSINESS PROCESSES WHILE HONING MY PARTICIPATORY STYLE AND MY PROACTIVE ATTITUDE, ALL WHILE VALUING DIVERSITY!
4/30/96 © 1996 United Feature Syndicate, Inc.(NYC)
YOU WATCHED THE MANDATORY TRAINING VIDEOS?
AND I LOST MY FREE WILL!

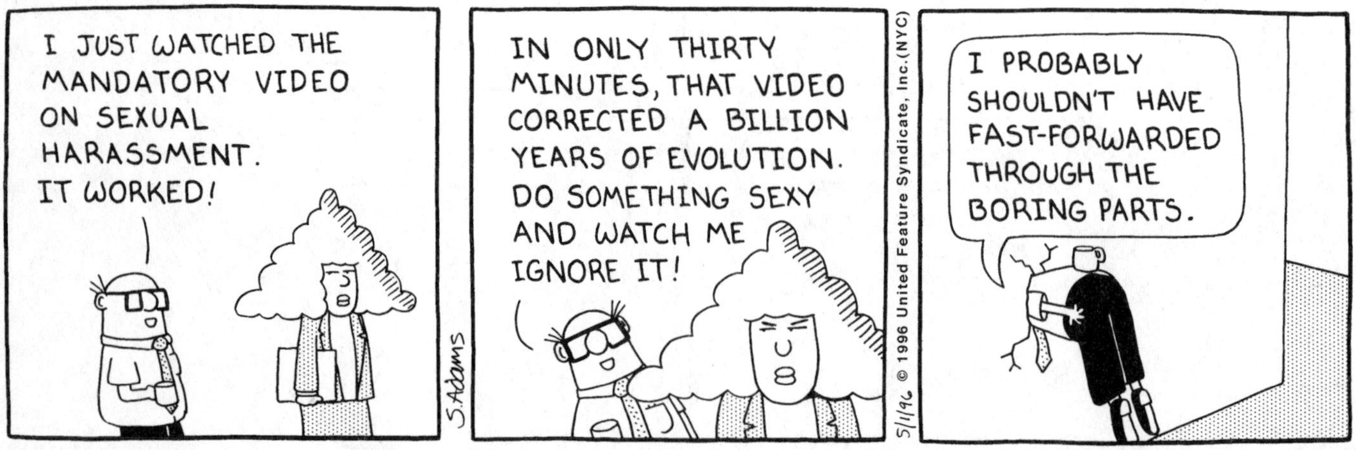
I JUST WATCHED THE MANDATORY VIDEO ON SEXUAL HARASSMENT. IT WORKED!
S. Adams
IN ONLY THIRTY MINUTES, THAT VIDEO CORRECTED A BILLION YEARS OF EVOLUTION. DO SOMETHING SEXY AND WATCH ME IGNORE IT!
5/1/96 © 1996 United Feature Syndicate, Inc.(NYC)
I PROBABLY SHOULDN'T HAVE FAST-FORWARDED THROUGH THE BORING PARTS.

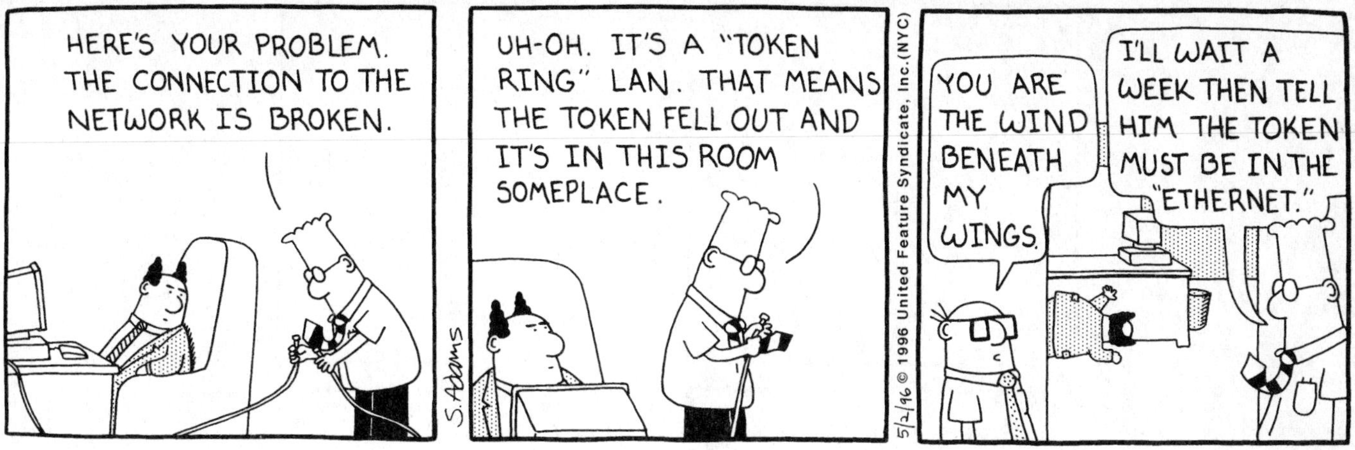
HERE'S YOUR PROBLEM. THE CONNECTION TO THE NETWORK IS BROKEN.
S. Adams
UH-OH. IT'S A "TOKEN RING" LAN. THAT MEANS THE TOKEN FELL OUT AND IT'S IN THIS ROOM SOMEPLACE.
YOU ARE THE WIND BENEATH MY WINGS.
I'LL WAIT A WEEK THEN TELL HIM THE TOKEN MUST BE IN THE "ETHERNET."

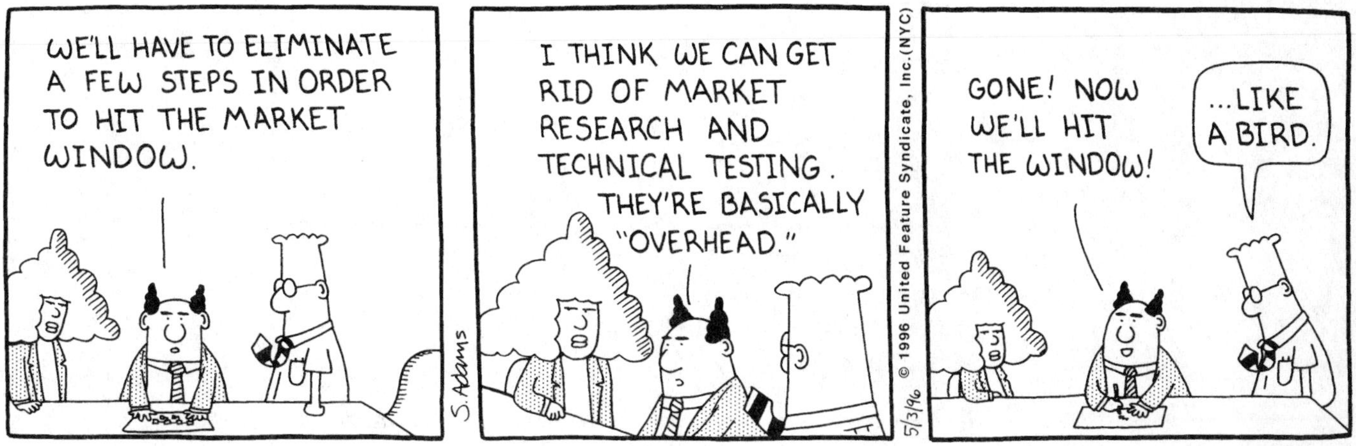
WE'LL HAVE TO ELIMINATE A FEW STEPS IN ORDER TO HIT THE MARKET WINDOW.
S. Adams
I THINK WE CAN GET RID OF MARKET RESEARCH AND TECHNICAL TESTING. THEY'RE BASICALLY "OVERHEAD."
GONE! NOW WE'LL HIT THE WINDOW!
...LIKE A BIRD.

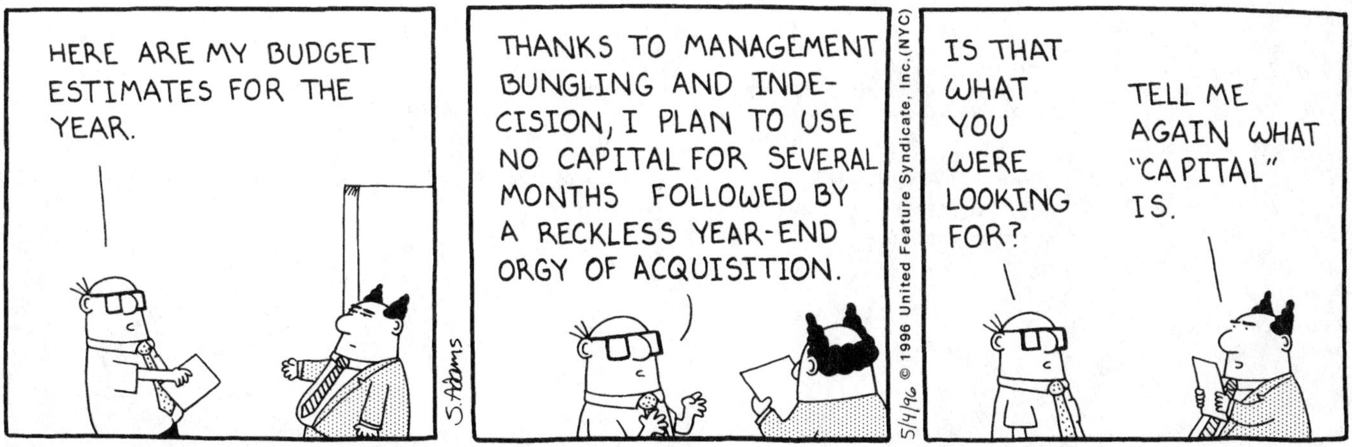
HERE ARE MY BUDGET ESTIMATES FOR THE YEAR.
S. Adams
THANKS TO MANAGEMENT BUNGLING AND INDECISION, I PLAN TO USE NO CAPITAL FOR SEVERAL MONTHS FOLLOWED BY A RECKLESS YEAR-END ORGY OF ACQUISITION.
IS THAT WHAT YOU WERE LOOKING FOR?
TELL ME AGAIN WHAT "CAPITAL" IS.

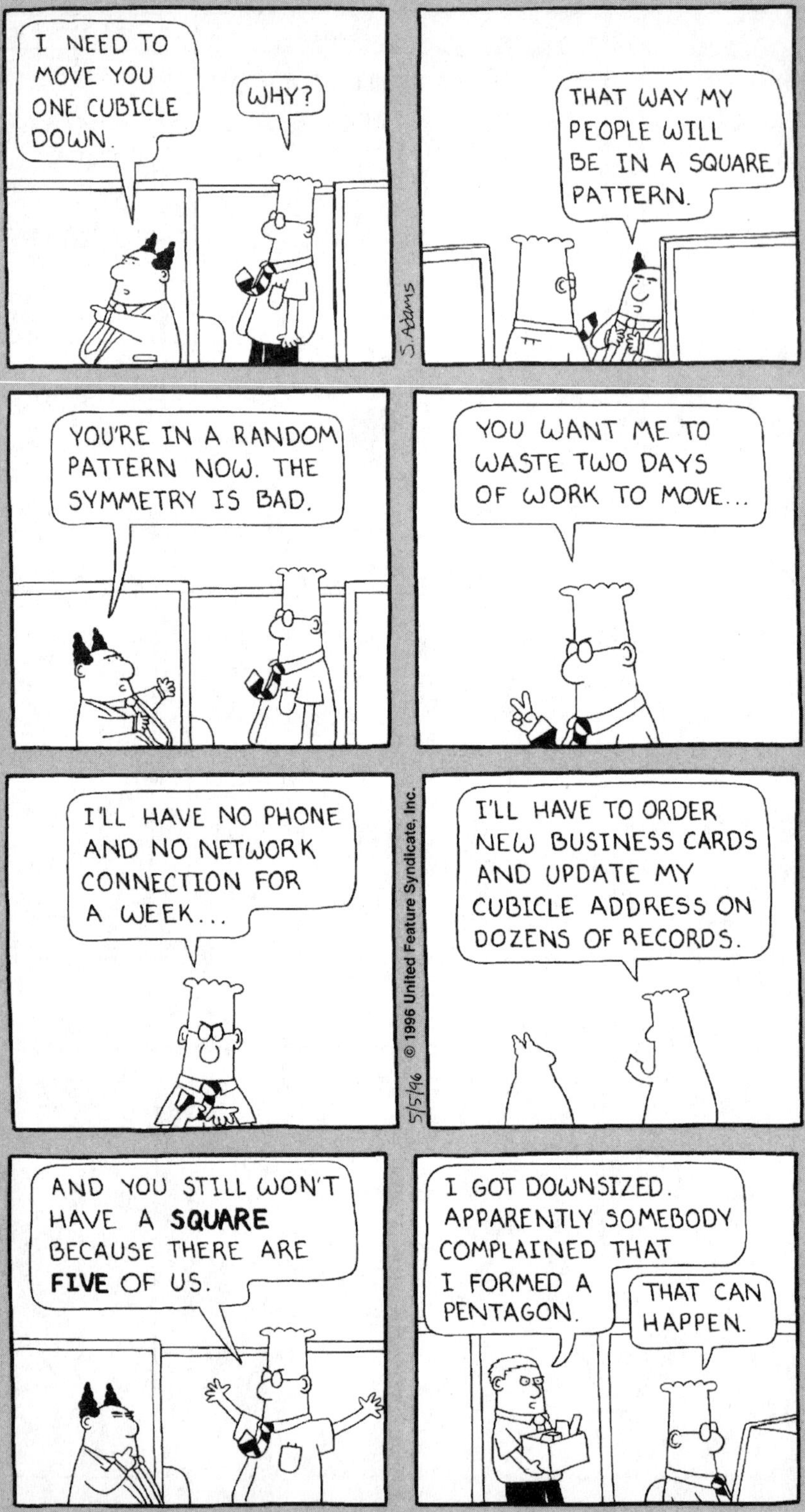
I NEED TO MOVE YOU ONE CUBICLE DOWN.
WHY?
THAT WAY MY PEOPLE WILL BE IN A SQUARE PATTERN.
S. Adams
YOU'RE IN A RANDOM PATTERN NOW. THE SYMMETRY IS BAD.
YOU WANT ME TO WASTE TWO DAYS OF WORK TO MOVE...
I'LL HAVE NO PHONE AND NO NETWORK CONNECTION FOR A WEEK...
© 1996 United Feature Syndicate, Inc.
5/5/96
I'LL HAVE TO ORDER NEW BUSINESS CARDS AND UPDATE MY CUBICLE ADDRESS ON DOZENS OF RECORDS.
AND YOU STILL WON'T HAVE A **SQUARE** BECAUSE THERE ARE **FIVE** OF US.
I GOT DOWNSIZED. APPARENTLY SOMEBODY COMPLAINED THAT I FORMED A PENTAGON.
THAT CAN HAPPEN.

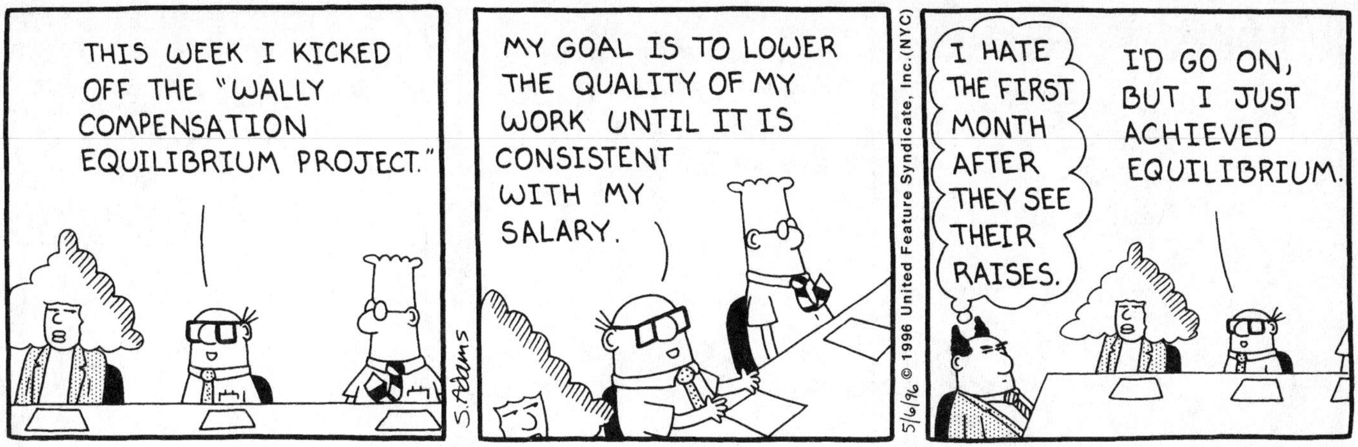
THIS WEEK I KICKED OFF THE "WALLY COMPENSATION EQUILIBRIUM PROJECT."
MY GOAL IS TO LOWER THE QUALITY OF MY WORK UNTIL IT IS CONSISTENT WITH MY SALARY.
I HATE THE FIRST MONTH AFTER THEY SEE THEIR RAISES.
I'D GO ON, BUT I JUST ACHIEVED EQUILIBRIUM.
S. Adams
5/6/96 © 1996 United Feature Syndicate, Inc.(NYC)

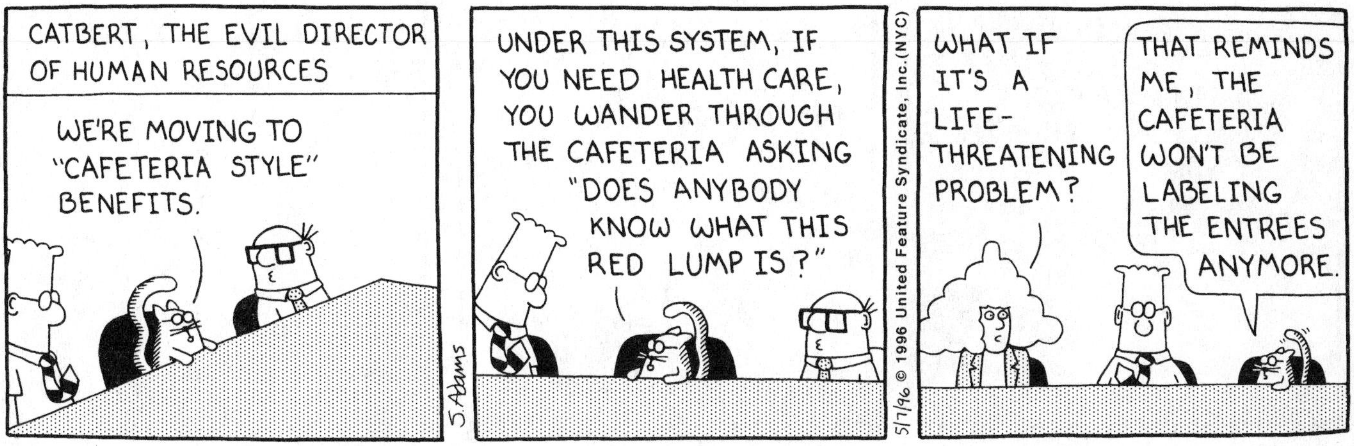
CATBERT, THE EVIL DIRECTOR OF HUMAN RESOURCES
WE'RE MOVING TO "CAFETERIA STYLE" BENEFITS.
UNDER THIS SYSTEM, IF YOU NEED HEALTH CARE, YOU WANDER THROUGH THE CAFETERIA ASKING "DOES ANYBODY KNOW WHAT THIS RED LUMP IS?"
WHAT IF IT'S A LIFE-THREATENING PROBLEM?
THAT REMINDS ME, THE CAFETERIA WON'T BE LABELING THE ENTREES ANYMORE.
S. Adams
5/7/96 © 1996 United Feature Syndicate, Inc.(NYC)

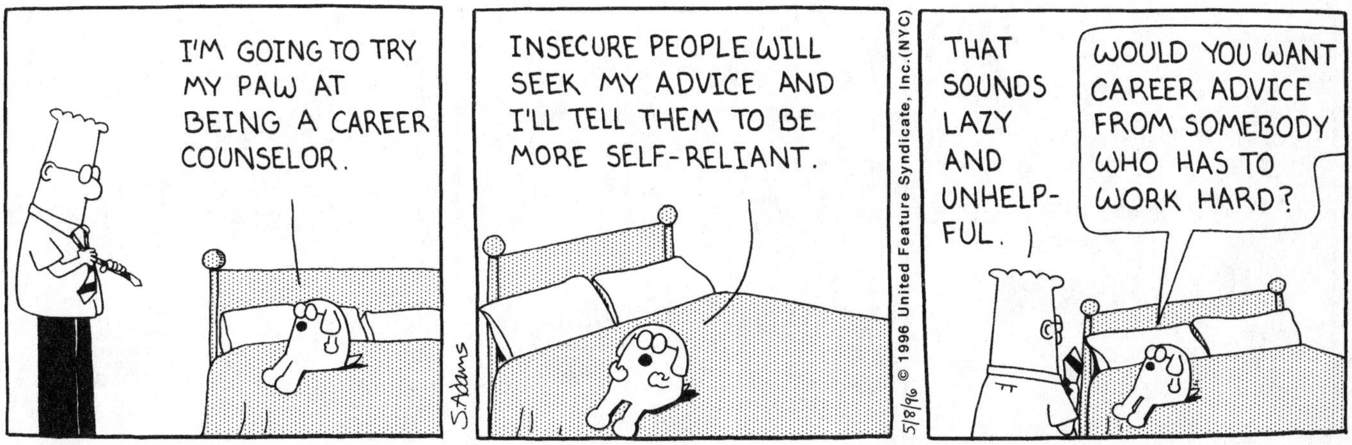
I'M GOING TO TRY MY PAW AT BEING A CAREER COUNSELOR.
INSECURE PEOPLE WILL SEEK MY ADVICE AND I'LL TELL THEM TO BE MORE SELF-RELIANT.
THAT SOUNDS LAZY AND UNHELP-FUL.
WOULD YOU WANT CAREER ADVICE FROM SOMEBODY WHO HAS TO WORK HARD?
S. Adams
5/8/96 © 1996 United Feature Syndicate, Inc.(NYC)

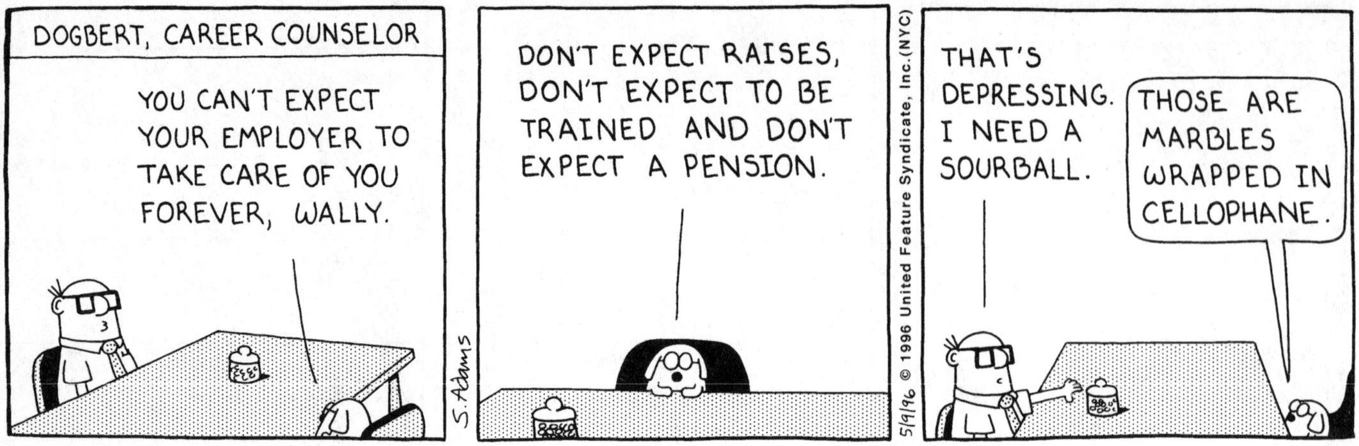
DOGBERT, CAREER COUNSELOR
YOU CAN'T EXPECT YOUR EMPLOYER TO TAKE CARE OF YOU FOREVER, WALLY.
S. Adams
DON'T EXPECT RAISES, DON'T EXPECT TO BE TRAINED AND DON'T EXPECT A PENSION.
5/9/96 © 1996 United Feature Syndicate, Inc.(NYC)
THAT'S DEPRESSING. I NEED A SOURBALL.
THOSE ARE MARBLES WRAPPED IN CELLOPHANE.

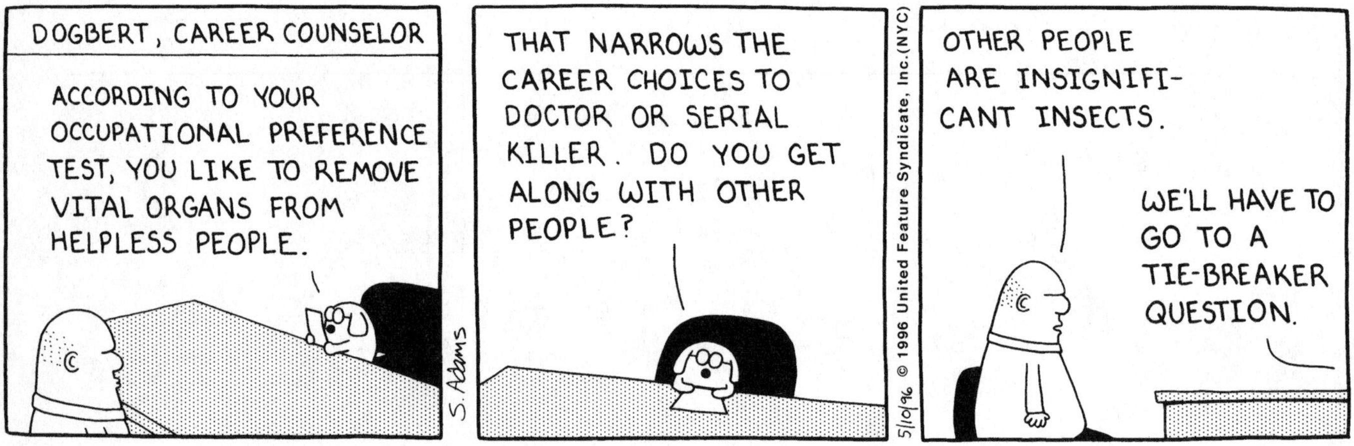
DOGBERT, CAREER COUNSELOR
ACCORDING TO YOUR OCCUPATIONAL PREFERENCE TEST, YOU LIKE TO REMOVE VITAL ORGANS FROM HELPLESS PEOPLE.
S. Adams
THAT NARROWS THE CAREER CHOICES TO DOCTOR OR SERIAL KILLER. DO YOU GET ALONG WITH OTHER PEOPLE?
5/10/96 © 1996 United Feature Syndicate, Inc.(NYC)
OTHER PEOPLE ARE INSIGNIFI- CANT INSECTS.
WE'LL HAVE TO GO TO A TIE-BREAKER QUESTION.

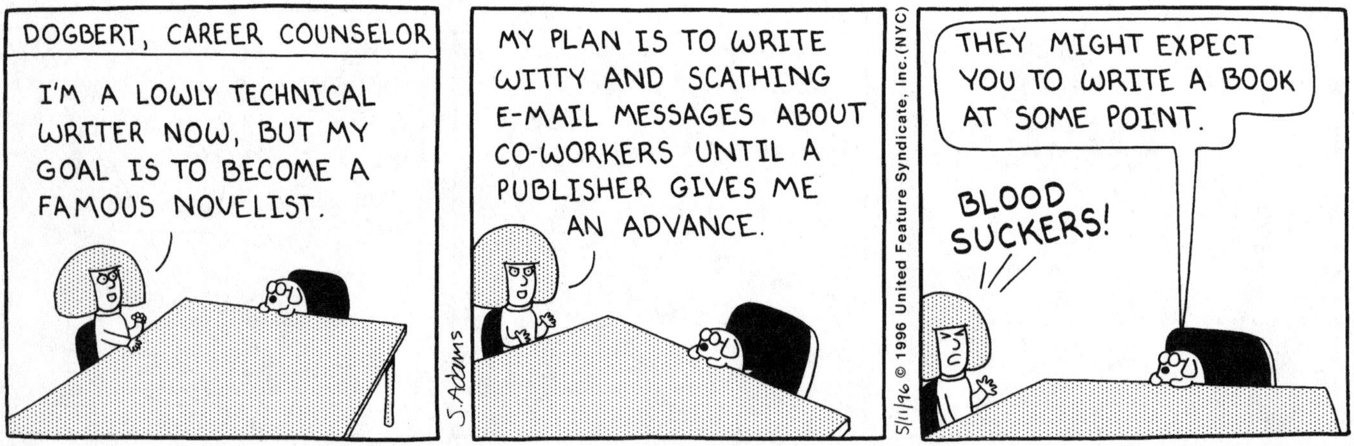
DOGBERT, CAREER COUNSELOR
I'M A LOWLY TECHNICAL WRITER NOW, BUT MY GOAL IS TO BECOME A FAMOUS NOVELIST.
S. Adams
MY PLAN IS TO WRITE WITTY AND SCATHING E-MAIL MESSAGES ABOUT CO-WORKERS UNTIL A PUBLISHER GIVES ME AN ADVANCE.
5/11/96 © 1996 United Feature Syndicate, Inc.(NYC)
THEY MIGHT EXPECT YOU TO WRITE A BOOK AT SOME POINT.
BLOOD SUCKERS!

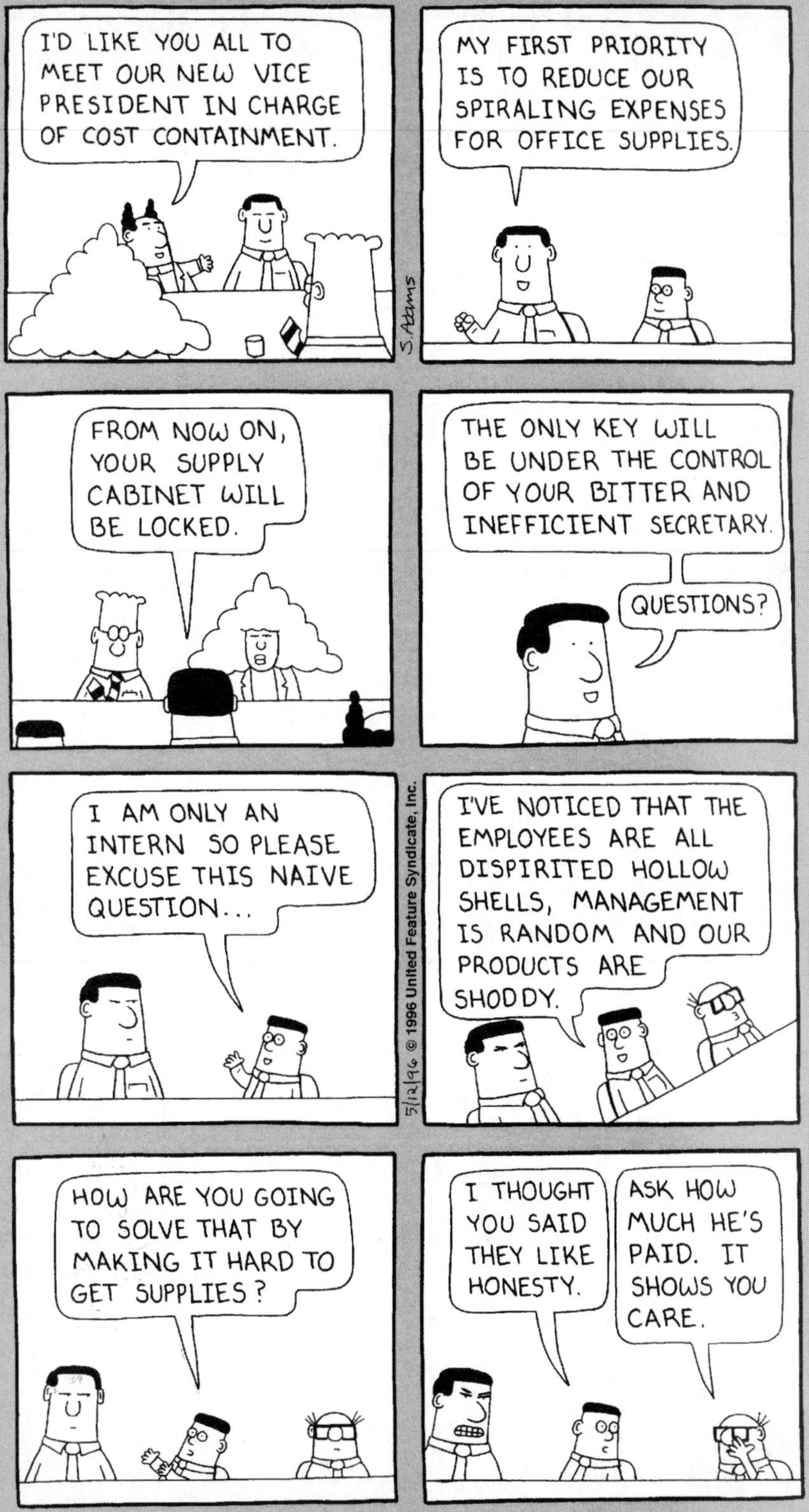
I'D LIKE YOU ALL TO MEET OUR NEW VICE PRESIDENT IN CHARGE OF COST CONTAINMENT.
S. Adams
MY FIRST PRIORITY IS TO REDUCE OUR SPIRALING EXPENSES FOR OFFICE SUPPLIES.
FROM NOW ON, YOUR SUPPLY CABINET WILL BE LOCKED.
THE ONLY KEY WILL BE UNDER THE CONTROL OF YOUR BITTER AND INEFFICIENT SECRETARY.
QUESTIONS?
I AM ONLY AN INTERN SO PLEASE EXCUSE THIS NAIVE QUESTION...
5/12/96 © 1996 United Feature Syndicate, Inc.
I'VE NOTICED THAT THE EMPLOYEES ARE ALL DISPIRITED HOLLOW SHELLS, MANAGEMENT IS RANDOM AND OUR PRODUCTS ARE SHODDY.
HOW ARE YOU GOING TO SOLVE THAT BY MAKING IT HARD TO GET SUPPLIES?
I THOUGHT YOU SAID THEY LIKE HONESTY.
ASK HOW MUCH HE'S PAID. IT SHOWS YOU CARE.

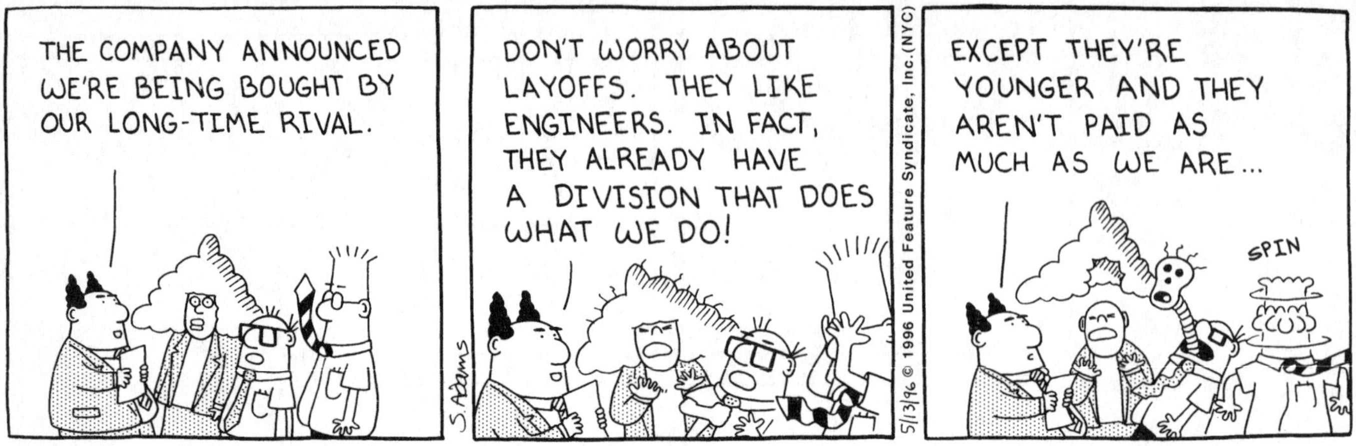
THE COMPANY ANNOUNCED WE'RE BEING BOUGHT BY OUR LONG-TIME RIVAL.
DON'T WORRY ABOUT LAYOFFS. THEY LIKE ENGINEERS. IN FACT, THEY ALREADY HAVE A DIVISION THAT DOES WHAT WE DO!
EXCEPT THEY'RE YOUNGER AND THEY AREN'T PAID AS MUCH AS WE ARE...
SPIN
S. Adams
5/13/96 © 1996 United Feature Syndicate, Inc.(NYC)

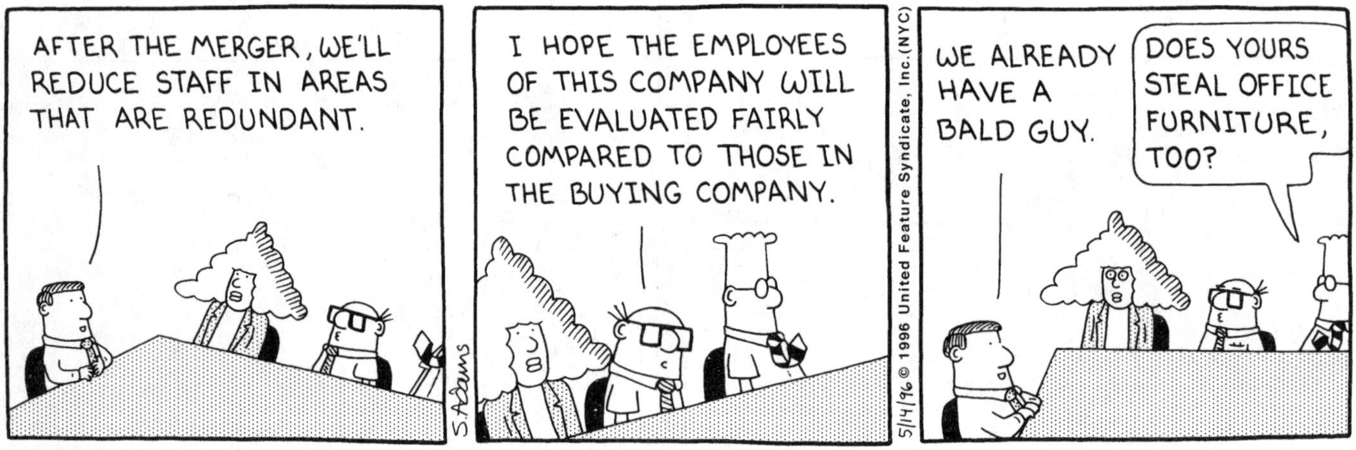
AFTER THE MERGER, WE'LL REDUCE STAFF IN AREAS THAT ARE REDUNDANT.
I HOPE THE EMPLOYEES OF THIS COMPANY WILL BE EVALUATED FAIRLY COMPARED TO THOSE IN THE BUYING COMPANY.
WE ALREADY HAVE A BALD GUY.
DOES YOURS STEAL OFFICE FURNITURE, TOO?
S. Adams
5/14/96 © 1996 United Feature Syndicate, Inc.(NYC)

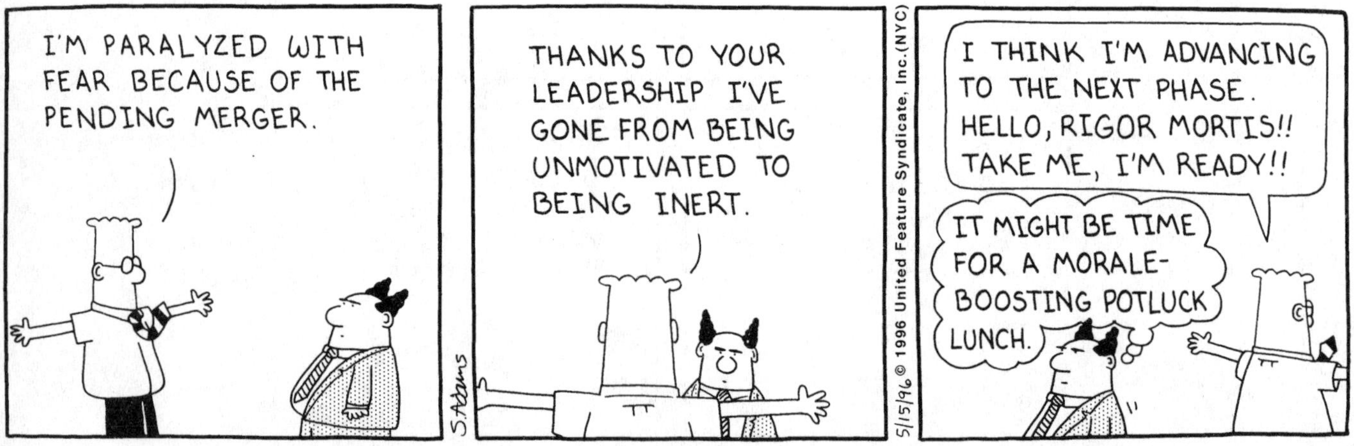
I'M PARALYZED WITH FEAR BECAUSE OF THE PENDING MERGER.
THANKS TO YOUR LEADERSHIP I'VE GONE FROM BEING UNMOTIVATED TO BEING INERT.
I THINK I'M ADVANCING TO THE NEXT PHASE. HELLO, RIGOR MORTIS!! TAKE ME, I'M READY!!
IT MIGHT BE TIME FOR A MORALE-BOOSTING POTLUCK LUNCH.
S. Adams
5/15/96 © 1996 United Feature Syndicate, Inc.(NYC)

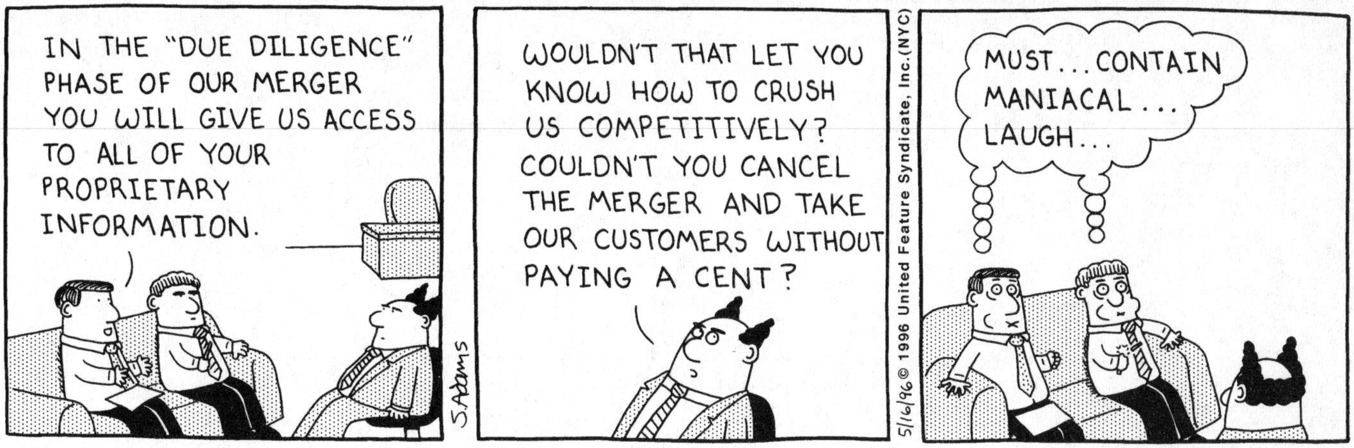
IN THE "DUE DILIGENCE" PHASE OF OUR MERGER YOU WILL GIVE US ACCESS TO ALL OF YOUR PROPRIETARY INFORMATION.
S. Adams
WOULDN'T THAT LET YOU KNOW HOW TO CRUSH US COMPETITIVELY? COULDN'T YOU CANCEL THE MERGER AND TAKE OUR CUSTOMERS WITHOUT PAYING A CENT?
5/16/96 © 1996 United Feature Syndicate, Inc.(NYC)
MUST... CONTAIN MANIACAL... LAUGH...

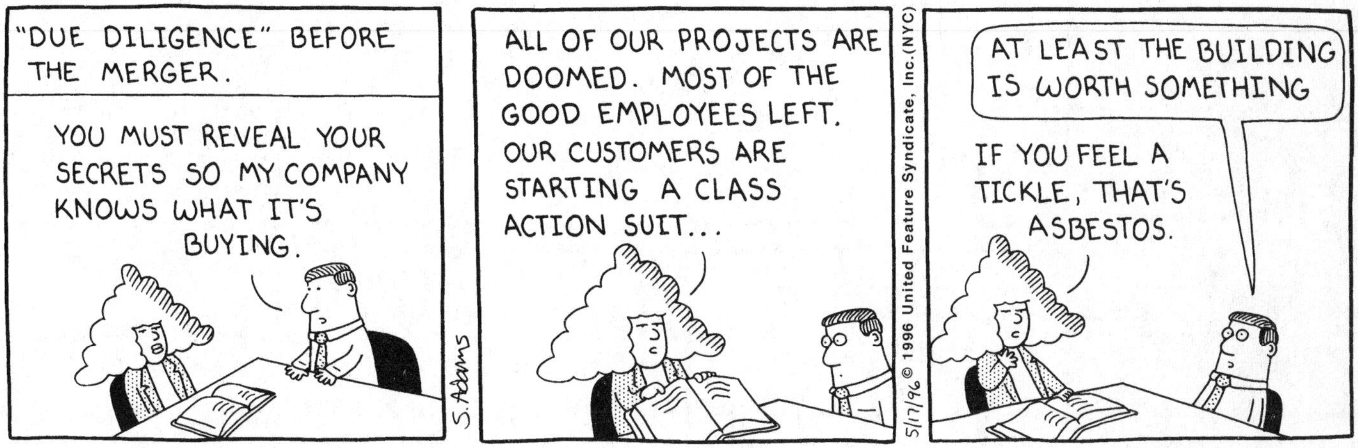
"DUE DILIGENCE" BEFORE THE MERGER.
YOU MUST REVEAL YOUR SECRETS SO MY COMPANY KNOWS WHAT IT'S BUYING.
S. Adams
ALL OF OUR PROJECTS ARE DOOMED. MOST OF THE GOOD EMPLOYEES LEFT. OUR CUSTOMERS ARE STARTING A CLASS ACTION SUIT...
5/17/96 © 1996 United Feature Syndicate, Inc.(NYC)
IF YOU FEEL A TICKLE, THAT'S ASBESTOS.
AT LEAST THE BUILDING IS WORTH SOMETHING

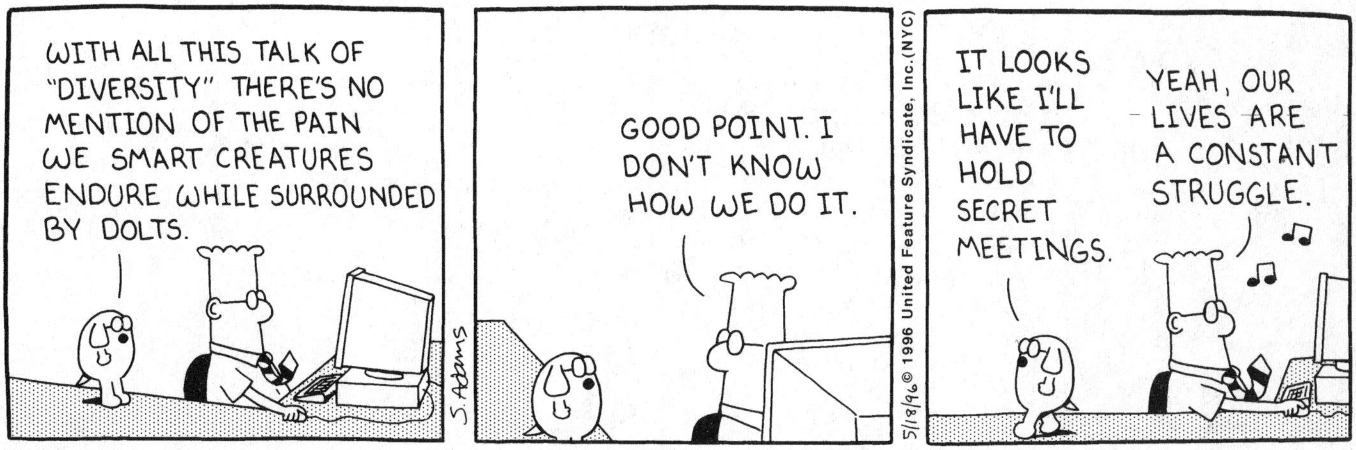
WITH ALL THIS TALK OF "DIVERSITY" THERE'S NO MENTION OF THE PAIN WE SMART CREATURES ENDURE WHILE SURROUNDED BY DOLTS.
S. Adams
GOOD POINT. I DON'T KNOW HOW WE DO IT.
5/18/96 © 1996 United Feature Syndicate, Inc.(NYC)
IT LOOKS LIKE I'LL HAVE TO HOLD SECRET MEETINGS.
YEAH, OUR LIVES ARE A CONSTANT STRUGGLE.

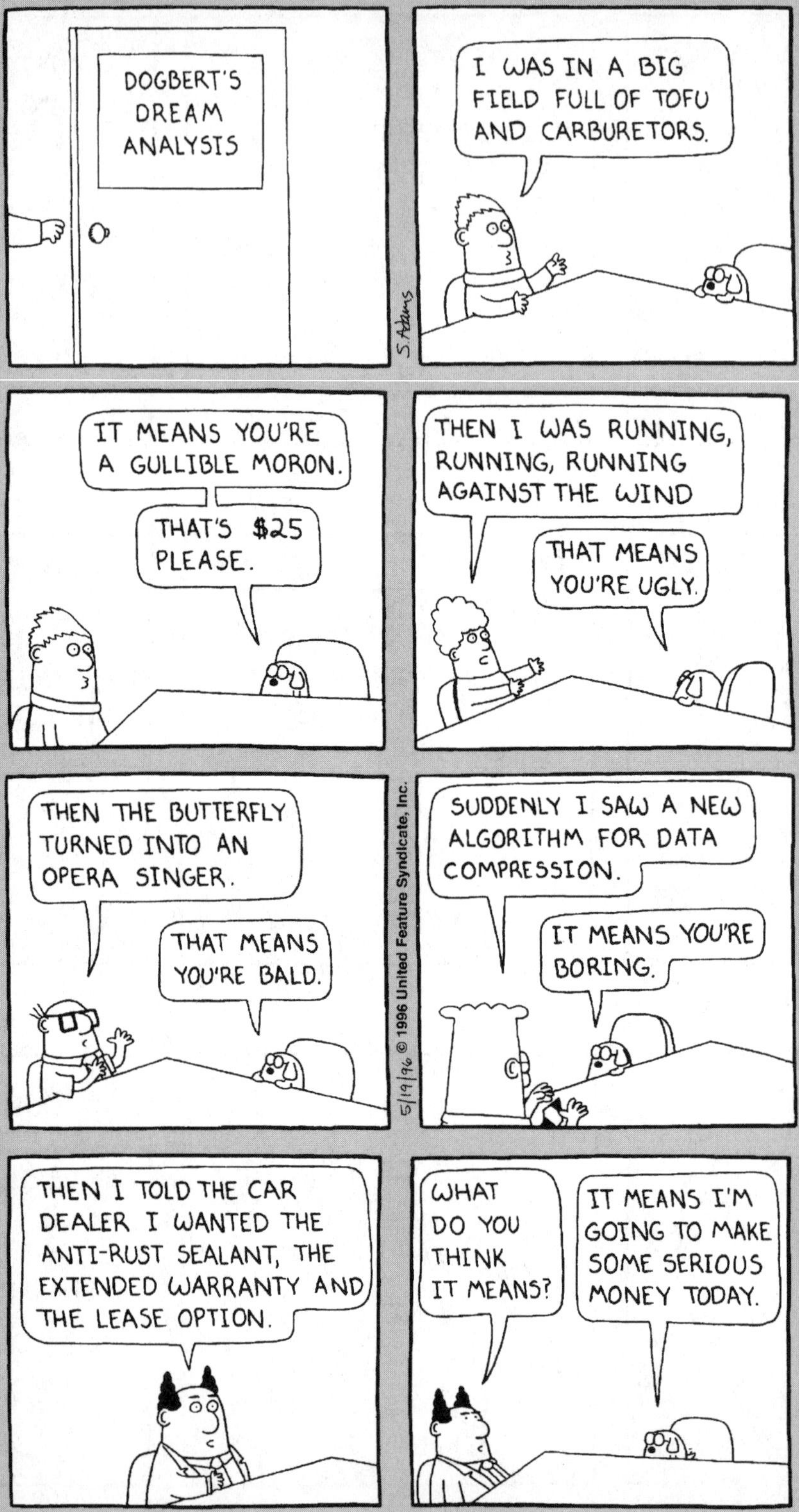
DOGBERT'S DREAM ANALYSIS
I WAS IN A BIG FIELD FULL OF TOFU AND CARBURETORS.
S. Adams
IT MEANS YOU'RE A GULLIBLE MORON.
THAT'S $25 PLEASE.
THEN I WAS RUNNING, RUNNING, RUNNING AGAINST THE WIND
THAT MEANS YOU'RE UGLY.
THEN THE BUTTERFLY TURNED INTO AN OPERA SINGER.
THAT MEANS YOU'RE BALD.
5/19/96 © 1996 United Feature Syndicate, Inc.
SUDDENLY I SAW A NEW ALGORITHM FOR DATA COMPRESSION.
IT MEANS YOU'RE BORING.
THEN I TOLD THE CAR DEALER I WANTED THE ANTI-RUST SEALANT, THE EXTENDED WARRANTY AND THE LEASE OPTION.
WHAT DO YOU THINK IT MEANS?
IT MEANS I'M GOING TO MAKE SOME SERIOUS MONEY TODAY.

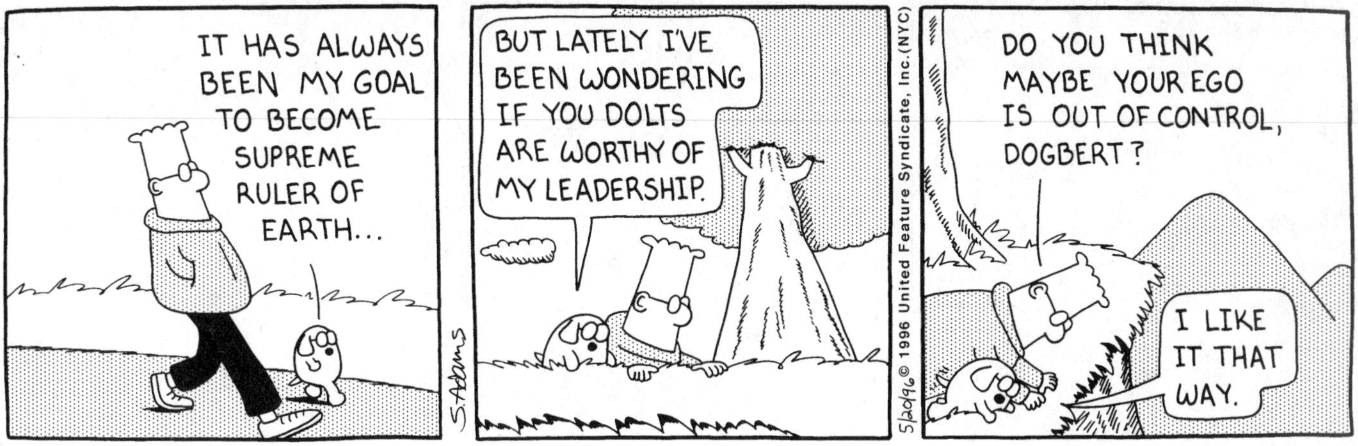
IT HAS ALWAYS BEEN MY GOAL TO BECOME SUPREME RULER OF EARTH...
BUT LATELY I'VE BEEN WONDERING IF YOU DOLTS ARE WORTHY OF MY LEADERSHIP.
DO YOU THINK MAYBE YOUR EGO IS OUT OF CONTROL, DOGBERT?
I LIKE IT THAT WAY.
5/20/96 © 1996 United Feature Syndicate, Inc.(NYC)

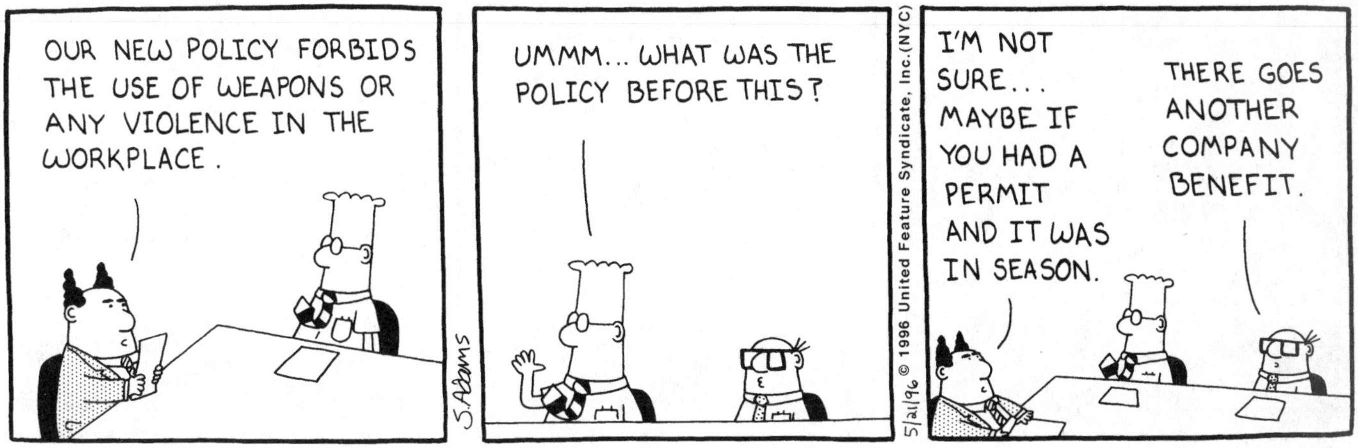
OUR NEW POLICY FORBIDS THE USE OF WEAPONS OR ANY VIOLENCE IN THE WORKPLACE.
UMMM... WHAT WAS THE POLICY BEFORE THIS?
I'M NOT SURE... MAYBE IF YOU HAD A PERMIT AND IT WAS IN SEASON.
THERE GOES ANOTHER COMPANY BENEFIT.
5/21/96 © 1996 United Feature Syndicate, Inc.(NYC)

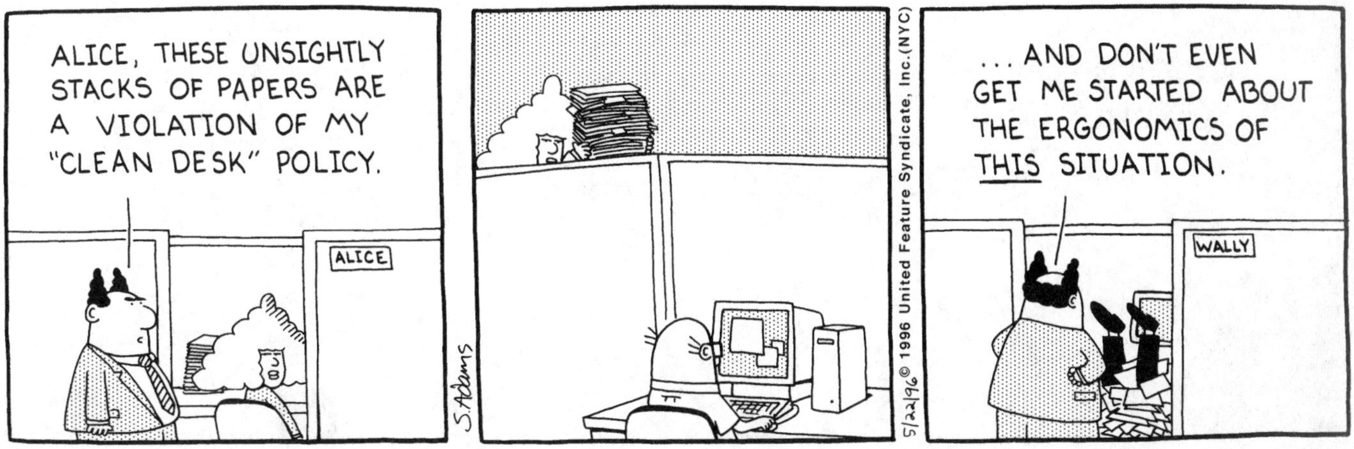
ALICE, THESE UNSIGHTLY STACKS OF PAPERS ARE A VIOLATION OF MY "CLEAN DESK" POLICY.
ALICE
5/22/96 © 1996 United Feature Syndicate, Inc.(NYC)
...AND DON'T EVEN GET ME STARTED ABOUT THE ERGONOMICS OF THIS SITUATION.
WALLY

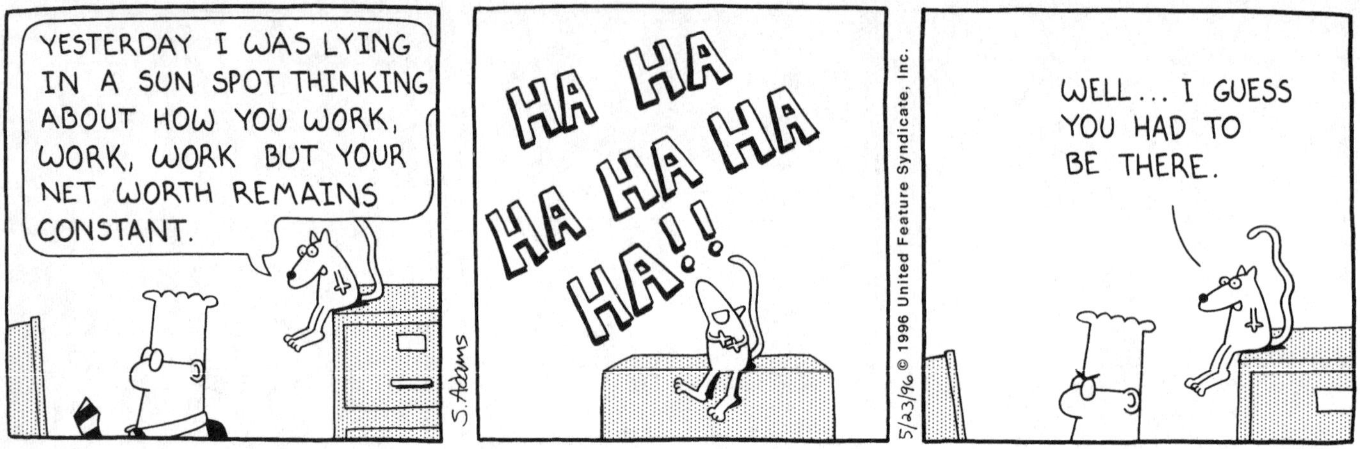
YESTERDAY I WAS LYING IN A SUN SPOT THINKING ABOUT HOW YOU WORK, WORK, WORK BUT YOUR NET WORTH REMAINS CONSTANT.
S. Adams
HA HA HA HA HA HA!!
5/23/96 © 1996 United Feature Syndicate, Inc.
WELL... I GUESS YOU HAD TO BE THERE.

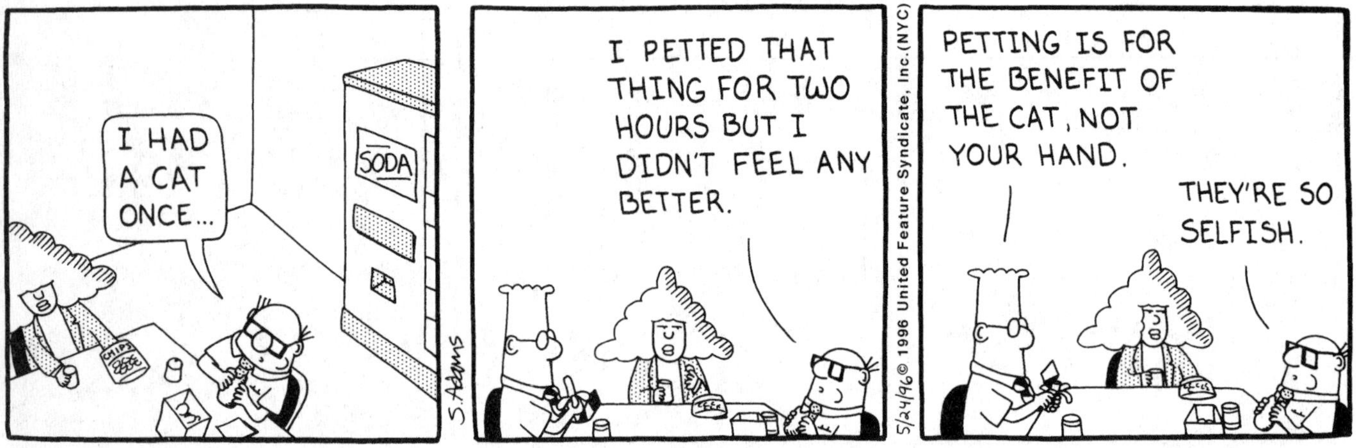
I HAD A CAT ONCE...
SODA
CHIPS
S. Adams
I PETTED THAT THING FOR TWO HOURS BUT I DIDN'T FEEL ANY BETTER.
5/24/96 © 1996 United Feature Syndicate, Inc.(NYC)
PETTING IS FOR THE BENEFIT OF THE CAT, NOT YOUR HAND.
THEY'RE SO SELFISH.

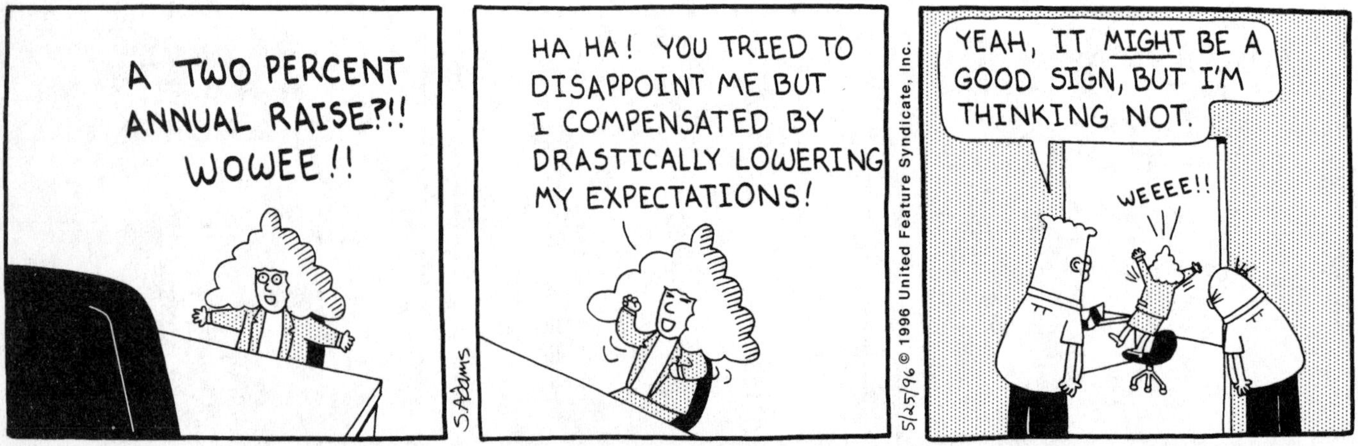
A TWO PERCENT ANNUAL RAISE?!! WOWEE!!
S. Adams
HA HA! YOU TRIED TO DISAPPOINT ME BUT I COMPENSATED BY DRASTICALLY LOWERING MY EXPECTATIONS!
5/25/96 © 1996 United Feature Syndicate, Inc.
YEAH, IT MIGHT BE A GOOD SIGN, BUT I'M THINKING NOT.
WEEEE!!

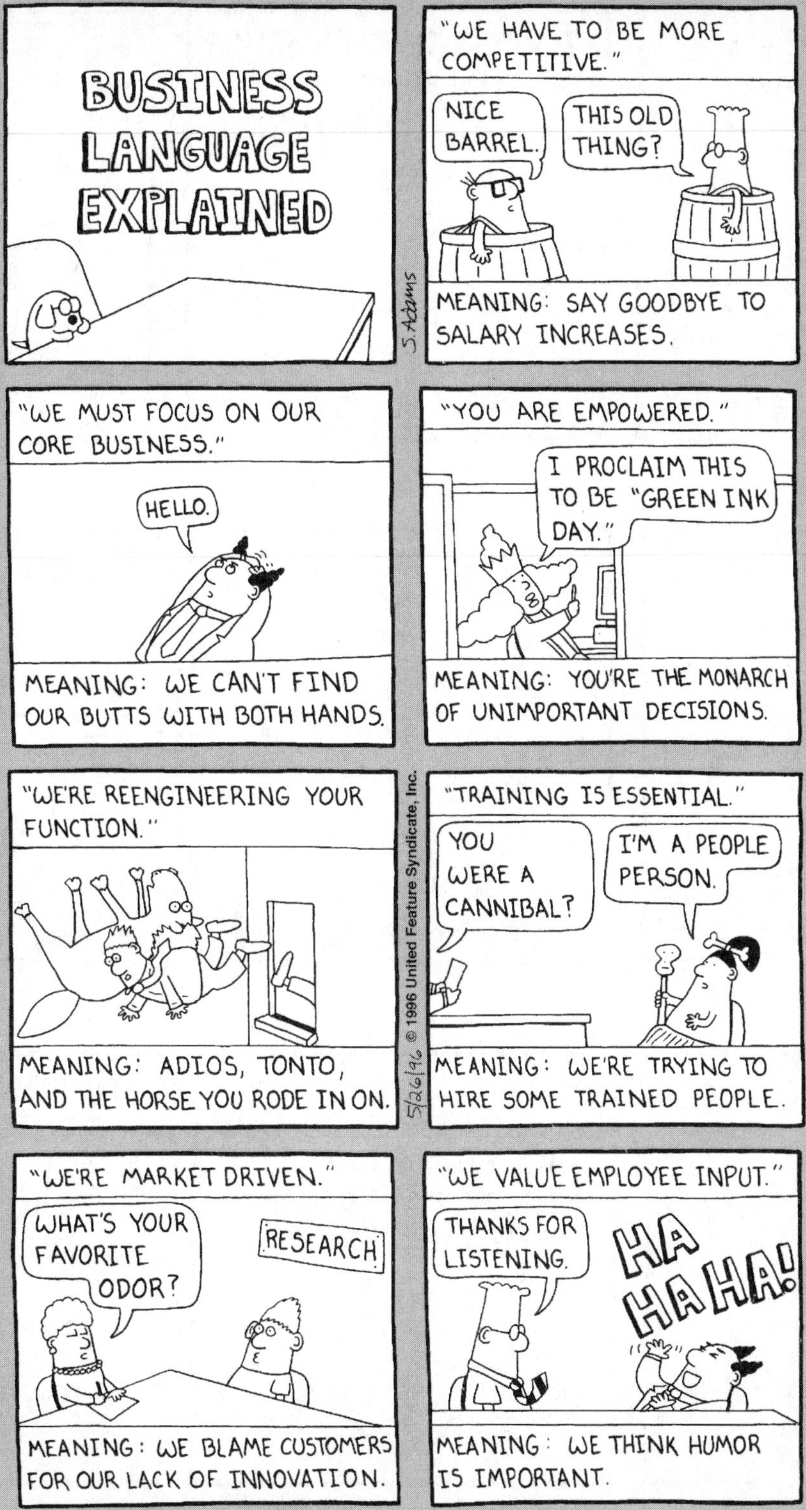
BUSINESS LANGUAGE EXPLAINED
S. Adams
"WE HAVE TO BE MORE COMPETITIVE."
NICE BARREL.
THIS OLD THING?
MEANING: SAY GOODBYE TO SALARY INCREASES.
"WE MUST FOCUS ON OUR CORE BUSINESS."
HELLO.
MEANING: WE CAN'T FIND OUR BUTTS WITH BOTH HANDS.
"YOU ARE EMPOWERED."
I PROCLAIM THIS TO BE "GREEN INK DAY."
MEANING: YOU'RE THE MONARCH OF UNIMPORTANT DECISIONS.
"WE'RE REENGINEERING YOUR FUNCTION."
MEANING: ADIOS, TONTO, AND THE HORSE YOU RODE IN ON.
5/26/96 © 1996 United Feature Syndicate, Inc.
"TRAINING IS ESSENTIAL."
YOU WERE A CANNIBAL?
I'M A PEOPLE PERSON.
MEANING: WE'RE TRYING TO HIRE SOME TRAINED PEOPLE.
"WE'RE MARKET DRIVEN."
WHAT'S YOUR FAVORITE ODOR?
RESEARCH
MEANING: WE BLAME CUSTOMERS FOR OUR LACK OF INNOVATION.
"WE VALUE EMPLOYEE INPUT."
THANKS FOR LISTENING.
HA HA HA!
MEANING: WE THINK HUMOR IS IMPORTANT.

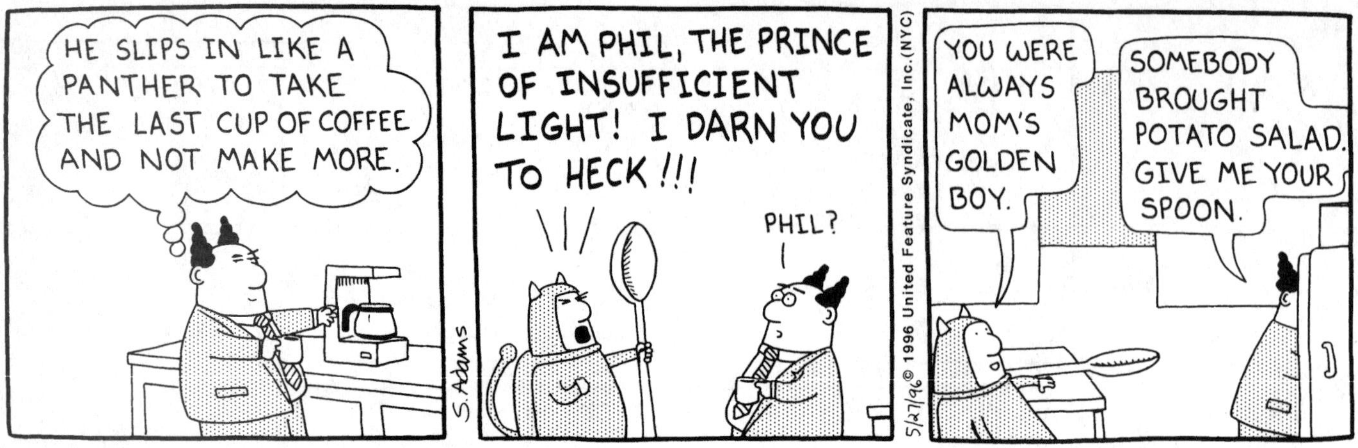
HE SLIPS IN LIKE A PANTHER TO TAKE THE LAST CUP OF COFFEE AND NOT MAKE MORE.
S. Adams
I AM PHIL, THE PRINCE OF INSUFFICIENT LIGHT! I DARN YOU TO HECK!!!
PHIL?
5/27/96 © 1996 United Feature Syndicate, Inc.(NYC)
YOU WERE ALWAYS MOM'S GOLDEN BOY.
SOMEBODY BROUGHT POTATO SALAD. GIVE ME YOUR SPOON.

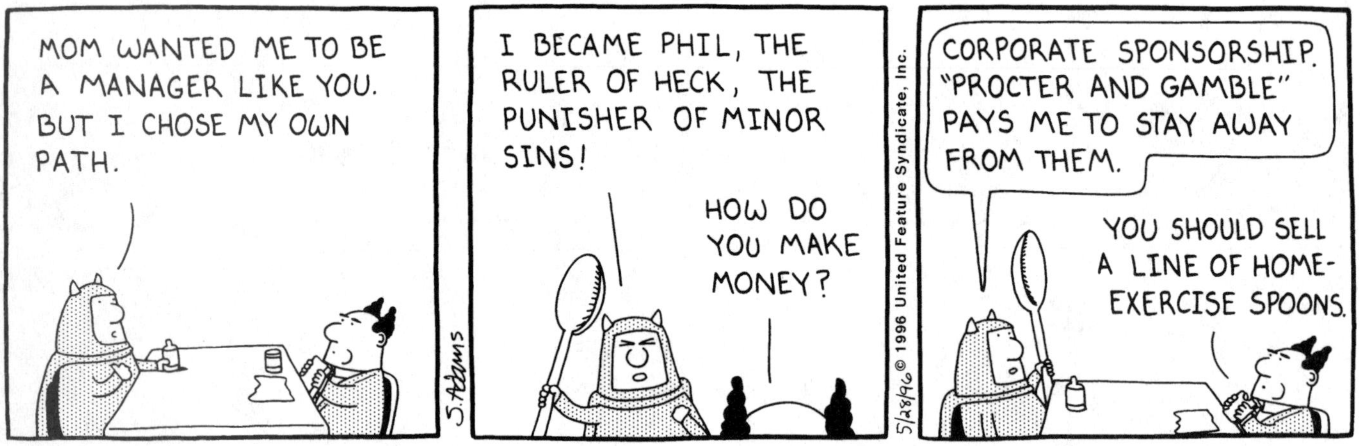
MOM WANTED ME TO BE A MANAGER LIKE YOU. BUT I CHOSE MY OWN PATH.
S. Adams
I BECAME PHIL, THE RULER OF HECK, THE PUNISHER OF MINOR SINS!
HOW DO YOU MAKE MONEY?
5/28/96 © 1996 United Feature Syndicate, Inc.
CORPORATE SPONSORSHIP. "PROCTER AND GAMBLE" PAYS ME TO STAY AWAY FROM THEM.
YOU SHOULD SELL A LINE OF HOME-EXERCISE SPOONS.

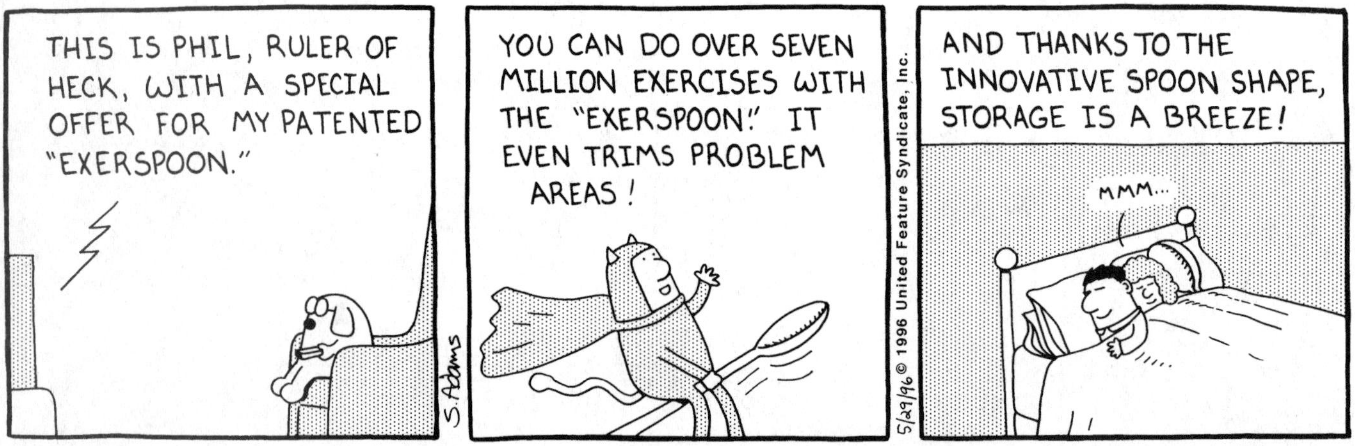
THIS IS PHIL, RULER OF HECK, WITH A SPECIAL OFFER FOR MY PATENTED "EXERSPOON."
S. Adams
YOU CAN DO OVER SEVEN MILLION EXERCISES WITH THE "EXERSPOON." IT EVEN TRIMS PROBLEM AREAS!
5/29/96 © 1996 United Feature Syndicate, Inc.
AND THANKS TO THE INNOVATIVE SPOON SHAPE, STORAGE IS A BREEZE!
MMM...

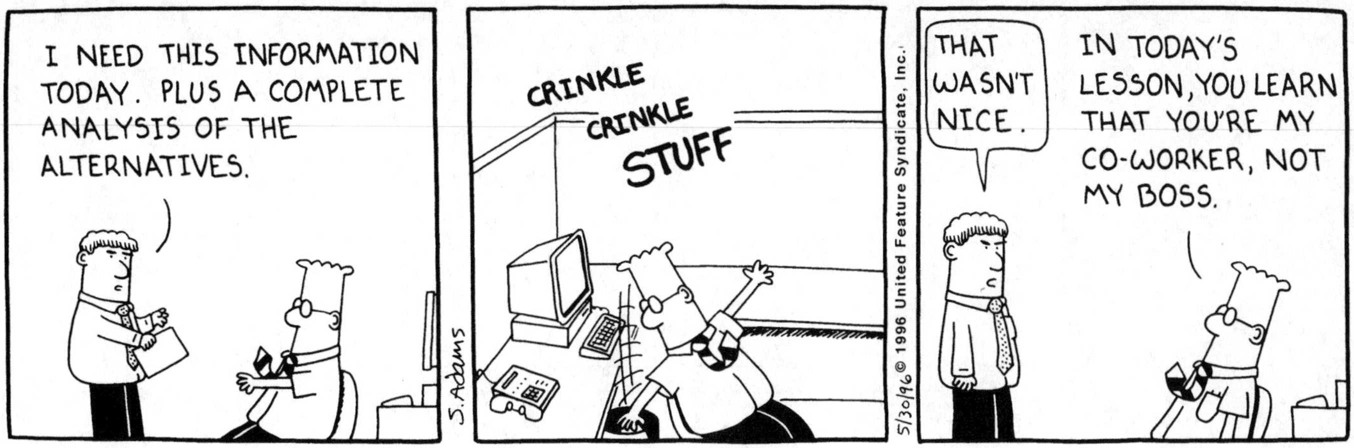
I NEED THIS INFORMATION TODAY. PLUS A COMPLETE ANALYSIS OF THE ALTERNATIVES.
S. Adams
CRINKLE
CRINKLE
STUFF
5/30/96 © 1996 United Feature Syndicate, Inc.
THAT WASN'T NICE.
IN TODAY'S LESSON, YOU LEARN THAT YOU'RE MY CO-WORKER, NOT MY BOSS.

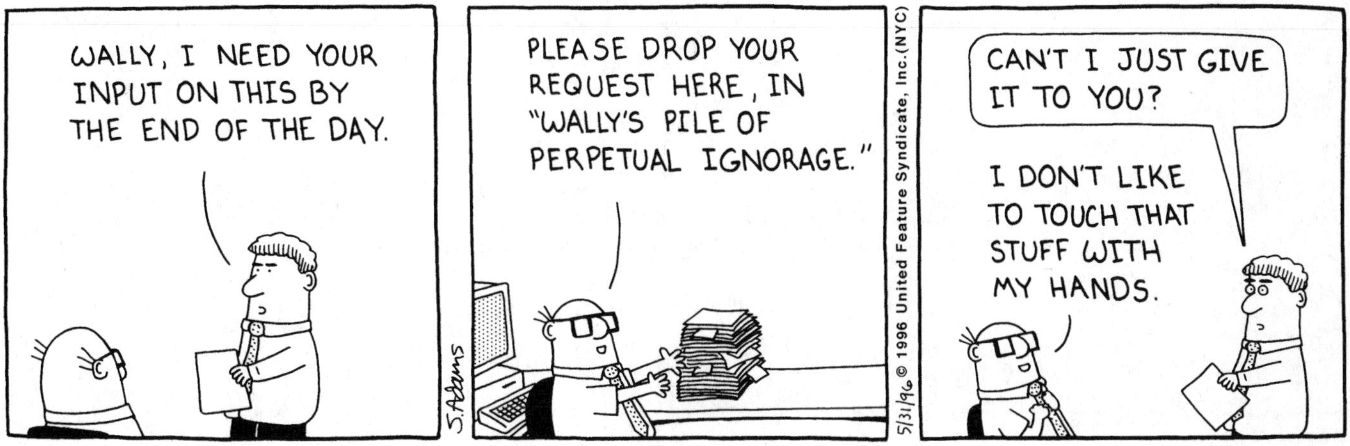
WALLY, I NEED YOUR INPUT ON THIS BY THE END OF THE DAY.
S. Adams
PLEASE DROP YOUR REQUEST HERE, IN "WALLY'S PILE OF PERPETUAL IGNORAGE."
5/31/96 © 1996 United Feature Syndicate, Inc.(NYC)
CAN'T I JUST GIVE IT TO YOU?
I DON'T LIKE TO TOUCH THAT STUFF WITH MY HANDS.

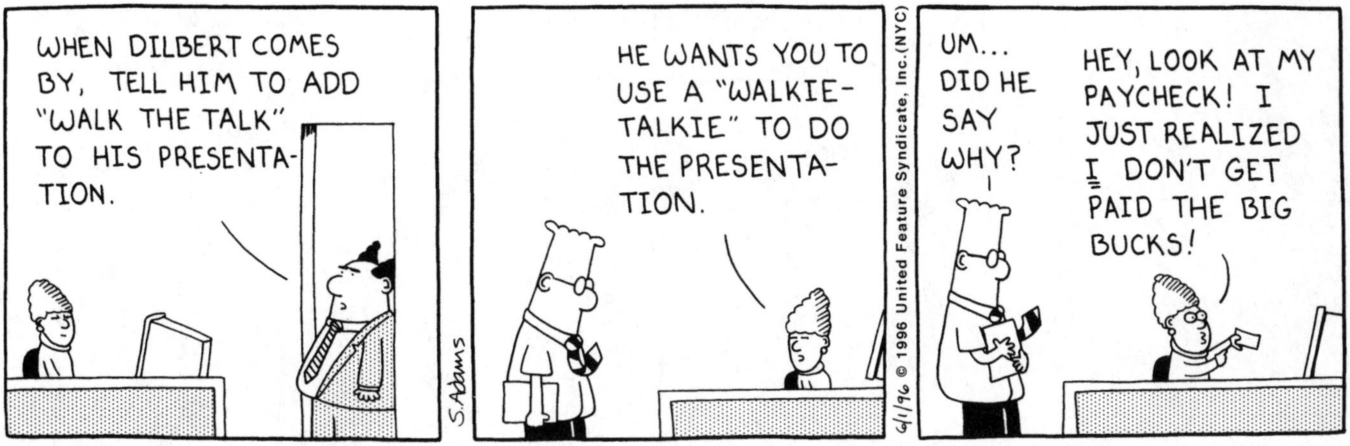
WHEN DILBERT COMES BY, TELL HIM TO ADD "WALK THE TALK" TO HIS PRESENTATION.
S. Adams
HE WANTS YOU TO USE A "WALKIE-TALKIE" TO DO THE PRESENTATION.
6/1/96 © 1996 United Feature Syndicate, Inc.(NYC)
UM... DID HE SAY WHY?
HEY, LOOK AT MY PAYCHECK! I JUST REALIZED I DON'T GET PAID THE BIG BUCKS!

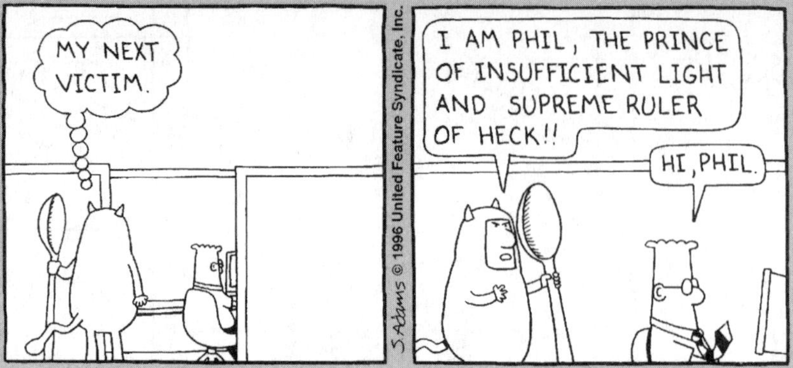
MY NEXT VICTIM.
S. Adams © 1996 United Feature Syndicate, Inc.
I AM PHIL, THE PRINCE OF INSUFFICIENT LIGHT AND SUPREME RULER OF HECK!!
HI, PHIL.

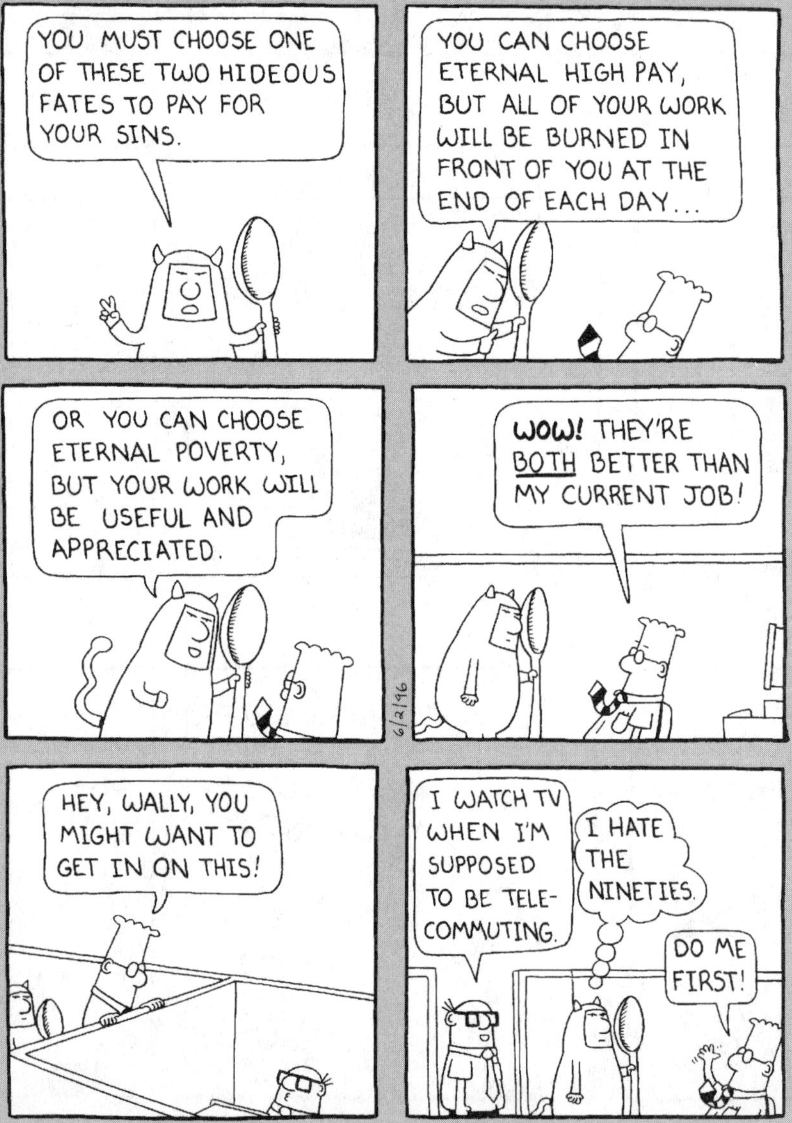
YOU MUST CHOOSE ONE OF THESE TWO HIDEOUS FATES TO PAY FOR YOUR SINS.
YOU CAN CHOOSE ETERNAL HIGH PAY, BUT ALL OF YOUR WORK WILL BE BURNED IN FRONT OF YOU AT THE END OF EACH DAY...
OR YOU CAN CHOOSE ETERNAL POVERTY, BUT YOUR WORK WILL BE USEFUL AND APPRECIATED.
6/2/96
WOW! THEY'RE BOTH BETTER THAN MY CURRENT JOB!
HEY, WALLY, YOU MIGHT WANT TO GET IN ON THIS!
I WATCH TV WHEN I'M SUPPOSED TO BE TELE-COMMUTING.
I HATE THE NINETIES.
DO ME FIRST!

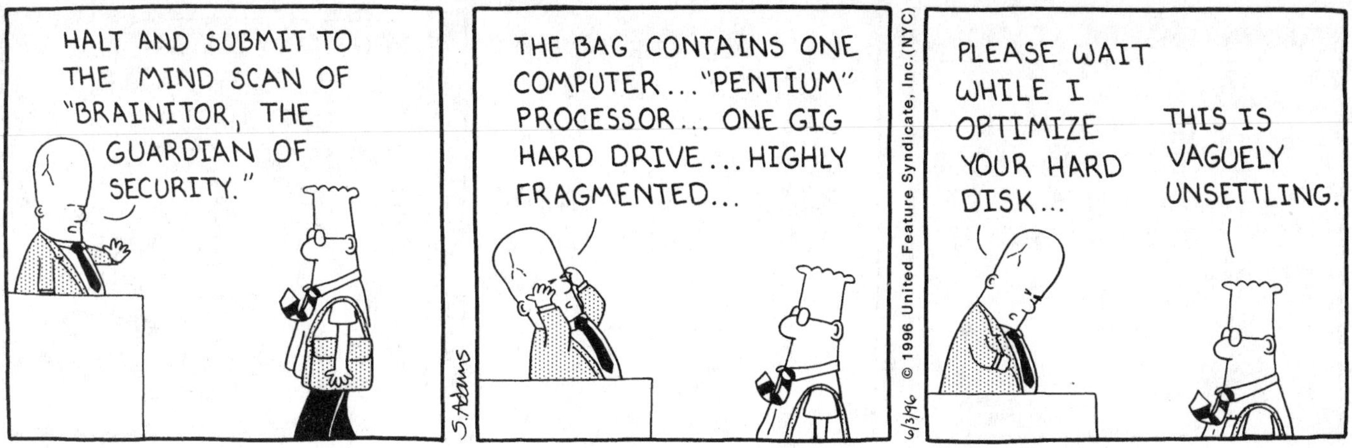
HALT AND SUBMIT TO THE MIND SCAN OF "BRAINITOR, THE GUARDIAN OF SECURITY."
THE BAG CONTAINS ONE COMPUTER ... "PENTIUM" PROCESSOR ... ONE GIG HARD DRIVE ... HIGHLY FRAGMENTED ...
PLEASE WAIT WHILE I OPTIMIZE YOUR HARD DISK ...
THIS IS VAGUELY UNSETTLING.
S. Adams
6/3/96 © 1996 United Feature Syndicate, Inc.(NYC)

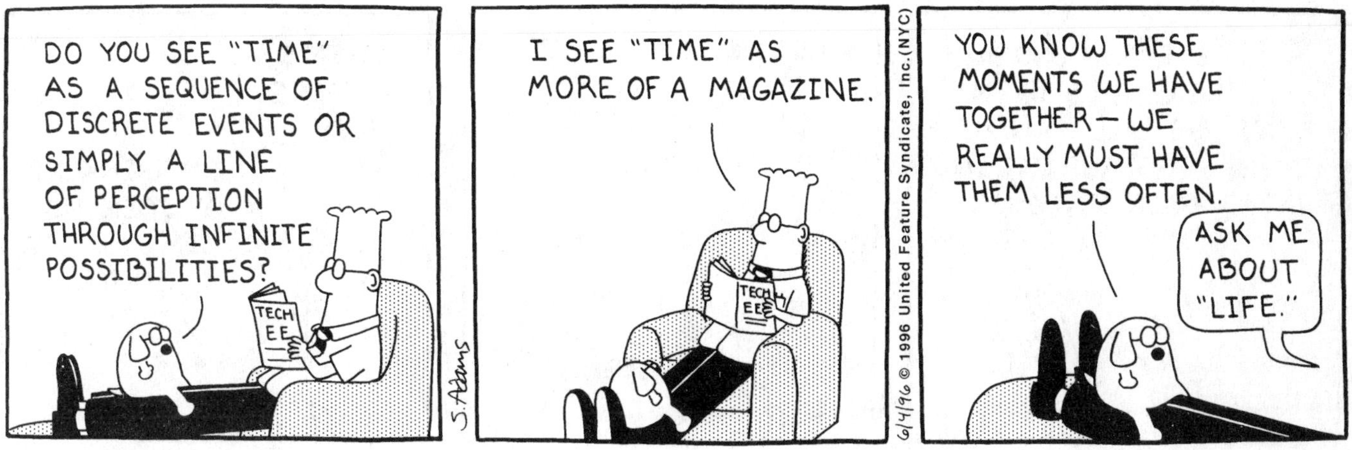
DO YOU SEE "TIME" AS A SEQUENCE OF DISCRETE EVENTS OR SIMPLY A LINE OF PERCEPTION THROUGH INFINITE POSSIBILITIES?
TECH EE
I SEE "TIME" AS MORE OF A MAGAZINE.
YOU KNOW THESE MOMENTS WE HAVE TOGETHER — WE REALLY MUST HAVE THEM LESS OFTEN.
ASK ME ABOUT "LIFE."
S. Adams
6/4/96 © 1996 United Feature Syndicate, Inc.(NYC)

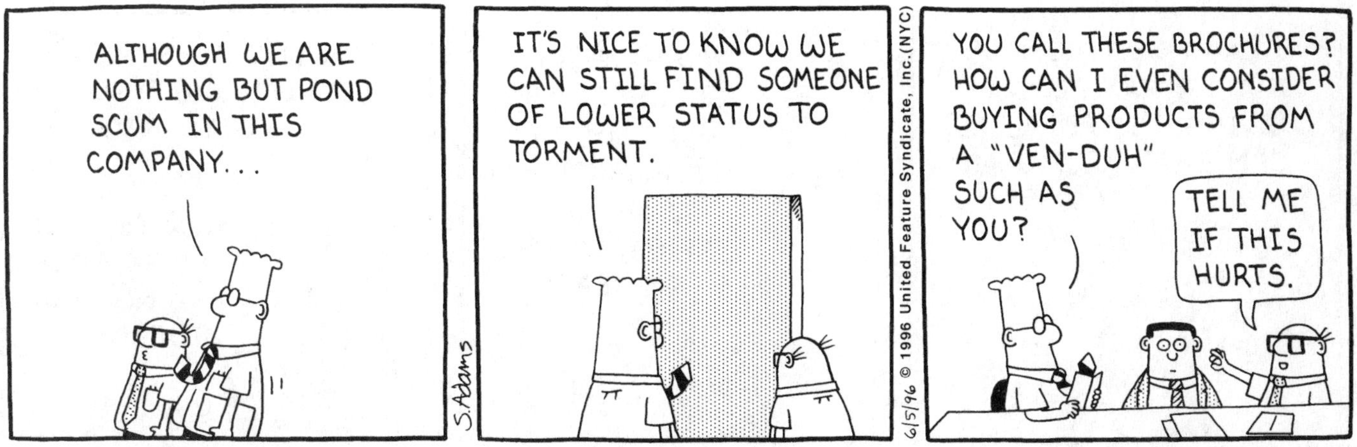
ALTHOUGH WE ARE NOTHING BUT POND SCUM IN THIS COMPANY...
IT'S NICE TO KNOW WE CAN STILL FIND SOMEONE OF LOWER STATUS TO TORMENT.
YOU CALL THESE BROCHURES? HOW CAN I EVEN CONSIDER BUYING PRODUCTS FROM A "VEN-DUH" SUCH AS YOU?
TELL ME IF THIS HURTS.
S. Adams
6/5/96 © 1996 United Feature Syndicate, Inc.(NYC)

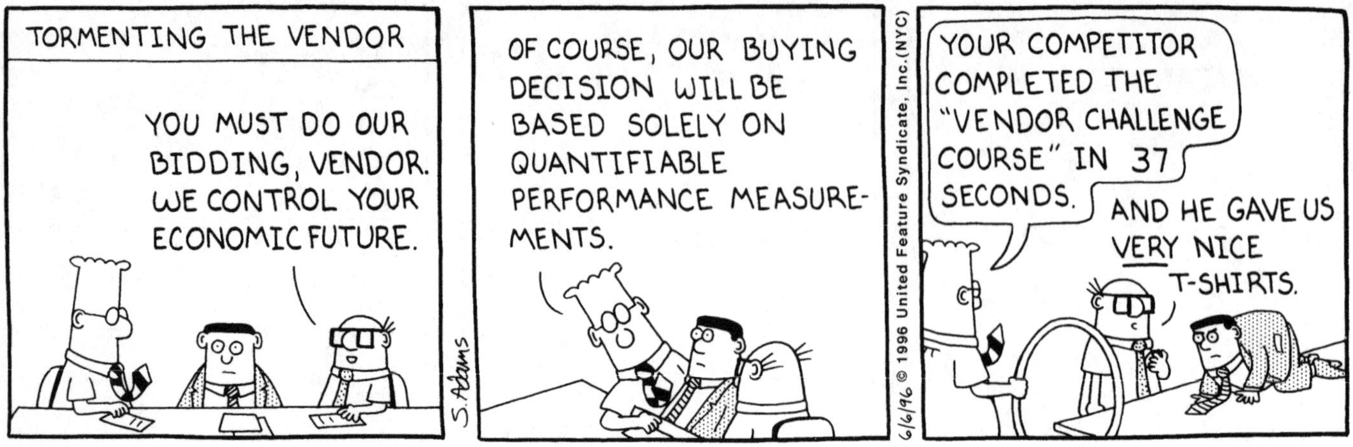
TORMENTING THE VENDOR
YOU MUST DO OUR BIDDING, VENDOR. WE CONTROL YOUR ECONOMIC FUTURE.
OF COURSE, OUR BUYING DECISION WILL BE BASED SOLELY ON QUANTIFIABLE PERFORMANCE MEASUREMENTS.
YOUR COMPETITOR COMPLETED THE "VENDOR CHALLENGE COURSE" IN 37 SECONDS.
AND HE GAVE US VERY NICE T-SHIRTS.
S. Adams
6/6/96 © 1996 United Feature Syndicate, Inc.(NYC)

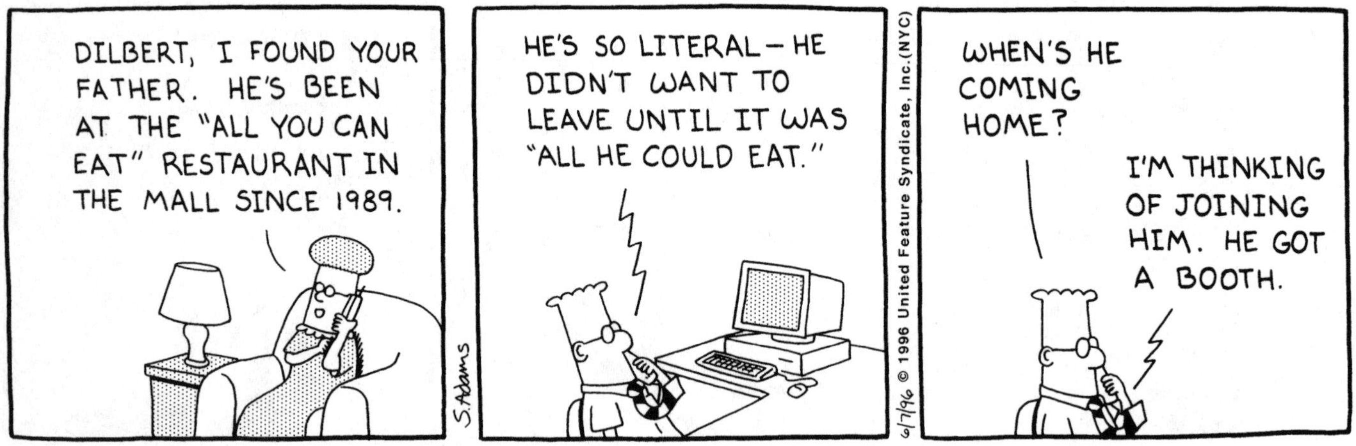
DILBERT, I FOUND YOUR FATHER. HE'S BEEN AT THE "ALL YOU CAN EAT" RESTAURANT IN THE MALL SINCE 1989.
HE'S SO LITERAL — HE DIDN'T WANT TO LEAVE UNTIL IT WAS "ALL HE COULD EAT."
WHEN'S HE COMING HOME?
I'M THINKING OF JOINING HIM. HE GOT A BOOTH.
S. Adams
6/7/96 © 1996 United Feature Syndicate, Inc.(NYC)

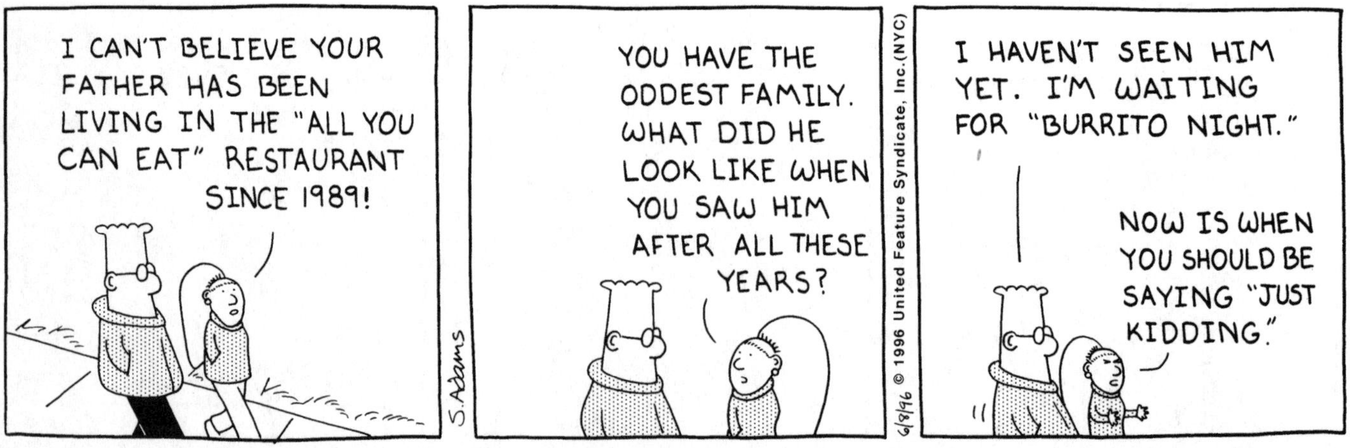
I CAN'T BELIEVE YOUR FATHER HAS BEEN LIVING IN THE "ALL YOU CAN EAT" RESTAURANT SINCE 1989!
YOU HAVE THE ODDEST FAMILY. WHAT DID HE LOOK LIKE WHEN YOU SAW HIM AFTER ALL THESE YEARS?
I HAVEN'T SEEN HIM YET. I'M WAITING FOR "BURRITO NIGHT."
NOW IS WHEN YOU SHOULD BE SAYING "JUST KIDDING."
S. Adams
6/8/96 © 1996 United Feature Syndicate, Inc.(NYC)

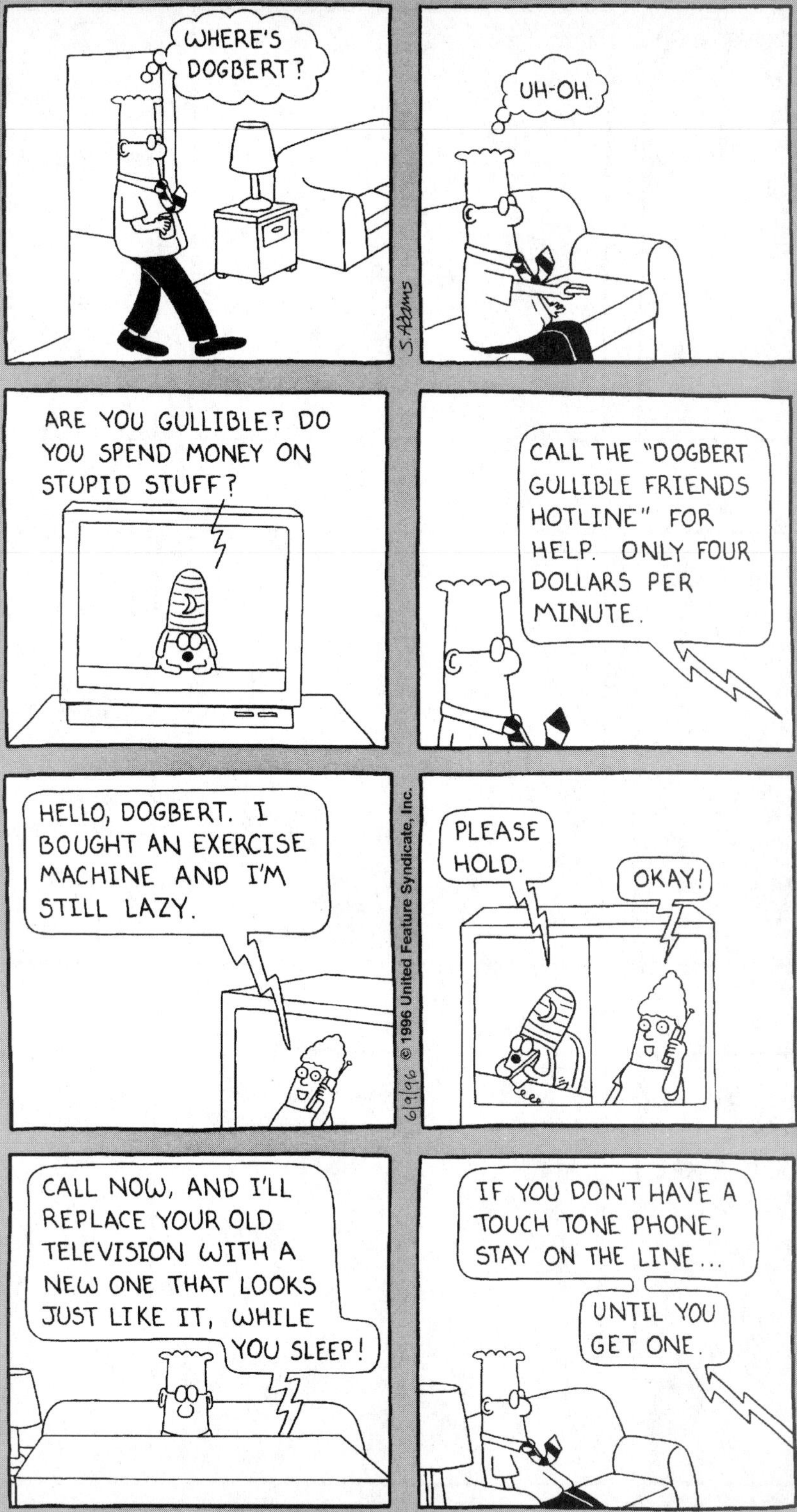
WHERE'S DOGBERT?
UH-OH.
ARE YOU GULLIBLE? DO YOU SPEND MONEY ON STUPID STUFF?
CALL THE "DOGBERT GULLIBLE FRIENDS HOTLINE" FOR HELP. ONLY FOUR DOLLARS PER MINUTE.
HELLO, DOGBERT. I BOUGHT AN EXERCISE MACHINE AND I'M STILL LAZY.
PLEASE HOLD.
OKAY!
CALL NOW, AND I'LL REPLACE YOUR OLD TELEVISION WITH A NEW ONE THAT LOOKS JUST LIKE IT, WHILE YOU SLEEP!
IF YOU DON'T HAVE A TOUCH TONE PHONE, STAY ON THE LINE...
UNTIL YOU GET ONE.
S.ADAMS
6/9/96 © 1996 United Feature Syndicate, Inc.

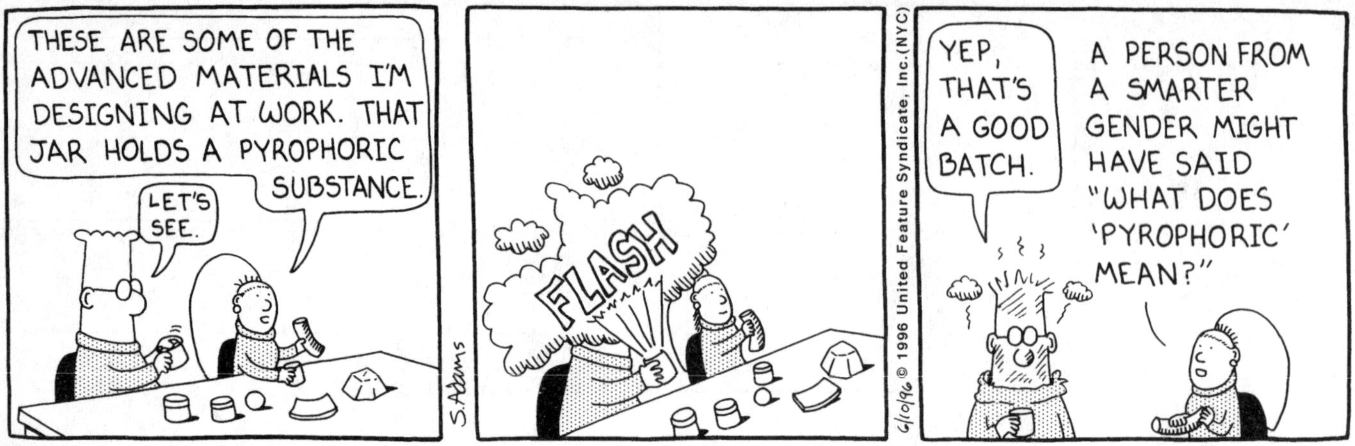
THESE ARE SOME OF THE ADVANCED MATERIALS I'M DESIGNING AT WORK. THAT JAR HOLDS A PYROPHORIC SUBSTANCE.
LET'S SEE.
S. Adams
FLASH
6/10/96 © 1996 United Feature Syndicate, Inc.(NYC)
YEP, THAT'S A GOOD BATCH.
A PERSON FROM A SMARTER GENDER MIGHT HAVE SAID "WHAT DOES 'PYROPHORIC' MEAN?"

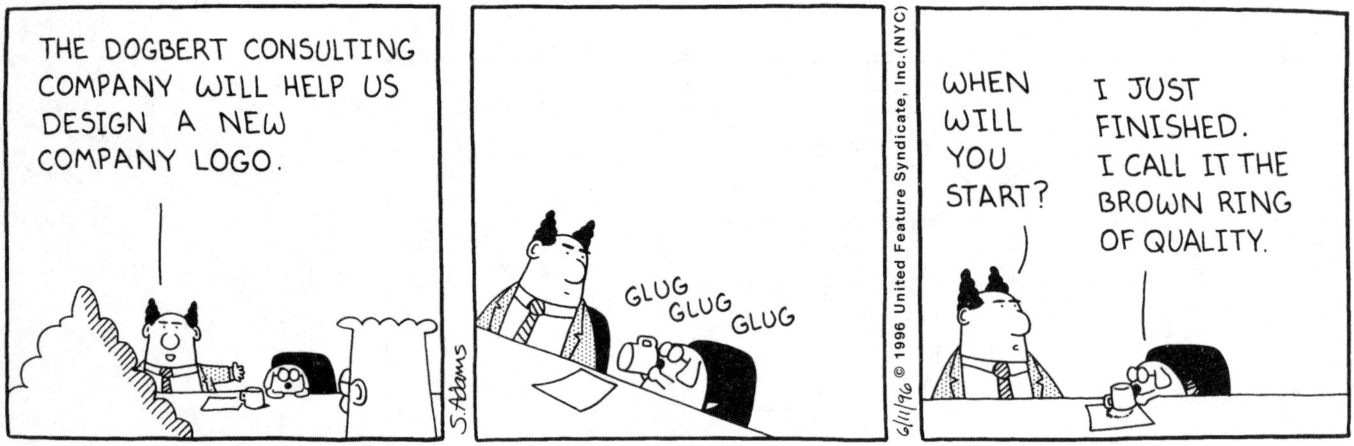
THE DOGBERT CONSULTING COMPANY WILL HELP US DESIGN A NEW COMPANY LOGO.
S. Adams
GLUG GLUG GLUG
6/11/96 © 1996 United Feature Syndicate, Inc.(NYC)
WHEN WILL YOU START?
I JUST FINISHED. I CALL IT THE BROWN RING OF QUALITY.

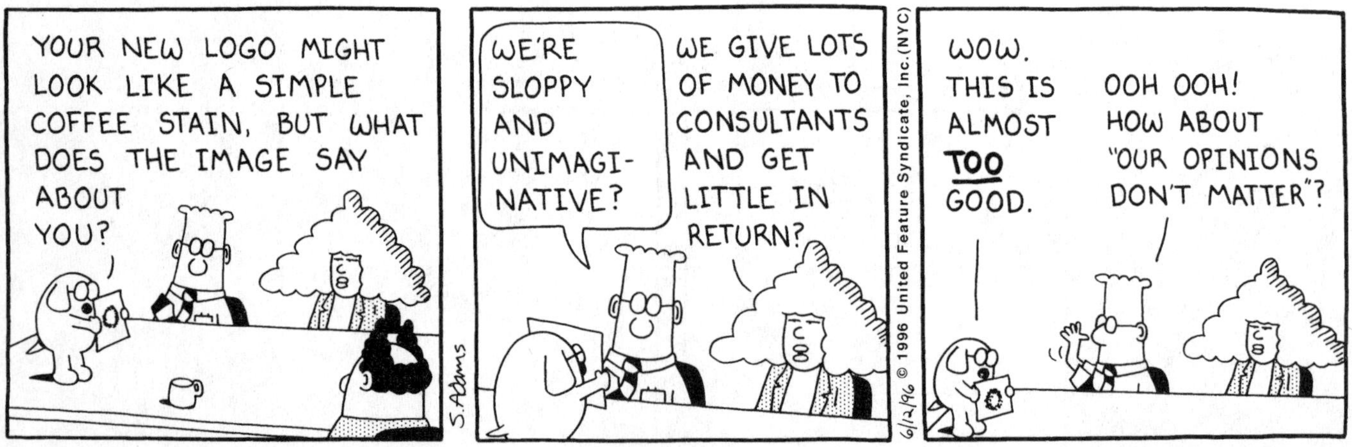
YOUR NEW LOGO MIGHT LOOK LIKE A SIMPLE COFFEE STAIN, BUT WHAT DOES THE IMAGE SAY ABOUT YOU?
S. Adams
WE'RE SLOPPY AND UNIMAGI-NATIVE?
WE GIVE LOTS OF MONEY TO CONSULTANTS AND GET LITTLE IN RETURN?
6/12/96 © 1996 United Feature Syndicate, Inc.(NYC)
WOW. THIS IS ALMOST TOO GOOD.
OOH OOH! HOW ABOUT "OUR OPINIONS DON'T MATTER"?

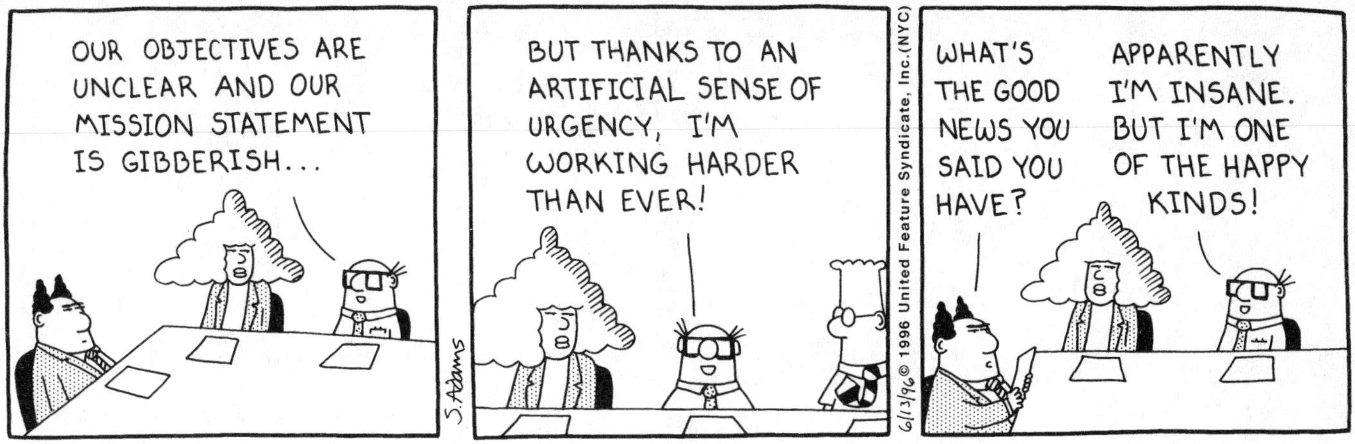
OUR OBJECTIVES ARE UNCLEAR AND OUR MISSION STATEMENT IS GIBBERISH...
S.Adams
BUT THANKS TO AN ARTIFICIAL SENSE OF URGENCY, I'M WORKING HARDER THAN EVER!
6/13/96 © 1996 United Feature Syndicate, Inc.(NYC)
WHAT'S THE GOOD NEWS YOU SAID YOU HAVE?
APPARENTLY I'M INSANE. BUT I'M ONE OF THE HAPPY KINDS!

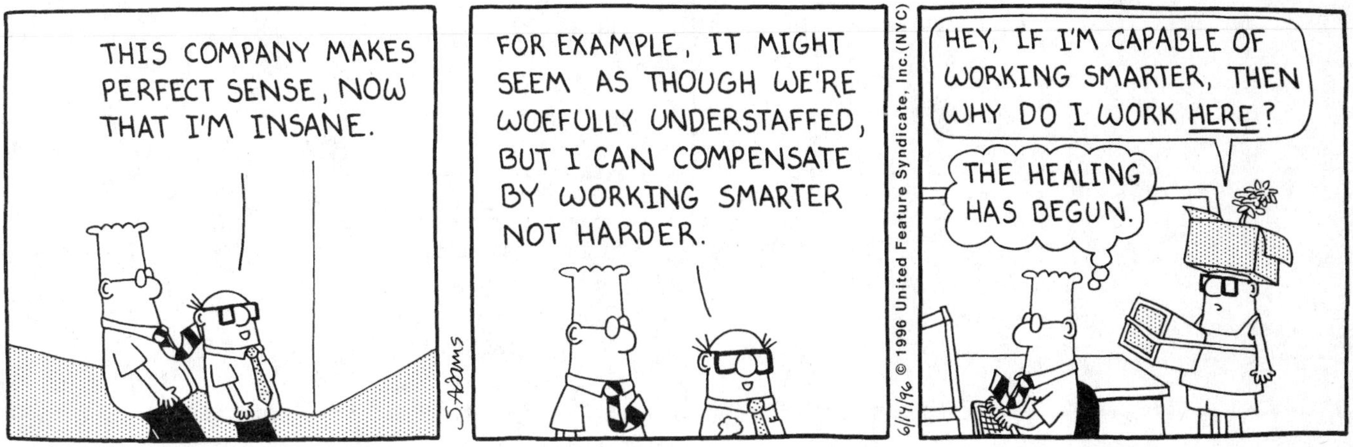
THIS COMPANY MAKES PERFECT SENSE, NOW THAT I'M INSANE.
S.Adams
FOR EXAMPLE, IT MIGHT SEEM AS THOUGH WE'RE WOEFULLY UNDERSTAFFED, BUT I CAN COMPENSATE BY WORKING SMARTER NOT HARDER.
6/14/96 © 1996 United Feature Syndicate, Inc.(NYC)
HEY, IF I'M CAPABLE OF WORKING SMARTER, THEN WHY DO I WORK HERE?
THE HEALING HAS BEGUN.

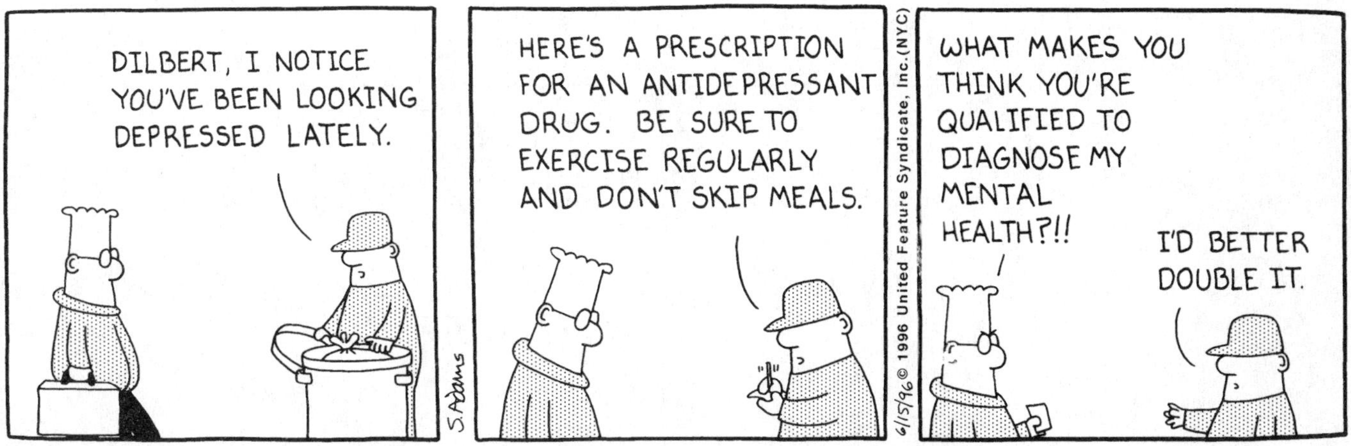
DILBERT, I NOTICE YOU'VE BEEN LOOKING DEPRESSED LATELY.
S.Adams
HERE'S A PRESCRIPTION FOR AN ANTIDEPRESSANT DRUG. BE SURE TO EXERCISE REGULARLY AND DON'T SKIP MEALS.
6/15/96 © 1996 United Feature Syndicate, Inc.(NYC)
WHAT MAKES YOU THINK YOU'RE QUALIFIED TO DIAGNOSE MY MENTAL HEALTH?!!
I'D BETTER DOUBLE IT.

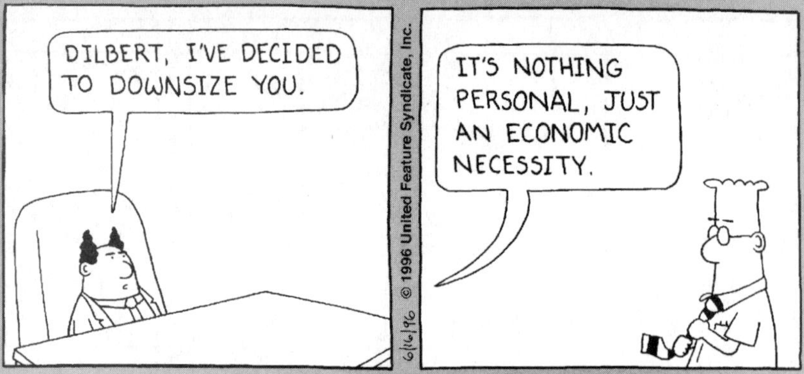
DILBERT, I'VE DECIDED TO DOWNSIZE YOU.
IT'S NOTHING PERSONAL, JUST AN ECONOMIC NECESSITY.
6/16/96 © 1996 United Feature Syndicate, Inc.

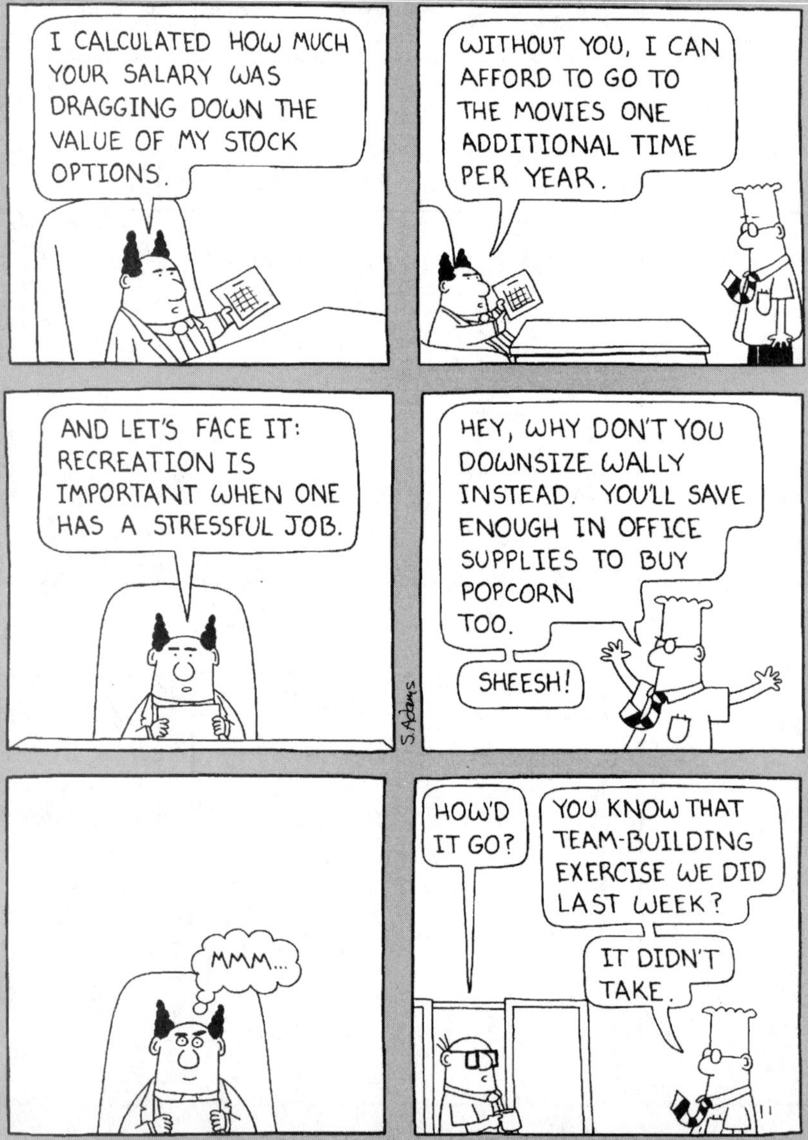
I CALCULATED HOW MUCH YOUR SALARY WAS DRAGGING DOWN THE VALUE OF MY STOCK OPTIONS.
WITHOUT YOU, I CAN AFFORD TO GO TO THE MOVIES ONE ADDITIONAL TIME PER YEAR.
AND LET'S FACE IT: RECREATION IS IMPORTANT WHEN ONE HAS A STRESSFUL JOB.
HEY, WHY DON'T YOU DOWNSIZE WALLY INSTEAD. YOU'LL SAVE ENOUGH IN OFFICE SUPPLIES TO BUY POPCORN TOO.
SHEESH!
S.Adams
MMM...
HOW'D IT GO?
YOU KNOW THAT TEAM-BUILDING EXERCISE WE DID LAST WEEK?
IT DIDN'T TAKE.

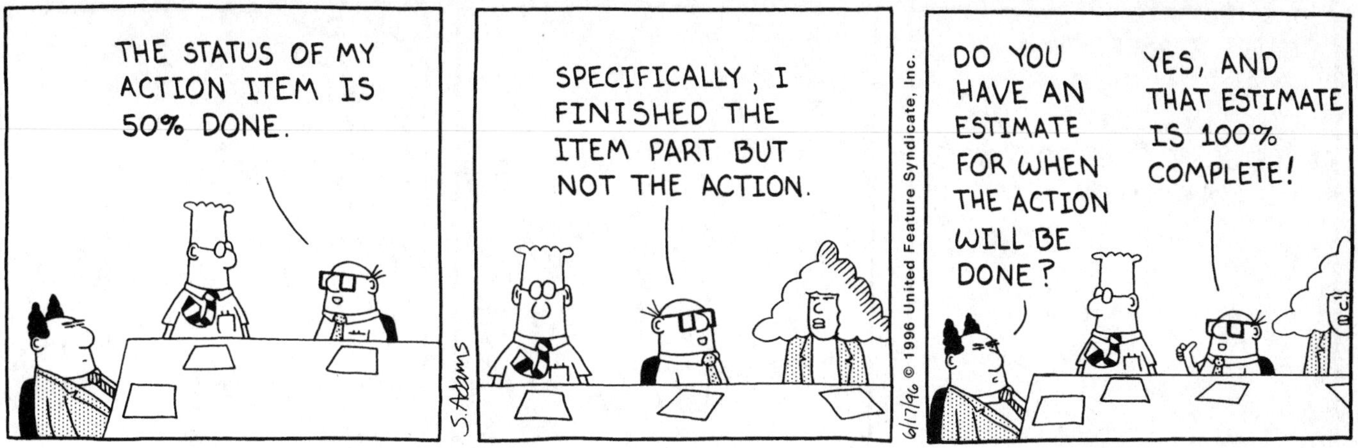
THE STATUS OF MY ACTION ITEM IS 50% DONE.
SPECIFICALLY, I FINISHED THE ITEM PART BUT NOT THE ACTION.
DO YOU HAVE AN ESTIMATE FOR WHEN THE ACTION WILL BE DONE?
YES, AND THAT ESTIMATE IS 100% COMPLETE!
S. Adams
6/17/96 © 1996 United Feature Syndicate, Inc.

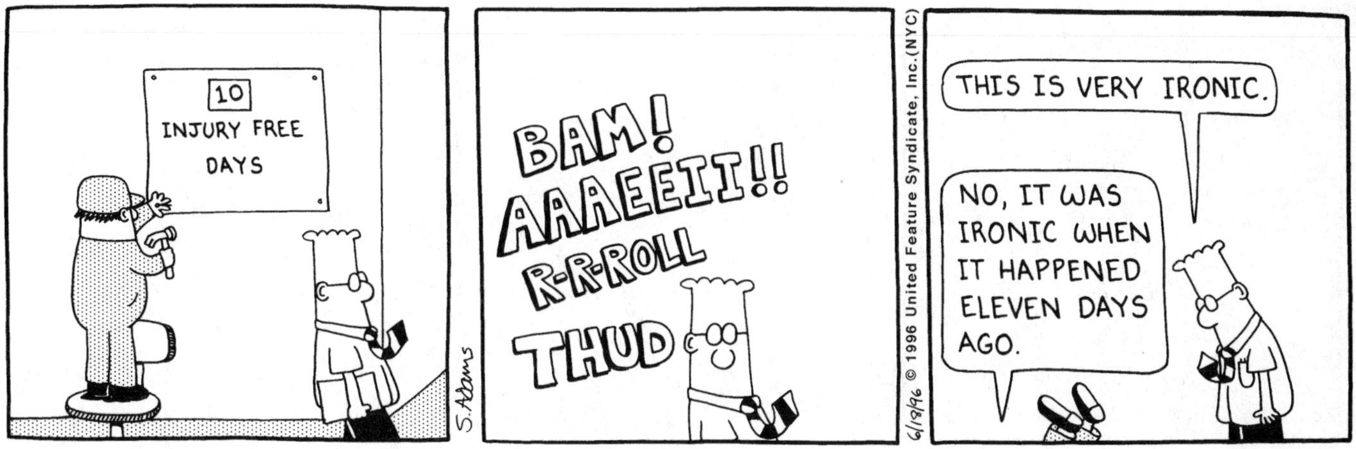
10
INJURY FREE DAYS
BAM!
AAAEEII!!
R-R-ROLL
THUD
THIS IS VERY IRONIC.
NO, IT WAS IRONIC WHEN IT HAPPENED ELEVEN DAYS AGO.
S. Adams
6/18/96 © 1996 United Feature Syndicate, Inc.(NYC)

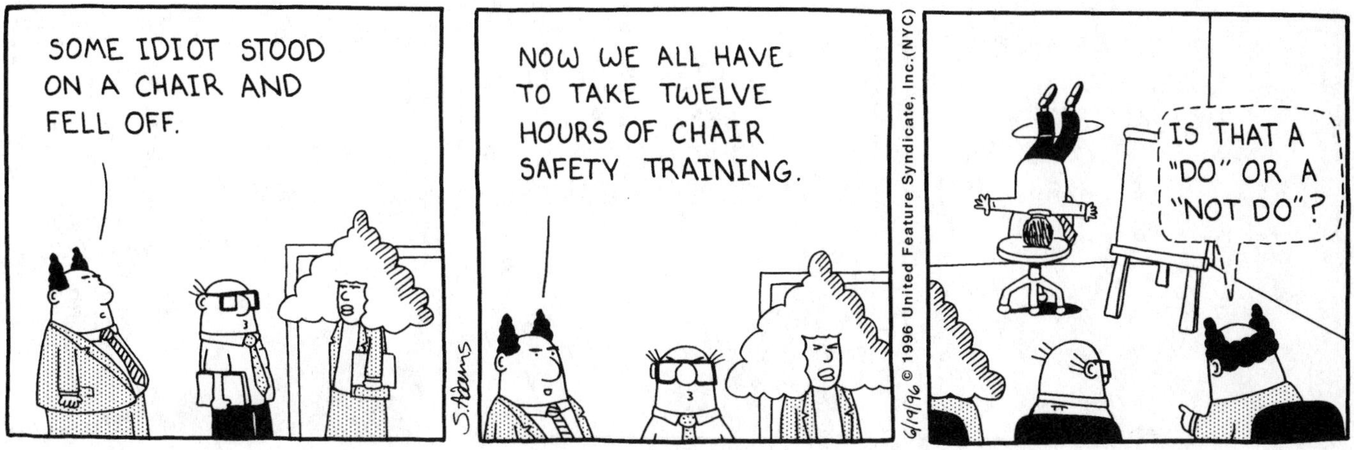
SOME IDIOT STOOD ON A CHAIR AND FELL OFF.
NOW WE ALL HAVE TO TAKE TWELVE HOURS OF CHAIR SAFETY TRAINING.
IS THAT A "DO" OR A "NOT DO"?
S. Adams
6/19/96 © 1996 United Feature Syndicate, Inc.(NYC)

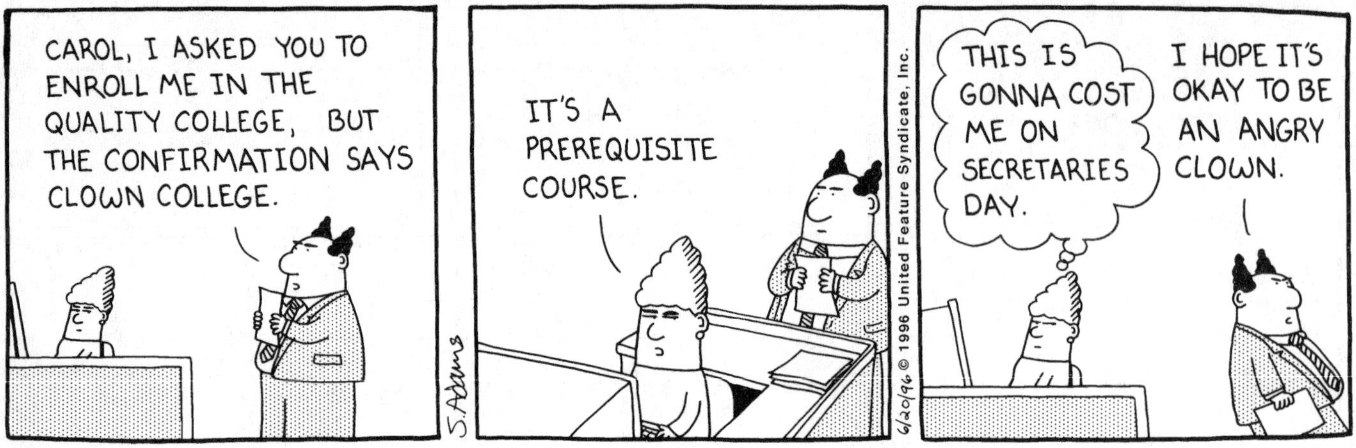
CAROL, I ASKED YOU TO ENROLL ME IN THE QUALITY COLLEGE, BUT THE CONFIRMATION SAYS CLOWN COLLEGE.
IT'S A PREREQUISITE COURSE.
THIS IS GONNA COST ME ON SECRETARIES DAY.
I HOPE IT'S OKAY TO BE AN ANGRY CLOWN.
S. Adams
6/20/96 © 1996 United Feature Syndicate, Inc.

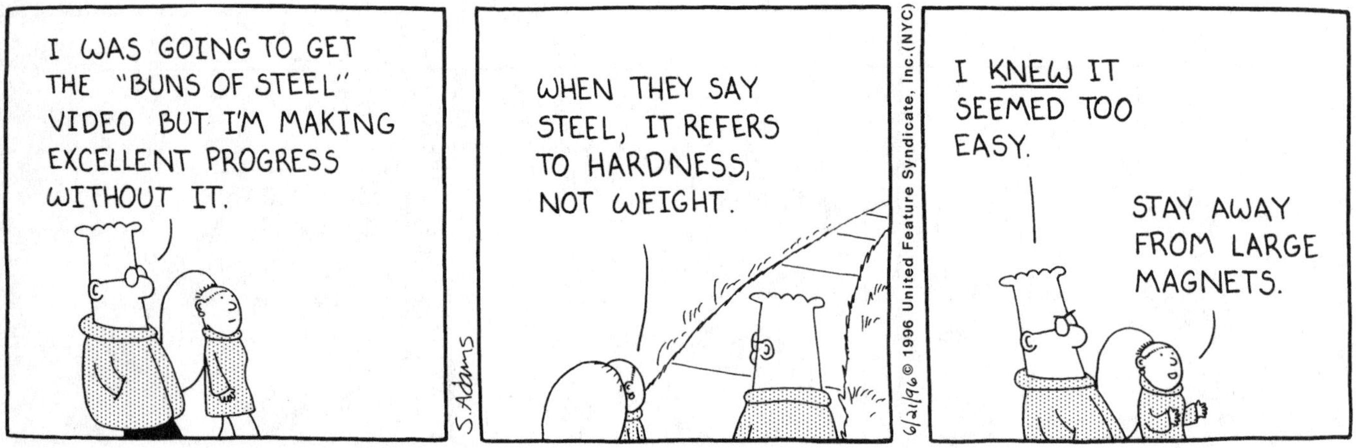
I WAS GOING TO GET THE "BUNS OF STEEL" VIDEO BUT I'M MAKING EXCELLENT PROGRESS WITHOUT IT.
WHEN THEY SAY STEEL, IT REFERS TO HARDNESS, NOT WEIGHT.
I KNEW IT SEEMED TOO EASY.
STAY AWAY FROM LARGE MAGNETS.
S. Adams
6/21/96 © 1996 United Feature Syndicate, Inc.(NYC)

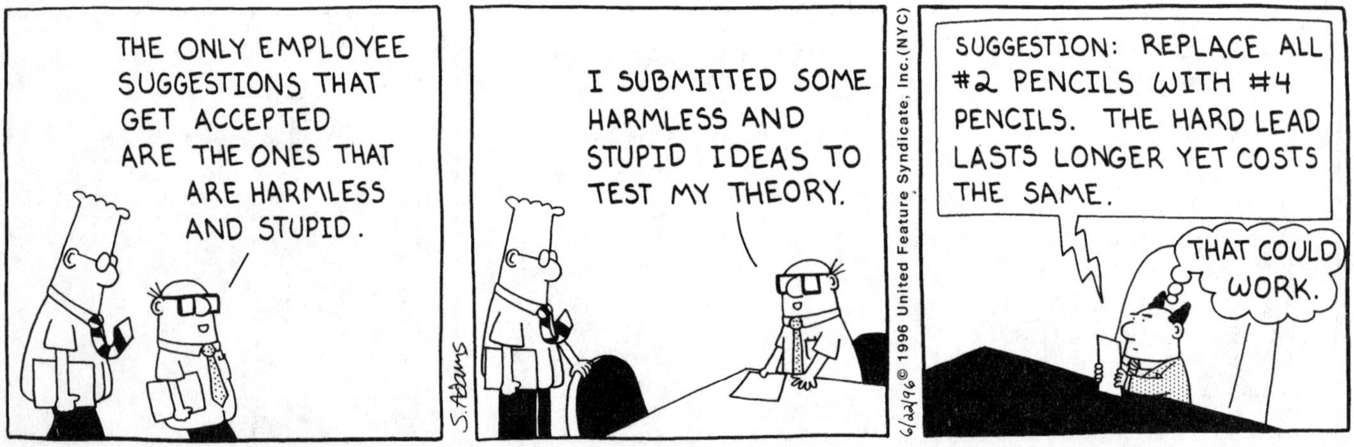
THE ONLY EMPLOYEE SUGGESTIONS THAT GET ACCEPTED ARE THE ONES THAT ARE HARMLESS AND STUPID.
I SUBMITTED SOME HARMLESS AND STUPID IDEAS TO TEST MY THEORY.
SUGGESTION: REPLACE ALL #2 PENCILS WITH #4 PENCILS. THE HARD LEAD LASTS LONGER YET COSTS THE SAME.
THAT COULD WORK.
S. Adams
6/22/96 © 1996 United Feature Syndicate, Inc.(NYC)

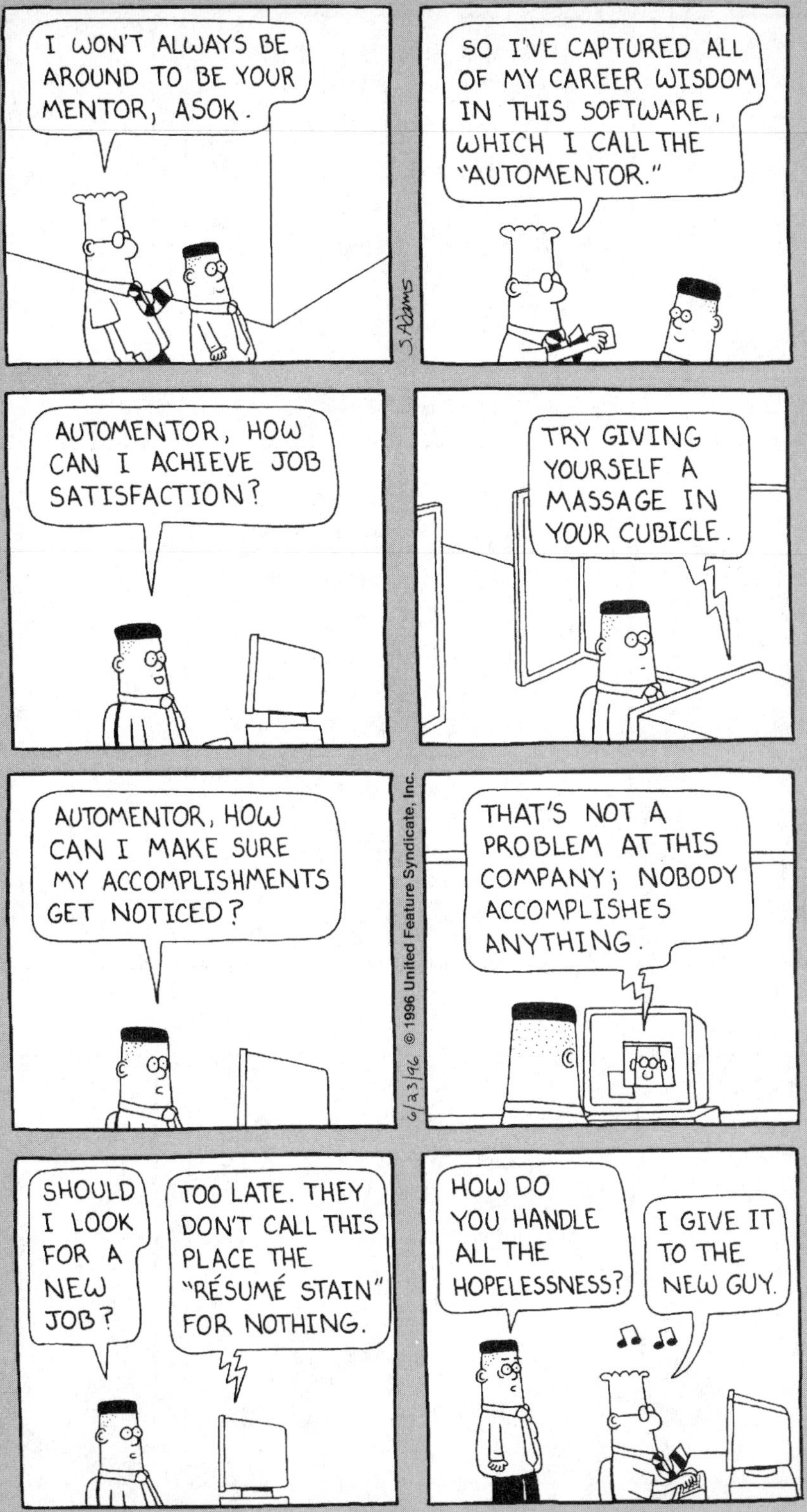
I WON'T ALWAYS BE AROUND TO BE YOUR MENTOR, ASOK.
SO I'VE CAPTURED ALL OF MY CAREER WISDOM IN THIS SOFTWARE, WHICH I CALL THE "AUTOMENTOR."
S. Adams
AUTOMENTOR, HOW CAN I ACHIEVE JOB SATISFACTION?
TRY GIVING YOURSELF A MASSAGE IN YOUR CUBICLE.
AUTOMENTOR, HOW CAN I MAKE SURE MY ACCOMPLISHMENTS GET NOTICED?
6/23/96 © 1996 United Feature Syndicate, Inc.
THAT'S NOT A PROBLEM AT THIS COMPANY; NOBODY ACCOMPLISHES ANYTHING.
SHOULD I LOOK FOR A NEW JOB?
TOO LATE. THEY DON'T CALL THIS PLACE THE "RÉSUMÉ STAIN" FOR NOTHING.
HOW DO YOU HANDLE ALL THE HOPELESSNESS?
I GIVE IT TO THE NEW GUY.

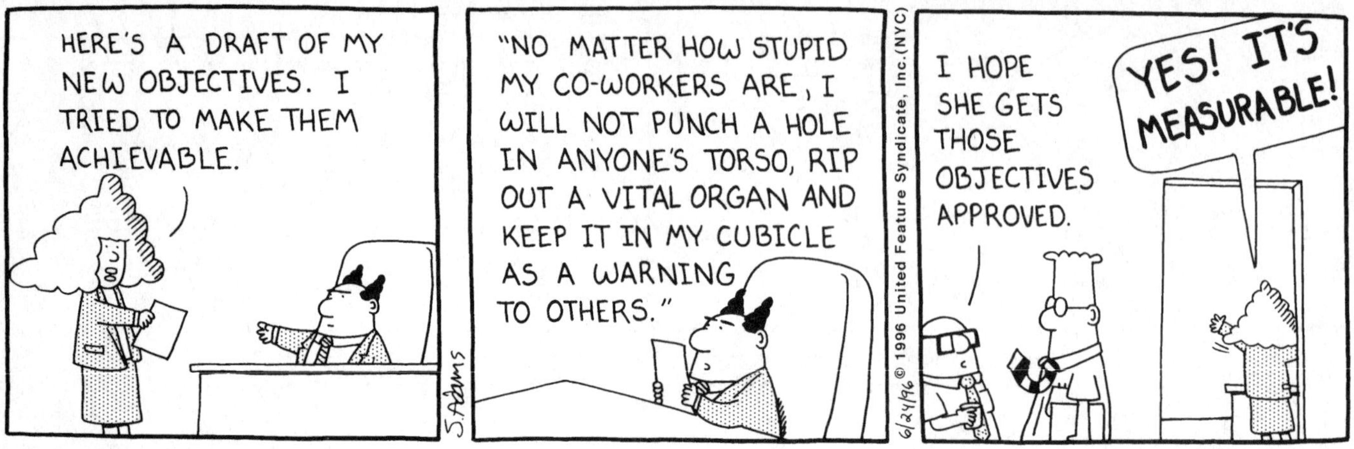
HERE'S A DRAFT OF MY NEW OBJECTIVES. I TRIED TO MAKE THEM ACHIEVABLE.
S.Adams
"NO MATTER HOW STUPID MY CO-WORKERS ARE, I WILL NOT PUNCH A HOLE IN ANYONE'S TORSO, RIP OUT A VITAL ORGAN AND KEEP IT IN MY CUBICLE AS A WARNING TO OTHERS."
6/24/96 © 1996 United Feature Syndicate, Inc.(NYC)
I HOPE SHE GETS THOSE OBJECTIVES APPROVED.
YES! IT'S MEASURABLE!

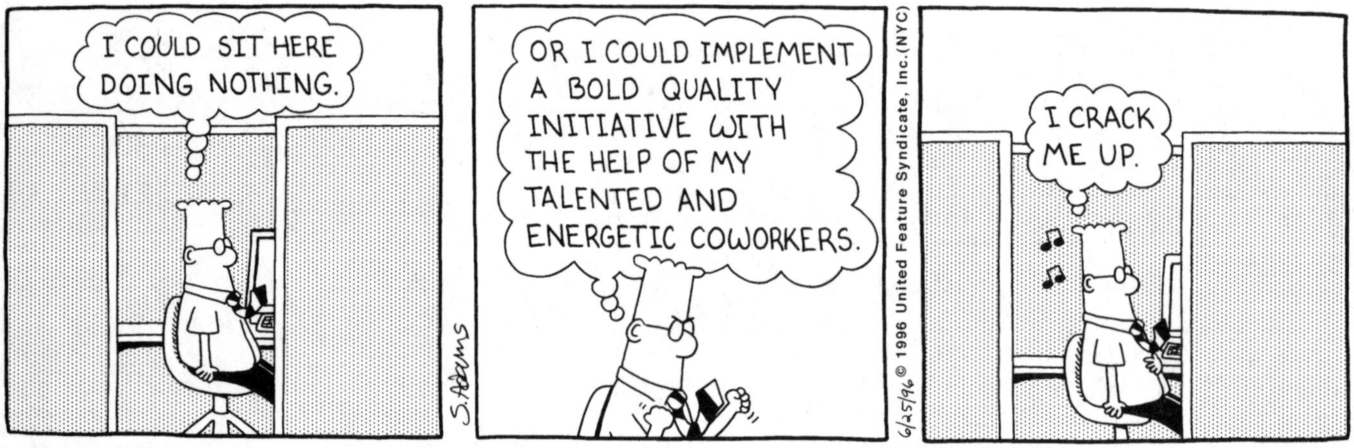
I COULD SIT HERE DOING NOTHING.
S.Adams
OR I COULD IMPLEMENT A BOLD QUALITY INITIATIVE WITH THE HELP OF MY TALENTED AND ENERGETIC COWORKERS.
6/25/96 © 1996 United Feature Syndicate, Inc.(NYC)
I CRACK ME UP.

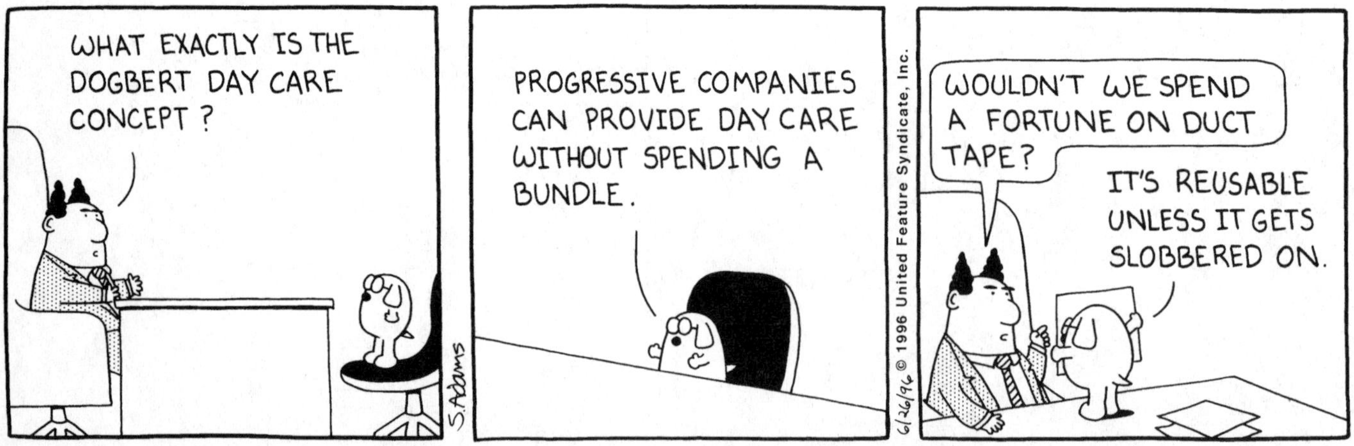
WHAT EXACTLY IS THE DOGBERT DAY CARE CONCEPT ?
S.Adams
PROGRESSIVE COMPANIES CAN PROVIDE DAY CARE WITHOUT SPENDING A BUNDLE.
6/26/96 © 1996 United Feature Syndicate, Inc.
WOULDN'T WE SPEND A FORTUNE ON DUCT TAPE?
IT'S REUSABLE UNLESS IT GETS SLOBBERED ON.

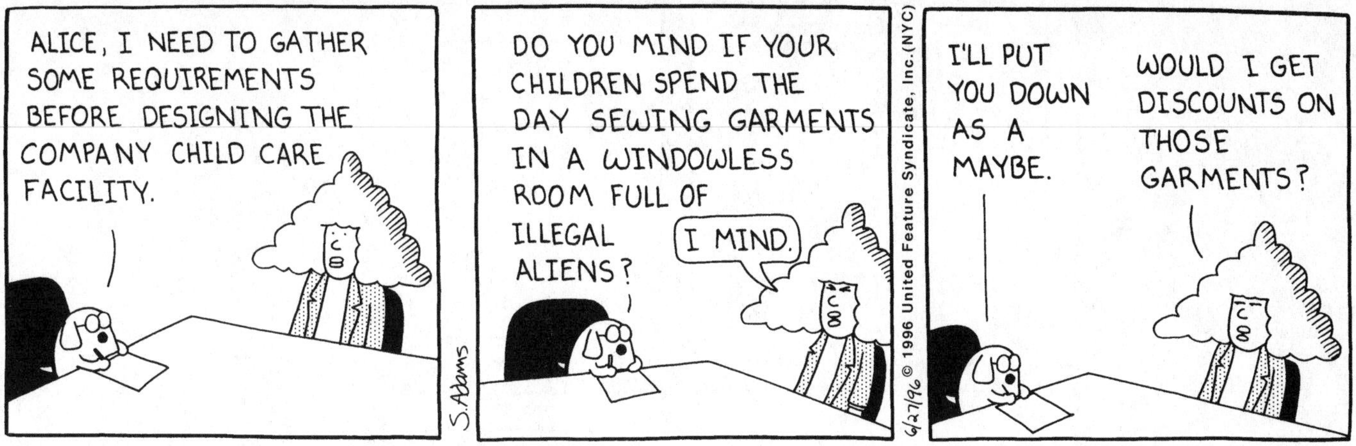
ALICE, I NEED TO GATHER SOME REQUIREMENTS BEFORE DESIGNING THE COMPANY CHILD CARE FACILITY.
S. Adams
DO YOU MIND IF YOUR CHILDREN SPEND THE DAY SEWING GARMENTS IN A WINDOWLESS ROOM FULL OF ILLEGAL ALIENS?
I MIND.
6/27/96 © 1996 United Feature Syndicate, Inc.(NYC)
I'LL PUT YOU DOWN AS A MAYBE.
WOULD I GET DISCOUNTS ON THOSE GARMENTS?

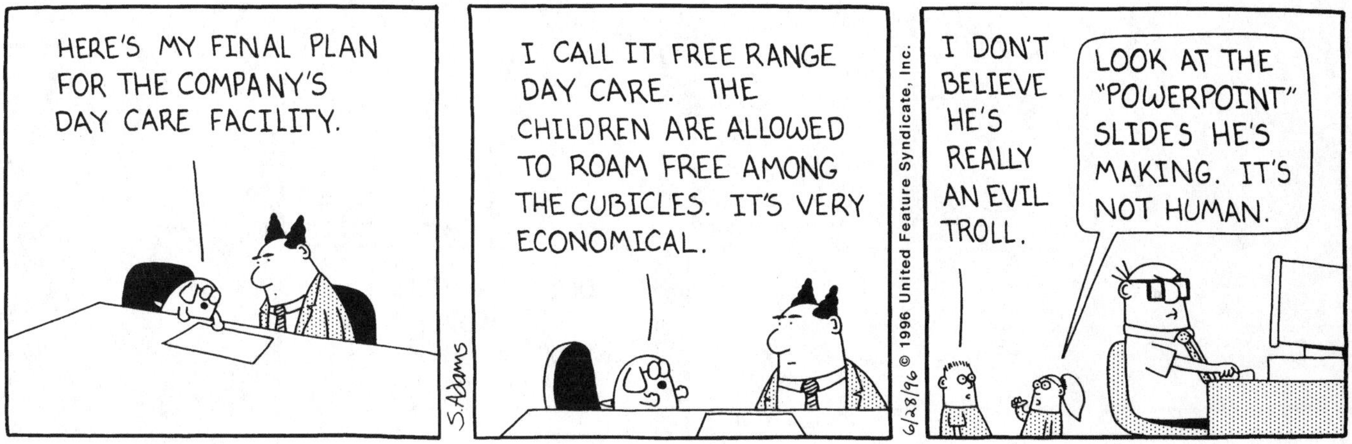
HERE'S MY FINAL PLAN FOR THE COMPANY'S DAY CARE FACILITY.
S. Adams
I CALL IT FREE RANGE DAY CARE. THE CHILDREN ARE ALLOWED TO ROAM FREE AMONG THE CUBICLES. IT'S VERY ECONOMICAL.
6/28/96 © 1996 United Feature Syndicate, Inc.
I DON'T BELIEVE HE'S REALLY AN EVIL TROLL.
LOOK AT THE "POWERPOINT" SLIDES HE'S MAKING. IT'S NOT HUMAN.

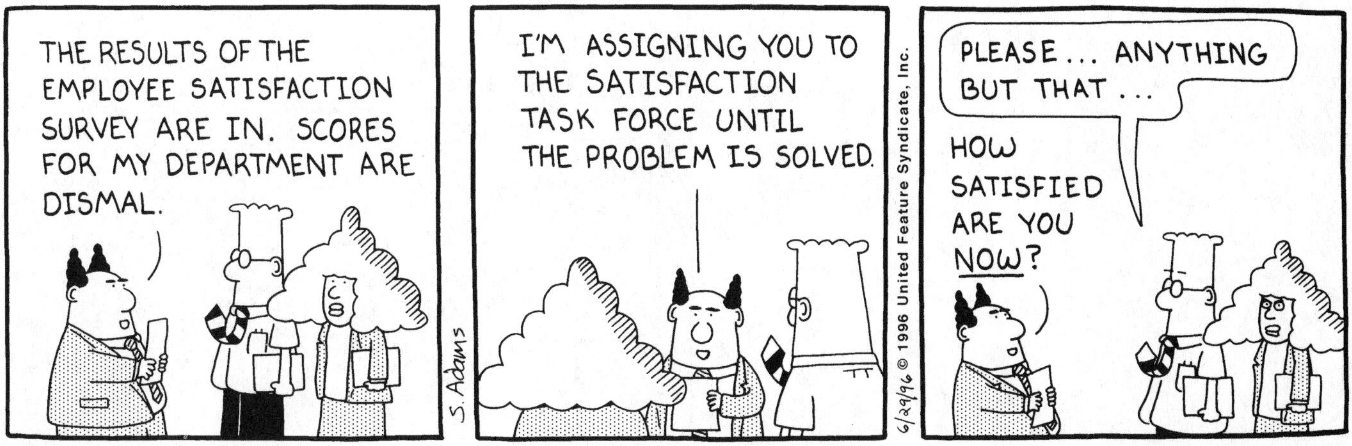
THE RESULTS OF THE EMPLOYEE SATISFACTION SURVEY ARE IN. SCORES FOR MY DEPARTMENT ARE DISMAL.
S. Adams
I'M ASSIGNING YOU TO THE SATISFACTION TASK FORCE UNTIL THE PROBLEM IS SOLVED.
6/29/96 © 1996 United Feature Syndicate, Inc.
PLEASE... ANYTHING BUT THAT...
HOW SATISFIED ARE YOU NOW?

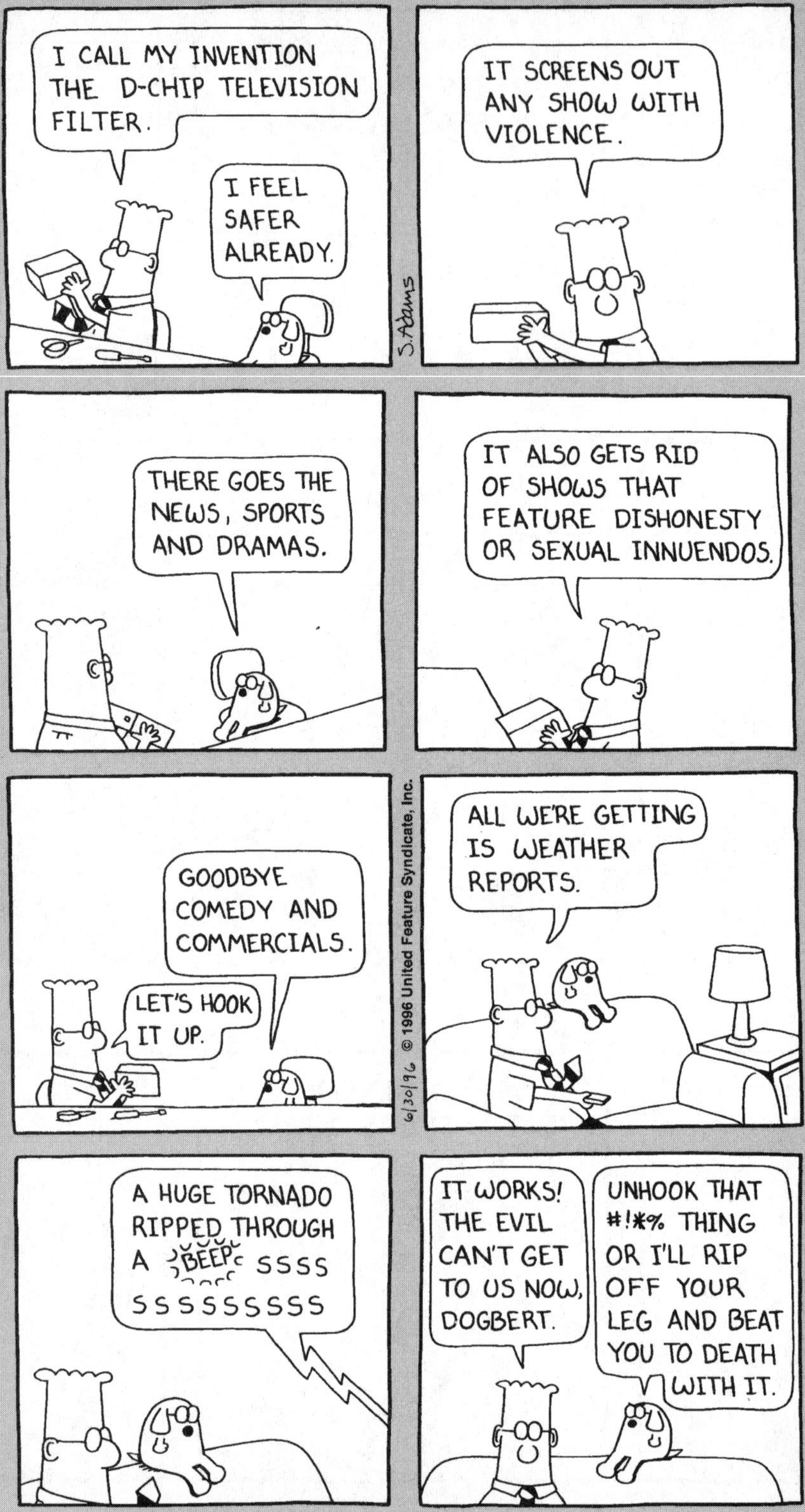
I CALL MY INVENTION THE D-CHIP TELEVISION FILTER.
I FEEL SAFER ALREADY.
S. Adams
IT SCREENS OUT ANY SHOW WITH VIOLENCE.
THERE GOES THE NEWS, SPORTS AND DRAMAS.
IT ALSO GETS RID OF SHOWS THAT FEATURE DISHONESTY OR SEXUAL INNUENDOS.
GOODBYE COMEDY AND COMMERCIALS.
LET'S HOOK IT UP.
6/30/96 © 1996 United Feature Syndicate, Inc.
ALL WE'RE GETTING IS WEATHER REPORTS.
A HUGE TORNADO RIPPED THROUGH A BEEP SSSS SSSSSSSSS
IT WORKS! THE EVIL CAN'T GET TO US NOW, DOGBERT.
UNHOOK THAT #!*% THING OR I'LL RIP OFF YOUR LEG AND BEAT YOU TO DEATH WITH IT.

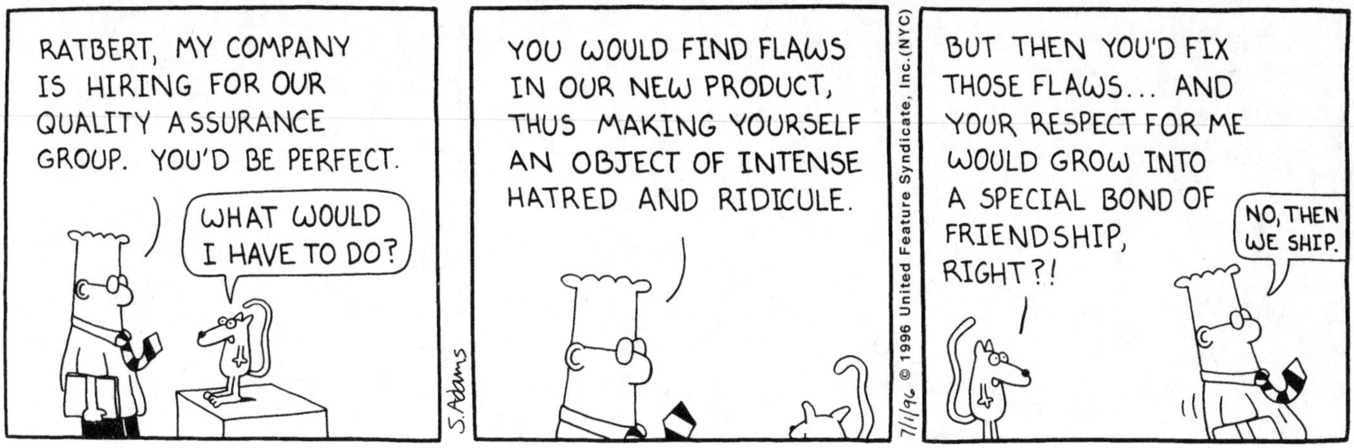
RATBERT, MY COMPANY IS HIRING FOR OUR QUALITY ASSURANCE GROUP. YOU'D BE PERFECT.
WHAT WOULD I HAVE TO DO?
S. Adams
YOU WOULD FIND FLAWS IN OUR NEW PRODUCT, THUS MAKING YOURSELF AN OBJECT OF INTENSE HATRED AND RIDICULE.
7/1/96 © 1996 United Feature Syndicate, Inc.(NYC)
BUT THEN YOU'D FIX THOSE FLAWS... AND YOUR RESPECT FOR ME WOULD GROW INTO A SPECIAL BOND OF FRIENDSHIP, RIGHT?!
NO, THEN WE SHIP.

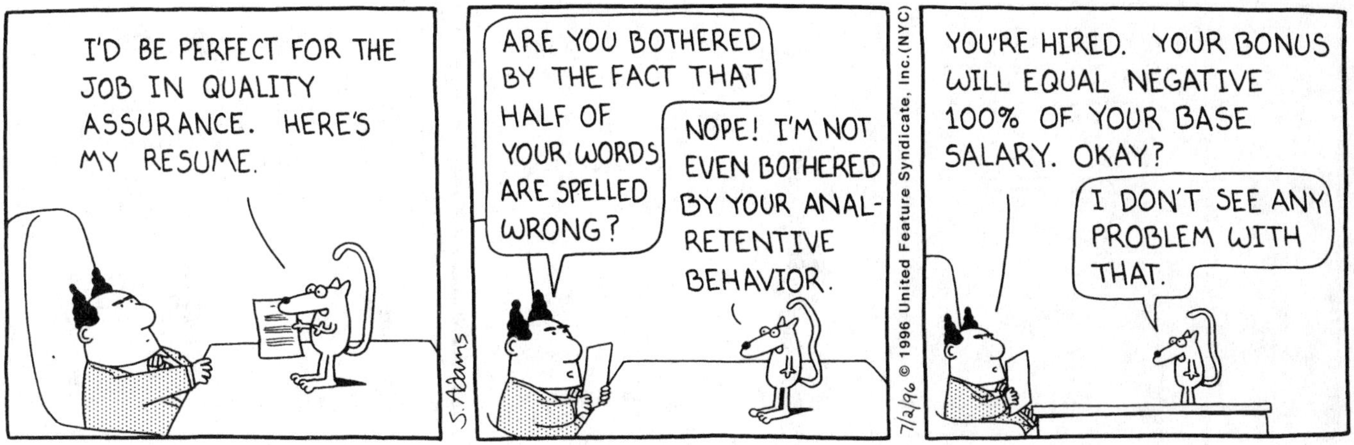
I'D BE PERFECT FOR THE JOB IN QUALITY ASSURANCE. HERE'S MY RESUME.
S. Adams
ARE YOU BOTHERED BY THE FACT THAT HALF OF YOUR WORDS ARE SPELLED WRONG?
NOPE! I'M NOT EVEN BOTHERED BY YOUR ANAL-RETENTIVE BEHAVIOR.
7/2/96 © 1996 United Feature Syndicate, Inc.(NYC)
YOU'RE HIRED. YOUR BONUS WILL EQUAL NEGATIVE 100% OF YOUR BASE SALARY. OKAY?
I DON'T SEE ANY PROBLEM WITH THAT.

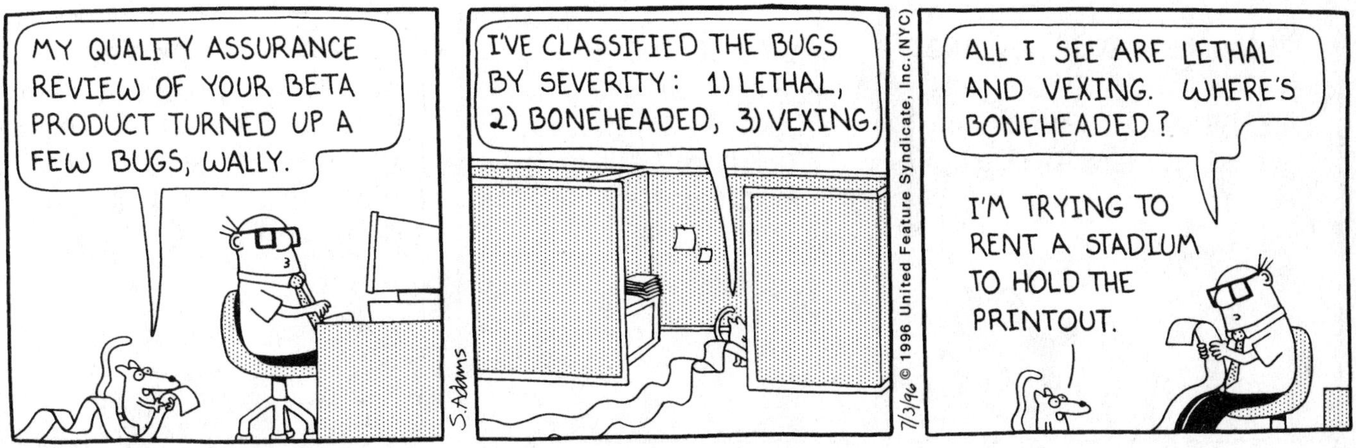
MY QUALITY ASSURANCE REVIEW OF YOUR BETA PRODUCT TURNED UP A FEW BUGS, WALLY.
S. Adams
I'VE CLASSIFIED THE BUGS BY SEVERITY: 1) LETHAL, 2) BONEHEADED, 3) VEXING.
7/3/96 © 1996 United Feature Syndicate, Inc.(NYC)
ALL I SEE ARE LETHAL AND VEXING. WHERE'S BONEHEADED?
I'M TRYING TO RENT A STADIUM TO HOLD THE PRINTOUT.

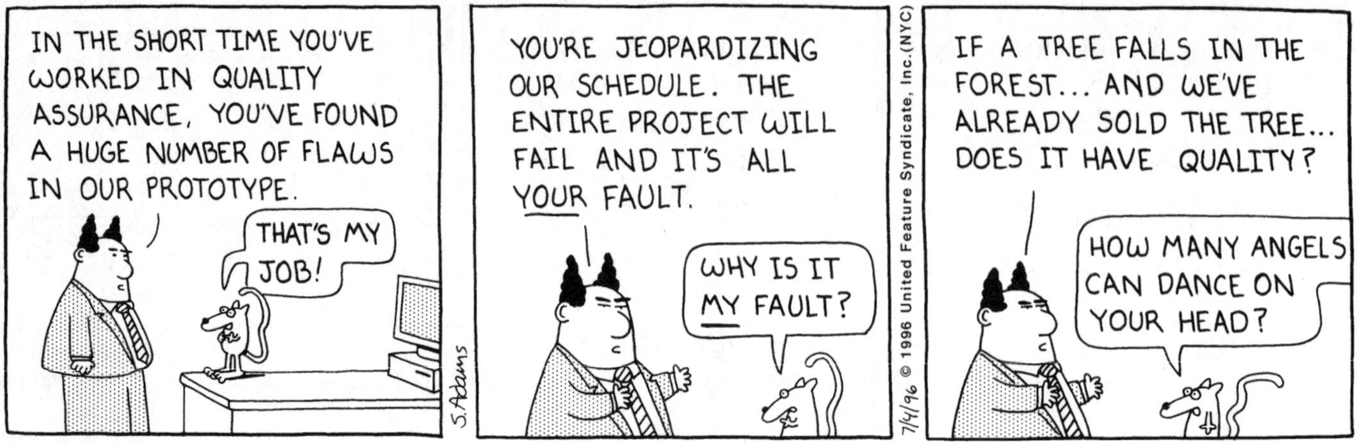
IN THE SHORT TIME YOU'VE WORKED IN QUALITY ASSURANCE, YOU'VE FOUND A HUGE NUMBER OF FLAWS IN OUR PROTOTYPE.
THAT'S MY JOB!
S. Adams
YOU'RE JEOPARDIZING OUR SCHEDULE. THE ENTIRE PROJECT WILL FAIL AND IT'S ALL YOUR FAULT.
WHY IS IT MY FAULT?
7/4/96 © 1996 United Feature Syndicate, Inc.(NYC)
IF A TREE FALLS IN THE FOREST... AND WE'VE ALREADY SOLD THE TREE... DOES IT HAVE QUALITY?
HOW MANY ANGELS CAN DANCE ON YOUR HEAD?

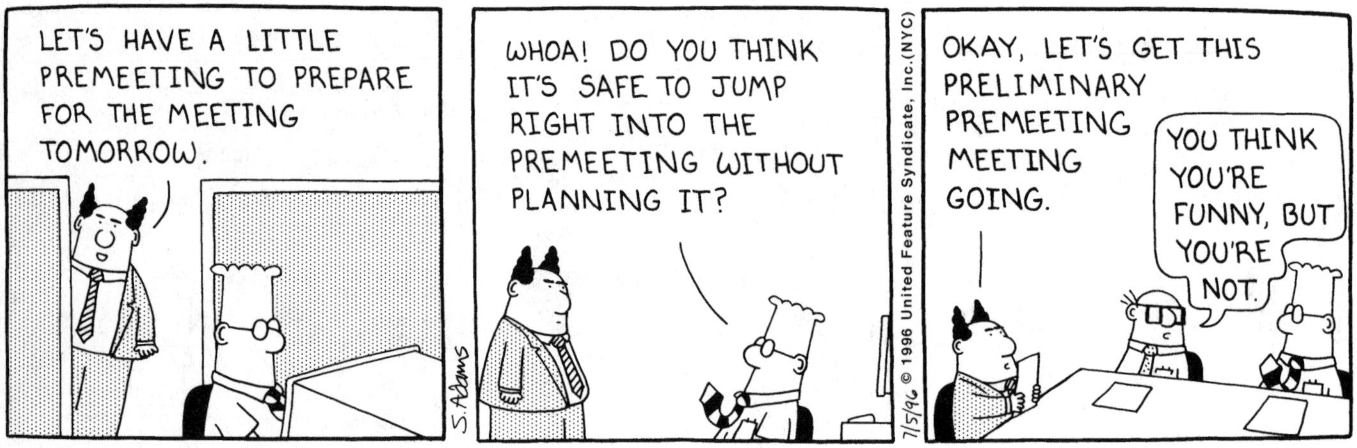
LET'S HAVE A LITTLE PREMEETING TO PREPARE FOR THE MEETING TOMORROW.
S. Adams
WHOA! DO YOU THINK IT'S SAFE TO JUMP RIGHT INTO THE PREMEETING WITHOUT PLANNING IT?
7/5/96 © 1996 United Feature Syndicate, Inc.(NYC)
OKAY, LET'S GET THIS PRELIMINARY PREMEETING MEETING GOING.
YOU THINK YOU'RE FUNNY, BUT YOU'RE NOT.

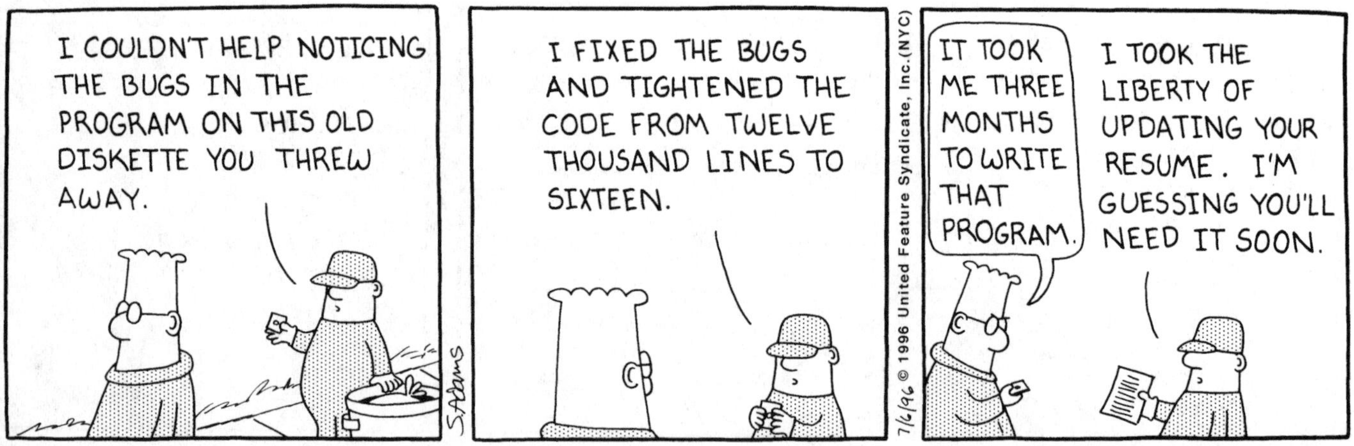
I COULDN'T HELP NOTICING THE BUGS IN THE PROGRAM ON THIS OLD DISKETTE YOU THREW AWAY.
S. Adams
I FIXED THE BUGS AND TIGHTENED THE CODE FROM TWELVE THOUSAND LINES TO SIXTEEN.
7/6/96 © 1996 United Feature Syndicate, Inc.(NYC)
IT TOOK ME THREE MONTHS TO WRITE THAT PROGRAM.
I TOOK THE LIBERTY OF UPDATING YOUR RESUME. I'M GUESSING YOU'LL NEED IT SOON.

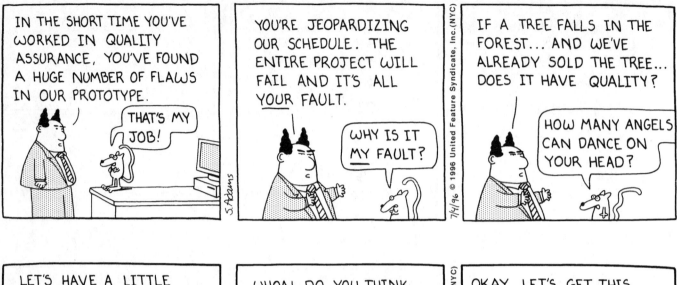

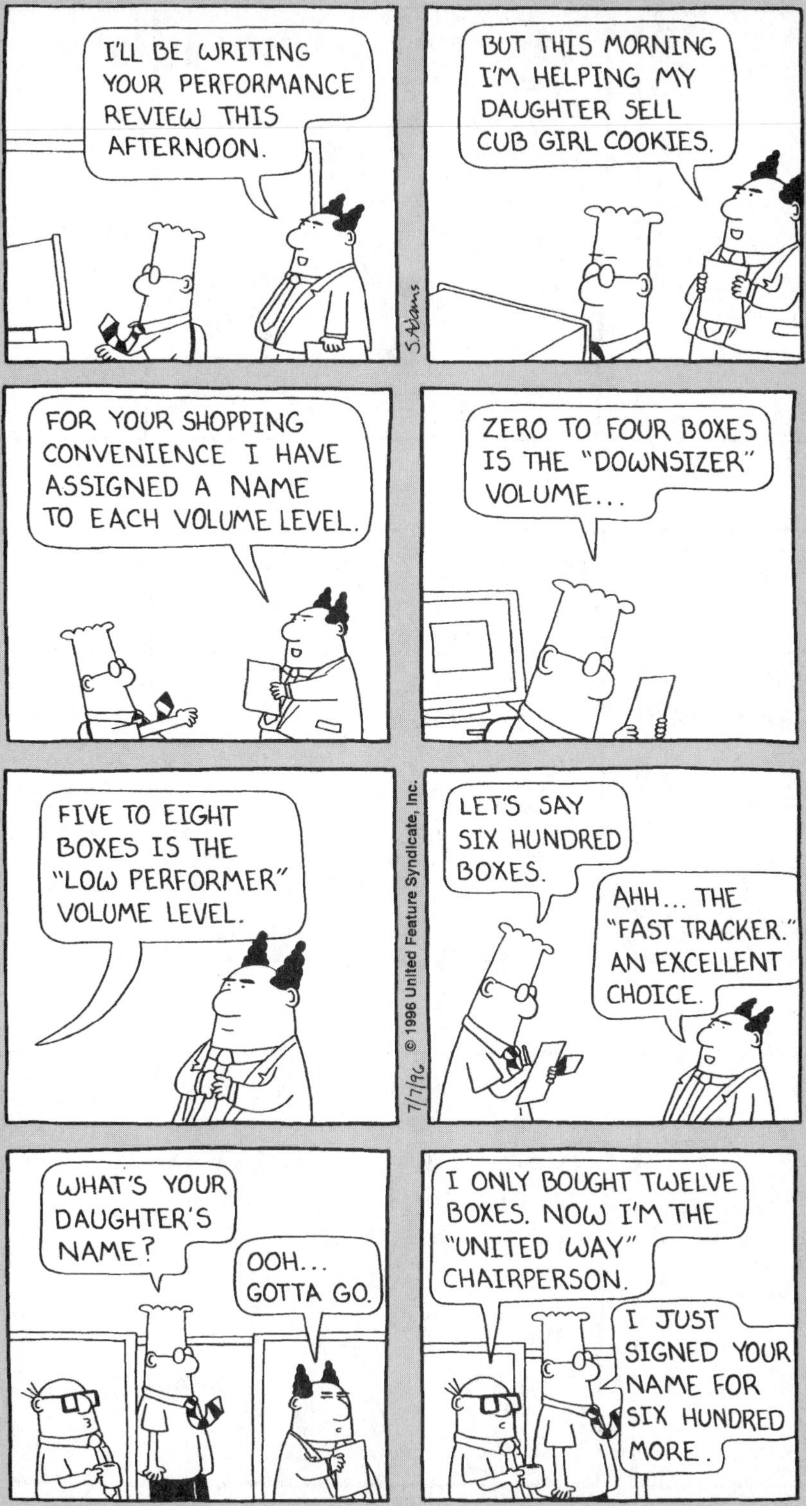
I'LL BE WRITING YOUR PERFORMANCE REVIEW THIS AFTERNOON.
BUT THIS MORNING I'M HELPING MY DAUGHTER SELL CUB GIRL COOKIES.
S.Adams
FOR YOUR SHOPPING CONVENIENCE I HAVE ASSIGNED A NAME TO EACH VOLUME LEVEL.
ZERO TO FOUR BOXES IS THE "DOWNSIZER" VOLUME...
FIVE TO EIGHT BOXES IS THE "LOW PERFORMER" VOLUME LEVEL.
7/7/96 © 1996 United Feature Syndicate, Inc.
LET'S SAY SIX HUNDRED BOXES.
AHH... THE "FAST TRACKER." AN EXCELLENT CHOICE.
WHAT'S YOUR DAUGHTER'S NAME?
OOH... GOTTA GO.
I ONLY BOUGHT TWELVE BOXES. NOW I'M THE "UNITED WAY" CHAIRPERSON.
I JUST SIGNED YOUR NAME FOR SIX HUNDRED MORE.

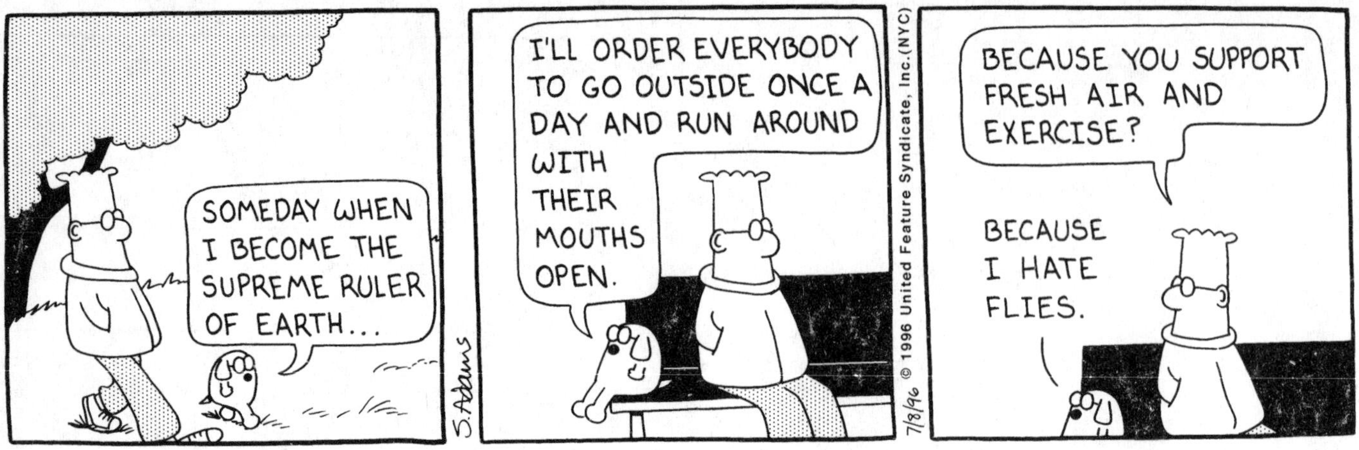
SOMEDAY WHEN I BECOME THE SUPREME RULER OF EARTH...
S. Adams
I'LL ORDER EVERYBODY TO GO OUTSIDE ONCE A DAY AND RUN AROUND WITH THEIR MOUTHS OPEN.
7/8/96 © 1996 United Feature Syndicate, Inc.(NYC)
BECAUSE YOU SUPPORT FRESH AIR AND EXERCISE?
BECAUSE I HATE FLIES.

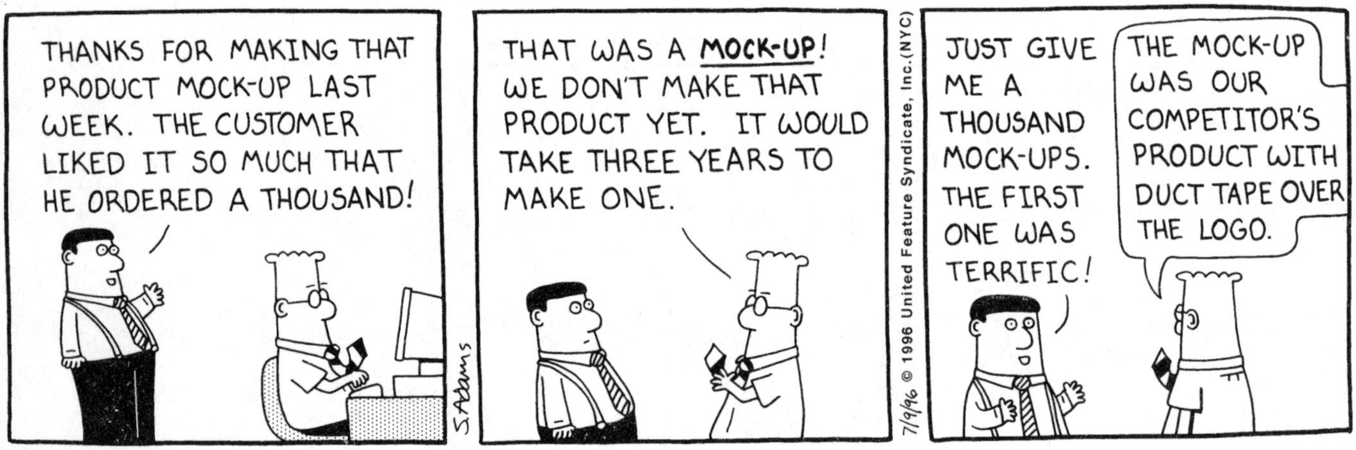
THANKS FOR MAKING THAT PRODUCT MOCK-UP LAST WEEK. THE CUSTOMER LIKED IT SO MUCH THAT HE ORDERED A THOUSAND!
S. Adams
THAT WAS A MOCK-UP! WE DON'T MAKE THAT PRODUCT YET. IT WOULD TAKE THREE YEARS TO MAKE ONE.
7/9/96 © 1996 United Feature Syndicate, Inc.(NYC)
JUST GIVE ME A THOUSAND MOCK-UPS. THE FIRST ONE WAS TERRIFIC!
THE MOCK-UP WAS OUR COMPETITOR'S PRODUCT WITH DUCT TAPE OVER THE LOGO.

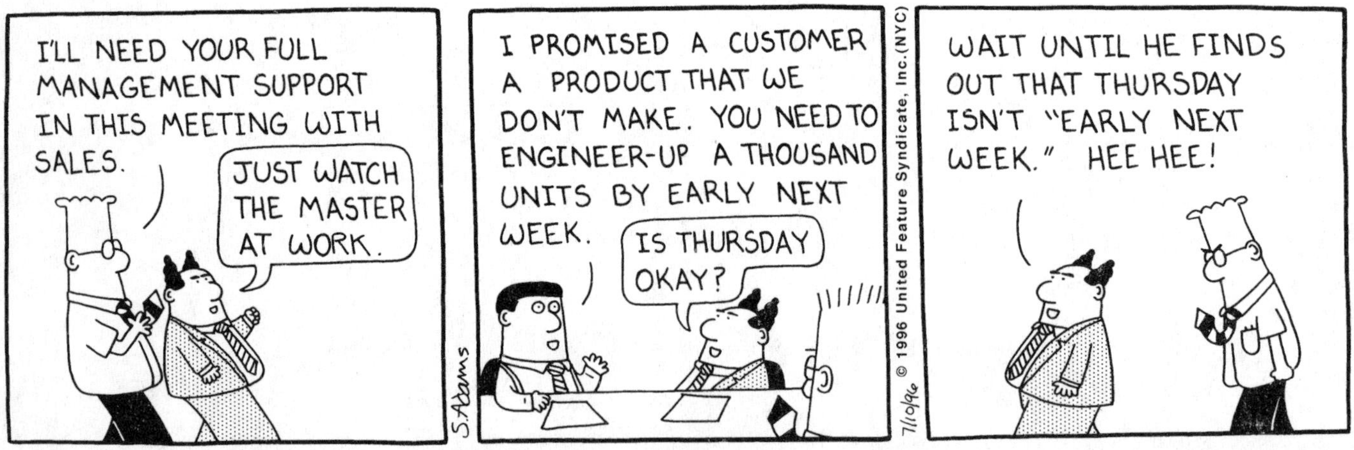
I'LL NEED YOUR FULL MANAGEMENT SUPPORT IN THIS MEETING WITH SALES.
JUST WATCH THE MASTER AT WORK.
S. Adams
I PROMISED A CUSTOMER A PRODUCT THAT WE DON'T MAKE. YOU NEED TO ENGINEER-UP A THOUSAND UNITS BY EARLY NEXT WEEK.
IS THURSDAY OKAY?
7/10/96 © 1996 United Feature Syndicate, Inc.(NYC)
WAIT UNTIL HE FINDS OUT THAT THURSDAY ISN'T "EARLY NEXT WEEK." HEE HEE!

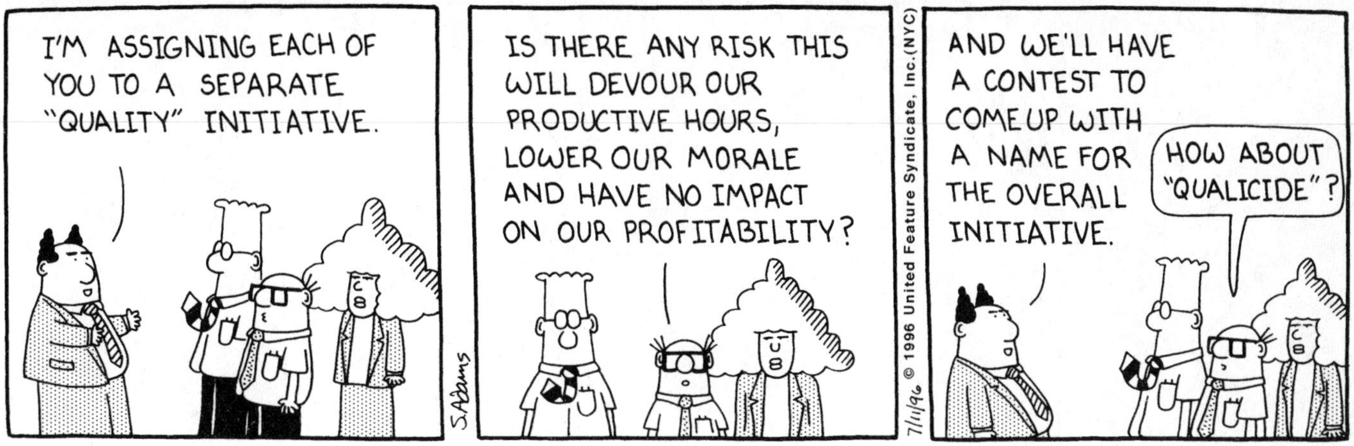
I'M ASSIGNING EACH OF YOU TO A SEPARATE "QUALITY" INITIATIVE.
S. Adams
IS THERE ANY RISK THIS WILL DEVOUR OUR PRODUCTIVE HOURS, LOWER OUR MORALE AND HAVE NO IMPACT ON OUR PROFITABILITY?
7/1/96 © 1996 United Feature Syndicate, Inc.(NYC)
AND WE'LL HAVE A CONTEST TO COME UP WITH A NAME FOR THE OVERALL INITIATIVE.
HOW ABOUT "QUALICIDE"?

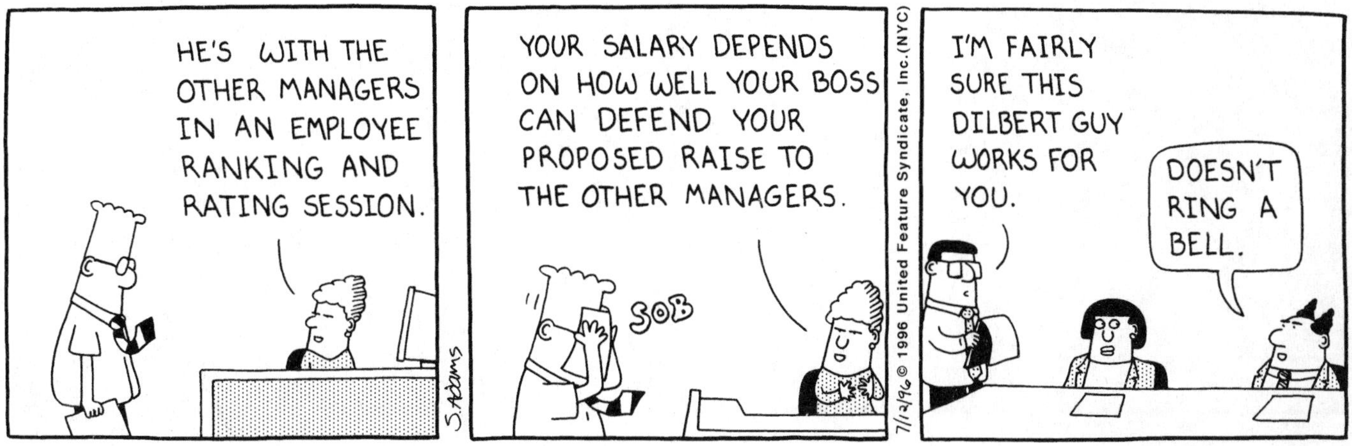
HE'S WITH THE OTHER MANAGERS IN AN EMPLOYEE RANKING AND RATING SESSION.
S. Adams
YOUR SALARY DEPENDS ON HOW WELL YOUR BOSS CAN DEFEND YOUR PROPOSED RAISE TO THE OTHER MANAGERS.
SOB
7/2/96 © 1996 United Feature Syndicate, Inc.(NYC)
I'M FAIRLY SURE THIS DILBERT GUY WORKS FOR YOU.
DOESN'T RING A BELL.

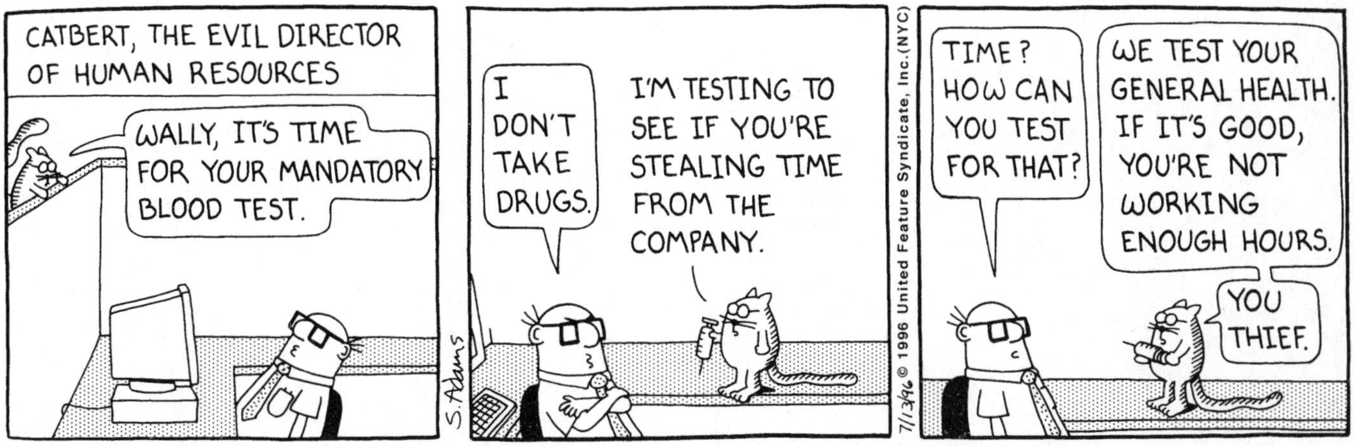
CATBERT, THE EVIL DIRECTOR OF HUMAN RESOURCES
WALLY, IT'S TIME FOR YOUR MANDATORY BLOOD TEST.
S. Adams
I DON'T TAKE DRUGS.
I'M TESTING TO SEE IF YOU'RE STEALING TIME FROM THE COMPANY.
7/3/96 © 1996 United Feature Syndicate, Inc.(NYC)
TIME? HOW CAN YOU TEST FOR THAT?
WE TEST YOUR GENERAL HEALTH. IF IT'S GOOD, YOU'RE NOT WORKING ENOUGH HOURS.
YOU THIEF.

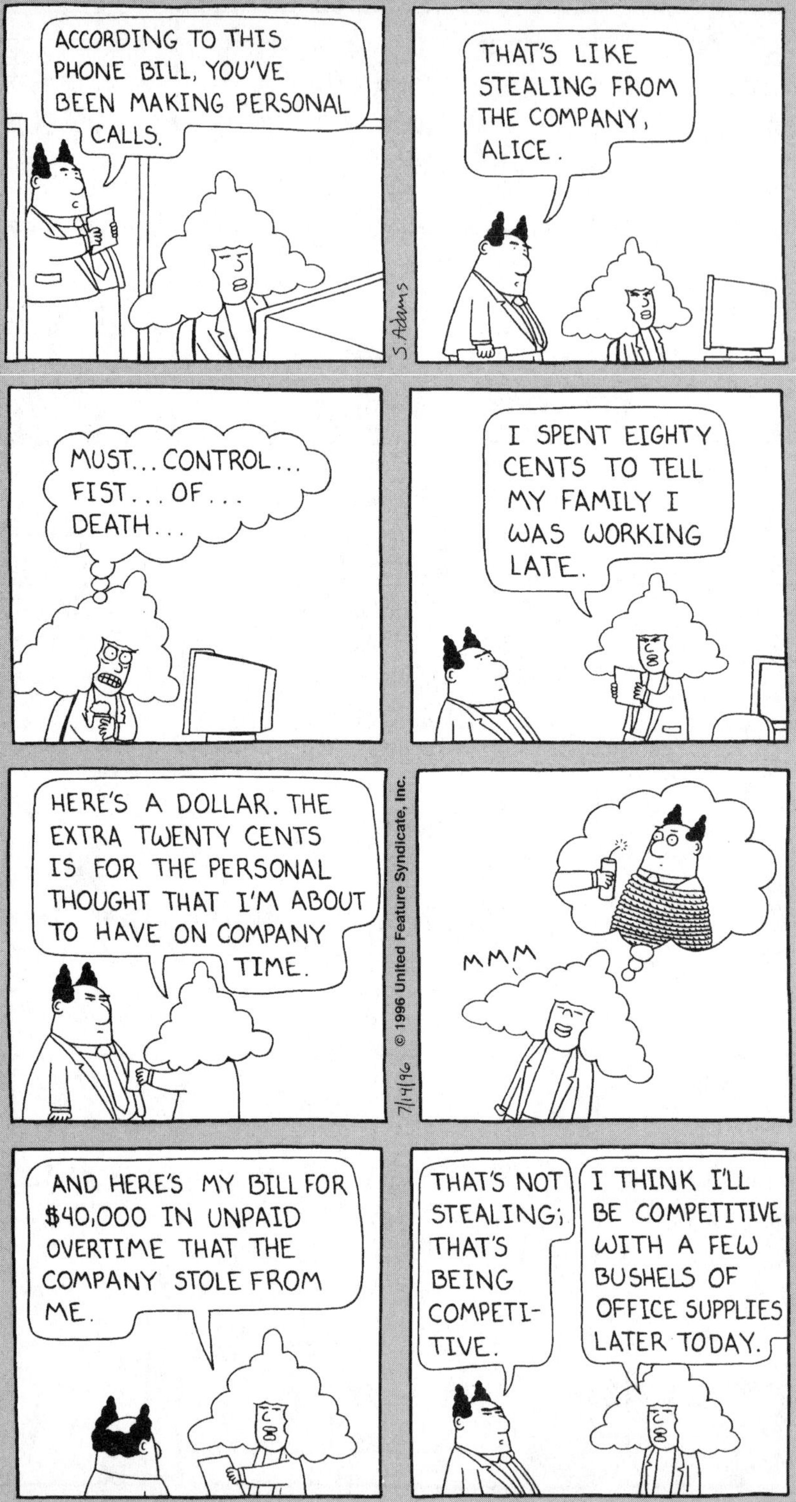

ACCORDING TO THIS PHONE BILL, YOU'VE BEEN MAKING PERSONAL CALLS.
THAT'S LIKE STEALING FROM THE COMPANY, ALICE.
S. Adams
MUST... CONTROL... FIST... OF... DEATH...
I SPENT EIGHTY CENTS TO TELL MY FAMILY I WAS WORKING LATE.
HERE'S A DOLLAR. THE EXTRA TWENTY CENTS IS FOR THE PERSONAL THOUGHT THAT I'M ABOUT TO HAVE ON COMPANY TIME.
7/14/96 © 1996 United Feature Syndicate, Inc.
MMM
AND HERE'S MY BILL FOR $40,000 IN UNPAID OVERTIME THAT THE COMPANY STOLE FROM ME.
THAT'S NOT STEALING; THAT'S BEING COMPETI-TIVE.
I THINK I'LL BE COMPETITIVE WITH A FEW BUSHELS OF OFFICE SUPPLIES LATER TODAY.

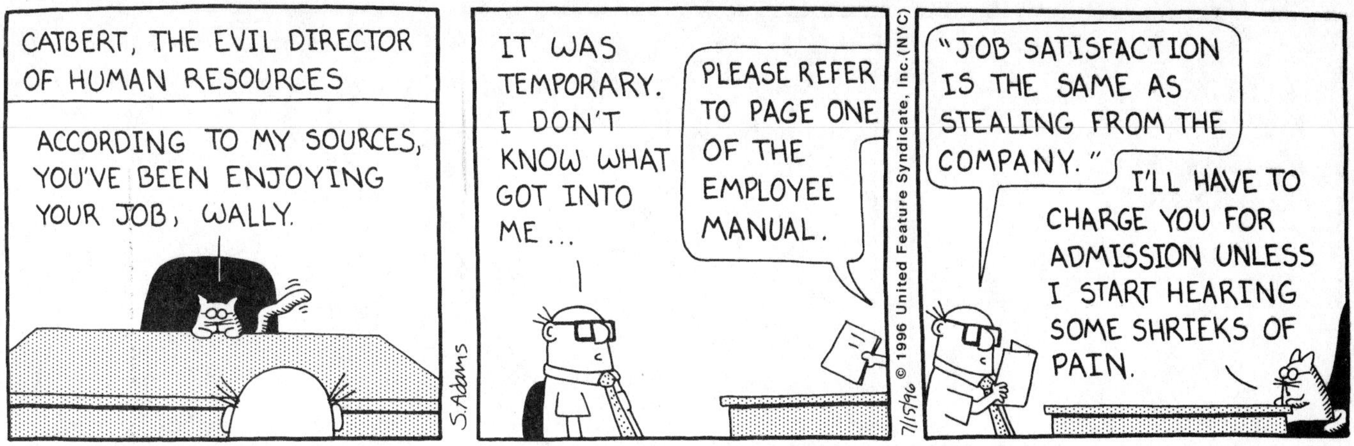
CATBERT, THE EVIL DIRECTOR OF HUMAN RESOURCES
ACCORDING TO MY SOURCES, YOU'VE BEEN ENJOYING YOUR JOB, WALLY.
S. Adams
IT WAS TEMPORARY. I DON'T KNOW WHAT GOT INTO ME...
PLEASE REFER TO PAGE ONE OF THE EMPLOYEE MANUAL.
7/15/96 © 1996 United Feature Syndicate, Inc.(NYC)
"JOB SATISFACTION IS THE SAME AS STEALING FROM THE COMPANY."
I'LL HAVE TO CHARGE YOU FOR ADMISSION UNLESS I START HEARING SOME SHRIEKS OF PAIN.

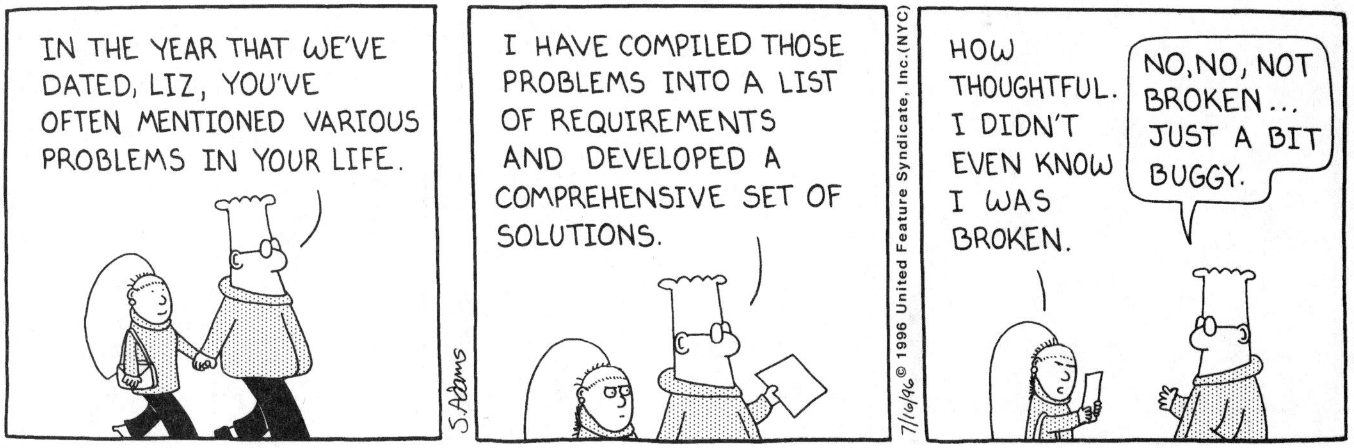
IN THE YEAR THAT WE'VE DATED, LIZ, YOU'VE OFTEN MENTIONED VARIOUS PROBLEMS IN YOUR LIFE.
S. Adams
I HAVE COMPILED THOSE PROBLEMS INTO A LIST OF REQUIREMENTS AND DEVELOPED A COMPREHENSIVE SET OF SOLUTIONS.
7/16/96 © 1996 United Feature Syndicate, Inc.(NYC)
HOW THOUGHTFUL. I DIDN'T EVEN KNOW I WAS BROKEN.
NO, NO, NOT BROKEN... JUST A BIT BUGGY.

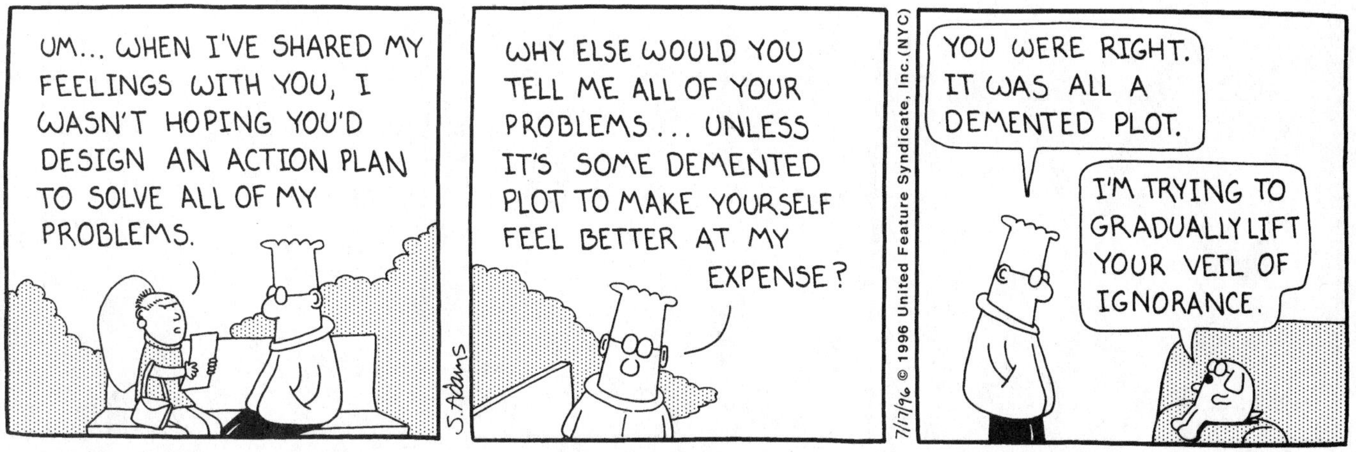
UM... WHEN I'VE SHARED MY FEELINGS WITH YOU, I WASN'T HOPING YOU'D DESIGN AN ACTION PLAN TO SOLVE ALL OF MY PROBLEMS.
S. Adams
WHY ELSE WOULD YOU TELL ME ALL OF YOUR PROBLEMS... UNLESS IT'S SOME DEMENTED PLOT TO MAKE YOURSELF FEEL BETTER AT MY EXPENSE?
7/17/96 © 1996 United Feature Syndicate, Inc.(NYC)
YOU WERE RIGHT. IT WAS ALL A DEMENTED PLOT.
I'M TRYING TO GRADUALLY LIFT YOUR VEIL OF IGNORANCE.

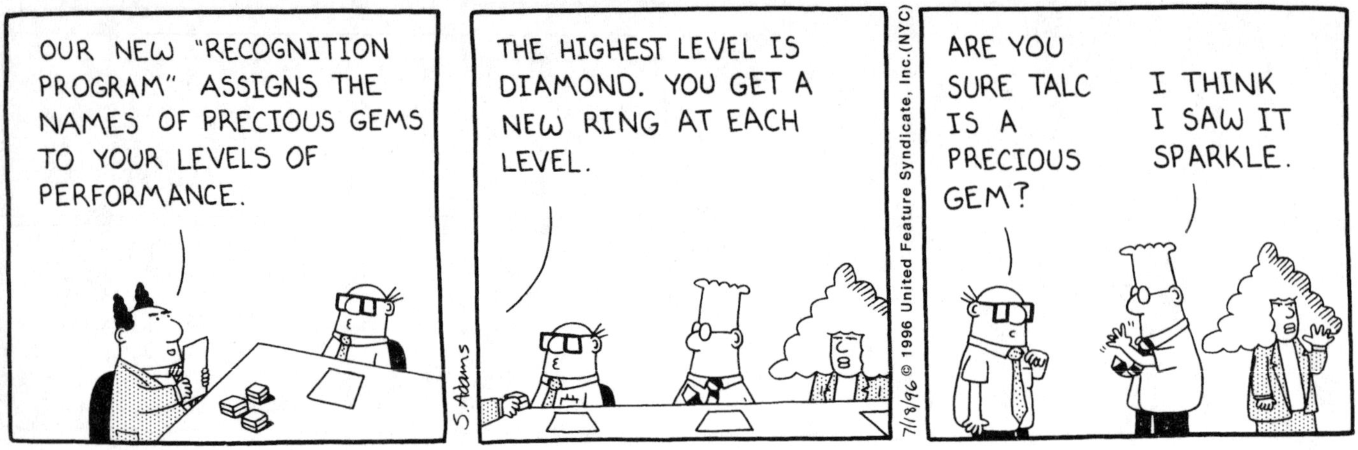
OUR NEW "RECOGNITION PROGRAM" ASSIGNS THE NAMES OF PRECIOUS GEMS TO YOUR LEVELS OF PERFORMANCE.
S. Adams
THE HIGHEST LEVEL IS DIAMOND. YOU GET A NEW RING AT EACH LEVEL.
7/8/96 © 1996 United Feature Syndicate, Inc.(NYC)
ARE YOU SURE TALC IS A PRECIOUS GEM?
I THINK I SAW IT SPARKLE.

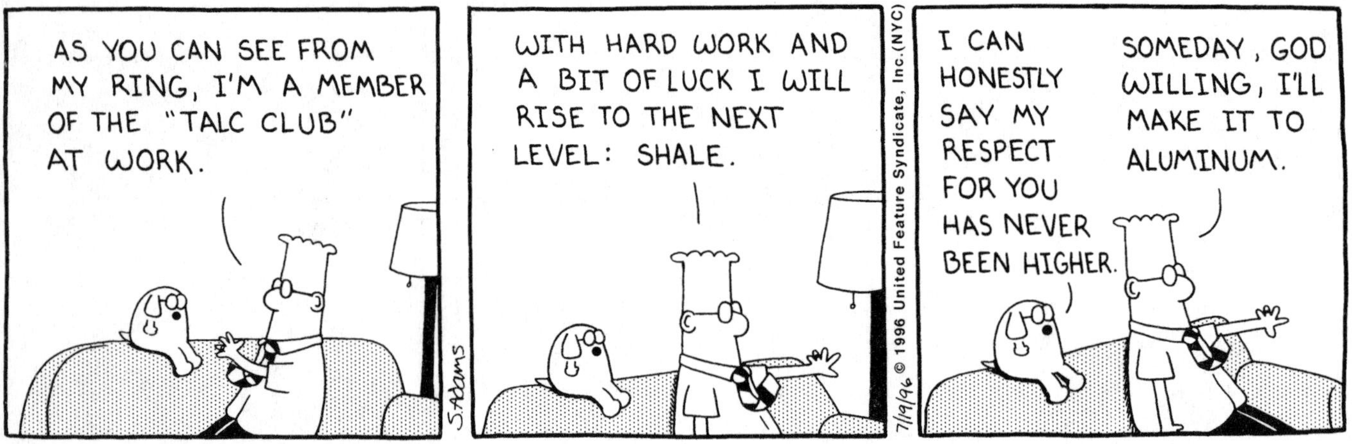
AS YOU CAN SEE FROM MY RING, I'M A MEMBER OF THE "TALC CLUB" AT WORK.
S. Adams
WITH HARD WORK AND A BIT OF LUCK I WILL RISE TO THE NEXT LEVEL: SHALE.
7/9/96 © 1996 United Feature Syndicate, Inc.(NYC)
I CAN HONESTLY SAY MY RESPECT FOR YOU HAS NEVER BEEN HIGHER.
SOMEDAY, GOD WILLING, I'LL MAKE IT TO ALUMINUM.

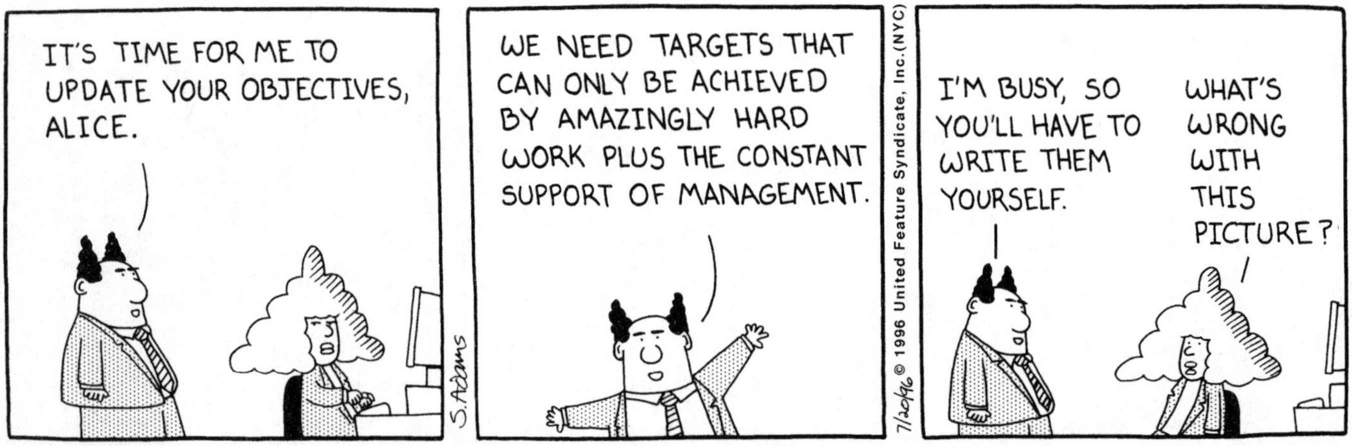
IT'S TIME FOR ME TO UPDATE YOUR OBJECTIVES, ALICE.
S. Adams
WE NEED TARGETS THAT CAN ONLY BE ACHIEVED BY AMAZINGLY HARD WORK PLUS THE CONSTANT SUPPORT OF MANAGEMENT.
7/20/96 © 1996 United Feature Syndicate, Inc.(NYC)
I'M BUSY, SO YOU'LL HAVE TO WRITE THEM YOURSELF.
WHAT'S WRONG WITH THIS PICTURE?

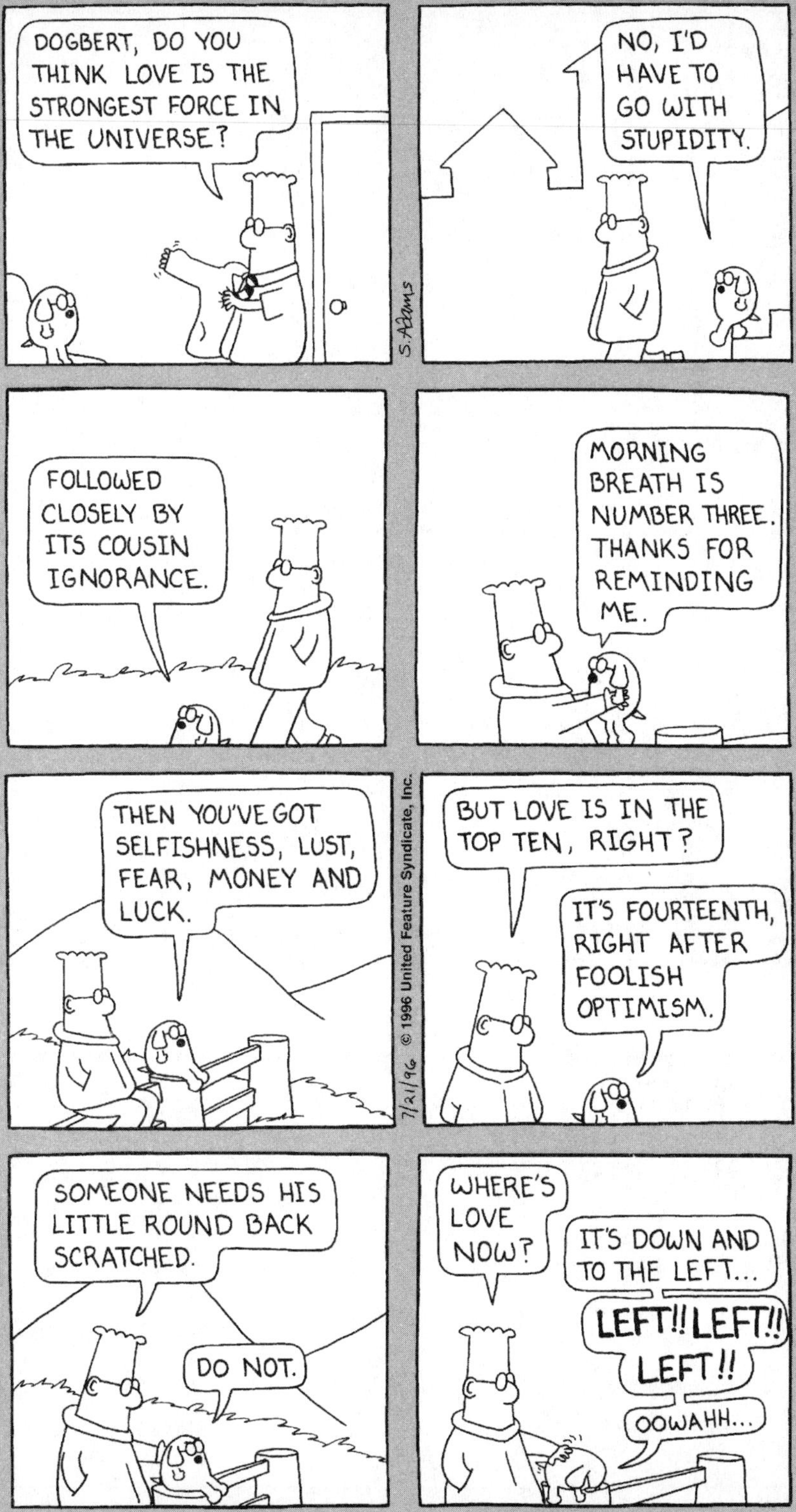
DOGBERT, DO YOU THINK LOVE IS THE STRONGEST FORCE IN THE UNIVERSE?
S. ADAMS
NO, I'D HAVE TO GO WITH STUPIDITY.
FOLLOWED CLOSELY BY ITS COUSIN IGNORANCE.
MORNING BREATH IS NUMBER THREE. THANKS FOR REMINDING ME.
THEN YOU'VE GOT SELFISHNESS, LUST, FEAR, MONEY AND LUCK.
7/21/96 © 1996 United Feature Syndicate, Inc.
BUT LOVE IS IN THE TOP TEN, RIGHT?
IT'S FOURTEENTH, RIGHT AFTER FOOLISH OPTIMISM.
SOMEONE NEEDS HIS LITTLE ROUND BACK SCRATCHED.
DO NOT.
WHERE'S LOVE NOW?
IT'S DOWN AND TO THE LEFT...
LEFT!! LEFT!!
LEFT!!
OOWAHH...

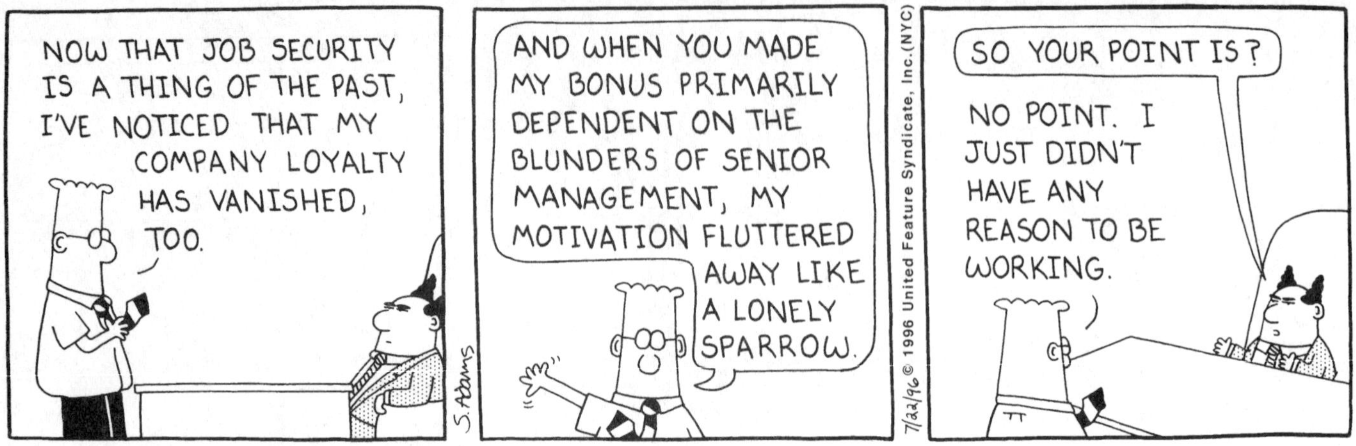
NOW THAT JOB SECURITY IS A THING OF THE PAST, I'VE NOTICED THAT MY COMPANY LOYALTY HAS VANISHED, TOO.
AND WHEN YOU MADE MY BONUS PRIMARILY DEPENDENT ON THE BLUNDERS OF SENIOR MANAGEMENT, MY MOTIVATION FLUTTERED AWAY LIKE A LONELY SPARROW.
SO YOUR POINT IS?
NO POINT. I JUST DIDN'T HAVE ANY REASON TO BE WORKING.
S. Adams
7/22/96 © 1996 United Feature Syndicate, Inc.(NYC)

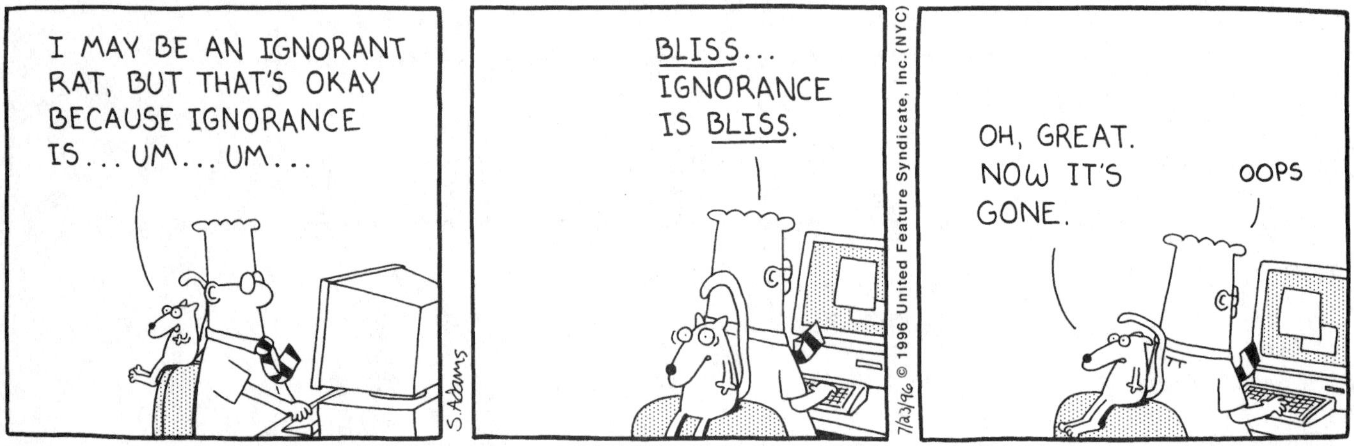
I MAY BE AN IGNORANT RAT, BUT THAT'S OKAY BECAUSE IGNORANCE IS... UM... UM...
BLISS... IGNORANCE IS BLISS.
OH, GREAT. NOW IT'S GONE.
OOPS
S. Adams
7/23/96 © 1996 United Feature Syndicate, Inc.(NYC)

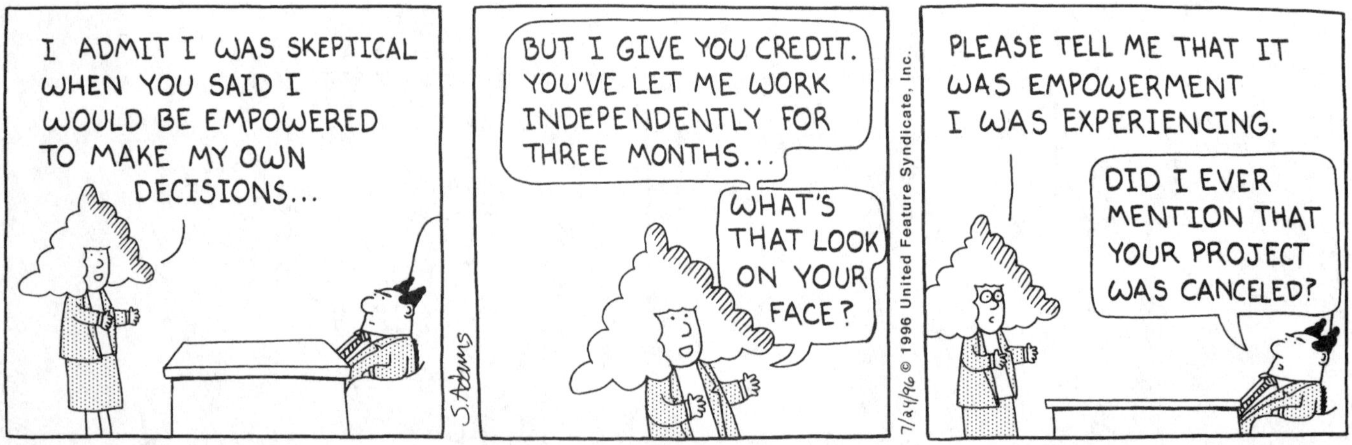
I ADMIT I WAS SKEPTICAL WHEN YOU SAID I WOULD BE EMPOWERED TO MAKE MY OWN DECISIONS...
BUT I GIVE YOU CREDIT. YOU'VE LET ME WORK INDEPENDENTLY FOR THREE MONTHS...
WHAT'S THAT LOOK ON YOUR FACE?
PLEASE TELL ME THAT IT WAS EMPOWERMENT I WAS EXPERIENCING.
DID I EVER MENTION THAT YOUR PROJECT WAS CANCELED?
S. Adams
7/24/96 © 1996 United Feature Syndicate, Inc.

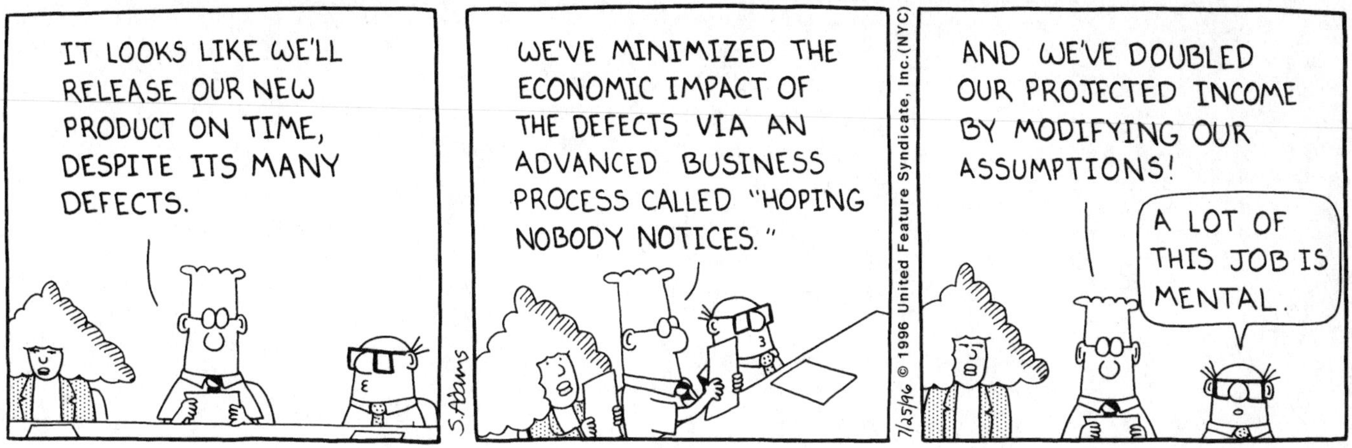
IT LOOKS LIKE WE'LL RELEASE OUR NEW PRODUCT ON TIME, DESPITE ITS MANY DEFECTS.
S.Adams
WE'VE MINIMIZED THE ECONOMIC IMPACT OF THE DEFECTS VIA AN ADVANCED BUSINESS PROCESS CALLED "HOPING NOBODY NOTICES."
7/25/96 © 1996 United Feature Syndicate, Inc.(NYC)
AND WE'VE DOUBLED OUR PROJECTED INCOME BY MODIFYING OUR ASSUMPTIONS!
A LOT OF THIS JOB IS MENTAL.

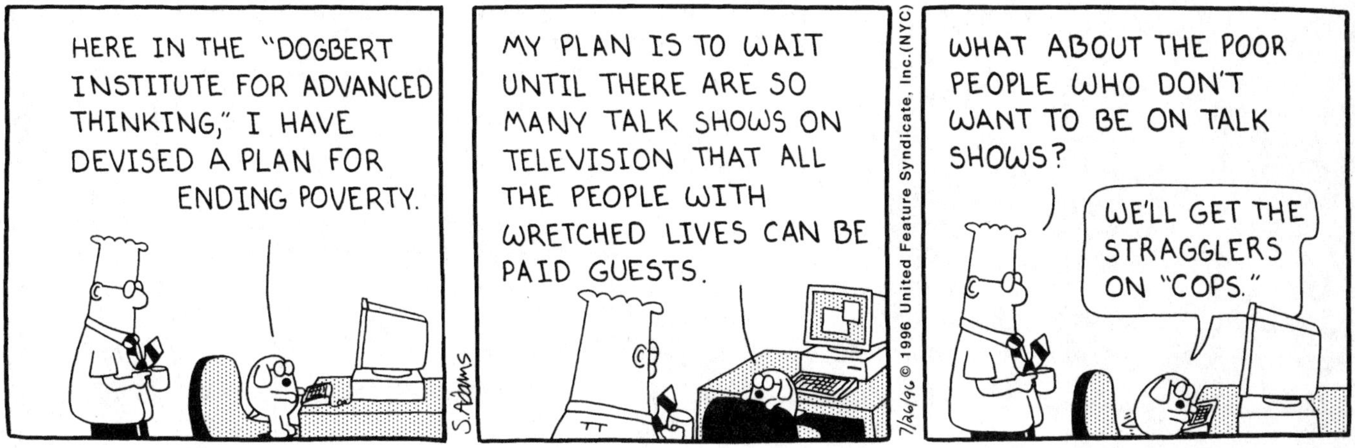
HERE IN THE "DOGBERT INSTITUTE FOR ADVANCED THINKING," I HAVE DEVISED A PLAN FOR ENDING POVERTY.
S.Adams
MY PLAN IS TO WAIT UNTIL THERE ARE SO MANY TALK SHOWS ON TELEVISION THAT ALL THE PEOPLE WITH WRETCHED LIVES CAN BE PAID GUESTS.
7/26/96 © 1996 United Feature Syndicate, Inc.(NYC)
WHAT ABOUT THE POOR PEOPLE WHO DON'T WANT TO BE ON TALK SHOWS?
WE'LL GET THE STRAGGLERS ON "COPS."

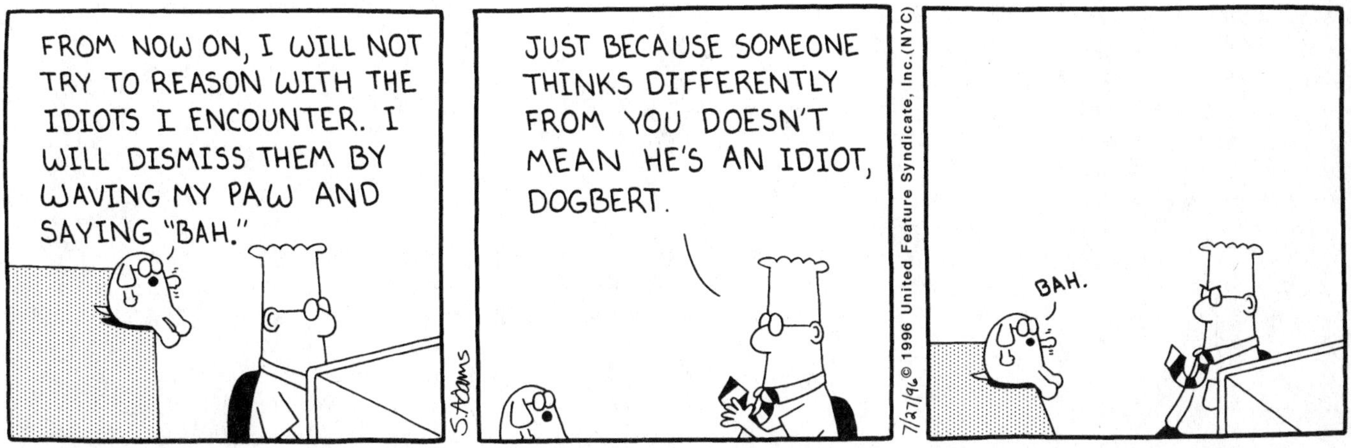
FROM NOW ON, I WILL NOT TRY TO REASON WITH THE IDIOTS I ENCOUNTER. I WILL DISMISS THEM BY WAVING MY PAW AND SAYING "BAH."
S.Adams
JUST BECAUSE SOMEONE THINKS DIFFERENTLY FROM YOU DOESN'T MEAN HE'S AN IDIOT, DOGBERT.
7/27/96 © 1996 United Feature Syndicate, Inc.(NYC)
BAH.

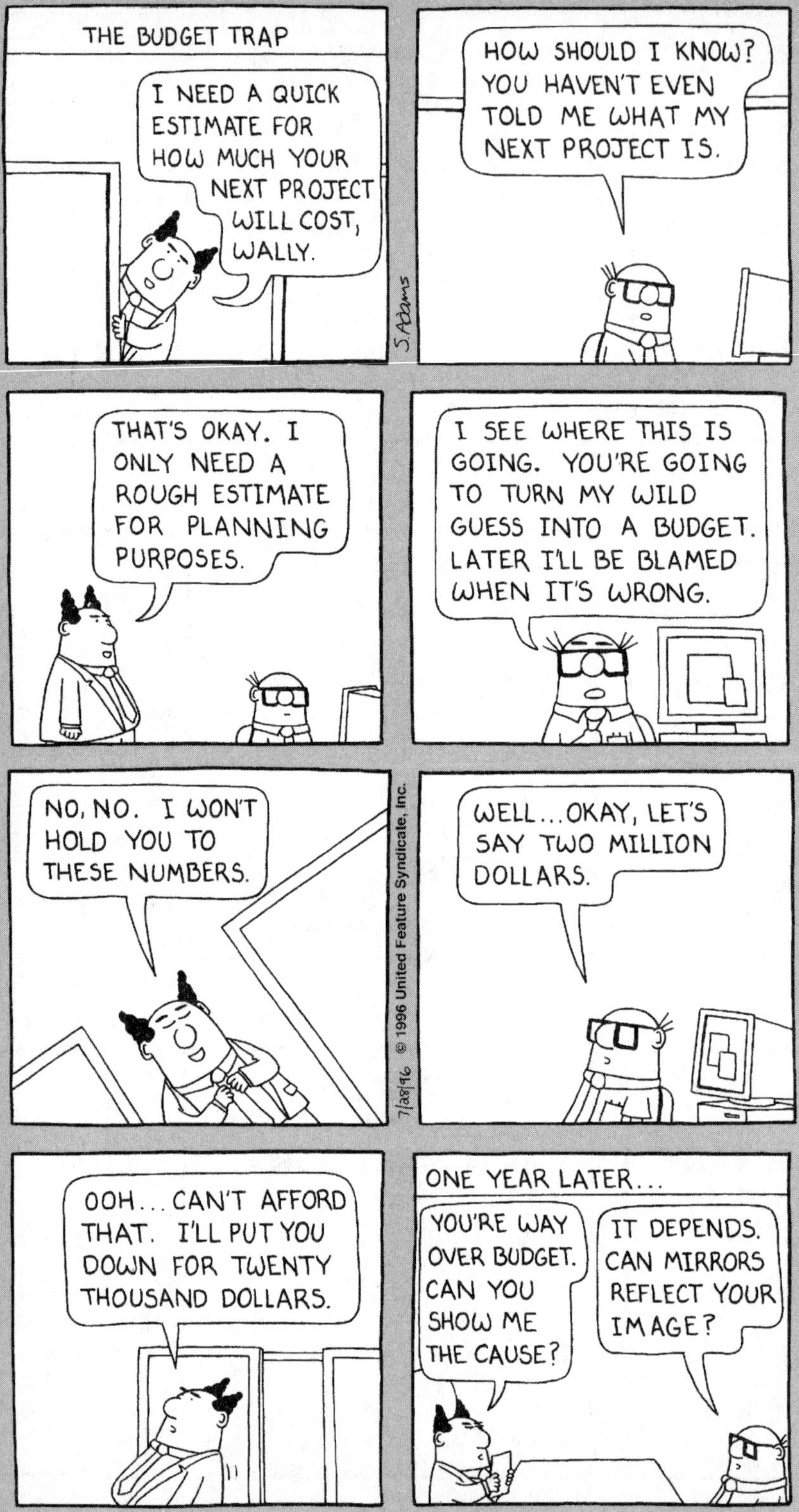
THE BUDGET TRAP
I NEED A QUICK ESTIMATE FOR HOW MUCH YOUR NEXT PROJECT WILL COST, WALLY.
S.Adams
HOW SHOULD I KNOW? YOU HAVEN'T EVEN TOLD ME WHAT MY NEXT PROJECT IS.
THAT'S OKAY. I ONLY NEED A ROUGH ESTIMATE FOR PLANNING PURPOSES.
I SEE WHERE THIS IS GOING. YOU'RE GOING TO TURN MY WILD GUESS INTO A BUDGET. LATER I'LL BE BLAMED WHEN IT'S WRONG.
NO, NO. I WON'T HOLD YOU TO THESE NUMBERS.
7/28/96 © 1996 United Feature Syndicate, Inc.
WELL...OKAY, LET'S SAY TWO MILLION DOLLARS.
OOH... CAN'T AFFORD THAT. I'LL PUT YOU DOWN FOR TWENTY THOUSAND DOLLARS.
ONE YEAR LATER...
YOU'RE WAY OVER BUDGET. CAN YOU SHOW ME THE CAUSE?
IT DEPENDS. CAN MIRRORS REFLECT YOUR IMAGE?

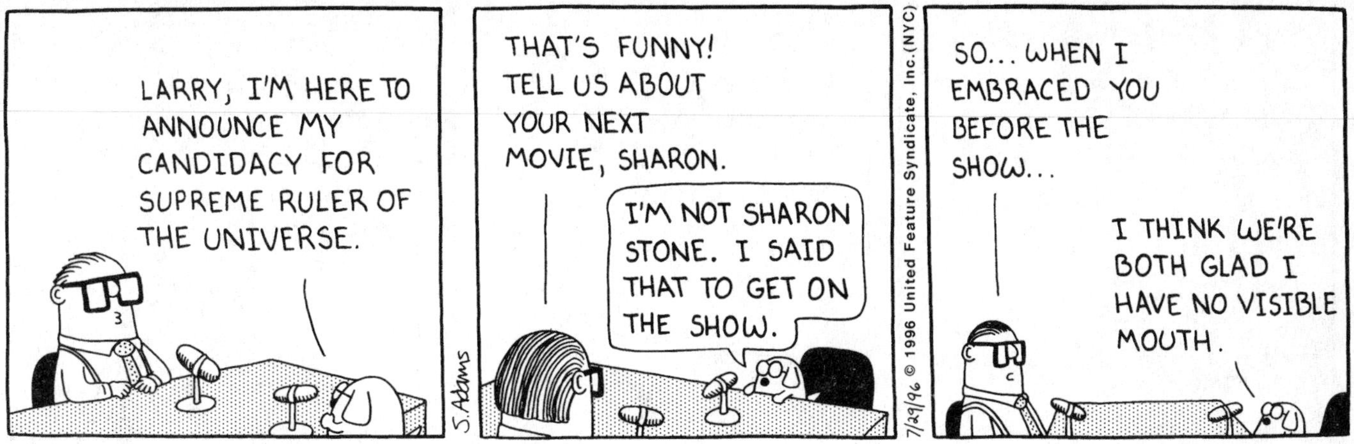
LARRY, I'M HERE TO ANNOUNCE MY CANDIDACY FOR SUPREME RULER OF THE UNIVERSE.
S. Adams
THAT'S FUNNY! TELL US ABOUT YOUR NEXT MOVIE, SHARON.
I'M NOT SHARON STONE. I SAID THAT TO GET ON THE SHOW.
7/29/96 © 1996 United Feature Syndicate, Inc.(NYC)
SO... WHEN I EMBRACED YOU BEFORE THE SHOW...
I THINK WE'RE BOTH GLAD I HAVE NO VISIBLE MOUTH.

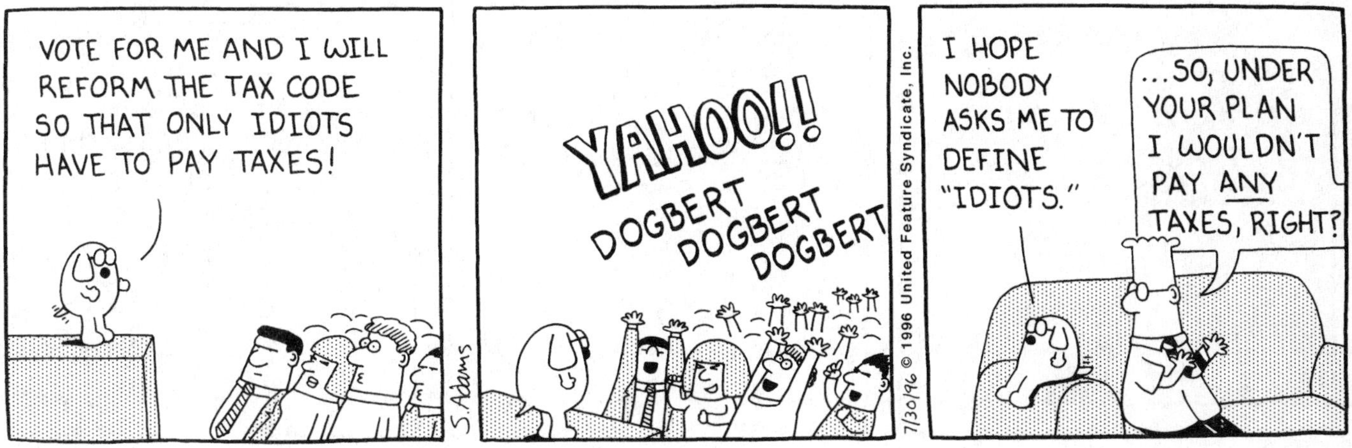
VOTE FOR ME AND I WILL REFORM THE TAX CODE SO THAT ONLY IDIOTS HAVE TO PAY TAXES!
S. Adams
YAHOO!!
DOGBERT DOGBERT DOGBERT
7/30/96 © 1996 United Feature Syndicate, Inc.
I HOPE NOBODY ASKS ME TO DEFINE "IDIOTS."
...SO, UNDER YOUR PLAN I WOULDN'T PAY ANY TAXES, RIGHT?

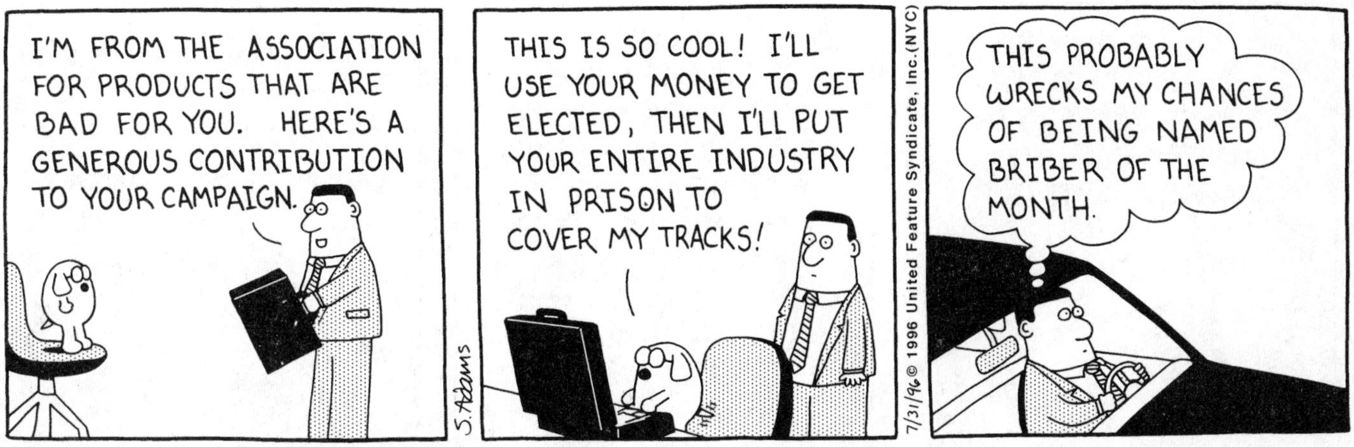
I'M FROM THE ASSOCIATION FOR PRODUCTS THAT ARE BAD FOR YOU. HERE'S A GENEROUS CONTRIBUTION TO YOUR CAMPAIGN.
S. Adams
THIS IS SO COOL! I'LL USE YOUR MONEY TO GET ELECTED, THEN I'LL PUT YOUR ENTIRE INDUSTRY IN PRISON TO COVER MY TRACKS!
7/31/96 © 1996 United Feature Syndicate, Inc.(NYC)
THIS PROBABLY WRECKS MY CHANCES OF BEING NAMED BRIBER OF THE MONTH.

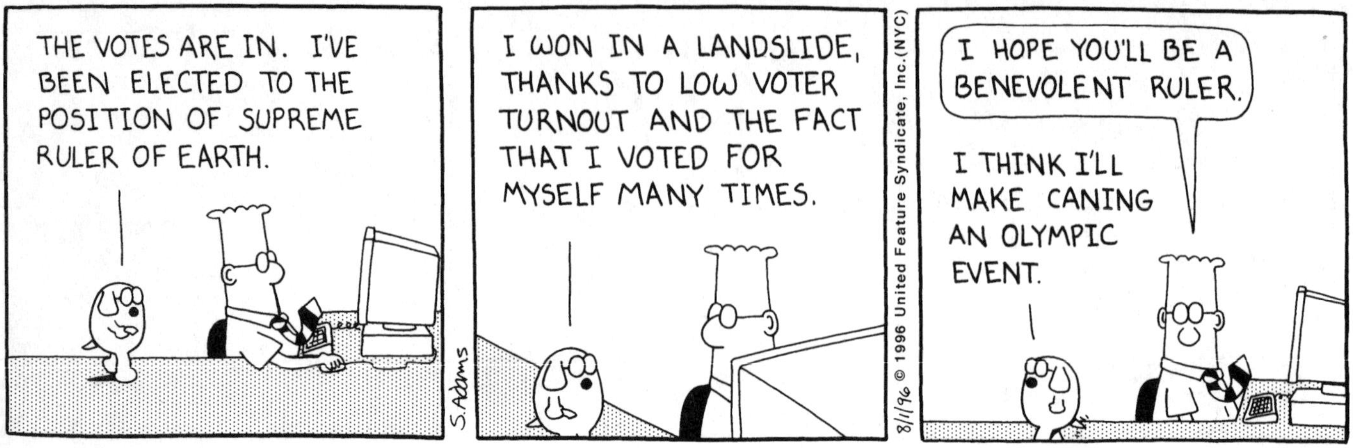
THE VOTES ARE IN. I'VE BEEN ELECTED TO THE POSITION OF SUPREME RULER OF EARTH.
I WON IN A LANDSLIDE, THANKS TO LOW VOTER TURNOUT AND THE FACT THAT I VOTED FOR MYSELF MANY TIMES.
I HOPE YOU'LL BE A BENEVOLENT RULER.
I THINK I'LL MAKE CANING AN OLYMPIC EVENT.
S. Adams
8/1/96 © 1996 United Feature Syndicate, Inc.(NYC)

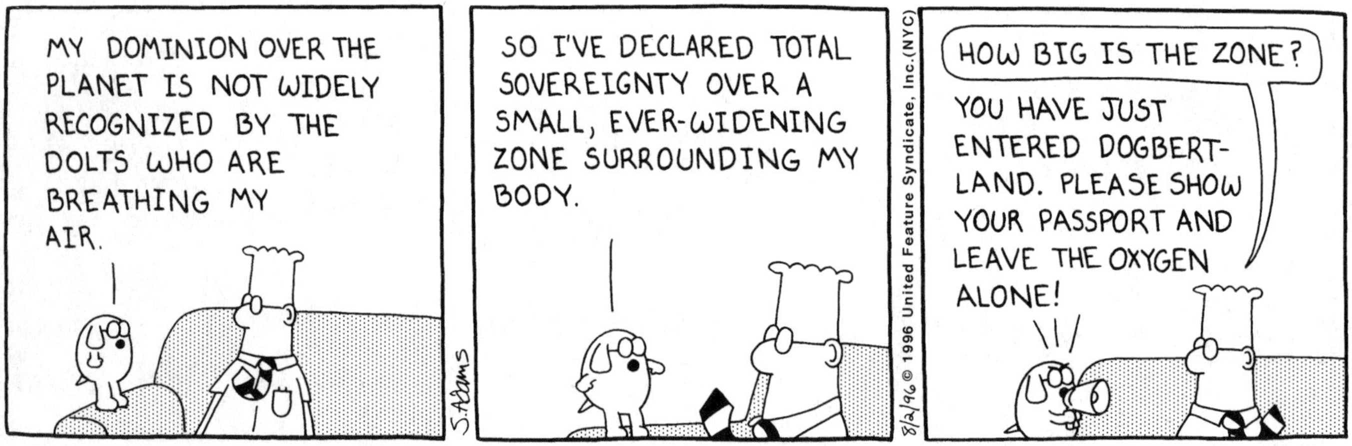
MY DOMINION OVER THE PLANET IS NOT WIDELY RECOGNIZED BY THE DOLTS WHO ARE BREATHING MY AIR.
SO I'VE DECLARED TOTAL SOVEREIGNTY OVER A SMALL, EVER-WIDENING ZONE SURROUNDING MY BODY.
HOW BIG IS THE ZONE?
YOU HAVE JUST ENTERED DOGBERT-LAND. PLEASE SHOW YOUR PASSPORT AND LEAVE THE OXYGEN ALONE!
S. Adams
8/2/96 © 1996 United Feature Syndicate, Inc.(NYC)

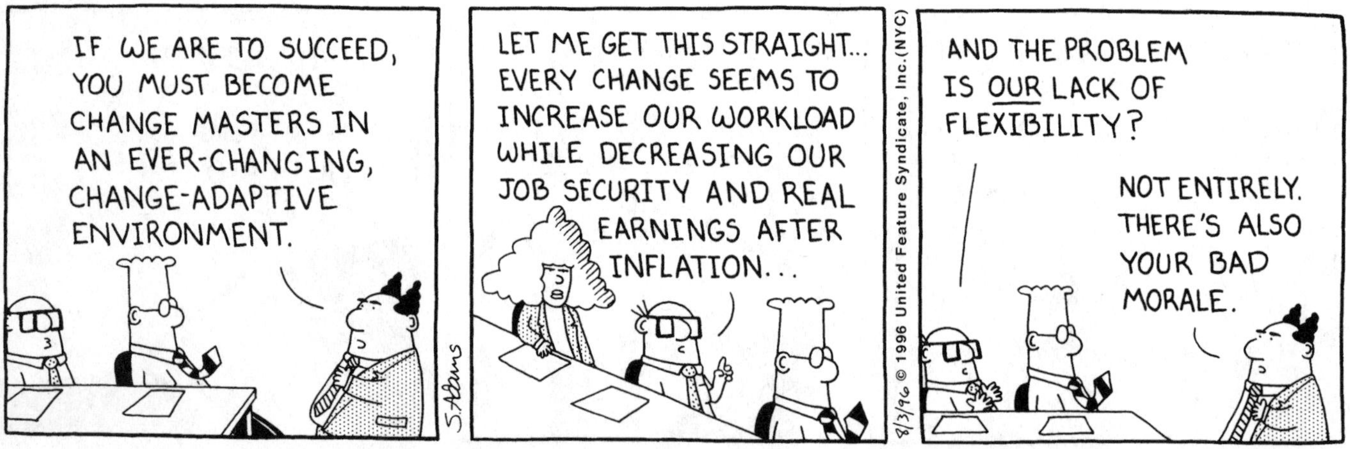
IF WE ARE TO SUCCEED, YOU MUST BECOME CHANGE MASTERS IN AN EVER-CHANGING, CHANGE-ADAPTIVE ENVIRONMENT.
LET ME GET THIS STRAIGHT... EVERY CHANGE SEEMS TO INCREASE OUR WORKLOAD WHILE DECREASING OUR JOB SECURITY AND REAL EARNINGS AFTER INFLATION...
AND THE PROBLEM IS OUR LACK OF FLEXIBILITY?
NOT ENTIRELY. THERE'S ALSO YOUR BAD MORALE.
S. Adams
8/3/96 © 1996 United Feature Syndicate, Inc.(NYC)

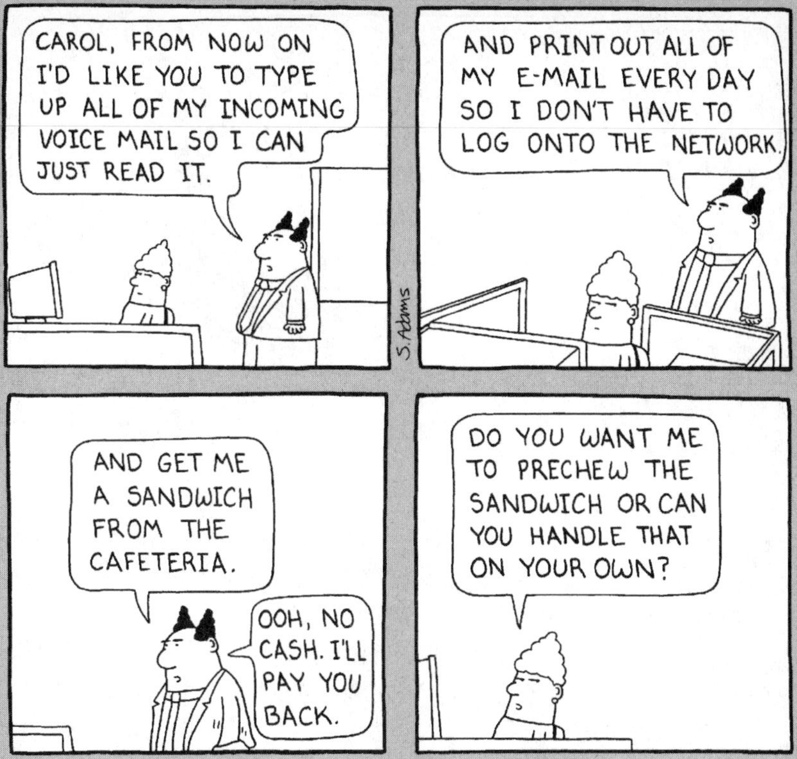
CAROL, FROM NOW ON I'D LIKE YOU TO TYPE UP ALL OF MY INCOMING VOICE MAIL SO I CAN JUST READ IT.
S. Adams
AND PRINT OUT ALL OF MY E-MAIL EVERY DAY SO I DON'T HAVE TO LOG ONTO THE NETWORK.
AND GET ME A SANDWICH FROM THE CAFETERIA.
OOH, NO CASH. I'LL PAY YOU BACK.
DO YOU WANT ME TO PRECHEW THE SANDWICH OR CAN YOU HANDLE THAT ON YOUR OWN?

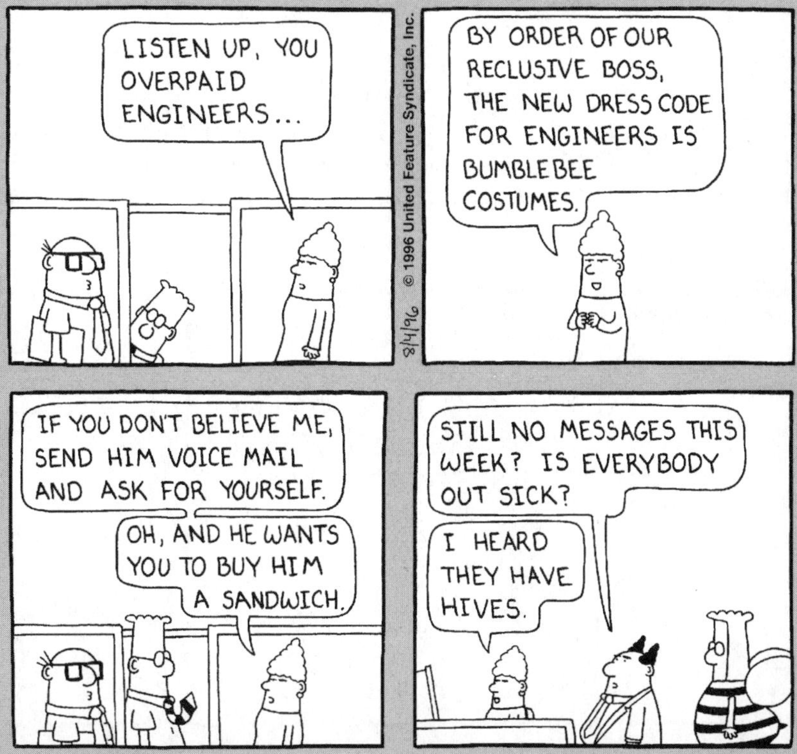
LISTEN UP, YOU OVERPAID ENGINEERS...
© 1996 United Feature Syndicate, Inc.
8/4/96
BY ORDER OF OUR RECLUSIVE BOSS, THE NEW DRESS CODE FOR ENGINEERS IS BUMBLEBEE COSTUMES.
IF YOU DON'T BELIEVE ME, SEND HIM VOICE MAIL AND ASK FOR YOURSELF.
OH, AND HE WANTS YOU TO BUY HIM A SANDWICH.
STILL NO MESSAGES THIS WEEK? IS EVERYBODY OUT SICK?
I HEARD THEY HAVE HIVES.

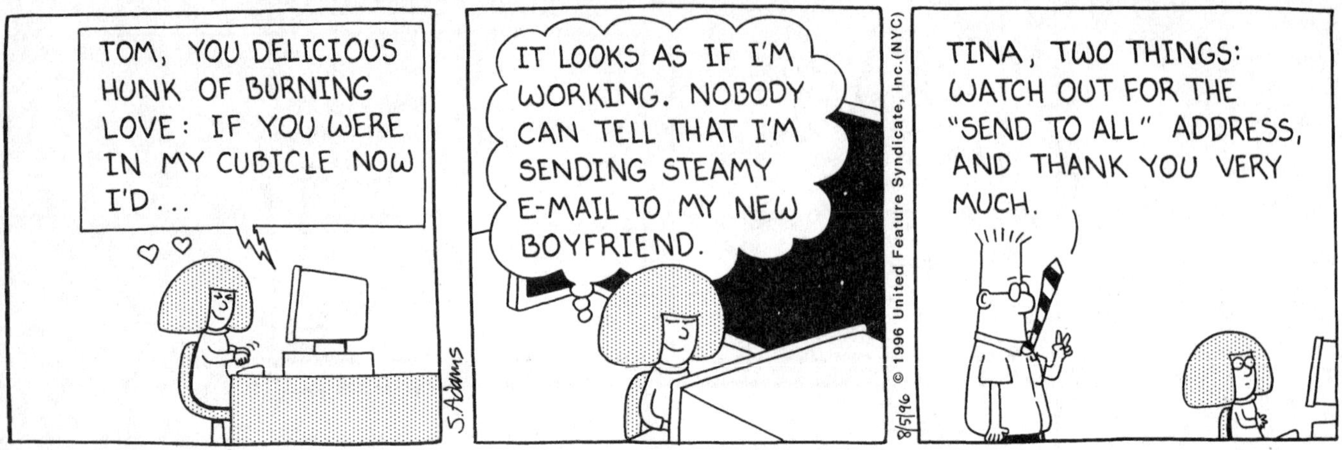
TOM, YOU DELICIOUS HUNK OF BURNING LOVE: IF YOU WERE IN MY CUBICLE NOW I'D...
S. Adams
IT LOOKS AS IF I'M WORKING. NOBODY CAN TELL THAT I'M SENDING STEAMY E-MAIL TO MY NEW BOYFRIEND.
8/5/96 © 1996 United Feature Syndicate, Inc.(NYC)
TINA, TWO THINGS: WATCH OUT FOR THE "SEND TO ALL" ADDRESS, AND THANK YOU VERY MUCH.

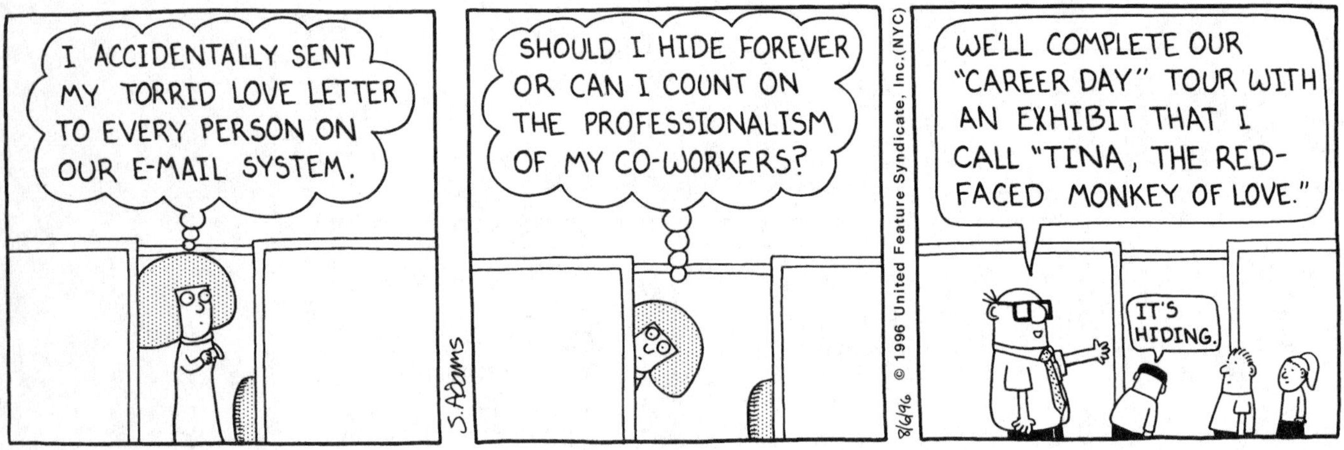
I ACCIDENTALLY SENT MY TORRID LOVE LETTER TO EVERY PERSON ON OUR E-MAIL SYSTEM.
S. Adams
SHOULD I HIDE FOREVER OR CAN I COUNT ON THE PROFESSIONALISM OF MY CO-WORKERS?
8/6/96 © 1996 United Feature Syndicate, Inc.(NYC)
WE'LL COMPLETE OUR "CAREER DAY" TOUR WITH AN EXHIBIT THAT I CALL "TINA, THE RED-FACED MONKEY OF LOVE."
IT'S HIDING.

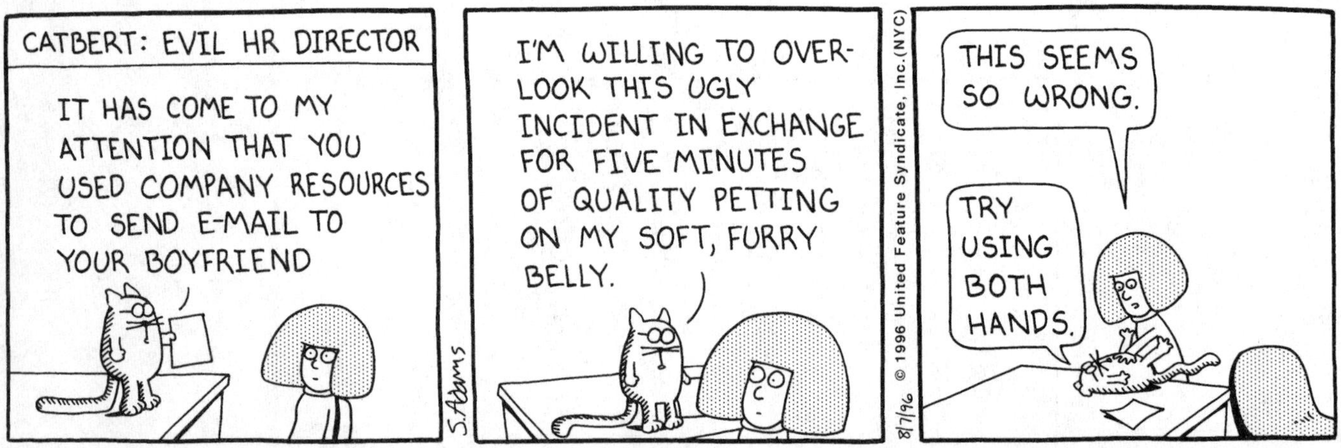
CATBERT: EVIL HR DIRECTOR
IT HAS COME TO MY ATTENTION THAT YOU USED COMPANY RESOURCES TO SEND E-MAIL TO YOUR BOYFRIEND
S. Adams
I'M WILLING TO OVER-LOOK THIS UGLY INCIDENT IN EXCHANGE FOR FIVE MINUTES OF QUALITY PETTING ON MY SOFT, FURRY BELLY.
8/7/96 © 1996 United Feature Syndicate, Inc.(NYC)
THIS SEEMS SO WRONG.
TRY USING BOTH HANDS.

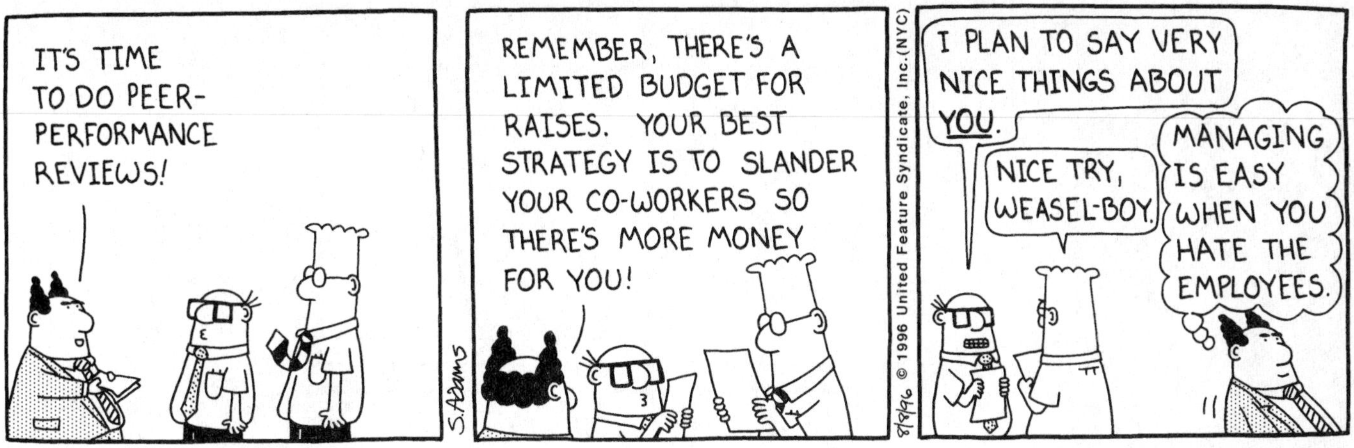
IT'S TIME TO DO PEER-PERFORMANCE REVIEWS!
REMEMBER, THERE'S A LIMITED BUDGET FOR RAISES. YOUR BEST STRATEGY IS TO SLANDER YOUR CO-WORKERS SO THERE'S MORE MONEY FOR YOU!
S. Adams
8/8/96 © 1996 United Feature Syndicate, Inc.(NYC)
I PLAN TO SAY VERY NICE THINGS ABOUT YOU.
NICE TRY, WEASEL-BOY.
MANAGING IS EASY WHEN YOU HATE THE EMPLOYEES.

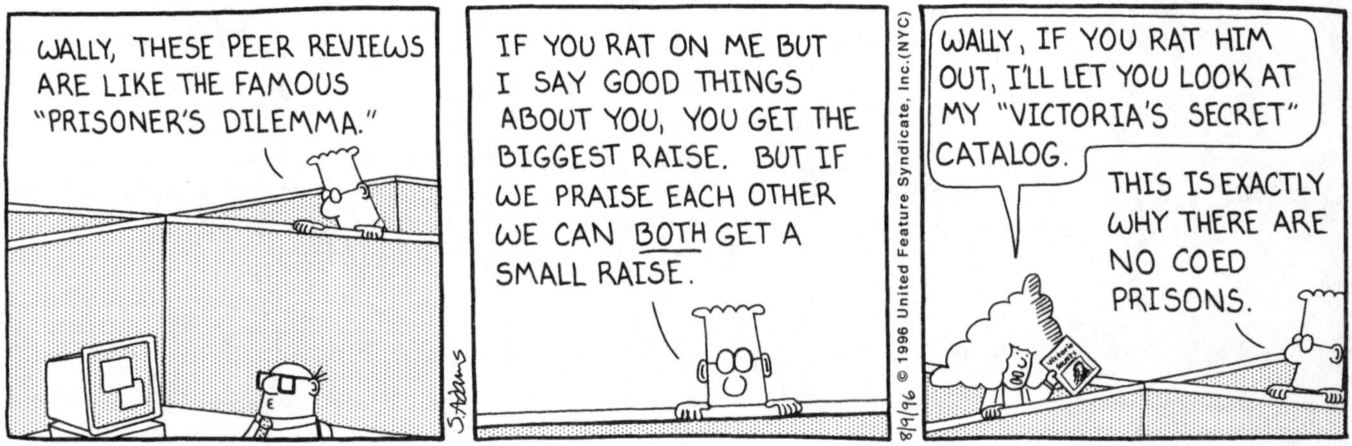
WALLY, THESE PEER REVIEWS ARE LIKE THE FAMOUS "PRISONER'S DILEMMA."
S. Adams
IF YOU RAT ON ME BUT I SAY GOOD THINGS ABOUT YOU, YOU GET THE BIGGEST RAISE. BUT IF WE PRAISE EACH OTHER WE CAN BOTH GET A SMALL RAISE.
8/9/96 © 1996 United Feature Syndicate, Inc.(NYC)
WALLY, IF YOU RAT HIM OUT, I'LL LET YOU LOOK AT MY "VICTORIA'S SECRET" CATALOG.
THIS IS EXACTLY WHY THERE ARE NO COED PRISONS.

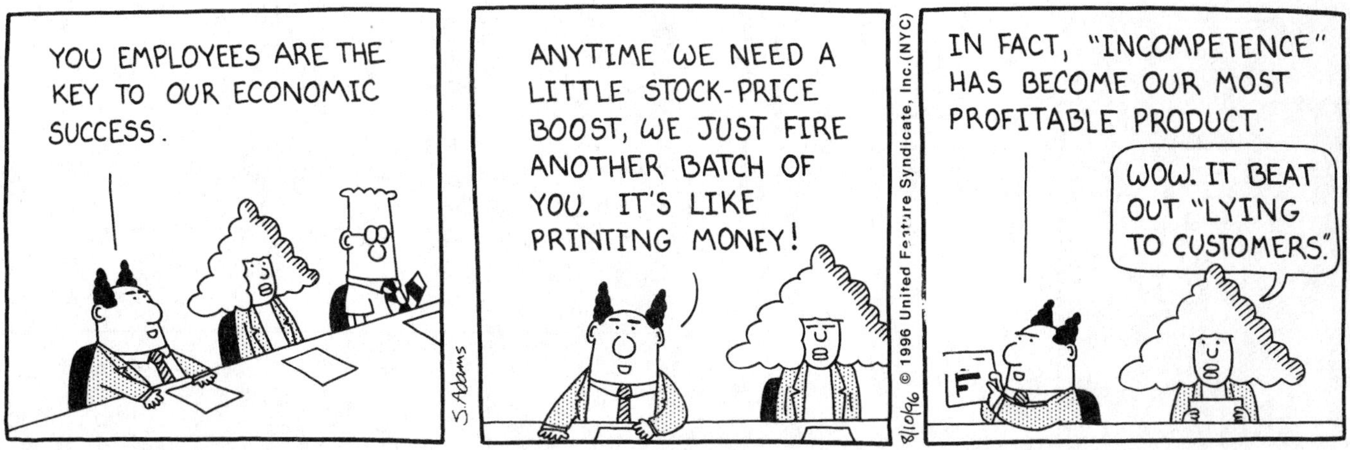
YOU EMPLOYEES ARE THE KEY TO OUR ECONOMIC SUCCESS.
S. Adams
ANYTIME WE NEED A LITTLE STOCK-PRICE BOOST, WE JUST FIRE ANOTHER BATCH OF YOU. IT'S LIKE PRINTING MONEY!
8/10/96 © 1996 United Feature Syndicate, Inc.(NYC)
IN FACT, "INCOMPETENCE" HAS BECOME OUR MOST PROFITABLE PRODUCT.
WOW. IT BEAT OUT "LYING TO CUSTOMERS."

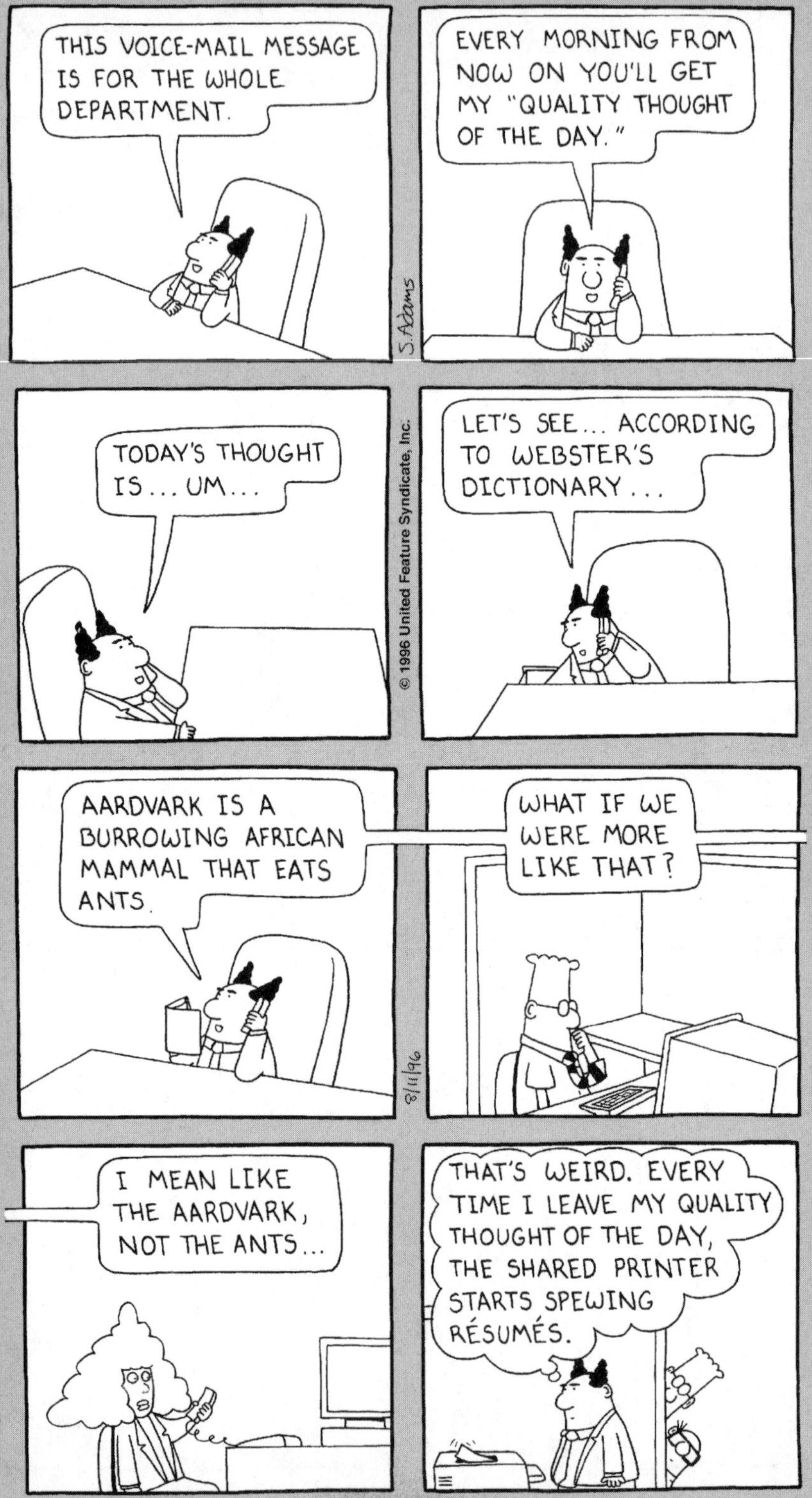
THIS VOICE-MAIL MESSAGE IS FOR THE WHOLE DEPARTMENT.
EVERY MORNING FROM NOW ON YOU'LL GET MY "QUALITY THOUGHT OF THE DAY."
S. Adams
TODAY'S THOUGHT IS... UM...
© 1996 United Feature Syndicate, Inc.
LET'S SEE... ACCORDING TO WEBSTER'S DICTIONARY...
AARDVARK IS A BURROWING AFRICAN MAMMAL THAT EATS ANTS.
8/1/96
WHAT IF WE WERE MORE LIKE THAT?
I MEAN LIKE THE AARDVARK, NOT THE ANTS...
THAT'S WEIRD. EVERY TIME I LEAVE MY QUALITY THOUGHT OF THE DAY, THE SHARED PRINTER STARTS SPEWING RÉSUMÉS.

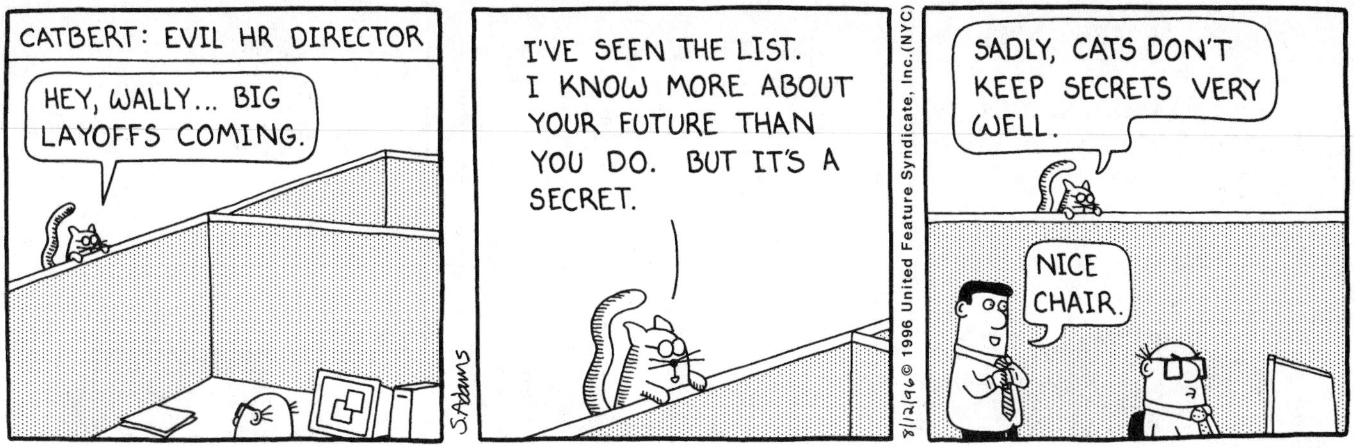
CATBERT: EVIL HR DIRECTOR
HEY, WALLY... BIG LAYOFFS COMING.
I'VE SEEN THE LIST. I KNOW MORE ABOUT YOUR FUTURE THAN YOU DO. BUT IT'S A SECRET.
S. Adams
8/12/96 © 1996 United Feature Syndicate, Inc.(NYC)
SADLY, CATS DON'T KEEP SECRETS VERY WELL.
NICE CHAIR.

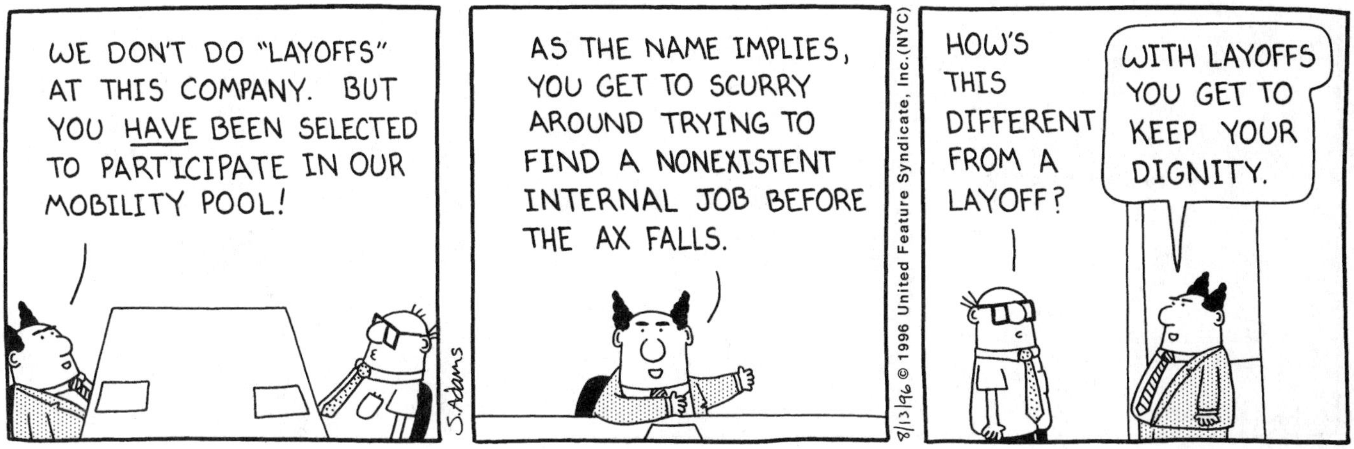
WE DON'T DO "LAYOFFS" AT THIS COMPANY. BUT YOU HAVE BEEN SELECTED TO PARTICIPATE IN OUR MOBILITY POOL!
S. Adams
AS THE NAME IMPLIES, YOU GET TO SCURRY AROUND TRYING TO FIND A NONEXISTENT INTERNAL JOB BEFORE THE AX FALLS.
8/13/96 © 1996 United Feature Syndicate, Inc.(NYC)
HOW'S THIS DIFFERENT FROM A LAYOFF?
WITH LAYOFFS YOU GET TO KEEP YOUR DIGNITY.

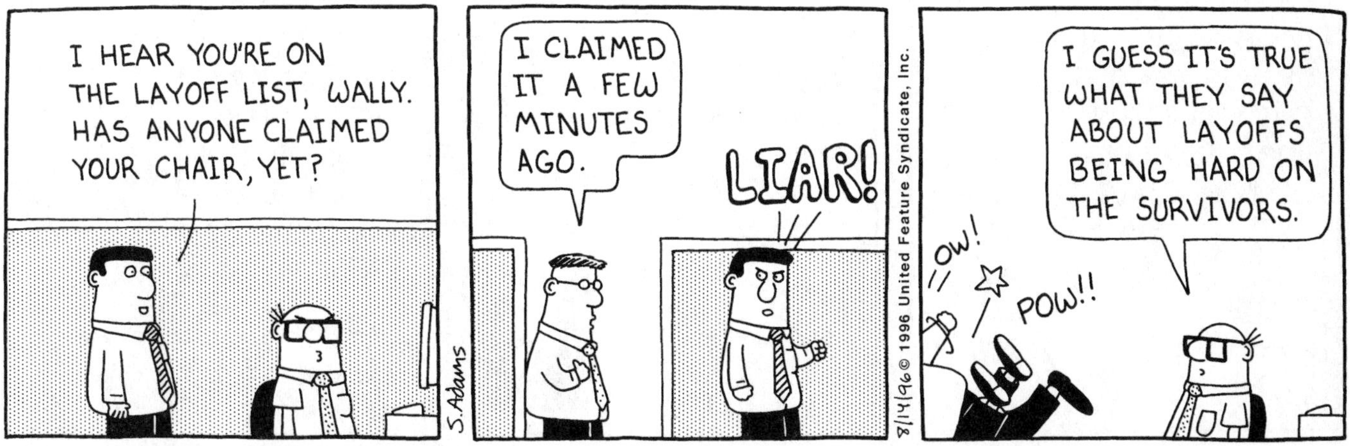
I HEAR YOU'RE ON THE LAYOFF LIST, WALLY. HAS ANYONE CLAIMED YOUR CHAIR, YET?
S. Adams
I CLAIMED IT A FEW MINUTES AGO.
LIAR!
8/14/96 © 1996 United Feature Syndicate, Inc.
OW!
POW!!
I GUESS IT'S TRUE WHAT THEY SAY ABOUT LAYOFFS BEING HARD ON THE SURVIVORS.

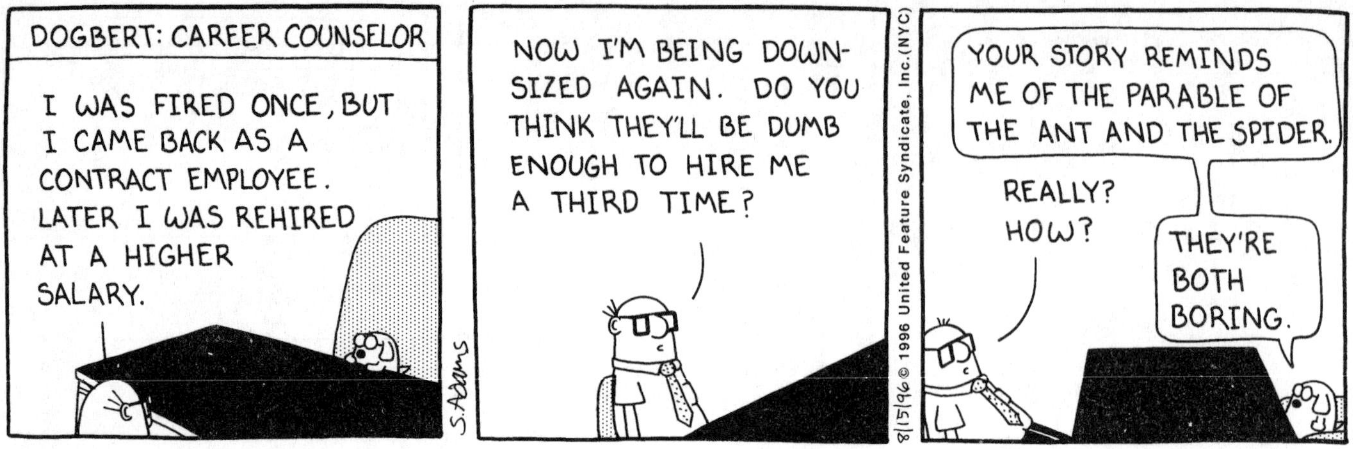
DOGBERT: CAREER COUNSELOR
I WAS FIRED ONCE, BUT I CAME BACK AS A CONTRACT EMPLOYEE. LATER I WAS REHIRED AT A HIGHER SALARY.
S. Adams
NOW I'M BEING DOWN-SIZED AGAIN. DO YOU THINK THEY'LL BE DUMB ENOUGH TO HIRE ME A THIRD TIME?
8/15/96 © 1996 United Feature Syndicate, Inc.(NYC)
YOUR STORY REMINDS ME OF THE PARABLE OF THE ANT AND THE SPIDER.
REALLY? HOW?
THEY'RE BOTH BORING.

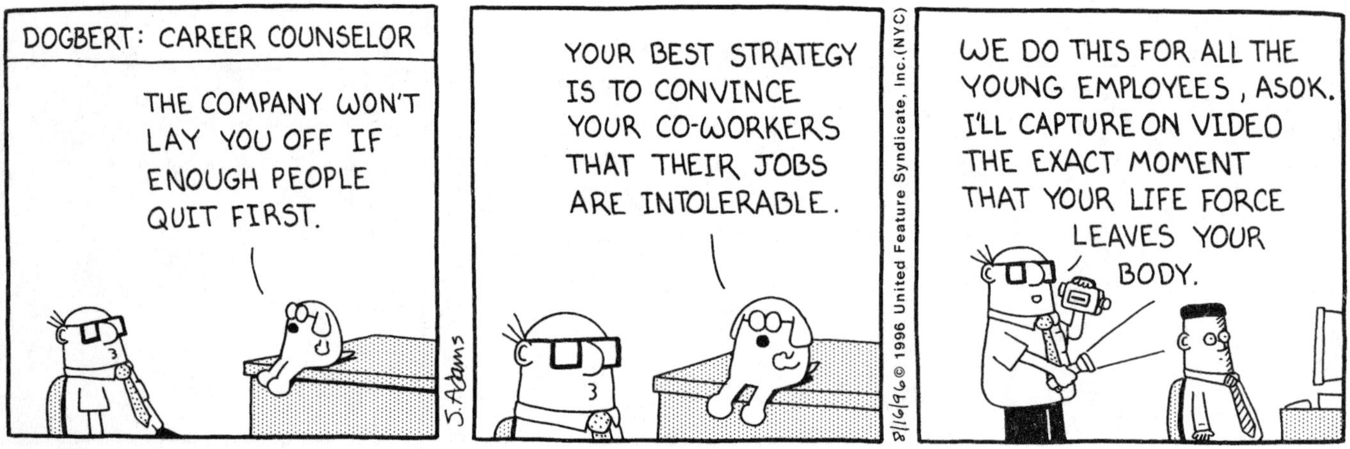
DOGBERT: CAREER COUNSELOR
THE COMPANY WON'T LAY YOU OFF IF ENOUGH PEOPLE QUIT FIRST.
S. Adams
YOUR BEST STRATEGY IS TO CONVINCE YOUR CO-WORKERS THAT THEIR JOBS ARE INTOLERABLE.
8/16/96 © 1996 United Feature Syndicate, Inc.(NYC)
WE DO THIS FOR ALL THE YOUNG EMPLOYEES, ASOK. I'LL CAPTURE ON VIDEO THE EXACT MOMENT THAT YOUR LIFE FORCE LEAVES YOUR BODY.

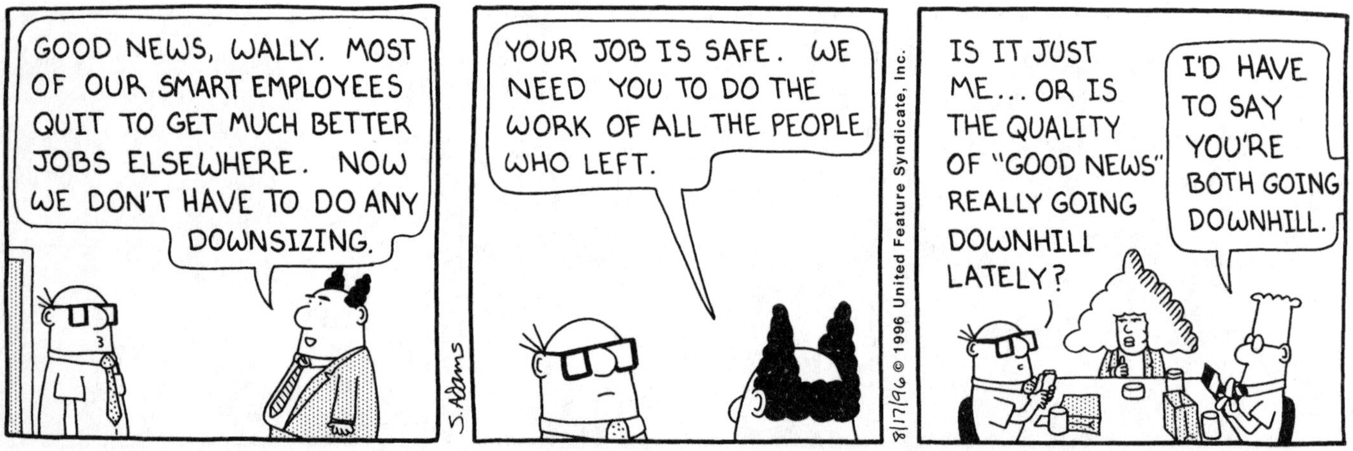
GOOD NEWS, WALLY. MOST OF OUR SMART EMPLOYEES QUIT TO GET MUCH BETTER JOBS ELSEWHERE. NOW WE DON'T HAVE TO DO ANY DOWNSIZING.
S. Adams
YOUR JOB IS SAFE. WE NEED YOU TO DO THE WORK OF ALL THE PEOPLE WHO LEFT.
8/17/96 © 1996 United Feature Syndicate, Inc.
IS IT JUST ME... OR IS THE QUALITY OF "GOOD NEWS" REALLY GOING DOWNHILL LATELY?
I'D HAVE TO SAY YOU'RE BOTH GOING DOWNHILL.

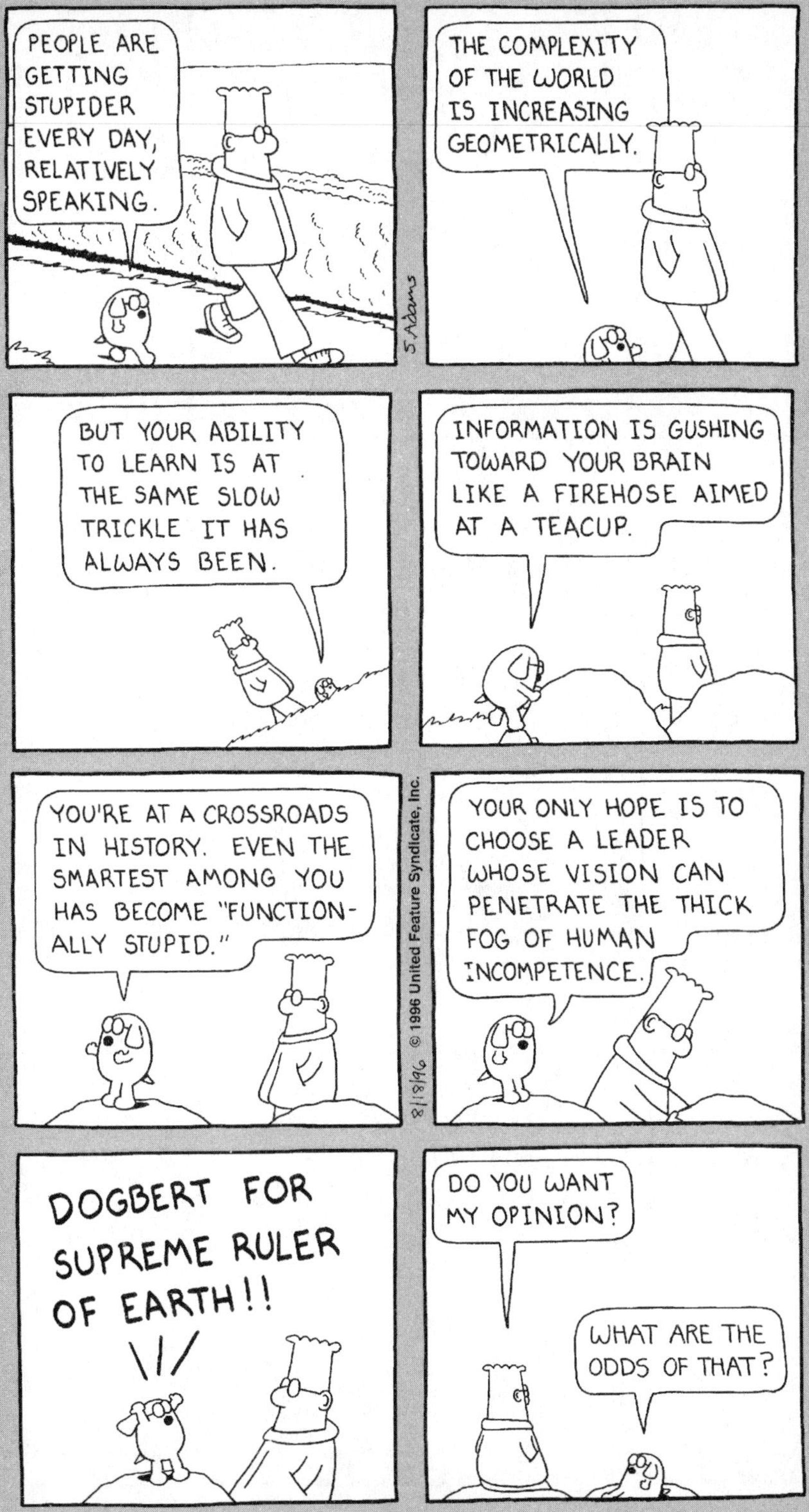
PEOPLE ARE GETTING STUPIDER EVERY DAY, RELATIVELY SPEAKING.
S. Adams
THE COMPLEXITY OF THE WORLD IS INCREASING GEOMETRICALLY.
BUT YOUR ABILITY TO LEARN IS AT THE SAME SLOW TRICKLE IT HAS ALWAYS BEEN.
INFORMATION IS GUSHING TOWARD YOUR BRAIN LIKE A FIREHOSE AIMED AT A TEACUP.
YOU'RE AT A CROSSROADS IN HISTORY. EVEN THE SMARTEST AMONG YOU HAS BECOME "FUNCTION-ALLY STUPID."
8/18/96 © 1996 United Feature Syndicate, Inc.
YOUR ONLY HOPE IS TO CHOOSE A LEADER WHOSE VISION CAN PENETRATE THE THICK FOG OF HUMAN INCOMPETENCE.
DOGBERT FOR SUPREME RULER OF EARTH!!
DO YOU WANT MY OPINION?
WHAT ARE THE ODDS OF THAT?

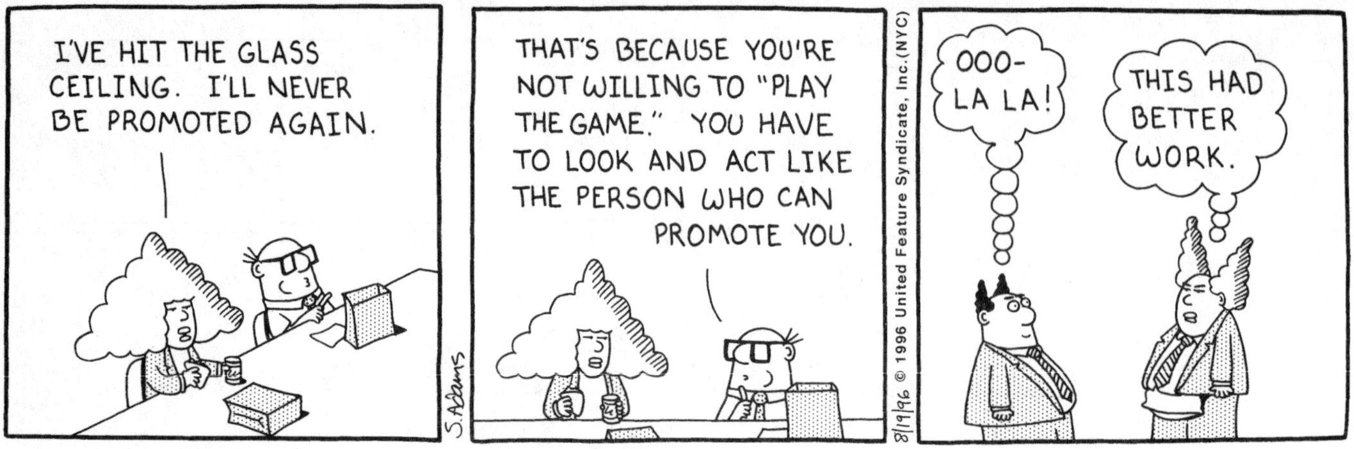
I'VE HIT THE GLASS CEILING. I'LL NEVER BE PROMOTED AGAIN.
THAT'S BECAUSE YOU'RE NOT WILLING TO "PLAY THE GAME." YOU HAVE TO LOOK AND ACT LIKE THE PERSON WHO CAN PROMOTE YOU.
S. Adams
8/19/96 © 1996 United Feature Syndicate, Inc.(NYC)
OOO-LA LA!
THIS HAD BETTER WORK.

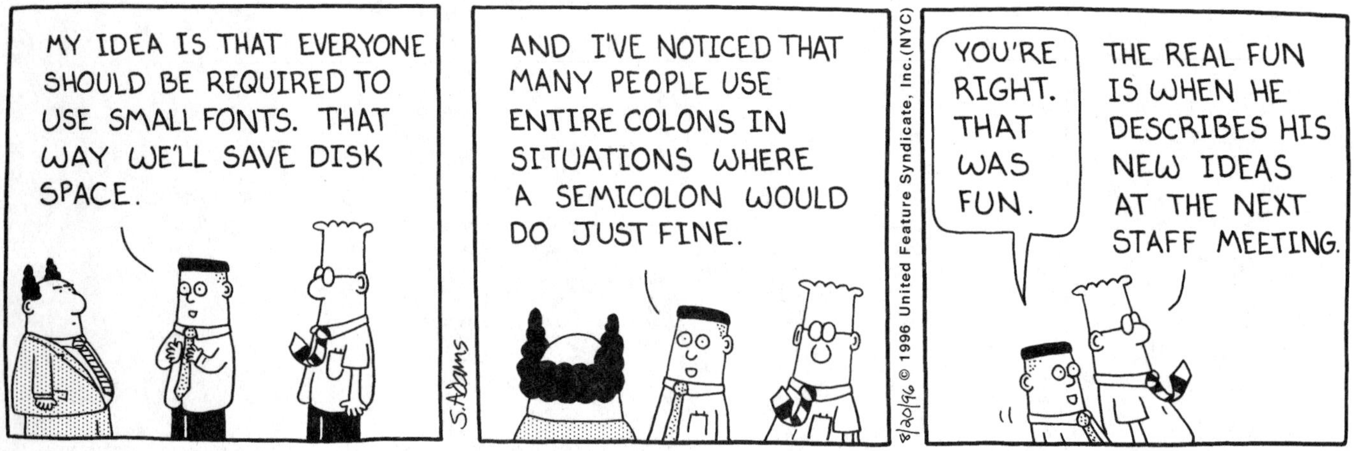
MY IDEA IS THAT EVERYONE SHOULD BE REQUIRED TO USE SMALL FONTS. THAT WAY WE'LL SAVE DISK SPACE.
AND I'VE NOTICED THAT MANY PEOPLE USE ENTIRE COLONS IN SITUATIONS WHERE A SEMICOLON WOULD DO JUST FINE.
S. Adams
8/20/96 © 1996 United Feature Syndicate, Inc.(NYC)
YOU'RE RIGHT. THAT WAS FUN.
THE REAL FUN IS WHEN HE DESCRIBES HIS NEW IDEAS AT THE NEXT STAFF MEETING.

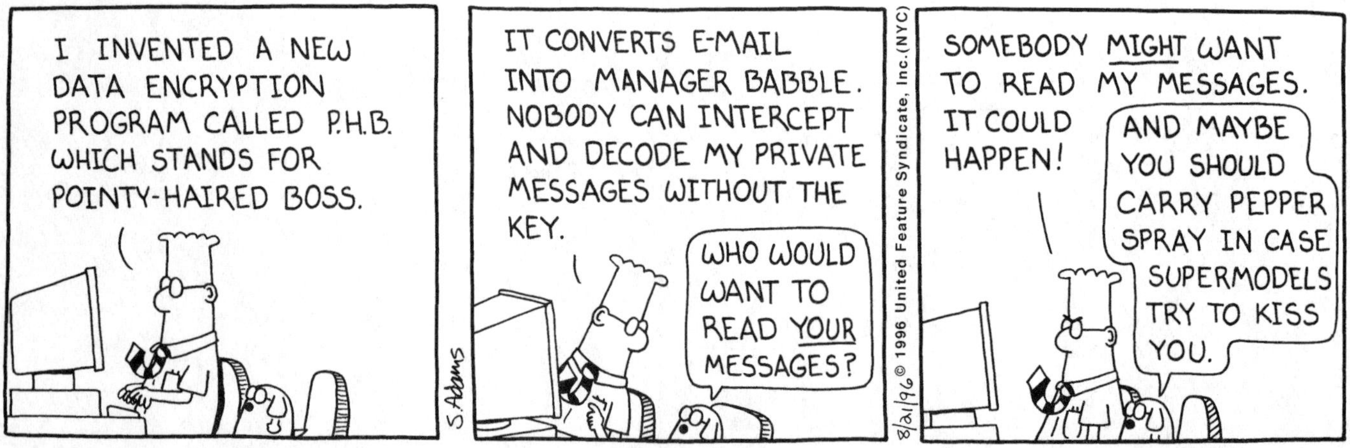
I INVENTED A NEW DATA ENCRYPTION PROGRAM CALLED P.H.B. WHICH STANDS FOR POINTY-HAIRED BOSS.
IT CONVERTS E-MAIL INTO MANAGER BABBLE. NOBODY CAN INTERCEPT AND DECODE MY PRIVATE MESSAGES WITHOUT THE KEY.
WHO WOULD WANT TO READ YOUR MESSAGES?
S. Adams
8/21/96 © 1996 United Feature Syndicate, Inc.(NYC)
SOMEBODY MIGHT WANT TO READ MY MESSAGES. IT COULD HAPPEN!
AND MAYBE YOU SHOULD CARRY PEPPER SPRAY IN CASE SUPERMODELS TRY TO KISS YOU.

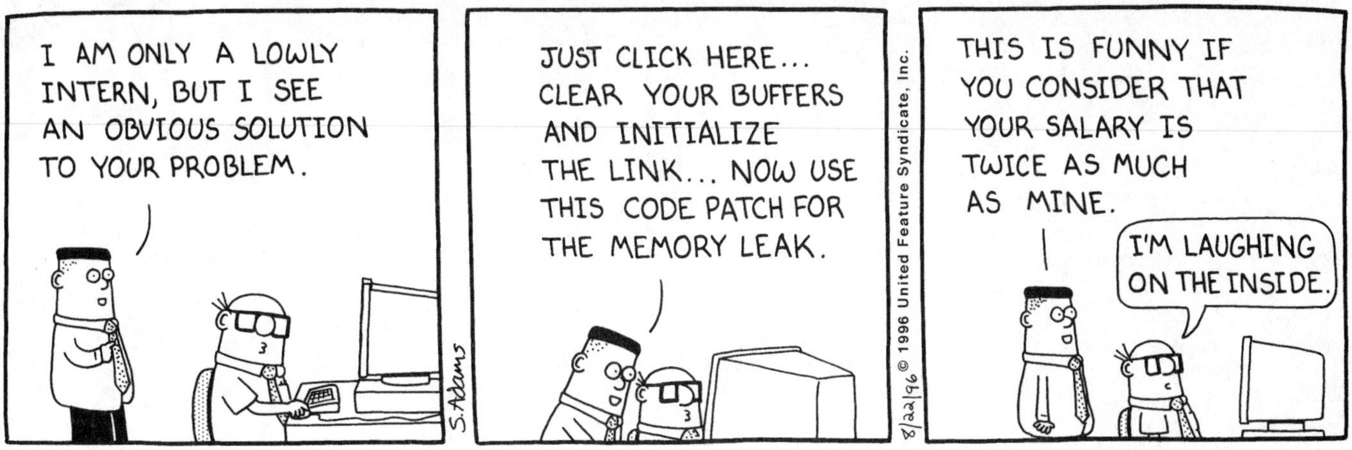
I AM ONLY A LOWLY INTERN, BUT I SEE AN OBVIOUS SOLUTION TO YOUR PROBLEM.
S. Adams
JUST CLICK HERE... CLEAR YOUR BUFFERS AND INITIALIZE THE LINK... NOW USE THIS CODE PATCH FOR THE MEMORY LEAK.
8/22/96 © 1996 United Feature Syndicate, Inc.
THIS IS FUNNY IF YOU CONSIDER THAT YOUR SALARY IS TWICE AS MUCH AS MINE.
I'M LAUGHING ON THE INSIDE.

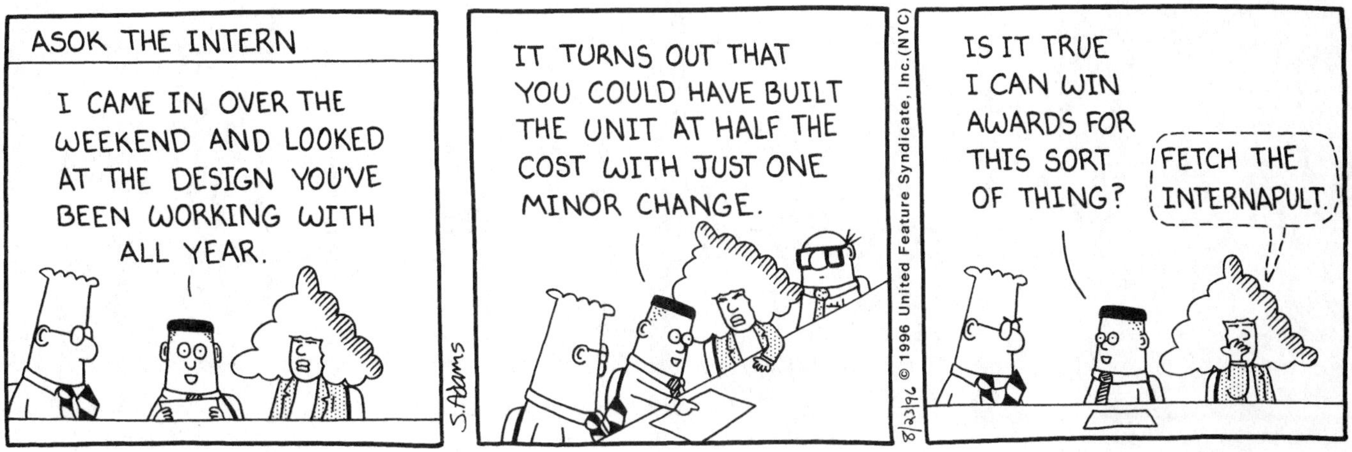
ASOK THE INTERN
I CAME IN OVER THE WEEKEND AND LOOKED AT THE DESIGN YOU'VE BEEN WORKING WITH ALL YEAR.
S. Adams
IT TURNS OUT THAT YOU COULD HAVE BUILT THE UNIT AT HALF THE COST WITH JUST ONE MINOR CHANGE.
8/23/96 © 1996 United Feature Syndicate, Inc.(NYC)
IS IT TRUE I CAN WIN AWARDS FOR THIS SORT OF THING?
FETCH THE INTERNAPULT.

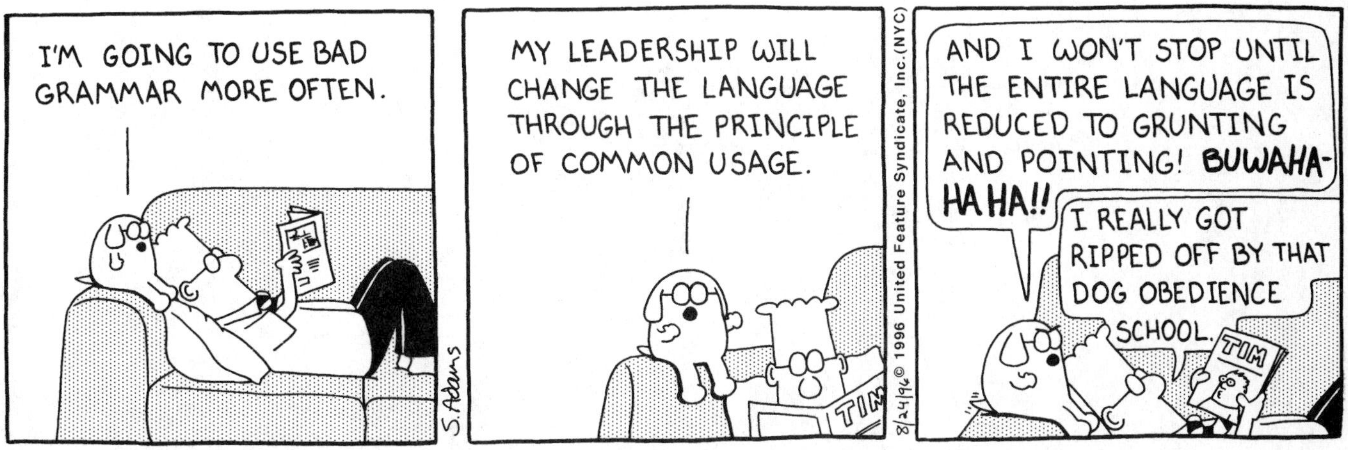
I'M GOING TO USE BAD GRAMMAR MORE OFTEN.
S. Adams
MY LEADERSHIP WILL CHANGE THE LANGUAGE THROUGH THE PRINCIPLE OF COMMON USAGE.
TIM
8/24/96 © 1996 United Feature Syndicate, Inc.(NYC)
AND I WON'T STOP UNTIL THE ENTIRE LANGUAGE IS REDUCED TO GRUNTING AND POINTING! BUWAHAHAHA!!
I REALLY GOT RIPPED OFF BY THAT DOG OBEDIENCE SCHOOL.
TIM

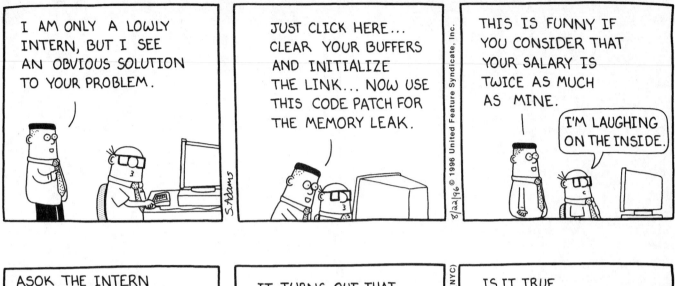

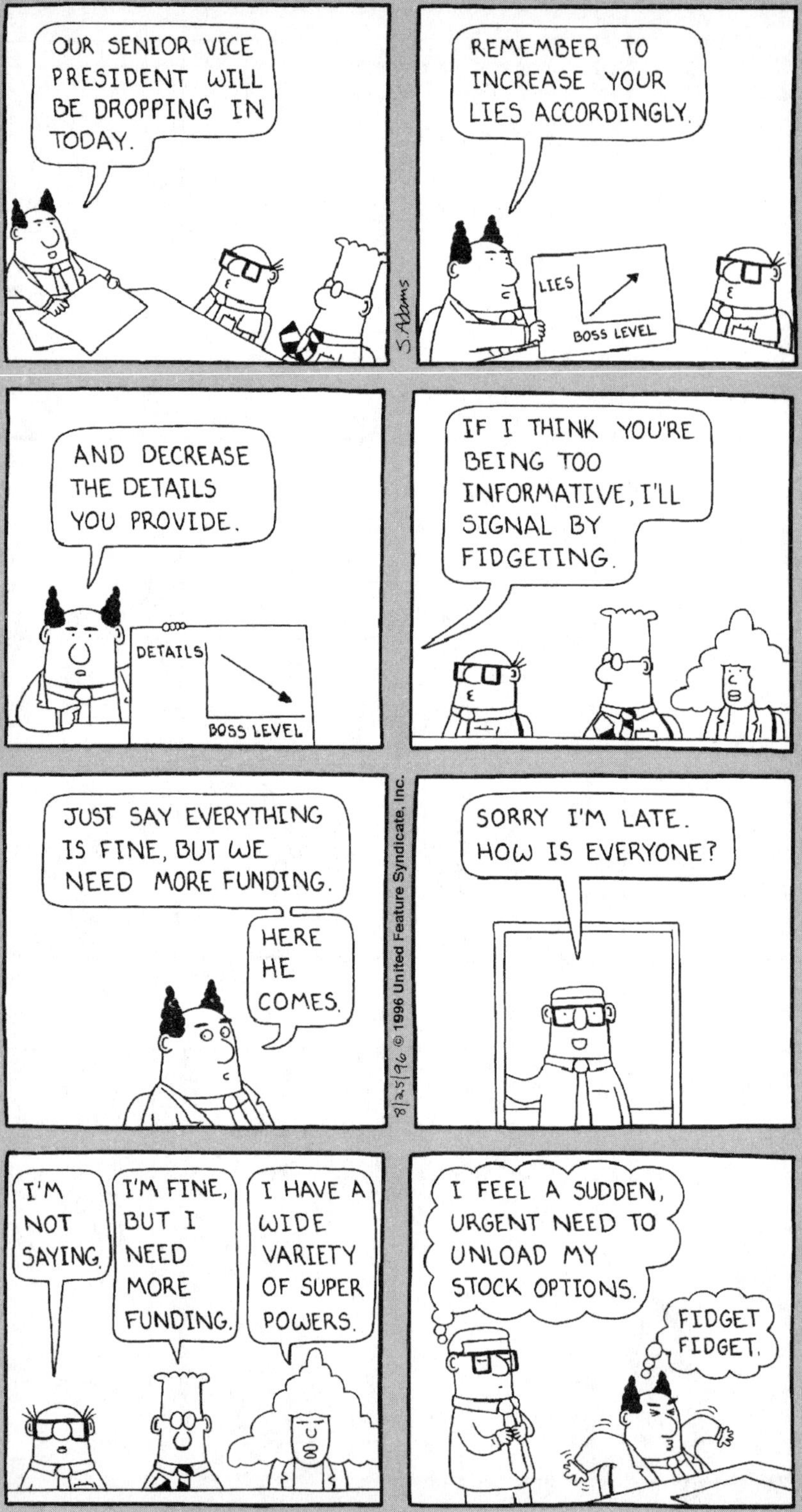
OUR SENIOR VICE PRESIDENT WILL BE DROPPING IN TODAY.
S. Adams
REMEMBER TO INCREASE YOUR LIES ACCORDINGLY.
LIES
BOSS LEVEL
AND DECREASE THE DETAILS YOU PROVIDE.
DETAILS
BOSS LEVEL
IF I THINK YOU'RE BEING TOO INFORMATIVE, I'LL SIGNAL BY FIDGETING.
JUST SAY EVERYTHING IS FINE, BUT WE NEED MORE FUNDING.
HERE HE COMES.
8/25/96 © 1996 United Feature Syndicate, Inc.
SORRY I'M LATE. HOW IS EVERYONE?
I'M NOT SAYING.
I'M FINE, BUT I NEED MORE FUNDING.
I HAVE A WIDE VARIETY OF SUPER POWERS.
I FEEL A SUDDEN, URGENT NEED TO UNLOAD MY STOCK OPTIONS.
FIDGET FIDGET.

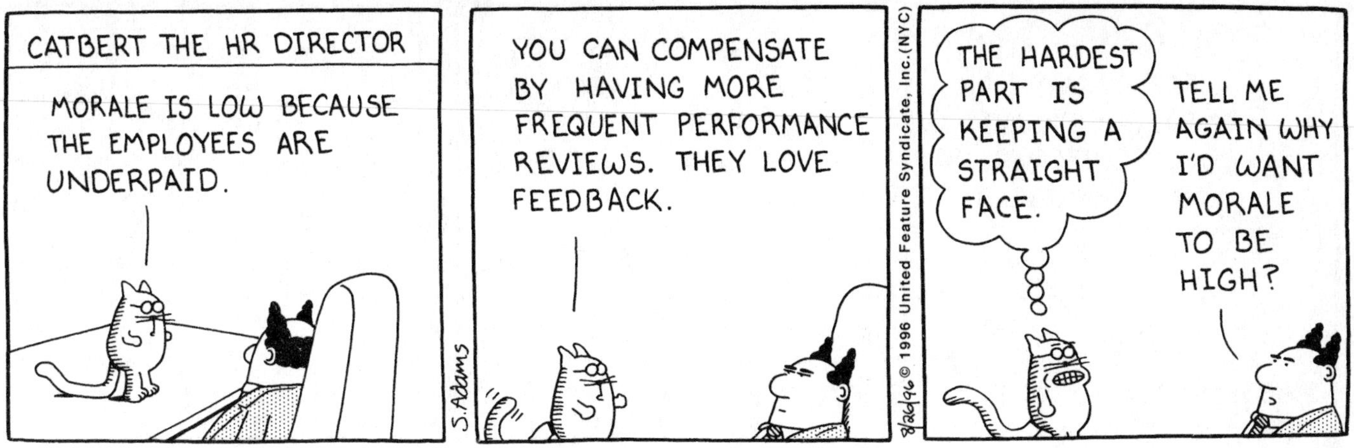
CATBERT THE HR DIRECTOR
MORALE IS LOW BECAUSE THE EMPLOYEES ARE UNDERPAID.
YOU CAN COMPENSATE BY HAVING MORE FREQUENT PERFORMANCE REVIEWS. THEY LOVE FEEDBACK.
S. Adams
8/26/96 © 1996 United Feature Syndicate, Inc.(NYC)
THE HARDEST PART IS KEEPING A STRAIGHT FACE.
TELL ME AGAIN WHY I'D WANT MORALE TO BE HIGH?

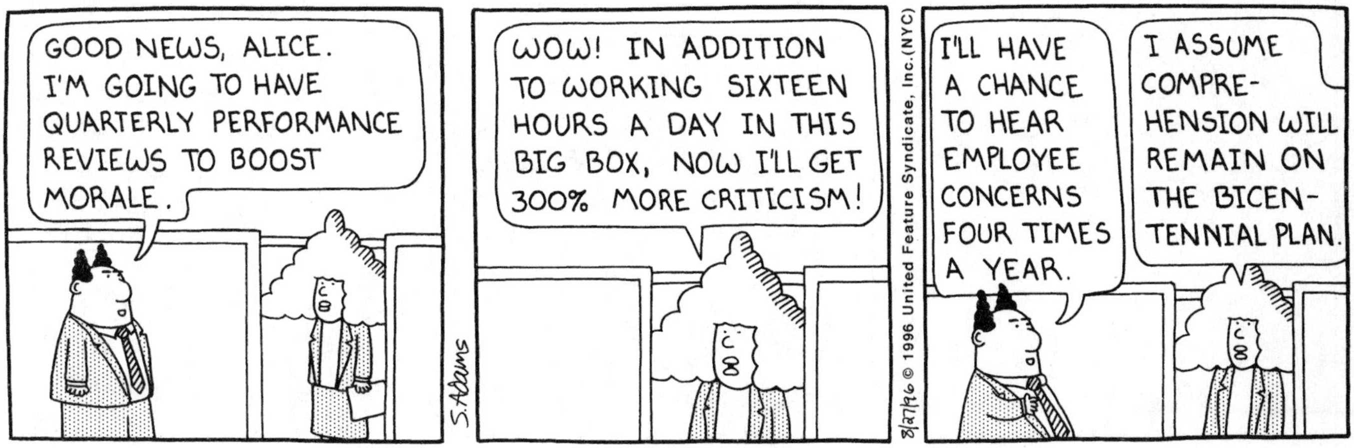
GOOD NEWS, ALICE. I'M GOING TO HAVE QUARTERLY PERFORMANCE REVIEWS TO BOOST MORALE.
WOW! IN ADDITION TO WORKING SIXTEEN HOURS A DAY IN THIS BIG BOX, NOW I'LL GET 300% MORE CRITICISM!
S. Adams
8/27/96 © 1996 United Feature Syndicate, Inc.(NYC)
I'LL HAVE A CHANCE TO HEAR EMPLOYEE CONCERNS FOUR TIMES A YEAR.
I ASSUME COMPRE-HENSION WILL REMAIN ON THE BICEN-TENNIAL PLAN.

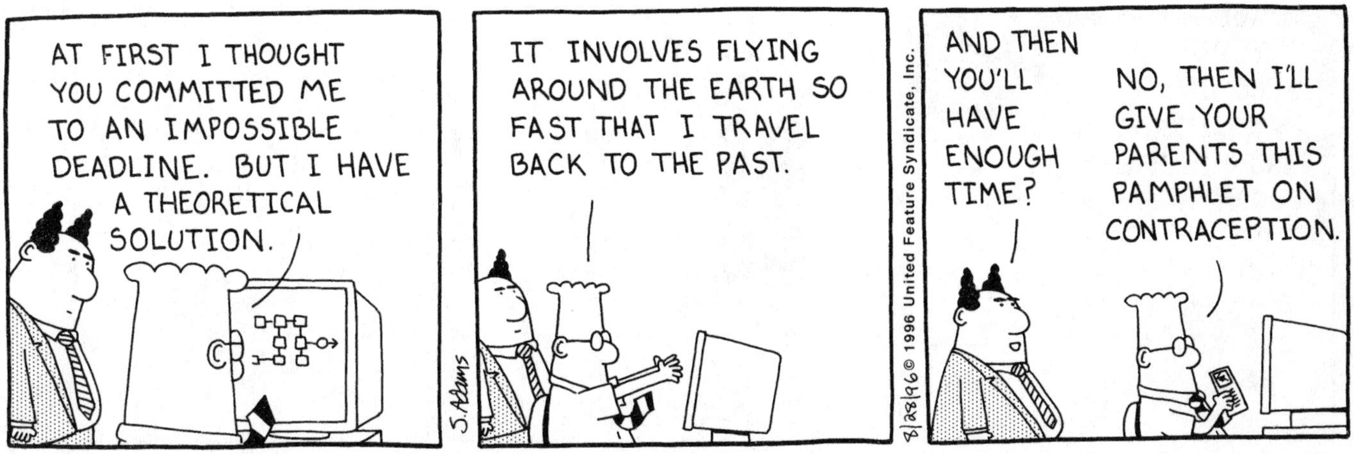
AT FIRST I THOUGHT YOU COMMITTED ME TO AN IMPOSSIBLE DEADLINE. BUT I HAVE A THEORETICAL SOLUTION.
IT INVOLVES FLYING AROUND THE EARTH SO FAST THAT I TRAVEL BACK TO THE PAST.
S. Adams
8/28/96 © 1996 United Feature Syndicate, Inc.
AND THEN YOU'LL HAVE ENOUGH TIME?
NO, THEN I'LL GIVE YOUR PARENTS THIS PAMPHLET ON CONTRACEPTION.

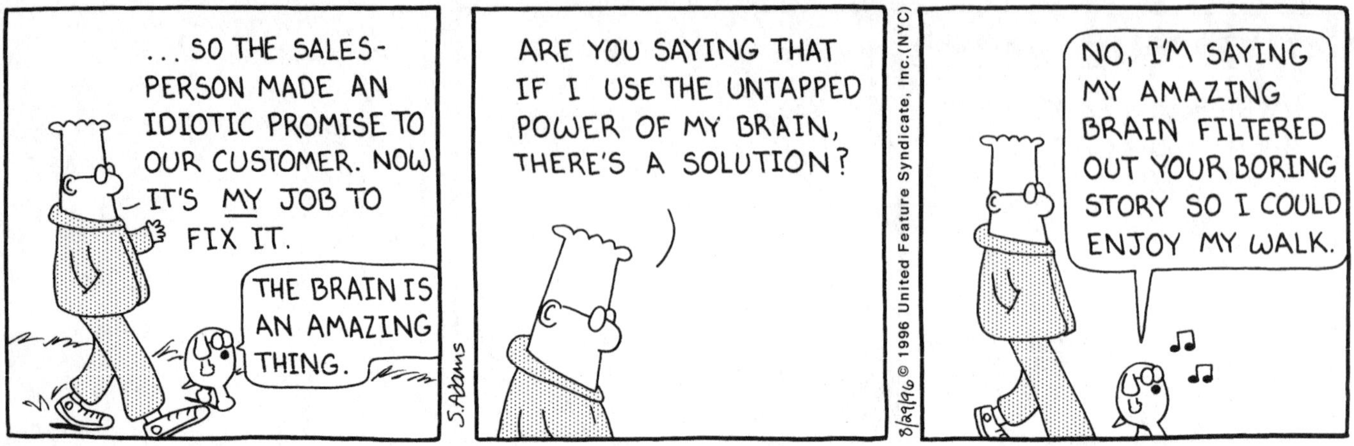
... SO THE SALES-PERSON MADE AN IDIOTIC PROMISE TO OUR CUSTOMER. NOW IT'S MY JOB TO FIX IT.
THE BRAIN IS AN AMAZING THING.
S. Adams
ARE YOU SAYING THAT IF I USE THE UNTAPPED POWER OF MY BRAIN, THERE'S A SOLUTION?
8/29/96 © 1996 United Feature Syndicate, Inc.(NYC)
NO, I'M SAYING MY AMAZING BRAIN FILTERED OUT YOUR BORING STORY SO I COULD ENJOY MY WALK.

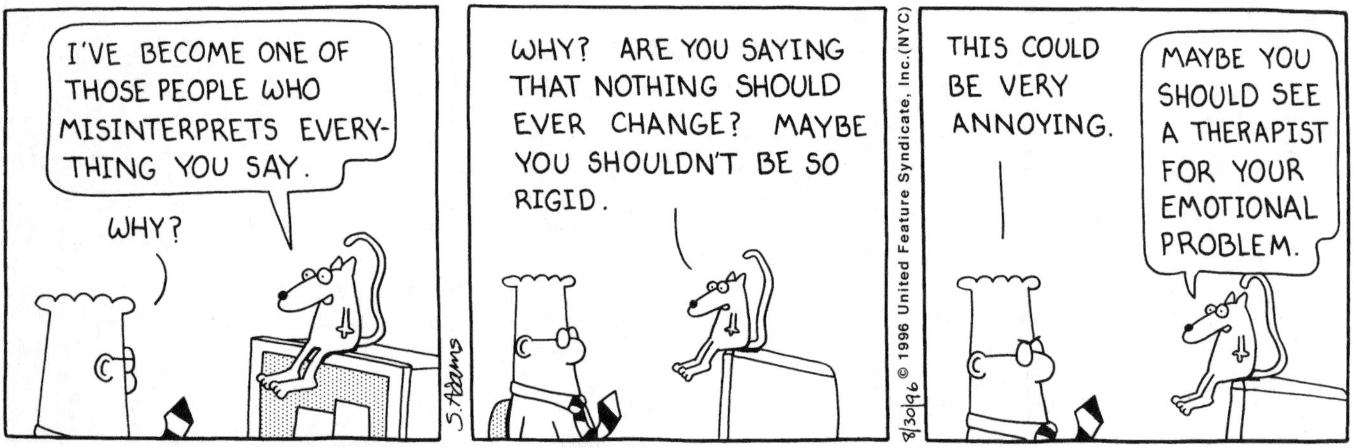
I'VE BECOME ONE OF THOSE PEOPLE WHO MISINTERPRETS EVERY-THING YOU SAY.
WHY?
S. Adams
WHY? ARE YOU SAYING THAT NOTHING SHOULD EVER CHANGE? MAYBE YOU SHOULDN'T BE SO RIGID.
8/30/96 © 1996 United Feature Syndicate, Inc.(NYC)
THIS COULD BE VERY ANNOYING.
MAYBE YOU SHOULD SEE A THERAPIST FOR YOUR EMOTIONAL PROBLEM.

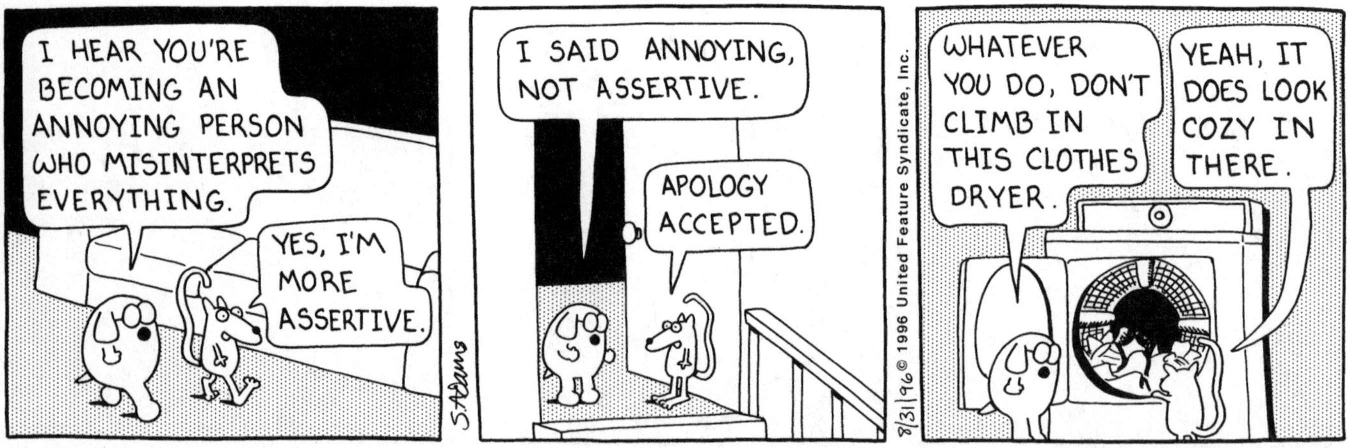
I HEAR YOU'RE BECOMING AN ANNOYING PERSON WHO MISINTERPRETS EVERYTHING.
YES, I'M MORE ASSERTIVE.
S. Adams
I SAID ANNOYING, NOT ASSERTIVE.
APOLOGY ACCEPTED.
8/31/96 © 1996 United Feature Syndicate, Inc.
WHATEVER YOU DO, DON'T CLIMB IN THIS CLOTHES DRYER.
YEAH, IT DOES LOOK COZY IN THERE.